PENGUIN BOOKS

BOWERING'S B.C.

George Bowering is the author of several historical novels set in British Columbia. One day his editor told him to get off the pot and write a real history of the place. Not knowing any better, he set out to do so, and nearly pulled it off. He is now contemplating a number of novels set in the present.

BOWERING'S B.C.
A SWASHBUCKLING HISTORY

GEORGE BOWERING

Penguin Books

PENGUIN BOOKS
Published by the Penguin Group
Penguin Books Canada Ltd, 10 Alcorn Avenue, Toronto, Ontario, Canada
M4V 3B2
Penguin Books Ltd, 27 Wrights Lane, London W8 5TZ, England
Viking Penguin, a division of Penguin Books USA Inc., 375 Hudson Street,
New York, New York 10014, U.S.A.
Penguin Books Australia Ltd, Ringwood, Victoria, Australia
Penguin Books (NZ) Ltd, cnr Rosedale and Airborne Roads, Albany,
Auckland 1310, New Zealand

Penguin Books Ltd, Registered Offices: Harmondsworth, Middlesex, England

First published in Viking by Penguin Books Canada Limited, 1996
Published in Penguin Books, 1997

1 3 5 7 9 10 8 6 4 2

Manufactured in Canada.

Canadian Cataloguing in Publication Data

Bowering, George, 1935-
Bowering's B.C.

Includes index.

ISBN 0-14-024040-3

1. British Columbia - History. I. Title.

FC3811.B69 1997   971.1   C95-933115-B
F1088.B69 1997

Photo credits: B.C. Archives & Records Service: pages 16, 59, 63, 68, 88, 94, 104,
119, 131, 174, 176, 182, 188, 197, 213, 220, 254, 257, 264, 285, and 309.
Vancouver Public Library: pages 117, 226, 228, 311, and 372.
City of Vancouver Archives: page 233.

Visit Penguin Canada's web site at **www.penguin.ca**

This book is for
the memory of
Sophia McLean
and Mourning Dove

Acknowledgments

I was pleased to find that archivists are very pleasant people, and that they are dedicated to helping an amateur researcher learn the ropes. I would like to thank the people at the Provincial Archives in Victoria, the Vancouver City Archives, the Vancouver Public Library, The University of British Columbia Library, the En'owkin Centre and the museums in Kamloops, Ashcroft, Oliver, Merritt, Greenwood, Penticton, Cape Mudge, New Westminster, Cumberland, Coulee City, Peachland, Vancouver and Victoria. Also, thanks to all those writers whose books I found in our good second-hand bookstores: you have been a big help. Same to you, Mary Adachi, you tenacious editor.

Contents

Hist & Geog { Hist. perspective
              { Ind vs Wht

BOWERING'S B.C.
A SWASHBUCKLING HISTORY

Digging for History

"See? That was ha-HA."
—Harry Robinson, "The First People"

The land created

In the beginning the Great Spirit, or as some people called him the Great Chief, or as a lot of people said, the Old Man—well this very strong person was interested in light, so he made the sun. After that he made the water, so then there was lots of light and lots of water. There was more water than you could shake a stick at, but there were no sticks.

The Old Man thought about sticks, and he thought about people that could shake those sticks. So he made about five people. Then he got them together and said, "Look at this."

He was holding a grain of sand between his finger and his thumb. While the five people watched, he tossed the grain of sand into the water, where it sank out of sight.

"Now I need somebody to dive down and get that grain of sand," he said.

A lot of people know this story, and a lot of people have told it, so it is the real story. Harry Robinson told this story, and he knew everything, and it is his story, too. Mourning Dove told this story. Windy Bone told this story in Oliver, B.C. This is the real story about the Old Man and his grains of sand.

The Old Man had been around forever. When the white tribes moved in and told the people about a big father figure in the sky named God, the people recognized him as a skewed version of Old Man.

Then the white men said that this God had only one son. His only begotten son, they said. The people thought about that and decided that maybe this God fellow was a less virile relative of Old Man.

Then the white men said that the people were going to go to a terrible place called Hell if they did not decide to believe that this only begotten son of their man God had died to set them on the road to the happy place after death.

"How can a person *decide* to believe in something?" the people asked.

"It's just that sort of talk that will send you to everlasting perdition," was the measured reply.

Well, that grain of sand fell right down to the bottom of the water. Four of the five people that the Old Man had created started diving for it. They dived and dived, and the sun shone bright on the water, but no one could bring back that grain of sand.

All this while Coyote, the fifth of Old Man's begotten people, was lying back, watching the aquatic adventures. He was biding his time. When Old Man looked over at him Coyote winked. All afternoon he leaned back with his eyes half-closed in the bright sunshine, until the other four people were completely exhausted from their useless diving. They were leaning over, trying to catch their breath. That's when Coyote did his dive.

Down he went in the water. At first the water was brilliantly lit by the sunshine, but the deeper Coyote swam the darker it became. Pretty soon it was totally dark, but still Coyote descended.

And when he came back up and broke the surface of the water, he had the grain of sand between his finger and his thumb.

"OK, that's a start," said Old Man.

"Heh heh heh," said Coyote.

"Now what are you going to do with that little chunk of sand?" asked Old Man.

Coyote started rolling the grain of sand between his hands. These animal people had hands instead of just paws or claws in those days. Pretty soon the grain of sand started growing. It grew and grew. Old Man watched with a benign smile on his face. The sand was now a big ball of dirt. It grew faster and faster, until it was bigger than Coyote. Coyote jumped on top of it and rolled it along with his feet. The chunk of dirt grew and grew till it was too big for anyone to see it all. It grew and grew until it was the whole earth. All from one little grain of sand that Old Man had held between his finger and his thumb.

So Coyote was there right at the beginning. Trouble for everyone. What we would in our recent time come to call British Columbia was part of what Coyote helped Old Man make.

You might want to spend some time every day saying thank you to Old

Man. You don't want to turn your back on Coyote.

That is how the place got started. How did the people get here?

At first there were the animal people. They could all talk to one another, and they could all understand what Old Man was telling them, but they were still the animal people. The regular people would come later.

Some say that Coyote created the regular people, or at least helped Old man create the regular people. Some say that Coyote was the father of all the regular people. Look at the regular people's eyes, they said. They have Coyote's eyes.

However it happened, Coyote had something to do with it.

There are some places where the people do not know that they are under Coyote's eye. They have their own problems. Some of the people on the Coast have to worry about birds that land on your head, for instance. And crack your head open.

Or this other bird, Raven. On the Coast, Raven is a kind of flying Coyote. On the Coast, they say that when Old Man was starting things up he got Raven to drop that grain of sand in the water. Well, that grain of sand turned into a little island, and pretty soon there the world was.

In any case, first there was no world at all. Then there was a world with the animal people in it. Then there was a world with the regular people. Later on some white people would arrive, and the world would start going away.

Many nations

Here is a description of some land.

The soil is beaten by the sun until it falls in dry slides whenever a passing animal disturbs it. Rattlesnakes doze in that sun, or slither past some low-lying cactus and speargrass, looking for the shade of some crumbling shale. Small owls burrow in the dust, and once in a while a scorpion can be seen walking on his shadow across a lump of basalt. In the bright sunlight the wrinkles of clay on the bare hillsides are becoming what people call hoodoos, pillars of grey soil with stone caps balanced on their tops. If a breeze comes up, it blows through crisp sagebrush and greasewood, scenting the air with a kind of spice. Turtles look in vain for mud. Coyotes scamper.

Is that the kind of image people in eastern Canada have of British Columbia? That's doubtful. People in eastern Canada, like potential tourists in the USA and elsewhere, probably swallow the version offered by tourism bosses in Vancouver. They see sailboats on the sunset-golden water of some inlet, a mountain of tall cedars rising behind everything. If you look at advertisements for B.C. in glossy US magazines, you will think that the province is filled with water-skiers and hot-tub sitters. People back east keep referring to the mountains just outside Vancouver as "the Rockies."

Coast chauvinism, I usually call it.

I was brought up among the cactuses and rattlesnakes in the South Okanagan Valley, four hundred kilometres by highway east of Vancouver. It's really dry there. I always used to be amused by easterners who describe B.C. as a place where it rains a lot. In the South Okanagan when I was a kid it rained about seven inches a year. If it started to rain, you stepped into a doorway and waited for it to stop. Most of B.C. is really dry. The Interior is a lot like the Interior of California.

Some of the Interior, that is. B.C. is larger than most countries in the world, and has a lot of regions. It was always hard to get from one region to another. Hardly any citizens of B.C. have seen more than a few of the various kinds of B.C. there are. Before the people from Europe showed up, there were already many nations living here. Here are the historic names for these nations, with their modern names in brackets:

Tlingit
Tahltan
Kaska
Slave (Dene-thah)
Beaver (Dunne-za)
Sekani
Gitksan
Nisga'a
Haida
Tsimshian
Carrier
Bella Coola (Nuxalk)
Kwakiutl (Kwakwaka'waku)
Chilcotin (Tsilhgot'in)
Shuswap (Secwepemc)
Kootenay (Ktunaxa-Kinbasket)
Bella Bella (Heiltsuk)
Okanagan
Nicola
Thompson (Nlaka'pamux)
Kitimat (Haisla)
Lillooet (Stl'atl'imx)
Coast Salish
Nootka (Nuu-cha-nulth)

If you were a Kootenay there was next to no chance you would ever meet a Haida. If you did, you wouldn't understand his language.

The regions of B.C. are separated by high mountains, gorges, waterfalls, piles of rocks, long distances and severely different climates. That's why a thousand years ago the area comprised a lot of countries. In many ways it still does.

Digging for history

When I was a student at UBC, I knew hardly anything about B.C. I was a history major who took a bus that crossed Discovery Street, and didn't have a clue. Gabriola Island I saw from the ferry. Who was that? Nootka? Sounds kind of Indian.

After a while it dawned on me that a college student could go and find stuff out. I don't remember how I wangled permission to go on a little dig. We went to a midden somewhere down near Boundary Bay. I had never heard of a midden. A midden, I was told by an archaeology student, is a sort of dump, kind of like the Oliver town dump up by where the city of Fairview used to be, only a lot older. Dr. Charles Borden, the famous archaeologist, was in charge, but at the moment he was looking at a site near Yale. The Indians who spent the winter down here by the ocean made a little mountain out of sea shells, and threw some of their other useless stuff there as well. The oldest middens we have were started about five thousand years ago. A midden is a treasure trove for archaeologists.

It's made mainly of clam shells and mussel shells, but it has a lot of other things that people would throw away, or lose. In the really early days of middens they had human bodies in them.

When I was a boy, people on the Coast and on the Island made driveways out of old piles of clamshells, and ashtrays out of their favourites. People living in coastal towns are still turning ancient Indian shells into their carrot gardens.

So I was not part of a crew. I didn't know anything about cutting straight holes and sifting dirt. But I had a day to kill, wandering around an actual site. I don't eat oysters, but I dug around the oyster mountain, and I found a curved bone. It was part of a cranium, someone told me. Really old.

In those days the diggers were shaking up people by announcing that the Native people had been in B.C. for four thousand years. Pretty soon some diggers up the Fraser River said make that eight thousand years. Then some diggers in the eastern mountains of the province said eleven thousand. Every year or so the population of the Canadian West becomes a few thousand years older. I think that the latest figure I heard was forty thousand years.

But the actual carbon-dated period is so far between 10,500 and 11,000 years.

What were the Europeans doing eleven thousand years ago?

The conventional wisdom has been for some time that the "Natives" of the Americas came across a land bridge from northern Asia some time during the last ice age, which started eighty thousand years ago. They used what is now British Columbia as a highway. They headed south and built the great civilizations of South America and Mexico. Then as the ice slowly receded, some of the people followed northward, marvelling at the nice new hunting ground where there used to be ice. Centuries later the people who called themselves Americans would do much the same.

One thing we do know is that the sites in the Interior are older than the sites on the Coast. The oyster people were Johnny-come-latelies. People in the mountains were making knives out of old volcano glass when the islands were only the playgrounds for the otter people and the cormorant people.

At the end of the ice age there was a big corridor of bare earth between ice to the east and ice to the west. Here the Interior Salish people started their settlement, learning how to make pit houses in the winter and smoke houses in the summer. When things warmed up to the west they sent some people over the last range of mountains to learn how to handle the tide and become the Coast Salish people.

After the ice left the Coast, some other people came from the northwest and settled the north coast and northern islands. These would become known as the Haida and Kwakiutl and others. The last I heard, they arrived more than nine thousand years ago. They left middens on the Queen Charlotte Islands and over on the mainland.

But why didn't the Asians just keep on coming to North America all the way up to modern times? Of course, the ice melted. If there was a land bridge the new elevation of the water covered it over. But they didn't have to walk. The Inuit people always went back and forth, at least until the Russians and USAmericans started their own ice age. When the Europeans started coming to the New World (and bringing unwilling Africans with them), there was no stopping them. So why did the Asians quit coming until very recent times?

Sometimes there are no answers in history. It is as full of holes as archaeology.

Looking at the atlas

We've been hearing this story about Asians and the land bridge all our lives. Somehow it seems right. When we were kids looking at our school atlas, we saw that the east coast of the Americas sort of fits the west coast of the Old World. Later we were told that continental drift was likely responsible for the fact that you can't walk from St. John's to Brest any more.

So looking at the atlas again, we saw that the Aleutians seemed to be the beginning of that chain of islands that makes up the most easterly part of

Asia, and that further north, just below the Arctic Circle, Alaska and East Siberia are nearly touching each other. Maybe forty thousand years before the USAmericans and Russian Soviets learned to make ballistic missiles, people in parkas were walking from continent to continent.

I have never heard anyone talk about westward travel. They always talk about the Asians crossing the ice bridge to America, or Turtle Island, or Gold Mountain. America is the place that explorers and immigrants come to.

But then what happened to all that other stuff we were told about the racial divisions of mankind? Many of us have British forebears, and our British forebears sorted the human race into white, black, red and yellow. Even today our British contemporaries refer to the earliest North Americans as "Red Indians," to distinguish them from the people in another of their former colonial areas.

How did the yellow Asians become the red Indians?

The ice bridge is a wonderful idea, and so is the picture of ancient people in hairy clothes chasing hairy mastodons that are going to America for the summer. What school kid can resist hairy mastodons and brave cavemen with spears? They're right up there with dinosaurs.

But we all noticed that Cheyennes don't really look much like most east Asians we know. Chilcotin people don't look like Koreans. Inuit people do look as if some of those people in the Russian Arctic might be their relatives. Once, while watching a National Film Board movie about Inuit, I heard a Japanese guy said "Hey, they're us!" The shamanistic teepee-dwelling Tsaatan people of Mongolia have remarked on how familiar some pictures of North American Indians look.

Maybe Chilcotin people look a little like those Asians who live in that unimaginable country where western China meets central Siberia.

But think about this: how much do modern Danes and Portuguese look like the people who were wandering into Europe in 30,000 B.C.?

One thing I do know. I have never seen a Native Canadian who looked the least bit red. And I have never seen a Chinese person or a Japanese person who looks at all yellow. That's two things I know.

The Okanagan writer Mourning Dove said that her people, the Interior Salishan, had slightly tilted eyes. She said that those eyes show that her people were descended from Coyote.

The trickster.

Giant wood

It is common wisdom that the Coastal Indians were distinguished from the Interior Indians by their wealth. Certainly the ocean full of food and the warmth of the winters contributed to the material comfort of the peoples along the ocean, and probably to their greater attention to material possessions and social distinctions based on possessions. They also had more time. They did not have to spend as many days and months finding food and escaping from snow. They had leisure, and because of leisure they had time to make art and jewellery. They were setting a pattern that would be followed by white people in the twentieth century: if you want to spend your life making art or jewellery, head for the Coast. For white people in the Interior in the twentieth century, the Coast means Vancouver.

But if you were an Indian person from the Interior several hundred years ago, and you went to the Coast on a trade mission, you might be struck by a more obvious difference between these people and your own. Maybe you are bringing a chunk of obsidian down to the Coast from Chilcotin country, and you want to trade it for dentalium shells.

You would probably be impressed by the largeness.

The people live in long wooden plank houses. The ceiling is much higher than a man's head. There is a round stone fireplace in the middle, and room for several families. You are used to crowding into a pit house in the winter and a teepee in the summer. These people can stand up and walk around inside their houses. They can dance. The children can run around until their parents chase them outside, into the rain.

Outside these huge wooden houses are some really large boats. These are wooden boats carved from giant trees, burnt and chopped at, hollowed out. They will each contain a dozen or more men. They scoot across the surface of the ocean after fish or other people. They are large.

But some kind of largeness is required. Back in the dry country one can live a whole lifetime familiar with one little tree that was smaller than one's grandfather and is now smaller than one's youngest sister. Here on the Coast the cedar trees are enormous, frightening. To be in their presence is to know that human people are very small.

To live here, it is necessary to fell a giant tree and make large houses and boats.

Everything is larger than anything you have seen back home. There are more people living in one of these longhouses than there are in your whole band. The pile of clam and oyster shells is higher than anything in your home town.

Walking softly

About the time that the first Canadian railroad entered British Columbia, non-Indians became more than half the population of the province. The unmoving iron tracks lay where silent hunters had pursued silent animals. The people of the woods had to get out of the way of the iron men.

Put it this way: the Europeans were starting to fill the land with their hard artefacts.

Over the previous ten thousand years the first peoples had left a few hard artefacts, some small stone bowls held by carved stone figures, lots of spearheads, a smidgen of native copper brought down from the Bering Sea. But most of the things these people made were made of wood. On the Coast they were lucky enough to live among the cedar, and the cedar could be used to make boats and boxes and houses and nets and skirts. On rare occasions archaeologists are lucky too, and find some ancient Indian artefacts that had been caught in a mudslide. But usually their things did what nature needed—they rotted their way back into the forest.

If most of your cultural artefacts are made of materials that disappear over time, the human beings digging holes thousands of years in the future might think your culture less complex than it is. If later sites yield richer findings, that formula may be due to human progress, but only in part; it will also be due to the fact that time brings deterioration. Archaeologists always have to remember that.

The people of the Interior did not make as many things as did the people of the Coast. In their sense of the world, things were not very important. They moved around quite a lot, and they did not go in much for a class system, so they did not need to amass possessions. They did believe in property, but they believed that the closer anything approached the quality of the invisible and weightless the more valuable it was. So houses and spears and baskets made from roots were not all that precious. Old family hunting and berry-gathering territory was pretty important. Most valuable of all were songs and names and stories owned by specific families. To be given one of those was a great honour. To steal one was a great shame. Shame, invisible and weightless, was a great punishment.

The Athapaskan-speaking peoples of the sub-Arctic were very much interested in survival. Survival meant having skill and swiftness. Property that slowed a person down without compensating by helping one kill bison was unheard of.

The various Indian peoples regarded language and kinship ties as the determinants of their differences and associations. They were defined by speech and by family. These things are very hard to find in an archaeological dig. Invisible property is not going to show up in a midden. Tlingits and Kootenays are as different as Vikings and Greeks, and very much different *from* them.

People of a poetic bent might say that the first peoples were process. The newcomers from the sun or wherever they emanated were bringers of things that just stayed there. It was a strange concept: if you put something that would not move somewhere, nothing else would be able to pass through that space. The first peoples saw a lot of examples of this strange concept. When the newcomers laid down their iron tracks, they did so along ways that were already traced by the creeks. The newcomers used a brand-new European invention to make explosions in the canyons and drop millions of big rocks into the creeks, and after that the fish could not get home up those creeks.

The first peoples had a hard time learning to live without process.

Landing hard

If working in wood meant that the people of the Coast would not leave tools and art that was much over a few generations old, it also meant that they would create settlements more prosperous and permanent than anything to be found in the great plains. While the students of Socrates were cramming for their final exams, the artisans of the lower Fraser River were employing wedges, hammers and adzes to make lumber out of giant red cedars. Marpole, the southern neighbourhood of Vancouver, where the remnants of these people's architecture have been found, is still the site of a lumber mill.

What a great place to live, the mouth of the Fraser River! The long cedar canoes these artisans made with their adzes and fires could reach far inland on the large waterway, and also travel up and down the Coast, looking into the countless inlets for trade or trouble. The ocean brought clams and mussels. The river conveyed huge shoals of salmon as well as the giant sturgeon that was as long as three men, sometimes four.

These carpenters were also sitting pretty when it came to trade. According to the archaeological record, the whole Coast and the whole of the southern Interior and even the prairies were markets and marketplaces. Graves in the Okanagan Valley sometimes contain dentalium shells from the Pacific deeps. The ground at Marpole reveals copper brought from the far north and mountain goat horn transformed into ostentatious serving spoons.

Also found in the ancient Vancouver site were the hard parts of the sculptor's tools, sharpened animal teeth, small jade adzes, little awls and chisels. The long canoes had eyes carved into their prows. Eyes of wood and paint looked out over the tidal river bank. The towns of the south never grew as elaborate or wealthy looking as the Haida towns of the Queen Charlotte Islands, but they impressed the traders who ventured down the Fraser from the mountains.

When the newcomers with the skin of ghosts came to the lower Fraser, they cut down the high cedars and they built sheds with no art on them. They made a field of mud for their high boots. Most of them were going somewhere else.

The potlatch

When the Europeans came to what is now British Columbia, they had little idea of how many cultures they were to meet in the last part of what was for them the eighteenth century. There were, depending on your sense of language and kinship, somewhere between ten and thirty cultural groups or areas. There were hundreds of bands, some moving around, some relatively settled. Within any language group there were dialects. Today the Shuswap of Kamloops and the Shuswap of Chase, a few kilometres east along the Trans-Canada Highway, like to make fun of each other's dialect.

Within each band there were families with their own histories. For the people of the Coast, there were highly developed clan loyalties, reflected in art, in the styles of poles and dances, as well as in property rights, fishing and hunting, especially. Clans included a class system, roughly marked into three levels: the aristocracy, the commonfolk and slaves, the last usually captured during forays into the territory of another culture, Kwakiutl into Salish, for instance. Each clan had a chief, a fact that puzzled European visitors, who did not understand how there could be two chiefs in one village.

In the Interior there were families, but no great formalized class system. Indian hunters or trappers in the Interior had to travel greater distances for their living than did the fishermen of the Coast. Their main reality was space. People who range over great distances to find their food do not have time or resources to pay artisans to make emblems of their family or clan history and power. The people of the Interior practised a necessary egalitarianism, or at least something far more democratic than the feudalism of the Coast.

So the people in the Interior did not have the time or the money for the potlatch.

Ever since the Europeans arrived on the Coast, they have had odd and contradictory ideas about the potlatch. Usually, they have been dismissive of it or hostile toward it. They have never really been able to understand it, and most tellingly, they have never been able to understand how deeply important it was and is to Native cultures. The various Coastal peoples have had differing ideas about the way to conduct a potlatch, but a few things remain common. The potlatch ensured the distribution of wealth that was necessary to a society's survival, or it provided a venue for passing down through the generations important names and stories and other valuable property. Marriages and compacts would be celebrated at the potlatches, thus bringing about peace and cooperation along the Coast.

The social system of a people would be encoded in the manner of its potlatches. The most powerful oligarchy was likely to stage the most extravagant celebration. In such a society, the potlatch was an enormous ceremonial feast hosted by a chief with the main purpose of affirming his power and wealth. A memorable potlatch would not only make his name live throughout time and the forest; it would redound upon all members of his clan, not counting the slaves, who had no right to life, much less acclaim.

If you could not afford to throw a big showy party, you had no place in the chief business. There were times when you had to hold a potlatch, and your invited guests had to come, because if they did not, they would be admitting that they did not have the resources to host an answering pot-latch of their own that winter. A man who had just attained the position of chief had to hold a potlatch to proclaim his name. Later his daughter might reach puberty or his son might earn a noble position. The father was obliged to hold a potlatch.

So clan leaders from near and not so near would arrive by dugout canoe, decked in their finest jewellery, attended by regalia-laden lords. They would step ashore and dance, shaking rattles decorated with colourful shells. They would go through costume changes, removing masks under which there would be faces like masks. Their back-up band would be costumed like ani-mals, birds, spirits of the sky and woods.

All this while the host chief would bide his time, allowing the visiting chiefs their moments, pretending to tolerate the music, counselling himself that the show he had prepared would put any road show to shame. He would display the greatest of respect, being certain, when the time came for sitting down, that all the visiting nobles and satraps were arranged in meticulous order. They were all there to celebrate his daughter's new status, not to begin a chain of minor wars. There was a lot of tension in the air. The blan-kets and headdress were heavy. The meat smelled delicious.

White people shivering in their stone castles on the Rhine had no idea that any of this was happening.

Each of the guests came armed with his beautifully carved spoon. The spoon might be carved of hemlock, or of mountain-sheep's horn, or of cold argillite. A nobleman would wield his spoon with pride, but he would have made certain that the spoon be as splendid as possible without being quite as splendid as his chief's spoon. And how the spoons were put to use, as the heaping dishes were brought out, more food in an hour than a band of Dene was likely to see in a winter. The bowls were art filled with fish and meat. It had to be the greatest meal ever seen by anyone here—that was the rule of the potlatch.

Meanwhile the host chief and his back-up singers and band were per-forming. He went through several costume changes as he sang all the songs and danced all the dances he owned. He wore the Raven mask while he per-formed the dance of his ancestor in the underworld. Between numbers he urged his audience to welcome more and more dishes of food brought into the longhouse from the kitchens next door.

Oolichan oil ran down upraised arms and glistened on chins. Each chief took note of every dish and every costume and calculated the expense of his next potlatch. Scallops in soapberry sauce were brought in. Who could resist?

And now the host was finished dancing. His poems were done. It was time for the giving of gifts, the heart of the potlatch. I can easily afford to give you this, boasted the host, sometimes with contempt in his voice. You think that canoe you arrived on was something? I will give you a craft that will put it to shame. You will give yours to a slave.

The gifts were extravagant but carefully accorded to rank. While his assistants brought them in and displayed them the chief spoke dismissively of their worth to him. Each guest would receive a gift more splendid than he had given to his host when his host was guest. It was a fine gesture to outdo your guest's last benevolence, putting it to shame. It would have been a shame and an insult to do less. An insult of generosity was honourable, but an insult of parsimony would have meant a bad future.

Suffering the boastful speeches of his host, the visiting chief played his role, the inferior for the moment. Disdainfully the host disbursed boats and copper, weapons and furs. Showing no untoward excitement the guests received their gifts, already calculating future orgies.

You have probably seen the disdain with which the truly rich can drop money on a counter. Nothing displays one's wealth as much as the disdain that one shows toward it. So the potlatch became not only the event at which valuables were given away, but also the theatre in which the propertied destroyed their belongings. The host might cause resplendent blankets to be rent and scattered. He might own a canoe that his artists had spent half a year in making, that would be the envy of noblemen up and down the coast. At his potlatch he would show contempt for this trifle and burn it, feeding the flames with bowl after bowl of oil.

Slaves were property too, of course. The host might cause a half-dozen slaves to be brought into the feast house and brained with stone clubs made for this purpose. Their lifeless or nearly lifeless bodies might then be thrown on the midden or into the blazing boat. A few slaves? There are piles more where they came from. If we need more, our warriors can pick them up easily next time they are on a business trip to Bella Coola country.

A chief might just about impoverish his clan by throwing a potlatch, but the output was worth it. For one thing, it left no doubt about the class system of which the chief was the apex, just as his figure might be seen at the top of a pole after his death. And by throwing a successful potlatch the chief ensured that he would be a guest at his neighbour's next potlatch, and by the rule, it should be even more spectacular than his. In the meantime his people, convinced of the rightness of the social order, will go about amassing wealth once more, from the forest and the sea and the enemy.

Strange law

Few Coastal Indian activities bothered the Europeans as much as did the potlatch. The serious Scots who ran the Hudson's Bay Company in the colony hated the idea of giving away or ostentatiously destroying property. They thought that it might set a bad example for Interior Indians who hadn't thought of the idea. Indeed, by the time the whites had reached the country, some Carrier Indians were beginning to throw a few potlatches, though of necessity these were not the extravagant affairs of the Coast.

The representatives of the European Christian churches were also unhappy about the ceremony. They saw the Archfiend's hand in a ritual based on pride in impoverishing oneself. William Duncan, the most famous of the Anglican missionaries of the nineteenth century, spent a lot of time on the north coast. He was amazed by the high quality of the peoples' sculpture, or carving, as aboriginal art is called by colonial Europeans. But he was appalled by the winter festivals, when the business of making a living was put aside and the people of the Coast devoted their time to dancing and singing and other spiritual works. In an 1875 letter to David Laird, the federal minister of the interior, he called the potlatch "the most formidable of all obstacles in the way of the Indians becoming Christian, or even civilized."

Mr. Duncan was assuming that Mr. Laird was assuming that civilization did not precede Christianity. That was not an unusual assumption in the nineteenth century, and even into the twentieth. It would show up in twentieth-century resistance to extending the franchise to immigrants from Asia.

But the potlatch was intricately connected with every part of Coastal Indian life. It ensured a distribution of wealth, as well as an industriousness among the people who had to work for years to prepare for a potlatch or to recover from one. It was only part of a spiritual life that included the magic of shamans and other healers, winter dance festivals, the designs of poles and houses, prayers at work and so on. Thus, when the European churchmen set about attacking the potlatch, they had to attack nearly all other aspects of Indian life. As Victorians they bent their attack primarily upon the expression of a group ethos. They wanted to introduce Jesus and individuality.

So William Duncan tried to civilize the savages by creating a model Indian village, designed to make them Christians. In this village there were more commandments than Moses brought his crowd. Among the things that the inhabitants shalt not do are painting their faces, calling for shamans to ease their souls and giving stuff away.

Thou shalt not give thy stuff away.

The Catholics, primarily the Oblate Brothers, also built villages, and in these villages the church would be the biggest building. They also built schools, where Indian children could be educated to understand individual work, away from the influence of their families and clans, who might teach them to dance together.

The Oblate Brothers built a lot of villages in the Interior, where the pot-latch had not taken hold yet, though they did have to contend with the winter dances. There they built churches and persuaded the wide-ranging hunters to live in shacks around the churches, and to work in the fields to pay for these shacks. Thus the former savages were introduced to the notion of taxes and mortgages. No giving stuff away in those little towns.

Some Indians on Vancouver Island took a long time to understand Protestantism. In the 1860s some Indians at Nanaimo tried to make a deal with the hotshot young Methodist missionary, Thomas Crosby. We will come to church every Sunday if you will put up with a little dancing in between times, they said. Dancing, they said, was not such an evil thing. In fact, dancing had been considered by their people a way of being with God.

No deal, said young Crosby. Dancing and potlatching are bad. God hates dancing and potlatching. And there is no Raven. Birds are birds. And cover up those bare legs.

Actually, the spirit of the potlatch was being subverted by the business-men who were cousins at least of the religious men and political men. By the late nineteenth century the potlatch-givers were giving away fewer button-blankets and more goods manufactured by the white people. And the ancient clan lines had been disrupted so much by the interference of the white tradesmen that newly rich Natives were throwing potlatches simply because they could pay for them.

Still, the Christians did not like the idea of people giving away the fruits of their labour or business sense. And the governments wanted some kind of governable order they could understand. People giving all their stuff away had to be insane or seriously religious. The provincial government felt that way nearly a century later when the Sons of Freedom started taking off their clothes and burning down their own houses.

So when the amended Indian Act of 1884 was promulgated, the spirit dances and the potlatch were made illegal. "Every Indian or other person who engages in or assists in celebrating the Indian festival known as 'Potlatch' or in the Indian dance known as the 'Tamanawas' is guilty of a misdemeanor and shall be liable to imprisonment." That's interesting lan-guage. It suggests with its "other person" and "assists" that it is either (a) dis-interestedly free of racialist specificity, or (b) fearful of any example that might persuade white people that the Indians have a better idea.

Those who managed to get the act passed knew that if they could destroy the potlatch they could pretty well chop down the culture of the Coast Indians, and start a new religious and economic organization for them among the deadfall. Most British people of the colonialist nineteenth century thought that the Indian folkways and the Indians themselves were on the way out of history. Some would survive into the twentieth century. These would be the ones who had been redeemed and turned into something

Victoria's last potlatch in the 1890s.

resembling the labouring classes of Britain.

It took a while for the potlatch to die away, though. It was not an easy practice to stop, and it was easy to disguise on an extremely long coastline with thousands of inlets patrolled by few Indian agents. Some Indian people protested, petitioning the prime minister. Others, such as the tough Kwakiutl, simply ignored the ban. In 1889 a Kwakiutl chief named Hemasak was arrested and found guilty of giving stuff away and sentenced to six months in jail.

What was Hemasak supposed to do? When he went to a number of potlatches in recent years, it was expected that the self-impoverishing chiefs would be attending a magnificent ceremony at his place. It would be a matter of great shame if he called off the party. And it would have been a disaster for the system of sharing wealth. Besides that, the beings in the spirit world, including his ancestors, would be terribly offended by this human being. Hemasak and his community would be doomed should he fail to hold a potlatch.

Six months, said the court.

But Matthew Begbie, "the Hanging Judge," did not like the anti-potlatch law. He understood how calamitous it would be for an ancient society, and he noticed that the act did not define the word "potlatch," a sign that the Government of Canada did not have a clue about what the ceremony meant. Judge Begbie presided at Hemasak's appeal and threw the case out on a technicality.

Begbie went after the law, writing decisions against it, evading it, mocking it. The Crown was having a hard time enforcing the anti-potlatch law in British Columbia. Finally the government had to go back to the legislation, plugging all the holes and thwarting Begbie's campaign.

People still held potlatches when they could, but there were Christians singing hymns in the big churches across the way from the feast-house. There were children coming home for the school holiday and laughing at the old ways. There were *nouveau-riche* fishermen arriving back home in dories and stepping around town in fancy European military jackets.

In the early years of the twentieth century the Indian agents and their back-up groups kept up the attack against the potlatch, especially the insistent traditional potlatch of the Kwakiutl people. The people would prepare for a potlatch, heaping up the carved and painted masks and blankets and jewellery for gifts. The government people would then arrive and confiscate all the treasure, heaping it onto their boats and sailing to Victoria or Vancouver. Before you knew it, the booty was appearing in museums and private collections in Ottawa and Washington and Paris. A lot of people got rich, but the wealth was no longer being distributed along the Indian Coast of British Columbia.

When the anti-potlatch law was repealed in the Indian Act of 1951, a lot of people had to take courses on how to operate one. And now when an important potlatch is to be held, it is likely that the premier of the province and some federal MPs will be there for a photo-opportunity.

Shamans

If the Indians had suddenly showed up in Europe around the year 1100, who knows what the Europeans would have thought of them, or done to them? But when the Europeans started arriving on the northwest coast of America, they were entering the territory of peoples who had been learning all their lives to encounter strange creatures and spirits.

They had shamans, who would understand the ghost people's presence. The shaman embodies Indian belief in transformation. He or she can become an animal when it is necessary. He or she can leave the body behind and travel as a soul to the other places that humans might go, to heaven or to the underworld.

The shaman can travel and change in these ways because he is not the person he once was. He is not his mother's son. He has gone through a near-death experience, during which the spirits of the old dead shamans came to him and took him apart. They took him apart and rebuilt him from scratch. They showed him the way to a truly frightful place, and there he encountered a frightening figure who would from that night forward be his guardian spirit. This ecstatic experience would forever set the shaman apart from his fellows while giving him a place of respect.

The shaman's job was to heal. But there were other healers, notably the men or women who understood the curative powers of plants, or the physicians who could set broken bones. The shaman was responsible for the care of people beset by spirits, whether those spirits were acting for enemy groups or themselves.

The role of the shaman will depend on the kind of society in which he practises. Among the Coastal people with their elaborate caste system and their secret societies, the shaman had lots of rivals for respect and power. He retained his amazing ability to converse with the creatures in the spirit world, but he did not have the political power enjoyed by shamans of the Great Plains, where they might act as military commanders and legislative chiefs.

If some enormous irregularity occurs in nature, the shaman is expected to know why. The abnormal does not just happen. If Mount Mazama blows his top and darkens the sky and covers the earth with white muck, the shaman can explain to his fellow citizens why the forces in the spirit world are acting so violently. When ghost-skin people in floating houses first arrived in Coast Salish waters, the ordinary folk consulted the shamans to figure it out.

With blunt European categorization we can see the shamans as the centre of the Indians' religious life. But the way they see the world is also at the root of artistic life. At the height of European painting and sculpture and architecture and music and poetry the subject was in most cases religion, whether Ancient Greco-Roman or Christian. For the Christian Europeans the heart of their religious belief was transcendence, and all their art forms projected that belief. A Handel oratorio and a Michelangelo *pietà* both express great compassion for the human experience, but do so in the context of reaching toward something higher.

For the Coast Indian peoples the heart of their religious belief was mutability and transformation, and all their art forms projected that belief. Shape-shifters and tricksters, if they existed in Christian religions, would probably be cast as evil-doers, as witches and demons. In the metonymic world of the Indians, creatures such as Raven on the Coast and Coyote in the Interior are to be both feared and thanked, respected and laughed at. They are figures of magic change. Transformations seen in nature reflect their nature.

On the Coast and the Island mysterious dances incorporated the use of costumes and especially masks that suggested the crossing of boundaries among human, animal and spirit forms. The removal of a mask would be a frightening and suggestive gesture. Its replacement by another mask, perhaps worn beneath the first one, would be pretty frightening, whether in a rain-soaked longhouse or a twelfth-floor psychiatrist's office.

European people who see a Tlingit or Haida totem pole for the first time
have a difficulty in "figuring it out." If they look around, they might find similar figures carved in paddles or on walls or on the handles of spoons. They
are instructed that a certain figure is a rendition of a beaver, and then they
see that it looks a lot like the figure that is supposed to be a killer whale. And
why is the killer whale pointed straight down? Why does he seem to have an
eye in the middle of his back? It is as if he is becoming something else. The
Indian carvings, for all their massiveness, are verbs in wood.

In the Interior your guide might often point out small mountains or large
rocks or still ponds that were once people. They say that the opposite movement has also occurred. What you have heard is another art form, called
poetry or fiction back home in Europe.

Spirit people

But it is not as if the shamans were spiritual loners and the rest of the people were simple earthly types. In the shamanistic world a guardian spirit was
available to people who went upon spirit quests. Artists, hunters and warriors felt that their special work was inspired by a guardian spirit. The noble
families of the north coast hired artists to create their family crests, images of
brave family members confronting scary supernatural creatures. As the
Salishan peoples of the Coast and the Interior were more egalitarian than
the north coast peoples, every Salish person might be initiated into the
spirit world.

In her autobiography, the Okanagan writer Mourning Dove recounted
her spirit quests. When she turned twelve and reached puberty, she felt quite
ambivalent about the ordeals. But she was hoping to prepare herself for a
future as a renowned medicine woman, so she went alone and without provisions into the mountain wilderness east of the Okanogan River for ten
days. She prayed and made certain not to touch her hair with her hands,
and so on, but nothing happened. Then a shaman woman opened her bag
and gave the child eagle bones, and the child spent a night atop an eagle
mountain, but she had her dog with her, so the eagles circled high overhead
but never came to the child, little Christine Quintasket. The shaman had
her sleep with the rotting body of a horse, and undergo other trials, but none
of them took.

Then

when summer came I went out again and had a strange experience. I
went down by the river and walked very carefully through the tall
grass under the cottonwoods, fearing to step on a rattlesnake.
Suddenly a dog came at me with menace. I felt a sensation as if cold
water was thrown on me, and the dog got even larger, with a swirl of

fire around him. He began to sing. I became very fearful and was about to faint when I thought to pray to God. The dog vanished. When I felt able, I ran home without regard to the rattlers infesting that country.

I paid a boy a dollar to find and kill the dog. Several years later the dog came to me in a dream and said that if I had followed his song and dance, I would have become a great doctor, able to cure the sick and have good luck. If I did not accept him, he would go to a little boy with a pack of dogs as his power. I knew the boy. When I awoke, I decided to choose the Christian God. The dog left me for good. The little boy died shortly afterward, and I went to his funeral. Perhaps he had no right to the "ghost spirits" of my ancestors. This dog had been one of my grandmother's powers, and I was probably meant to inherit it.

So little Christine grew up not to be a doctor but a writer and a feminist and a political worker as well as an agricultural labourer. She chose Christianity, but she did not feel obliged therefore to deny the reality of the shaman.

The Christian priests who came to the Indian country did not exhibit such tolerance. They were on a mission to save the aboriginal people from just such perversions of the human soul as were to be found in a world-view that included spirits among the trees. For the Christians anything supernatural among the trees had always been the work of the Fiend.

Strange Visitors

"The trouble is, it is very difficult, to be both poet and,
an historian."
—Charles Olson, October 1953, Mayan Letters

North and south

People in British Columbia really do think of their place differently. For one thing, they think in terms of geography rather than history. The main directions of Canadian history are east and west. The main directions of B.C. geography are north and south. Granville Street in downtown Vancouver and Ste. Catherine Street in downtown Montreal run roughly parallel to one another. But in Montreal they say Ste. Catherine West and Ste. Catherine East. Granville Street runs north and south.

Central Canadians say that the 401 Highway between Montreal and Toronto runs west, whereas visiting British Columbians will know that it is running south. If you go west from Montreal you get to Ottawa. If you go what they call "south" from Montreal, you get to the Eastern Townships.

This is the subjugation of geography (the non-human) to history (the human—read European). As far as those white people in Montreal and Toronto are concerned, the discovery and settlement of Canada was a matter of Europeans going westward. They went westward across the ocean. They went westward from Ontario to the Canadian prairies.

So if they had to get to the Great Lakes via the St. Lawrence River, it must have been a westward voyage. If you want to take the train from Burlington, Ontario, to Niagara, Ontario, in which case you will be going mainly east, and a little bit south, you have to take the westbound train.

They like history back east. On that island that became Montreal, they are proud of some old stones. These are stones that have been made cubic by human hands, and piled on one another. This happened three or four hundred years ago. Those stones are three hundred and fifty years old, some Montrealer will tell you, a rube from the west.

But you've stood on some slippery rocks on the edge of North Vancouver. The city behind you might be made up largely of contemporary building materials, such as squashed cardboard or whatever, but these stones are millions of years old. You could use one to crack open an oyster.

Anyway, if you are like me, you grew up in a valley that runs north and south, beside a river that runs south. When you came to the Coast you came to a coast that runs north and south. Most of the radio stations you listened to as a kid were south of you. The valley you lived in existed also in another country, where they just spelled its name differently.

Recently I went into a store in a mall to ask about its name. It's apparently part of a chain of leather-jacket stores called "Hollywood West." I said "Isn't Hollywood already in the west?" They said "It's only a name, man." I knew that I was talking to the kind of people who think that you can claim a whole ocean in the name of a Spanish king.

Now that the malls are here, maybe these things are changing, but British Columbia people have always regarded themselves in a way that people in other provinces do not. Quebeckers may want to revision themselves as a separate nation, but they are still thinking of separating *from* something. British Columbians who want to see themselves as Canadians have to make a conscious effort to do so when they grow up.

Have you noticed that when prairie people talk or write about the "West" they mean Manitoba, Saskatchewan and Alberta. B.C. is something else. People on the prairie look eastward to Toronto when it comes to seeing themselves in place. They are the west, and the east is back there, where history happened earlier.

But people in B.C. know this fundamental difference: there is the Coast and there is the Interior. You situate yourself by how far you are from the ocean. So people in B.C. have to be taught to be Canadians. This is done by the Canadian Broadcasting Corporation and *The Globe and Mail*. But most British Columbians don't listen to the CBC or read the G&M. The more learned ones do. But even the more learned ones know that they are British Columbians first. Our most famous authors will tell you that. George Woodcock, for instance, and Ethel Wilson:

> But my interest in British Columbia as a place and a past grew more intense as the years went on, and made me more closely committed to my regional loyalties, so that in the end I would proclaim myself

to be "British Columbian first, and then Canadian." (George Woodcock, 1990)

I have a life-long love for this province of ours which I share with many people, this British Columbia, as if it were a person, as it is—and a person with infinite variety and inference. (Ethel Wilson, 1957)

Speaking of writers

The simple fact is that in British Columbia there is one hell of a lot of geography. There is more geography than there is history, always has been. There is a lot more geography than there are people.

Once the poet John Newlove, who wrote a great poem about the relationship between Indians and geography, was hitchhiking along the Trans-Canada Highway, somewhere around Sicamous. Along came a driver with New York licence plates and gave him a ride

&. asked me where all
the people were in Canada, the cities[.]

If you look at road-maps of New York and British Columbia, two differences make themselves known immediately. There are a lot more cities and towns along the highways in New York. And the highways in New York cover the entire state. A road-map of British Columbia will show how difficult it is to make highways in the province. They have to go long distances to connect small communities, and they have to find a way to get somewhere between mountains, alongside cliffs, over canyon rivers and through granite. The road-map of British Columbia is even a lot different from the road-map of Alberta, where they have the luxury of laying out a flat road every mile or so.

Unfold that road-map to the triangular grid that shows you how far the drive is from one town to another. You will see that the drive from Kelsey Bay, on Vancouver Island, to Atlin, which is just south of Yukon, is 2899 kilometres, or, if you are a USAmerican making the drive, 1812 miles. You will see a lot of beautiful scenery along the way.

If you want to drive a similar distance in the USA (over easier highways, of course), drive from Kansas City, Missouri, to Portland, Oregon.

Speaking of Canadian writers, Robert Kroetsch said that post-modern writers resemble archaeologists. Henry James had said that novelists are like historians. He said that novelists are to history as painters are to nature. That was a hundred years ago. Along came Kroetsch and said that now novelists are a lot more like archaeologists. He even called his collected poems *Field Notes*. He even made a dinosaur archaeologist the main character of his most famous novel. He said that writers nowadays are more like archaeologists because they admit that they are working with fragments, with holes between the fragments. Archaeologists are always longing for the complete story, but they have to work with fragments and holes.

Well, history is full of holes, too.

It's just that historians try to pretend it isn't so. Historians are fond of cause and effect. In high school, whenever they didn't know what else to do, they made us write an essay on "The Causes of the First World War." If you are working with cause and effect, you can't have any holes in history. Historians started thinking of themselves as scientists in the nineteenth century. But they are social scientists. The difference between social scientists and real scientists is that things don't have to work out the way you predict them all the time. They think that 60 per cent is pretty good.

But history is full of holes. At least 40 per cent of it is holes. In the old days the holes would have been seen as lapses, as gaps, as something that needed filling up, to make continuity. Now when we read history we read the holes as part of history. I don't know, says a historian, and we don't mark him down to 60 per cent any more. Historians are something like archaeologists now. They spend more of their time reading.

I am saying all this stuff about history and archaeology because it is making more sense these days to draw them together if we can. It used to be that the past would be separated into historical times and prehistory. Into a time full of holes and a time of cause and effect. But think about early historical times: now we can look back on that early history the way archaeologists might. And we can think of ourselves first as readers.

My theory is that reading came first, then writing. Then speech. First our grunting ancestors learned to read the clouds and the tracks made by mammoths. Then they figured out how to leave signs themselves. At long last some humans with accidental changes to their vocal cords became dominant.

But reading was first. Now we know that historians spend most of their time reading. They read other history books, of course, and they read old deeds and treaties and trial cases. They read other people's writing. The historical period and the age of writing are the same thing. But then someone made up a seeming oxymoron called "oral history." There are historians who cannot write an approved European or Asiatic language, but who have history to tell. In the old days this stuff was called folklore.

There is also reading material that was not written by human beings. It was scratched on canyon floors by receding ice. It was hurled into Asiatic Russia from outer space.

Here was geography being read as history. Marks on the land with stories to be told.

Just two centuries shy of seven thousand years ago a peak called Mount Mazama did some writing all over the southern part of British Columbia. Mount Mazama is now called Crater Lake, a beautiful landmark in Oregon. Airline pilots make sure that their passengers get a good view of Crater Lake, round blue water in the shell of a large volcano. Mount Mazama blew its top 6,800 years ago in an explosion that made the 1980 outburst of Mount Saint Helens sound like a hiccup. It was a huge event. It darkened the sky over the whole Interior plateau and then some. For days a wet ash fell from the dark sky and covered everything in a gooey way that no snow had ever done.

This must have been a terribly frightening moment of history for people who lived in a world populated by invisible beings. Depending on how close they were to Oregon, they would have heard the blast and felt it move the ground under them. Then they had to live under a sky in which the sun had been replaced by a red smear. They must have been frightened to know what the spirit world thought of them. They must have given some thought to their religious life. For them their religious life was minute-to-minute life-and-death at all times.

But these people, whose families had been on the Interior plateau for five thousand years, did not write down their experience of the ash on everything. We, however, can read it when we drive around southern British Columbia. If you dig a hole or cut a road in southern B.C., you will find a white line of old ash that was once burning earth in Oregon. It is some writing from prehistory.

So that is how geography becomes history. Archaeologists are people who read geography historically.

Dancing history

The Europeans wanted hard evidence. Hard evidence for archaeologists means stone axe-heads. Hard evidence for historians means words written on sheep bellies centuries ago.

The Europeans brought hard evidence with them. From the sea they brought iron weapons. From the land they brought parallel iron tracks. The path an Indian berry-picker and her grandmothers may have taken was invisible property, a family story. The railroad engines could go right through a mountain, and make a frightful noise before doing so.

So white people discounted the idea of Indian "history." They called it folklore. They said that it was more like magic than history, more like poetry. It favoured mutability, transformation, invisibility, metonymy. In the Indian "history" there were people, animals and spirits, and they could change places.

Worse, these stories were as likely to be told through dance as through words, and when they were told through words, the words were often sung, while someone banged a stick on some stretched animal skin.

Worse, the Indian "historians" did not have a rational sense of time, the element in which history lives. When they told stories about some great event that happened among their people, it might have happened a thousand years ago, or fifty years ago. It might be happening right now.

The Indians were stuck in their backward ways because they had not learned to separate history and myth, science and art. The reason for the astounding success of the expansionist Europeans in the nineteenth century was that they had shaken off the romance of literature and the sister arts, and replaced it with the doxology of science and commerce. Not all British people were happy with that change. In 1904, the young historian in an historian family, G.M. Trevelyan, wrote: "The last fifty years have witnessed great changes in the management of Clio's temple. Her inspired prophets and bards have passed away and been succeeded by the priests of an established church." History, he lamented, is now "proclaimed a 'science' for specialists, not 'literature' for the common reader of books."

Speaking of time, the length of time that Europeans and others from the east have been between the Cordillera and the Coast is tiny in comparison with the length of time that the first people have been here. The Eurocolumbians have been writing histories ever since they got here. The used-book stores are filled with B.C. histories, picture books and local chronicles. But the volume is tiny in comparison with the histories told and danced by the first peoples.

When the white people came into the valleys of the Indian country, they brought their various histories with them. One of the most ambitious was carried in by the Christians. They had a story to tell and in their opinion it was the most important story the Indians would ever hear. They also found it necessary to persuade the Indians to quit singing and dancing their own story.

There have been about ninety generations since the death and resurrection of Jesus Christ. The Indians have been in what the whites tell them is British Columbia for at least five hundred generations. No one in the world was trying to write history down five hundred generations ago. Back in those days people were still busy reading the sky and the ground.

If you think that you can understand Indian history from a European/white historical method, imagine trying to understand classic and medieval European history as told by Tlingit storytellers using their methods. Look: now the historian is doing the dance of the House of York, soon to be followed by a chant signifying the power of the House of Lancaster. See, he shakes a Plantagenet rattle. It is wrapped, as you will see, in native broom.

Archaeologists may seem more objective, dealing as they do with earth sifted through screens. But to some extent at least, the archaeologists are really studying their own *discoveries* of Indian artefacts and remains.

Ghost Ships

"Philanthropy is not the object of our visits to these Northern Indians."
—George Simpson, 1821

Balboa and others

In history classes we were always finding out about discovery. The Europeans were always sailing bravely around the world (and they had to be brave—you wouldn't catch me going around the Horn in a sixty-foot ship under ripping sails) discovering new lands. Planting a booted foot and a flag on the island that would one day become Montreal, and claiming it for the king of France. Telling the Amazonian natives that they were all at once living in Portugal.

Imagine this: V. Balboa gets half the way across the Panamanian isthmus, sees the Pacific Ocean, and declares that it belongs from now on to Spain. The ocean and every bit of land it washes against. All Spanish. Everyone in China, Australia, Patagonia and Alaska had better get used to it. Start speaking the language of Madrid.

Balboa said this on September 27, 1513. The Haida people didn't hear about it. The Slavey people were looking at the first snow in the air. They weren't interested in any Spanish sailors.

The peoples of this mountainous country had enough trouble with the fifty or so languages they were already speaking. They didn't have time for Spanish. They wouldn't have to bother with Spanish for a couple hundred years yet.

The Spanish were busy putting boots and flags on Peru and Mexico.

Here comes everybody

On the east coast there are a lot of stories about people who reached the New World before Columbus did. The best-known ones are the Vikings on the pointy part of Newfoundland, and the Irish monks in their little leather boats. I once read in a Soviet magazine that the Phoenicians had been to Mexico.

We have got used to the idea that the discovery of America is a matter of opinion, a fiction maybe, at least provisional, like so many other things these days. And really, do we know for sure that Columbus always told his employers the facts? After all, we on the west coast know that the explorer John Meares told some pretty wild stories about how far north he had sailed. We know that Juan de Fuca, though he has a strait named after him in British Columbia, never entered that water as he claimed. Even the redoubtable Captain Cook used to just sail across the mouths of inlets rather than going to all the work of exploring them. He said: oh, by the way, I found a great river that will probably get you at least part way across the continent. We're calling it Cook River. Young George Vancouver, a rookie on Cook's ship, held his tongue until he got his own command. Then he explored the great river and changed its name to Cook Inlet, and that is its name today, that wide waterway leading to Anchorage.

On the west coast too there are many stories about first non-Indian, historical times visitors to the New World. Thor Heyerdahl followers are forever trying to sail rafts from Southeast Asia to South America. On the west coast of Vancouver Island beachcombers are always finding glass fishing-net floats made in Japan. Of course nowadays the Japanese place driftnets just about all the way across the north Pacific.

One of the great mysteries of archaeology is the existence of the giant Olmec heads found in Vera Cruz, Mexico. Some observers observe that they look African. Others observe that they look Oriental. Actually, some of them look as if they are wearing football helmets. The mystery lies in the fact that they do not resemble other ancient Mexican art, and in the fact that they are both huge and made of a stone material not found in the region.

When the Spanish and British sailors arrived on the northwest coast of America in the eighteenth century of the Christian era, they occasionally found Natives using iron knives they did not recognize. This could mean (a) the Indians knew how to work iron, (b) some people with iron had visited here in earlier times or (c) the elaborate trading practices of the aboriginal peoples reached all the way to either Asia or eastern America.

In 1971 some archaeologists made a lucky find on the coast just south of Vancouver Island. Even today the Pacific coast of the Olympic Peninsula is lightly populated, and most of the population is First Peoples. Several major language groups, from Salishen to Kootenay, rub shoulders there. In 1971 someone found a sixteenth-century town that had been inundated in a mud slide. Cape Alava is not known to most white people who live along the coast from Seattle to Vancouver, people who could tell you lots of things historical and fanciful about Pompeii. But among archaeologists it is a legend. They found everything there.

Including copper and iron objects. Nowadays professionals can look at old metal and tell you where it was made. The iron things at Cape Alava were not made by Europeans. They were made in northern Asia. They probably got to the Olympic Peninsula because some Salish people did some trading with some Haida people who had done some trading with some Aleut people who had business associates in Kamchatka.

But the question I often ask myself remains: if the Vikings used to come year by year to Vinland to do some fishing, why didn't the Asians keep coming to the shores of Alaska and B.C.? Maybe the Asians were homebodies. But look at the modern globe. Chinese people live just about everywhere in the world. So why didn't they settle the coast of what they would later call Gold Mountain?

There are lots of fanciful stories of Chinese sailors and fishermen who were blown off course and fetched up on the shores of America, never to be seen again. One persistent fable tells of Japanese men who from time to time made involuntary landfall on the coast north of Vancouver and married into Indian communities, contributing their genes to the Salish or Haida gene pool. The most famous story shrouded in north-coast fog is the story of the Buddhist monks of the fifth century.

Early in the seventh century a Chinese historian by the name of Liyan Chiew wrote the story of a group of monks who went to the end of Siberia, cruised down the Alaskan coast, and eventually found a land called Fusang. They left in AD 458, and in 499, the last remaining monk, Huei Shin, came home and told his story. According to his story the monks had encountered a sophisticated people with domestic horned animals and a religion that sounded a lot like Buddhism.

There's got to be something to it, say a lot of people. Many of the details of Fusang, its elaborate buildings and writing system, sound like Mexico. But others sound like the B.C. coast. Maybe Huei Shin and some other monks made several voyages, and the historian put them all together. Maybe the historian was a seventh-century Jonathan Swift.

I hear that there is a scholar from China coming to B.C. to work on the monks' travels. He says that he has incontrovertible proof that Huei Shin and his fellows were here. Here's what I say: welcome, have a look around, let us know if you find anything.

Of all the pre-European visitors I have heard about, the strangest ones are to be found in the first chapter of *Pageant of B.C.* by B.A. McKelvie. This book was published in 1955, and in a "Centennial edition" in 1957. B.A.

McKelvie is the author of several books about the province, notably a history of romantic Fort Langley. McKelvie was a newspaperman, and as journalists often will, prided himself on being a non-academic historian. The blurb on the dust jacket of *Pageant of B.C.* reports that he "has had the unique honour of being acclaimed, by all the parties in the B.C. Legislature, 'the foremost historian of the Province.'" He had a mountain on Vancouver Island named after him.

His book is subtitled: "Glimpses into the romantic development of Canada's far western province." Hmm.

Who could resist such a book? On the first page we are introduced to "some definite facts" that support the idea of Asian visitors. He tells of Chinese coins from 2000 BC found by Cassiar miners, 2,000-year-old Buddhist ceremonial dishes found among the roots of trees at Telegraph Creek and an ancient Japanese sword found under the streets of Nanaimo. Unfortunately these objects appear to have remained in the hands of private collectors rather than B.C. museums.

But strangest of all are the Chinese Jews. "It is an historical fact," says the foremost historian of the province, "that Jews were once powerful in China." Apparently when Kublai Khan set out to attack Japan near the end of the thirteenth century, a big storm arose and blew the ships of his Jewish troops over to the Queen Charlotte Islands area. There these Jews instructed the Natives in many customs, and the Natives continued them long after the Jews had passed on. These customs include ceremonies concerning the first fish of the season, fasting and bathing regimens, wearing of fringed blankets by the religious leaders and Jewish measurement of time.

Better than that: two eminent Catholic clergymen noted similarities between the aboriginals and the people of the Old Testament. Father Adrien Morice apparently found similar customs forced upon adolescent females; Father Jean Marie LeJeune wrote that he found Hebrew words among the Native languages of the province.

I have also heard that people from outer space showed the Egyptians how to make the pyramids. So anything is possible.

One thing bothers me about these Jews from China. How did they feel about those great piles of clamshells?

In any case, B.A. McKelvie does not seem any more to be the major historian of his province. He does not show up in many bibliographies in recent years. That's too bad—a lot of romance seems to be going out of history on the west coast of Canada.

The Strait of Anian

> the problem that is ours and yours,
> that there is no clear Strait of Anian
> to lead us back to Europe,
> that men are isled in ocean or in ice
> —*Earle Birney, 1948*

In the late 1970s I was writing a novel about the Northwest Passage and the eighteenth century, and when it came to writing the first inky draft, I decided to sail away from home. So it happened that I was spending a few days in Florence, writing in the morning and sightseeing (research is the word I used then) in the afternoon.

One afternoon I went to visit a palace that was supposed to be open, but it was closed. Then there was the Palazzo Vecchio, which was supposed to be closed but which was open. As usual, going through the rooms upstairs, I found after a while that I was going the opposite way to the sequence described by the guidebook and followed by the few other tourists, some Japanese, a few German. So I didn't know where I was when I stumbled into a room whose walls, cupboards, really, were covered with fifty-three painted maps, surrounding a monumental *mappa mundi* in the middle of the room. The first map I spied, on my right upon entry, displayed a fanciful *Cina* and a fanciful *Giapan*. To the north and to the east, all the way to the top right corner of the painting, stretched a sea called the *Stretto di Annian*.

When I saw this, the guidebook fell from my hand and smacked the echoing marble floor.

The next room was the office of Secretary of the Republic, Niccolò Macchiavelli.

That map room, I was to learn later, is called the *Sala dei Guardarobe*, and was used by the Medici grand dukes for stashing their precious objects from around the world. The maps were painted by Fra Ignazio Danti (1563) and Don Stefano Buonsignori (1575). The painters were working from a description made by a Portuguese sailor named Gaspar Corte-Real, who found the Northwest Passage about 1500, and named it the Strait of Anian after his brother. The Northwest Passage would be found over and over again in the next few years, and sought by brave sailors for the next four centuries.

The Strait of Anian became the El Dorado of the north. It was a dream of all navigators and the obsession of all merchants. There was a Greek sea captain from Italy, Apostolos Valerianos, who claimed to have sailed for many years for Spain, using the name Juan de Fuca. There is no such word as *fuca* in Spanish, unless it is a coarse word I have not been exposed to. Maybe it means something in Greek. In Latin it means phony, counterfeit. In 1592, symbolically a hundred years after Columbus's first American voyage, Valerianos found the Northwest Passage. Around the 49th parallel he sailed into a strait that led him to an enormous sea filled with islands. He sailed the sea for twenty days and then sailed back out.

Incidentally, he met lots of well-dressed Indians and saw a lot of gold, silver and pearls. Enough to rival the fortunate finds to the Spanish south.

Valerianos's story was something he told in exchange for drinks in Venice. Now, when old sailors talk about silver and gold, they are usually trying to raise support for a new expedition, or at least a promotion. But the old Greek was on his way home to spend his last days in the Mediterranean. Fellow seamen brought his story back to the ports of Europe. Some listeners did not believe the giant inland sea. Others did not believe that the Greek had got as far as forty-nine degrees north latitude. But in the eighteenth century some navigators sailed between what would be Vancouver Island and the mainland, and named the waters the Strait of Juan de Fuca, the name it has now. There is no way of knowing whether Valerianos ever floated on the waters that bear his assumed name. It's too bad he didn't go by the name Juan de Anian.

In 1640 the Northwest Passage was discovered by the Spanish admiral Bartolemo de Fonte. De Fonte and his ships encountered, having entered at fifty-three degrees north, an intricate system of lakes and rivers and islands, which they sailed far, far to the east and north. They were certain that they were on waters that would lead to Baffin Bay, which is a nice bit of irony, because William Baffin, looking for the Northwest Passage from the other side had been an unusual pessimist among mariners. He had concluded that he was looking at three blind inlets that would not offer passage to the west. Each of them was, in fact, navigable in summer weather.

But according to Admiral de Fonte, he encountered, far inside the continent, a merchant ship from Boston, trading happily with the Indians along the water's edge. It was to be more than a century until the Boston traders were found on the west coast. It is no wonder that de Fonte's discovery inflamed the expeditionary imagination. It was not really that much different than the amazing corroborated tales of treasure and passage in Southeast Asia. It was just as romantic, if perhaps not as warm, not as jasmine-scented.

While Captain George Vancouver was making the long leg of his journey from Hawaii to the northwest coast in 1792, he spent long hours poring over a great array of charts—Spanish and British, fanciful and legitimate, inherited and made by his own hand on Cook's last voyage there. Some of those he inherited featured wide rivers leading deep into the continent. Some showed the Strait of Anian, the Strait of Juan de Fuca and the Strait of de Fonte.

George Vancouver loathed the French. In fact, while he was commissioned to explore in the Pacific, he was hankering to be in the Atlantic and Caribbean, blowing French sails to Kingdom Come. So in 1792 he was not using the French maps of a few decades earlier. These showed between forty-seven and fifty-three degrees north a huge inland sea, *La mer de l'ouest*, another body like Hudson Bay, extending into the heart of North America. A little exploring would soon find a way to get from one sea to the other, to send barks where birchbarks now went.

There were more Northwest Passages than you could shake a stick at.

And no wonder. In 1745, frustrated by the Spanish at Panama and the Dutch at the Cape, the English Parliament passed an act establishing a reward of £20,000 to any merchant vessel that should find a passage west of Hudson Bay. In the interesting year of 1776 the offer was extended to ships of the Royal Navy. In the eighteenth century £20,000 was a sum not to be sneezed at. Perhaps it was not a sum to freeze for, but some young men did that.

You could say that the search for the Northwest Passage was what Lief the Lucky was involved in. Nearly all the explorers we heard about in elementary school, Cartier and Cabot and Champlain, for example, were hoping to find a passage to the Pacific. The mighty St. Lawrence River made hearts race. Lake Ontario filled Europeans with hope. But Niagara Falls, beautiful as it was, was a heart-breaker.

But as long as you did not know what was out there, there was hope. For centuries the Spanish had been coming home with ships deep in the water with the weight of gold. West meant hardship and wealth, a land empty of people and full of resources waiting to be picked up.

Frozen ships

The first Arctic quest was made by the men under Sir Martin Frobisher in 1576. Queen Elizabeth had had it with the Spanish. She wanted their armada burnt to the waterline, and she wanted the Pacific to be yanked out from under their mastheads. She sent Frobisher north and west. Thus started three hundred years of small ships frozen in water to the north of America. Frobisher and some of the other early pícaros had to contend with missing islands. In 1558, an Italian named Niccolò Zeno (one would perhaps expect an explorer who endlessly halved the distance between his ship and a hoped-for landing) produced a map that most people who looked at maps credited. It showed a big island country called Friesland, lying between Iceland and Greenland. This map would confuse people: if that last place was Iceland, this one must be Friesland, or if this one is Greenland, we must have missed either Iceland or Friesland, or maybe we missed two of them and this is a new one, in which case what should we name it?

Martin Frobisher, anyway, gave up one dream for another, equally familiar to history. On a barren northern beach somebody brought him a rock that looked as if it might have gold in it, and there were lots of rocks where that one came from. Frobisher took some rocks back home from the New World.

Next the Virgin Queen sent John Davis into the western hemisphere's

Arctic. He went in 1585, 1586 and 1587. Davis was one of the most innovative of the English explorers. He took musicians aboard, and communicated with the native peoples of the Arctic by having his sailors dance for them. The reviews were pretty good for the first of the English bands to make a North American tour.

The most famous English sailor of Elizabeth's time was, of course, Sir Francis Drake. Drake was a *déclassé* bumpkin who was laughed at by the gentry, but Elizabeth liked him because of his unwavering hatred for the Catholics. He devoted his life to two things: buying a house that was as fancy as the houses of the gentry, and defeating Catholicism. He burned the Spanish Armada to the waterline. He became the Queen's pirate in the New World. He was the first Englishman in Balboa's Spanish Pacific. He sailed the *Golden Hind* around the Horn and started up the west coast, plundering Spanish ships and ports as he went. When he got back to the Thames, he was captain of a twenty-four-carat ship. The Queen stepped aboard the *Golden Hind* and made him a knight. Sir Francis, a pirate with a garter.

Drake sailed with two other ships that eventually disappeared; up the American coast he came. He ran out of Spanish ports and ships so he became an explorer instead of a pirate. Explorers name places. He called the coast from northern California to southern British Columbia "New Albion." He was looking for the Strait of Anian because he wanted to get back to England without going past a lot of angry Spanish (especially now that he had only one very heavy sixty-foot ship) and around the wintertime Horn. It was summer in the north, but in June of 1579 it was tremendously cold. The Englishmen would go no further north. They stayed ashore somewhere around forty-eight degrees north, they thought, and then turned their noses south and west.

So in addition to being the first Brit in the Pacific, Francis Drake also became the first person to sail his own ship around the globe.

And he may have been the first Englishman to stand on the soil of British Columbia—although if his calculations were precise, he was on the most northerly point of Washington State.

Close enough.

The English explorers were incredibly brave. There is nothing an English explorer likes better than to make a completely understated greeting to another English explorer thousands of miles from anywhere. English naval history would love to have had a meeting of British explorers penetrating the Northwest Passage from both ends: "Captain Baffin, I presume?"

Henry Hudson went out in 1610 and got the job half done. The year before that he had sailed for the Dutch and determined that the big river now named the Hudson did not go across America. The huge bay named after him became for a couple of centuries the main hope. Ships and boats covered every foot of the western reaches of the bay. But they were forced to turn their prows north again. Hudson became the victim of one of England's most famous mutinies in the summer of 1611. He and his son and some loyal crew members were set adrift in a boat, while the angry usurpers tried to go back to England. But they got some Inuit people angry too, and were killed in one of the few Inuit-English battles known to history.

Hudson did not get back to London to see the new plays, A Winter's Tale and The Tempest.

In the early nineteenth century there was a big rebirth of interest in the Northwest Passage, because after the conclusion of the Napoleonic Wars, the British had a really big navy about which the country would become quite sentimental. This little island ruling the waves. The most famous of the new expeditions is the last Franklin expedition of 1845, a disaster that has seized the imaginations of Canadian scientists and writers. Magazine articles show photographs of the skulls of the expedition's young sailors, and we have seen the frozen and preserved body and face of one of them.

The Northwest Passage was finally navigated by a Norwegian. Roald Amundsen had to wait out three frozen winters in his little yacht before reaching the western sea in 1906.

But to date there has been no commercial use made of the old route of dreams, even though the very snows of the high Arctic are polluted with by-products of our manufacturing craze.

The Russians are coming! The Russians are coming!

During the seventeenth century there was not a lot of European travel along the northwest coast of America. The Portuguese had made their deal with the Spanish and the Pope, and were pushing into the interior from the Brazilian coast. They also had a lot to do in Africa. They had a colony off the coast of China, and there would be rich trade between the Chinese coast and the North American coast, but a deal was a deal. And the numbers did not look good for the Portuguese navy in the New World.

The French were looking at a great deal of geography in New France and Acadia, and they were adding the area of the Mississippi delta. Struggling against the interests of Spain and Britain in the eastern half of the continent, they had no time to send ships into the Pacific.

The English, meanwhile, had pretty valuable colonies along the Atlantic coast to see to, as well as an empire abuilding in Africa and Asia. The Spanish were hauling home nearly everything of value in their half of South America, and maintaining the Caribbean ports through which it had to pass. In 1603 they checked Oregon and found that Balboa's claim was being respected. No one went north of California for another century and a half. The Dutch, meanwhile, had lost their territory in North America and were sitting on a few pieces in the Caribbean.

No one had found any of the gold that Juan de Fuca had seen in the northwest, and no one had sailed through the continent. Young coastal Indians began to doubt the traditional stories of ghost-skinned one-sexed people on floating cities.

But there was another European monarchy that spent the seventeenth century expanding like crazy. In the late sixteenth century the Russians had begun their great drive east of the Urals, gathering up lands occupied by Muslims and Mongols. By the time that Peter the Great came to power in 1682, the Russians had reached the Pacific.

It was impossible for anyone to know exactly what the Russians had gathered. Siberia reached northward in many peninsulas reaching into frozen seas. Immense distances were involved. It was possible that the lands claimed by Peter's explorers might include part of North America. That could lead to all kinds of interesting possibilities. It is an enormous distance from St. Petersburg to the Sea of Okhotsk, and it was even further in the early eighteenth century when the handlers of young Tsar Peter II had men and supplies sent to the east coast, where ships would be built for the discovery voyage of Vitus Bering, the intrepid Danish captain selling his expertise to the Russian navy.

In 1728 Bering made his first expedition and discovered that there was no land bridge between Asia and America. Actually, a Russian captain named Semyon Dezhnyov had sailed through what would be the Bering Strait in 1648. Unfortunately his report lay hidden in the naval records until it was dug up in 1736. By then Bering was planning his next trip east. In 1741 he left Petropavlovsk on the second expedition, with the ships *St. Peter* and *St. Paul*. The ships became separated, as so often happened to ships in the North Pacific, and by prior arrangement, went on with their jobs. Aboard the *St. Peter*, Bering landed on the North American coast just inside Kayak Island. He was at sixty degrees north, which would become the boundary between British Columbia and Yukon.

There Bering named the highest mountain he could see and the cape he was standing on after St. Elias, because he saw them on the saint's day. Later, the river of ice between those two sites would be named Bering Glacier. At that site Bering and his crew were probably not, as one historian has suggested, the first Europeans to see what is now British Columbia, even if Drake's landing was on the Olympic Peninsula south of Victoria. Mount St. Elias is at the Yukon border. It is just possible that the Dane and his Russian and Swedish crewmen saw the white tip of a B.C. mountain.

As it turned out, the sailors aboard the errant *St. Paul* went farther south on the American coast, at least to fifty-five degrees north. Some of them went ashore and never returned. Maybe some of them saw British Columbia.

Bering let his scientists loose for one day only, because it was already late in July, and the way back to Okhotsk was long and unpredictable. As a matter of fact he never got back to the Russian mainland. As the *St. Peter* hopped from island to island of the Aleutian chain, the winds became more and more unfriendly. By September many of the men were down with scurvy. Though they had sailed most of the way back to Kamchatka, in November Bering decided to make a landing and spend the winter on one of the islands near the peninsula. We now call it Bering Island. It is just west of Attu, on the 55th parallel.

The ship was rammed into the sand by a storm, and the explorers faced a hard winter made worse by the fear that even were spring to arrive they would not have the strength and resources to try for Petropavlovsk. As they grew weaker, the sick lay among the dead near the fire. Sand leaked through the roof of their hut. In December Vitus Bering died on a cold forlorn island in an icy sea.

In the spring the scurvy killed some of the men and began to leave the rest. The survivors managed to find fur seals and kill them and eat them. They used their skin for clothing and bedding. When they managed to build a seagoing craft from the beached *St. Peter* and return to Asian Russia, they took these skins with them. At St. Petersburg there were businessmen who saw the beauty and potential of these pelts. Thus was the North Pacific fur trade begun. In a few years the Russians had trading posts in Alaska.

They didn't give a hoot about Balboa. But they kept pretty quiet about Alaskan details when they were talking business in Europe.

A European world

Since its first publication in 1958, Margaret Ormsby's massive *British Columbia: a History* has pretty well been the standard history of the province. Here is its first sentence: "Distant from the travelled sea-lanes and girdled by mountains, British Columbia stood apart from the civilized world until late in the eighteenth century."

That's quite a thought. While men in wigs and silk stockings were sniffing snuff in a big stone house in Kent, and Marie Antoinette was perfuming her thighs for an in camera carriage ride, all to the strains of Bach's chorale preludes, the northwest coast of America was a scene of mud-eating brutes hitting each other with clubs.

The Europeans believed that white people were destined to carve up the world among them, and they treated the globe like a vast mining field, staking claims, sometimes faking claims, and registering them in writing. Balboa had claimed the biggest ocean in the world without even putting a toe in it.

Now the Spanish were sailing up and down the Pacific coastline of the Americas, sticking crosses in the ground and leaving bottles under them. Inside the bottles were messages to the effect that this beach belongs to the Spanish Crown.

When Spanish sailors erected crosses along the British Columbia coast, the Natives thought that they could have used a little carving, a little painting.

The English did not stick crosses in the ground, but they too left written claims in sealed bottles. The idea was that when someone of another European nationality arrived and opened the bottle and read the message, he was supposed to say something to the effect of "Oh drat!" and reseal the bottle. No throwing the bottle into the salt chuck.

A lot of the history of seagoing in the Pacific and Indian oceans was determined by wars and revolutions in Europe. France, for instance, pulled out of the North Pacific when it became preoccupied with the Bastille and the guillotine.

Finding it difficult to negotiate with the Dutch at the Cape of Good Hope, impossible to deal with the Spanish at Panama, time-consuming, seasonal and perilous to navigate Cape Horn, the British really could have used a Northwest Passage through America to the Oriental bazaars.

One big candy shop

When the Europeans, the fur seekers, the gold seekers, the timber men and the fishermen, first came into this immense place with its mountains after mountains, they must have been imagining fantastic and never-ending wealth. There were more beavers and otters than you could shake a stick at. When the salmon started upstream, you could have walked across the river on their backs. Under a skein of lichen or grass certain mountains were made of gold. All of Europe let loose with double-bitted axes could never bring down all the sky-high trees of this place.

It's a wonder that the European countries, who were busy fighting each other anyway, didn't meet here and blow each other's ships out of the water. Captain Vancouver, who wished he were on the Atlantic sending grapeshot through the midriffs of French sailors, was sitting at the Peruvian Captain Quadra's sumptuous table somewhere off the coast of New Dover. They were discussing the fur trade and geography in a friendly way. They agreed to ignore the Russians and be wary of the Yankees, and settle this coastline between them, Spanish to the south, British to the north.

Amazing.

The Indians had over a hundred centuries learned to live according to the things nature would give them. The people of the sub-Arctic were usually on the move, looking for big meat. They did not have the time or weather or resources to make houses and jewellery. The peoples of the Coast saw bounty rolling in. They learned to like clams and they made towns full of big houses with art on the front of them, and canoes parked in front of the houses. The people of the Great Plateau did not have to be as nomadic as the Athapaskan people of the north, nor were they as wealthy as the canoe people on the Coast. They made houses in the earth for the cool winters, and they chased animals and trapped fish and went berry-picking in the hot summers.

But the European fur seekers and gold seekers just wanted to get their stuff and go, either back home or to the next cornucopia. They never thought of settling.

Curiously, this desire on the part of the fur seekers and gold seekers to grab and go was not nearly as bad news for the first peoples as the desire to stay and spread of the aliens who arrived after the fur and gold were gone. The Hudson's Bay Company and its buyers treated the Indians only as badly as they could. If they killed them all or chased them away, they would not have anyone bringing pelts to their forts.

So they told the Indians that a pile of wolfskins was worth as much as a rifle of the same height, and they invented the fur press. But nobody had invented reserves yet.

What is scurvy?

When Vitus Bering got sick with scurvy, he knew that he was probably going to die a long way from home. A lot of explorers died a long way from home, on some beach or in some obscure sea. James Cook got cut into segments on the Sandwich Islands. Balboa was beheaded by a crooked politician in Panama. But a lot of sailors died of scurvy. In the early eighteenth century outfitters calculated the number of scurvy deaths they expected on any expedition.

Nowadays we tend to give boring names to our diseases, even when we have pretty well knocked them out. We think of "scurvy" as a word belonging in old sea adventures. If someone gets it now, we call it vitamin C deficiency. Can you imagine some adventurous pirate wielding his bent sword at a foe and insulting him thus: "Avast, ye vitamin C deficiency dog!"

Scurvy has probably always been around as long as people have gone on long voyages, or old men have lived alone and not eaten a sensible diet. Vitamin C, ascorbic acid, is found in fresh fruits and vegetables, especially citrus fruits. The English navy eventually learned to stock its ships, when they were sailing in the appropriate latitudes, with oranges and limes, or lots of juice. That is why Englishmen, especially military men, were called Limeys. In the 1950s we RCAF types used to call the RAF types "juicers," and we meant lime juice, not booze.

If you do suffer scurvy you have swollen and bleeding gums, loose teeth, stiff and aching joints, legs that hurt all the time, bleeding under the skin and a general slowing down. If you experience a wound, it might never heal. Eventually you are too tired to get up and leave the dead body beside you in a hut in a cold island that might be named after you.

Europeans suffered scurvy during their medieval crusades to the Holy Land. By the time of Columbus scurvy had become the main enemy of seamen who had to go great distances. There were a lot of fanciful notions about its cause, and many inventive methods to ward it off. In the eighteenth century, with all the world-conquering that had to be done, the British navy turned to Edinburgh scientists and physicians for help. Finally, in 1753, eleven years after Vitus Bering's death, Dr. James Lind proved that scurvy was related to diet and that there was such a thing as a deficiency disease. Furthermore, he proved that it could be cured within days by eating lemons, oranges or limes. It could also be prevented by a regular dose of citrus juice.

But sometimes you are sailing in places where citrus fruits are hard to come by. So the ship's doctor is always on the lookout for a substitute. In South America people eat begonias to prevent scurvy. Captain James Cook was to change the face of the earth more than any man in history, but perhaps just as important, he did it with crews that did not fall victim to scurvy. Cook was interested in health, and willing to listen to sensible Scottish doctors. Periodically he would have all the decks and walls and tables scoured with vinegar, scraping out the fat that accumulated and brought invisible dangers. He would also have smoky fires lit between decks, and burning gunpowder to clean the air and whatever the air touched. And he would have his sailors scamper ashore to find something to make into sauerkraut. All over the green world, where there are no begonias and no limes, you can find wild plants that resemble cabbages, and you can ferment them. You can also find spruce trees and make spruce beer. Sailors might not like the taste of wild sauerkraut and spruce beer, but there was no arguing with Captain Cook's remarkable record.

When his protégé George Vancouver succeeded him, he faithfully followed his teacher's methods. Sailors on Vancouver's ships knew that they might get murdered by Polynesians, or frozen in an arctic ocean, but they would not die of scurvy.

An unofficial language

When I was at Southern Okanagan High School, majoring in history, we never studied the Okanagan. We never studied B.C. We studied Canada a little bit—I remember drawing pictures of Talon and other figures from New France. When I majored in history at University of British Columbia, there was no course on B.C. There was a course on Canada. It was about Confederation and reciprocity and the CPR.

I didn't know that Discovery Street was named for Captain Vancouver's ship, though there was a model of that ship at the downtown library. Vancouver streets are filled with names from B.C. history, but the people who ride the streets don't know who they are named for. Some of them are named for premiers that bus riders know nothing about. Others have names like Valdez Road, Quadra Street, Narvaez Drive and Cardero Street. Those are Spanish names. They sound something like the names of all those islands off the B.C. coast—Galiano, Gabriola, Texada, Cortes, Aristazabal, Revillagigedo.

Just below the B.C. border the island group is called the San Juans. The Spanish names go all the way up the coast to Alaska. But in Alaska names such as Cape Chacon and Cordova Bay are scattered around that maze of inlets with names such as Kruzof Island and Kupreanof Island. The Spanish and the Russians have left their names, and we pronounce them as best we can.

But we never heard them in our history classes. According to our classes the languages of history in Canada were French and English. They were not Russian and Spanish. They certainly were not Salish and Bella Coola.

Southern crosses

When the Russians seemed to be getting interested in the eastern half of the North Pacific horseshoe, the Spanish decided that they had better pay more attention to the cooler part of their ocean. The north had never seemed promising in terms of resources, at least not when compared to Incan gold, for instance. But the Russians might be after something. There were rumours that animals were swimming around the coastal waters up there, with expensive coats on. After Carlos III climbed onto the Spanish throne in 1759, the year that General Wolfe and his soldiers took Canada for the British, he ordered a big ship-building project on the west coast of Mexico. There was California to settle with forts, and California Indians to convert to Catholicism. There were Russians farther north, who must be disillusioned if they had dreams about California, and Brits who would be more ambitious now that they controlled the east coast of the continent.

It was easier to build ships on the west coast of Mexico than it was on the Sea of Okhotsk. In 1773 the *Santiago* was christened and on the next New Year's Day, sent up the coast. At Monterey it took on two priests who would offer Christianity to any Indians they might encounter up north. When they weren't instructing savages, they were to be making notes and drawings of anything interesting along Spain's little-known coast. So little attention had the Spanish paid to it that the officers were using Russian maps.

The officers were headed by Don Juan José Pérez Hernández, who had lots of experience sailing the trade route between the Philippines and Mexico. His pilot was Don Estéban José Martínez, after whom a group of islands and Estevan Point are named. Pérez was told to go to the 60th parallel, where Vitus Bering had made his landing, but the early summer of 1774 was a time of terrible adverse winds, at least as far as the Mexican sailors were concerned. On July 18 Pérez made his first sighting, through the mist and rain, of Spain's forlorn land. They anchored off the west coast of one of the Queen Charlottes. This was the first recorded view of these islands by Europeans, though they did not know that they were not looking at the mainland.

For two days, the *Santiago* lay at anchor while Haida men and boys and women and girls approached in canoes nearly as long as the Spanish bark. Pérez traded for water and dried fish, and for the beautiful blankets placed inside boxes made without metal fasteners, offering in exchange abalone shells from the southern seas, and some affordable European trinkets. His priests looked carefully for signs of Russian intrusion, but saw only one piece of iron on a spear. They made lots of notes about the Indians, but were never able to introduce the subject of God. These people were attractive, they wrote, but must have given themselves to heathen ways, for they disfigured their faces with paint, and the women wore plates in the stretched skin beneath their mouths.

The weather discouraged any more northward travel, and the *Santiago*'s men were falling down with scurvy. Pérez turned the ship southward. The big wooden cross that they were supposed to drive into the ground on Bering's beach would go back with them. Their ship was named for the patron saint of sea voyagers, but the North Pacific had beaten them this time.

Still, they made an authentic sighting at nearly fifty-three degrees north, and they would make further contact on the way home. This would be at Nootka Sound, halfway down the west coast of Vancouver Island. It would turn out to be the most important fur town in the world. The priests suggested the big wooden cross again, but their captain said that the weather was too bad. So they anchored again, and met more indigenous people, the Nootka this time.

At first the Nootka people tried to keep the strangers away. Whether they thought that the Spanish were ghosts, or whether they had had some bad experience with earlier visitors that no one knows about, a few brave Nootka, perhaps a shaman and his assistants came out in the sea that even roughened the pleasant harbour of Nootka Sound, and sang the fearful songs that were intended to chase the spirits away. When that did not work, they did a little trading, offering furs and carvings for abalone shells. Rightly or wrongly, the Nootka were to gain a reputation as burglars. In the summer of 1774 they began by lifting four silver spoons from the quarters of Don Estéban Martínez.

When the *Santiago* got back to San Blas, its home port in Mexico, the Spanish viceroy announced his displeasure that Pérez still had the cross with him. He wanted land claims. Who else did you see up there, he asked. Only Indians, replied Pérez. Exactly, said the viceroy, you certainly don't expect the Indians to make land claims, do you?

In 1775, the *Santiago* went north again, this time under the command of Don Bruno de Heceta. Pérez went along as pilot. It was accompanied by a new and smaller vessel called the *Sonora*, under the control of the Peruvian who would become the most reknowned Spanish sailor on the B.C. coast, Don Juan Francisco de la Bodega y Quadra. They planted crosses here and there on their way north, but they still did not touch anything that was to become British Columbia. In what is now Washington, some of Quadra's men stood a cross and a Spanish flag. But on a search for drinking water, some of Quadra's men were killed by the inhabitants. When the latter, flushed with their success, set out in canoes after the *Sonora*, they were met by the phenomenon of gunpowder. When a shot hit a canoe, smashing it to bits and killing six men, the Indians called off their operation.

Quadra also planted a cross north of B.C. The *Santiago* again gave up, this time just north of Vancouver Island, but the little *Sonora*, only eleven metres long, got to the Alaska panhandle. Quadra's men did not quite reach Bering's Kayak Island, but they made the Spanish claim at a little north of fifty-seven degrees. Then weather and scurvy sent them south.

Meanwhile British troops entered Concord, Massachusetts, looking for contraband weapons. The U.S. War of Independence was beginning. This was good news for the French and Spanish. The French and Spanish had had their disagreements in the eighteenth century. They wanted each other's possessions in the Caribbean. They had to keep changing the language in Louisiana. But they had more trouble with the English. The English occupied Havana in 1762. Although the Seven Years' War had left France with little in the New World or India, the revolt of Britain's American colonies offered France an opportunity to find some revenge for the Treaty of Paris. The Spanish had their territorial reasons to help the rebels. Britain had to concentrate its attention on the uprising, while swatting at French and Spanish ships.

In 1779 San Blas sent a third expedition north. If Balboa's ocean was to be secured, the Spanish king's sailors had to defeat polar wind and scurvy, and establish landfall at least as far north as the 70th parallel. Don Ignacio de Arteaga commanded the *Princesa*, and Bodega y Quadra was in charge of the second ship again, this time the *Favorita*. On this trip a Spanish cross was planted at Bering's 60th parallel, in sight of high snowy Mt. St. Elias, named nearly four decades earlier. Spanish men liked warm waters and free gold. But now the Russians and the British had been instructed. The Pacific was still a Spanish sea.

While they were there, they did a little trading with the Natives. But this time the priests (there were always priests on the Spanish ships) traded shells and cutlery for five children. These lucky kids went to Monterey or maybe all the way to Mexico. They were going to become the first Christians born on the northwest coast of America.

That was to be the last voyage that the Spanish made to the north for a while. A lot of accidents happen in history. If the Spanish had paid more attention to the northwest in the 1780s, the history of British Columbia would have been more like the history of California. But a year before that third expedition, Captain Cook sailed into the area. Pretty soon the first US businessmen arrived.

Fur in the Ocean

"The well known generosity of my other Spanish friends,
will, I trust, pardon the warmth of expression with which
I must ever advert to the conduct of Señor Quadra; who,
regardless of the difference in opinion that had risen
between us in our diplomatic capacities at Nootka, had
uniformly maintained towards us a character infinitely
beyond the reach of my powers of encomium to describe."
—George Vancouver, 1792

Strange flowers

When you are in the South Pacific it is easy to forget that important things are happening in Europe. You can lie on a beach under palm fronds, your toes in the sand, the breeze in your hair, the scent of strange flowers in your forebrain, and forget about some war or revolution on that distant continent. That is true today, and it was true in the late eighteenth century. The second half of the eighteenth century was jammed with wars and revolutions for the European peoples, but there were sailing ships gliding from island to island in the Pacific, on the watery surface of another world.

The North Pacific has a lot of islands in it too, but once one is north of the Hawaiian Islands, few of them have palm trees on them. However, in the northernmost parts, from Bering Island to Vancouver Island, there were glossy creatures called sea otters. Rich people in China wanted the fur off these animals to trim their silken clothes, and they would pay European mariners handsomely for them. At the other end of the sealines, the native Aleuts and Nootkas would let their otter pelts go for a song.

A pattern was established.

What are sea otters?

You might well ask. They are almost all gone. Ecologists keep trying to re-establish them from California to Alaska, and human fishers keep shooting at them with high-power rifles.

The sea otter is part of a history that includes the plains bison and the Atlantic cod. First there were so many of them that early witnesses were astounded. You could walk from Newfoundland to Cape Breton on the backs of the cod, etc. Well, the cod is an ugly fish, but we ate them anyway. I don't know exactly why white men killed nearly all the bison. They were not as ugly as the Atlantic cod, and they did not have fur like the fur on the Pacific sea otter.

Really, all otters are part of the weasel family, and we generally use the word "weasel," as a noun or a verb, about something we have contempt for. Unfortunately for the otters, they have furs that people like a lot, and their furs are more durable than most. Men who can be persuaded to kill otters have to overcome their humour and friendliness, I would think. Anyone who has seen otters in a zoo knows how much fun it is to watch them, because the otters seem to be having so much fun, sliding down their slides into the water, swimming underwater on their backs, clambering over one another to get back to the top of the slide. They do this stuff in the wild, too. Who could kill an animal that looks so happy?

There are different kinds of otters all over the world, and they are all rare or becoming rare. The Brazilian giant otters should have been relatively safe because they had the sense to hide away in the rain forest. Lots of luck. They are now extremely rare.

All otters are cute, but the sea otter is perhaps cutest of all because of the way it eats seafood. It floats on its back with a stone on its chest, and opens a mollusc by bashing it on the stone. Oyster fishers in California choose this moment to shoot it. By the time that you read this, there may be eleven sea otters at Santa Catalina, the island of romance.

Of all the world's otters, the sea otter's fur was the most coveted and the most expensive. The sea otter spent its time in the cold water of kelp beds in the north Pacific, so its coat was luxuriant. It ranged in colour from reddish brown to blackish brown, and was sometimes shot through with white highlights. This thick hair was designed to help this playful animal survive. Unfortunately, being so beautiful was a bad survival tactic when the China clippers came around.

The sea otters didn't know anything about the Seven Years' War and the Treaty of Paris. They didn't know anything about the US War of Independence or the French Revolution. Those things were happening a planet away. They didn't know that the gleaming hair on their supple bodies would cause men to build sailing ships and allow them to be propelled into the unwelcoming weather of the North Pacific.

Captain Cook

The Spanish had gone to the northwest coast because they had heard rumours of the Russians being there. Now the English heard rumours of the Spanish being there.

In the summer of 1776, Captain James Cook, who would become Britain's most illustrious seaman since Francis Drake, set sail from England with two ships, the *Resolution* and the *Discovery*, the latter commanded by Mr. Charles Clerke. His entourage included young Mr. George Vancouver and young Mr. William Bligh, both of whom would prove to be great and famous sailors.

On the fourth of July the American Colonies declared their independence.

Cook sailed around the bottom of Africa and into the Orient. He spent all of 1777 charting the south seas. It was his third voyage there. In New Zealand they knew James Cook. He was forty-nine years old now, and he had been at sea for forty years. The French and Spanish and Austrians had learned respect for him in the war. He had been with the British forces that took Quebec. At the end of 1777 he set sail for the northwest coast of America. The Admiralty wanted him to keep an eye out for the Northwest Passage, make accurate maps of the serrated northernmost coastline, and show the Spanish that Balboa and the Pope mean nothing to Englishmen.

As on his second expedition in the south, Cook was using a new gadget called the Harrison Chronometer. It beat the moon and stars all to hell for telling longitude. It would be very useful for telling how long the Northwest Passage would have to be. Cook had a knack for being the first to do something, and he inspired young Vancouver to do likewise. Cook's ship was the first to sail across the Antarctic Circle, and of course the first to cross both the Antarctic and Arctic circles. He made the first charts of New Zealand's coastline, and rediscovered many places unvisited by Europeans for more than a century. Cook was always itching to see somewhere else. He also liked to prove things. He had proved that the fabulous Southern Continent did not exist. Now he would get busy doing the same for the Northwest Passage. On the way to Nootka from Tahiti he discovered the Sandwich Islands and showed the Hawaiians how to draw the Union Jack, which is still on their flags.

Cook's ships, beaten around by the Pacific Ocean, sailed right on by the Strait of Juan de Fuca, and fetched up at Nootka, near the end of March, 1778. Actually, no one there called the place Nootka. Pérez had not called it Nootka. But Captain Cook, who had been the first European commander to spend months talking with Polynesians, liked to use native names for places. He asked the people what they called their place. Unfortunately, they thought he was asking for directions and so told him to sail *around* the island, using the word *notka*.

The first people he saw were in three canoes. In one of the canoes stood a man covered with feathers and paint. This creature was shouting something and throwing white downy feathers toward the English ships. His companions were throwing some kind of red powder. The important-looking man was shaking something, which, when they got close enough to hear, turned out to be a rattle. Nowadays we think that this personage was Maquinna, which is a name worn by the most important man in the most important clan of the Nootka people. James Cook, in his elegant journals, does not mention the names of any Native people.

But Maquinna was the leader at his village of Yuquot, and he made the Englishmen welcome for four weeks. The seamen had to cut new masts for their vessels, plug up the leaks in their hulls, find a lot of water, and make spruce beer by the tun. The sailors were perhaps disappointed that the Nootka women did not have the unfettered attitude toward sex that was shown by the women of Tahiti. In fact they noticed that while the Nootka men could walk around or lie on the beach with their genitals showing, the women were, in James Cook's words, "always properly clothed, and behaved with the utmost propriety justly deserving all commendation for a bashfulness and modesty becoming their sex."

James Cook was being first again. As at Tahiti, he was making the first extended stay by any Europeans among the northwest Indians. He called the landing Friendly Cove.

Cook's description of his month at Yuquot is very informative, both of the village life of these new people, and of the attitudes of the world-travelling English. Cook again and again uses the word "monstrous" when describing Indian carvings and paintings and masks. But about the singing of the Nootka men he can praise "a very agreeable air, with a degree of softness and melody." When they are dressed in ceremonial outfits, with wooden animal masks and rows of deer hoofs, they inspire "horror," but when they are in their normal clothes, cedar bark cloaks and otter skins, they are friendly, and when they take the paint and insect repellent off they are light-skinned as southern Europeans and "plump," though never fat.

Many have rings of metal hanging from their noses. The women have discs in their bottom lips. These people like metal more than anything else the Europeans will trade. They scorn glass beads and they have no use for the white men's cloth. They like iron and copper.

They showed Captain Cook some silver spoons. Cook looked them over and gave his opinion that they were Spanish in manufacture. He was looking at the missing pieces from the silver service of Don Estéban Martínez of the *Santiago*.

The natives of Tahiti were like that, too, always on the lookout to steal something from the visiting ships. It was a good thing that the natives of Polynesia and the northwest coast did not understand real estate. They might conceive of coming to Europe and stealing land from the people who lived there.

In late April it was time to head north, so Cook listened to some songs, watched some frightening dances, and boarded the *Resolution*. Nootka men with their long canoes towed the two ships free of the snug harbour, and sang to them as they sailed toward the pole. Among the souvenirs of their stopover were furs of every kind, including three hundred sea otter pelts. Cook was not first in this—the survivors of the last Bering expedition had been the first to bring a bunch of otter furs to Europe.

Now the *Resolution* and the *Discovery*, a couple of old coal boats, headed for the Alaska coast. They got a lot further than the Spanish had; there was no scurvy on Cook's ships. At the 60th parallel, within eyeshot of Mt. St. Elias, Cook began his careful survey, checking out the immense and maddeningly intricate Prince William Sound and the westward coastline. If there had been a Northwest Passage, he would have welcomed it. There were hundreds of inlets, and none of them, so far, a passage. Cook studied the Harrison Chronometer. It told him that if he found a passage to Hudson Bay, it would have to traverse five hundred leagues and more. If there was a passage, Cook decided, it must be through the frozen latitudes past the Bering Strait.

The two ships turned south, to spend the winter in the Sandwich Islands. There the English and the Islanders were on amicable terms, but they started to steal from one another, and anxieties escalated, and one day there was a fight on the beach at Karakakoa. The upshot was that Cook, whom the Islanders thought might be a god, was killed and cut into pieces like Osiris. Eventually the pieces were brought back to the new commander, Captain Clerke, who interred the roughly assembled British hero, and sailed north again.

Clerke had been suffering from tuberculosis for some time, but he had a Northwest Passage to find or disprove. This time the *Resolution* and the *Discovery* stopped at Petropavlovsk on the way south, and heard all about the Russian fur trade. Captain Clerke's body was left in Russian soil, and the ships sailed for home, not through any newly found passage, but all the way around Asia and Africa. At Macao they stopped and sold the Nootka furs for a fortune. If some of the sailors had had their way, they would have headed straight back to Maquinna's village.

Strange

The secretive Russians were grabbing sea otter furs all this while. They hopped eastward along the hundred Aleutian Islands, eradicating the animals as they went. The supply lines from Kamchatka were getting longer. Eventually the intrepid Captain Gregory Shelikov built a trading post on

Kodiak Island, the large island at the root of the Alaska peninsula. He built a town, a church and a school. His wife, Natasha, was one of the first two European women to set foot on Northwest America. In a few more years the Russians would create a town further south, in the panhandle. They called it New Archangel, but we now call it Sitka. The Russians managed to do most of their business without fanfare.

But when the story of James Cook's month at Nootka spread around the mercantile world, it started a fur rush. The English got to Vancouver Island first. In 1785 the aptly named *Sea Otter*, under the command of James Hanna, came from Macao on the first visit by any Briton who was simply looking for business. Hanna was not a great diplomat. His visit featured a battle in which several of the outgunned Natives were killed. He was soon followed by others, and before the fur-bearing animals knew it, there were more than a hundred vessels out there looking for them.

One of the most interesting of the Englishmen was James Strange, who may have been animated by his surname. He was a partner in a two-ship expedition sent out from Bombay under the protection of the East India Company. The Native traders at Nootka probably favoured him because of his singing voice. Most Europeans were slow to appreciate the differences among Indian peoples, and most white businessmen were less thoughtful than they might have been about the ceremonial nature of Native life. It happened, for instance, that the Nootka fur traders observed two customs before transactions were to be made in earnest. There should be a ceremonial exchange of gifts that were considered outside the main business; and a trader should perform an appropriate song at the beginning and end of each trading session.

James Strange was an enthusiastic man. He had brought with him a pair of brass cymbals, and after he had laid out his wares, chisels and pieces of copper and iron rings, he slammed the cymbals together, performed a little dance, and sang a loud song which he improvised for the moment. He was as successful as the dancing sailors of John Davis's Arctic expedition two centuries earlier. The Nootkas called for encore after encore of Strange's music, and he could never make a non-musical deal at Friendly Cove. Other English traders must have wondered why the Indians were making a big gesture that looked like someone slapping things together.

When Strange had arrived in summer of 1786, he had brought with him a ship filled with scurvied men. Maquinna offered Strange a big house as a hospital. The Company man thought that he was buying it for pocket change, but chances are that the host was simply saying "Our home is your home." In any case, the able-bodied men remaining in the *Captain Cook* and the *Experiment* set to cleaning the cedar building. However, the sick men could not get used to the odour of old fish, and decided to finish their recuperation in tents. The people showed them what they had in the way of vitamin C, greens and roots and salmonberries, and the English soon revived. While they did, they dug a garden and planted it with seeds brought from England and Asia. This was the first farm on Vancouver Island.

Strange liked this place, and planned to return every summer. He wanted to establish a special relationship with Maquinna and his people, so he found a volunteer among his sailors to stay the winter in the village of Yuquot. This was the young surgeon Dr. John Mackay. Mackay would learn the language, tend to ailments if permitted, and curry favour. Maquinna took him into his own house, and said that he would take special care of him, that when Strange's ships returned next summer their young medical fellow would be as fat as a whale.

So Dr. John Mackay was the first European to live alone with the Indians of the Pacific slope.

The people in Bombay, however, decided that the South Sea Company could exercise their claimed monopoly on trade on the Northwest American coast. The East India Company had other plans for James Strange. John Mackay would have to make his own way back to India.

But before taking his vessels full of furs to China, Strange decided to do a little exploration and to correct an oversight of James Cook. Nowhere in his writings had Cook mentioned claiming the fur country for the British Crown. This Strange did on a pleasant beach at the northwest corner of the big island. He hoisted the colours and turned the soil and pronounced the name of His Britannic Majesty. He climbed a mountain and looked down at the pattern of trees and sea, and named the large body of water known as Queen Charlotte Sound. Queen Charlotte was the wife of King George III, and got her name on a lot of places. On Canada's east coast there is a city called Charlottetown, and on Canada's west coast there is a town called Queen Charlotte City.

Then Strange and his men found an old Indian village in which no one had lived for a long time. They dug a hole in a tree and left some copper and a message, to prove George III's claim to this land. In 1936 someone found the piece of copper in the tree on little Nigei Island. This was five years after the Statute of Westminster, which asserted the right of the Dominion of Canada to total legislative autonomy.

It's too bad that we don't have anything named for James Strange in northern Vancouver Island. According to the Island's well-known novelist Jack Hodgins, Islanders tend to be strange people. Strange named Cape Scott on the northwest corner after his Bombay partner.

Strangers still

Farther down the west coast of Vancouver Island there is a sound even larger than Nootka Sound. This is Barkley Sound. It is named after Charles

Barkley, who was in 1787 a young English captain of a 400-ton vessel regis-tered in Belgium under Austrian colours. When the ship had left London it was called the *Loudoun*. After a paint job in Ostend it was rechristened the *Imperial Eagle*. This was one of those ships that sailed for English interests under foreign flags so that the backing syndicates could sail around the monopolies—the South Seas Company along the American coast, the British East India Company along the Chinese coast.

Barkley, who was so courtly that friends called him "Sir Charles," had his new teenage bride, Frances, with him. Some sailors thought that meant bad luck. Some Vancouver Island Natives thought that she was some kind of vision, she with her long blonde hair in the wind at the taff-rail. She was the second European woman to see the northwest coast, and the first to visit what would become British Columbia. She had with her a maidservant, who was probably the first Hawaiian to see Vancouver Island. Mr. Barkley sprin-kled his wife's names around the map—Frances Hornby Trevor.

As soon as the *Imperial Eagle* dropped anchor in Friendly Cove, a canoe propelled by a single person came out to meet it. The canoer climbed aboard the "Austrian" ship. Mrs. Barkley took two steps backward. Several officers wrinkled their noses. No one stepped forward to assist the creature. And no wonder: he had oolichan grease in his tangled hair, his clothing was primar-ily filthy greased otter skins, there was dirt all over his face, and straggles of whiskers here and there growing out of the dirt. He smelled to high heaven, and took up a position upwind on the deck. He carried a bird-headed rattle in one hand, but no visible weapon. Just the same, several officers had their hands on theirs.

No one greeted this disgusting spectacle. Opinion of the local Natives ran low on the deck of the *Imperial Eagle*. There was a silence. Charles Barkley had been alerted that the Nootkas like to sing before they get down to talk-ing. They waited for whatever hideous air might escape the filthy lips of this apparition.

Then it spoke.

In nice Celtish-inflected English.

It was the surgeon from the *Experiment*. He had spent the last year among the Nootka people. He was not as fat as a whale.

But now he could speak the local language. He was on friendly terms with Nootka businessmen. Overcoming a certain revulsion, Captain Barkley invited the smelly doctor belowdecks for a wash and a change of clothing. Dressed as a Briton again, John Mackay happily accepted the invitation to join this expedition, and at the fur market made Barkley the most successful white trader of the summer.

With his own trade goods gone and their place taken by heaps of shining otter pelts, young Barkley set sail southward along the Vancouver Island coast. He found a big sound which he named after himself, then turned the corner and went eastward. There he found a big waterway that had been a legend among seamen for almost two centuries. Barkley called it the Strait of Juan de Fuca on his new map. Then with his treasure and his bride he hied to the Orient.

If you have written a book about Captain George Vancouver, you tend to think of all these sailors as pre-Vancouver figures. There were quite a few of them, and they were becoming more and more mercantile all the time. Already the west coast was beginning to acquire its reputation as a place where businessmen could play fast and loose with the rules while stripping nature of its bounty. Vancouver was not of that sort, but by the waning years of the eighteenth century he was in a minority.

One of the least savoury characters of the time was an energetic man named John Meares. If he had been around two centuries later, he would be a real-estate "developer" with interests in casinos and car dealerships. He would have friends in all levels of government, or if not friends, at least people who would be grateful for whatever he could give them. The only trees he would leave standing would be the ones on his estate high above the ordinary people. He would never read a book, except parts of his autobiography.

Meares owned an interest in the Bengal Fur Company, headed by a slickster named John Henry Cox. Another of Cox's captains was James Hanna, the man who thought it was a good idea to treat Indians with gunpowder. Cox noticed in the middle 1780s that the East India Company and the South Sea Company were paying less attention than they might have to the North American fur trade. He sent his poachers out, chief among them Meares and Hanna. Meares grabbed furs wherever he could, and made claims in his sailing log that would have embarrassed Juan de Fuca.

In the summer of 1786 Meares took two ships, the *Nootka* and the *Sea Otter*, to the north, picking up whatever he could lay his hands on in Russian and British waters, and wound up getting the *Nootka* trapped in the ice of Prince William Sound. *The Sea Otter* had sailed away from its lead vessel, never to be seen again. In May of 1787 the men of the *Nootka* were found and rescued by Nathaniel Portlock and George Dixon, who had both been officers under Captain Cook. Now they had legal contracts with the British East India Company, the South Sea Company and the British government. When they found the poachers frozen in the ice, twenty-three of Meares's men had died of scurvy, and the rest were on the brink of starvation.

Nowadays if the people at Canada Customs find hidden contraband in your car they can seize your car as well as imposing a fine on you. In the spring of 1787 Portlock and Dixon could have seized Meares's ships with all their contraband furs. Instead, they fed the stranded crew, supplied their ships with necessaries for a trip back to home port, and even gave Meares some sailors to help him get back across the ocean. From Meares they extracted a bond and a promise to cease illegal activities and sail straight to China. Not for the first time, Meares offered thanks and made the promise. As soon as the two legal ships were over the horizon, he started gathering more furs from whoever would sell them.

And the next year he was back for more, sailing under convenient Portuguese colours. He had seen the way the Russians were operating in the north, with their "permanent" land base, a place for Native people to bring their furs, a place for the furs and the goods they would be traded for to be stored. Meares would establish his trading post not at Prince William Sound with its unhappy memories, but at Nootka Sound, where the ice never grew.

When he arrived in May of 1788 he had twenty Chinese carpenters with him. From then on in British Columbia, whenever white people needed anything built they would bring a lot of Chinese workers to do it. Meares was carrying the materials he needed to build a coastal schooner and a big shelter for his men and materials. Why he brought lumber from China to the forested home of the longhouse-building Nootka, he did not explain. We do know that the Indians adjusted to the strangeness of the Europeans faster than the Europeans adjusted to them.

But Meares diversified his business now, or so he claimed, and this diversification was to have repercussions in a short while, when the Spanish returned. Meares claimed to have purchased some real estate from Maquinna, just as James Strange claimed to have bought a house and garden plot. But Meares proceeded to build a fort-like shelter on his land, to become the first developer in British Columbia. This was an elaborate two-storey structure, with rooms for officers and a bunkhouse for the men, areas for storage and areas for repair. And breastworks outside, and a cannon aimed toward the harbour. Then Meares headed south for a little exploring and trading. He spent most of the summer doing business in Clayoquot Sound. When the fur business slowed down, he looked around at the immense trees and wondered whether there was any money in them.

Meares set to expanding his enterprise. He built his schooner. He sent his ships north and south. He expanded his "property" at Friendly Cove, and worked his cunning ways with Maquinna and the other important Island chiefs, Callicum and Wickaninnish. He dressed Maquinna in ship's officer's clothing and exchanged feasts with him. Sign here, he said.

When the USAmerican ships came around, Meares said welcome to our little town. The USAmericans, who were used to coming around when the Brits went home for the winter, did not like the idea of a permanent English or Portuguese or Austrian post on the coast. But what could they do? The US navy was busy in Atlantic waters. But there were rumours that the Russians were thinking of how nice and warm it must be at Nootka. The USAmericans decided to keep in touch.

But it was the Spanish who came to Nootka.

No northern vision

Here is what Bernal Diaz del Castillo wrote about the Spanish approach to Tenochtitlan, the great capital of the Aztec people in 1519: "The great towns seemed like an enchanted vision from the tale of Amadis. Indeed, some of our soldiers asked whether it was not all a dream... It was so wonderful that I do not know how to describe this first glimpse of things never heard of, seen, or dreamed of before."

If the Spanish had been able to get over the European prejudice against a little grease and pigment on the face, they might have been pretty well impressed by the villages on the northwest coast. The houses and poles and canoes and masks and rattles and gleaming furs might have bespoken a people with their own share of wonder. But when the Spanish decided to come back to Nootka, it was not for wonder. They were resplendent *perros en el pesebre*. Perhaps during recent times they had not shown much interest in the Pacific north of California, but they could not be expected to handle their whole ocean all at once. There would be time in the future.

But now there were stories of swarming ships, Russians, British, USAmericans and all the flags of convenience. If the Spanish did not put these interlopers to flight now, they might have greater trouble asserting their ownership in the future. The Spanish were not involved in the Asian fur trade, but they were the emissaries of the Divine order of things. Churches in Iberia had walls that were coated with flattened gold that used to be shaped into false idols in the New World. Some day there would be a cathedral at Nootka Harbour. The Englishmen who were gorging themselves on the wealth of the Coast would not be giving any thought to the saving of the heathen souls.

The Nootka Crisis

The viceroy in Mexico did not want to go down in history as the commander who let the Russians and USAmericans take the northern part of their ocean from the Spanish. In February of 1789 he sent Captain Estéban José Martínez north with instructions to establish Spanish hegemony at that dirty little cove they were all sneaking into. Martínez was to build a military fort and make it self-sufficient, with cows and priests and grain.

When Martínez got to Nootka, he found that there were already four ships there, two Boston men and two of Meares's organization. Martínez did not like the odds. Although he had more firepower than did the traders, he had not been sent to create a huge international incident—only a little one. Besides, the USAmericans did not have the navy that Britain had. He would ignore the US ships and seize the Brits. This he did, with a certain military bluster, and when two more British ships entered Friendly Cove, he grabbed them, too. These two he sent to Mexico, with their officers and crews as prisoners. One of the first two was flying Portuguese colours, so he sent it back to Asia. What did he find on the fourth ship but a gang of Chinese workers sent across the sea to build Meares's empire of fur? Martínez gave these immigrants a new job. They would erect the Spanish settlement. In a year there would be fifty buildings in San Miguel, the first European town in what would become British Columbia.

I take possession of this whole place for the king of Spain, said Martínez, in an elaborate ceremony attended by some British people who kept their counsel. The Nootka people never did get a good explanation of what was going on.

The English sailors on the *Argonaut* were particularly incensed by the Spanish priests. According to the sailors the priests came aboard and sprinkled holy water on the decks, claiming the ship for both Spain and its Heaven. When the whole crisis was over, the Brits swabbed those decks, labouring to wash the water off the wood.

The English officers were piqued when the Fourth of July came round. Martínez joined the Boston men in celebrating their national day, commemorating the USAmerican victory over British rule. The Spanish fired thirteen guns and danced a Virginia reel. Captain Colnett of the *Argonaut*, while technically a prisoner, was invited to join in the celebration. He declined.

Martínez was as pushy as Meares. If the whole of the Nootka incident had been left to these two men, Friendly Cove would be a burnt hole in the ground today. Martínez was the kind of man who would shoot an Indian leader if he didn't like his song. Meares would let no man or truth stand in the way of his mercantile ambition. Martínez thought that his job was simple: he would remove any ownership Meares pretended to at Nootka, and make the foundation of a Spanish city. It is too bad that the two men did not meet.

Instead, Meares went to London, where he told his version of the story. He stressed the moral and legal rightness of his own claims and the perfidy of the foreigners. When this story was told in Parliament, members of that institution leapt to their feet, wild of eye, frothy of lip. The British, valiant champions of the bounding main for two centuries and more, had received enough insults from the Spanish. They began to line up their old team from the Seven Years' War. They worked out plans to send forces from Canada down the great rivers to New Orleans.

Meanwhile the Spanish were looking to their old allies, along with some new ones. Most important, of course, was Bourbon France, but there was trouble in France. Still, Madrid thought that a king was a king. Things would not get *that* bad in Paris.

If there was going to be outright war there would be war on three continents and all the seas. A little cove on a remote shore might be the flashpoint for a first world war. The Spanish garrisoned their forts. The British sent their warships out.

The Spanish position was based on tradition, on Balboa and the Pope. The British argued for the fact of their continuous occupation. The Indians had been at Friendly Cove for ten centuries, and they had their own popes. No one ever briefed them on the latest pronouncements in Madrid and London.

News travelled slowly across oceans in the last decade of the eighteenth century. While Meares was whipping the parliamentarians into a frenzy, the ships and men that had been captured and sent to Mexico were wending their free ways back to English-controlled waters. In fact, in the fall of 1789 the Spanish had for some strange reason ceased their building at Nootka. They even removed some of the buildings and replaced them with big crosses. The Spanish always thought that crosses were better than houses when it came to claiming territory.

They did come back in 1790, though, and began to build anew. They also started a second settlement at the doorway to the Strait of Juan de Fuca. It looked as if the Spanish had decided that there was a negotiation coming, and they wanted it to look as if they had always been interested in the country north of California.

The Nootka Convention

How strange that a world war was almost started over a place that the white people finally left to the original inhabitants. If the Spanish had stuck to their guns and retained what they thought was ownership, British Columbia would probably be part of the USA now. If war had raged up the coast, there would probably be fewer Spanish names in downtown streets in Vancouver.

But the Spanish saw what was happening in France in 1790. They knew that they would not be able to depend on their largest ally. On the other hand, Nootka looked as if it would become the most important fur-trading site in the world. If the Indios had been bringing gold rather than animal skins, the Spanish Armada would have been riding the chuck at Friendly Cove. But from his vantage spot in London, Pitt the Younger had a look around and threatened war against the distracted French. The Spanish agreed to sign an agreement on Nootka.

The essential theme of the Nootka Convention was that no government owned the place: "The officials of the two Crowns shall withdraw, respectively, their people from the said port of Nootka." It was signed by the Spanish and English in October 1790. Maquinna was not at the ceremony because it took place on another continent.

At Nootka John Meares was to get his putative property back, see his destroyed buildings rebuilt, and get compensation of 200,000 dollars. He always landed on his feet. The English were to keep ten leagues away from established Spanish territories. There was some disagreement over the location of the latter. In any case, the English now came out in favour of free trade, a sure sign that they considered themselves the strongest Europeans in the area. They adumbrated the East India Company monopoly, and left the trading lanes open.

But the Nootka Convention would take five years to be put in force. There were arguments about Meares's real estate. Spanish and British explorers swarmed the area, venturing into the Strait of Juan de Fuca and naming the smaller islands there. The Spanish sent Quimper and Narvaez, Galiano and Valdéz, Eliza and Malaspina. They claimed this place and that for the Spanish Crown. In later negotiations they could cede some of them, thus proving reasonable negotiators.

One day in June of 1792, the *Sutil* and the *Mexicana*, little ships under the command of Dionisio Galiano and Cayetano Valdéz, were perched off what they did not know was Point Grey, where the University of British Columbia now sprawls. We know the place as Spanish Banks. Along came some sailors in boats, rowing across Burrard Inlet. These were Captain George Vancouver and his crew, a bunch of tired and hungry men.

Vancouver was busy at his task of surveying the whole west coastline of the continent. He had left his ship the *Discovery*, a week before, with six days' food, to criss-cross inlets, drop sounding lines and create a map that would be used two hundred years later by the US Coast Guard. He did not know that the Spaniards had been doing similar work in these waters. He did not know that there would one day be a "world-class" city crowding these waters and mountains.

At first the proud young heir to James Cook was disappointed to find the Iberians. Damn it all to hell, he thought. "I cannot avoid acknowledging that, on this occasion, I experienced no small degree of mortification in finding the external shores of the gulf had been visited, and already examined a few miles beyond where my researches during the excursion had extended," he wrote. But he found the Spanish to be gracious, and more important, munificent with their food and drink. Then the Spanish and English captains showed each other their maps and sketches, and decided to work together. Vancouver had often let it be known that he would rather fight than explore, but upon meeting the Spanish officers in the North Pacific, he proved their equal in diplomacy. It was a quality that would serve him well in his wonderful association with Don Juan Francisco de la Bodega y Quadra.

Vancouver and Quadra

Vancouver Island was once known as Vancouver and Quadra Island. Here in British Columbia we call the Spanish-Peruvian explorer Quadra, after his mother's family. In Spanish America he was known as Bodega, after his father's family. That is one of the ways we handle history. Bodega, whom we call Quadra, came from one of the two Spanish viceroyages in the New World. In Peru the few white families would exploit the labour of the huge Indian population for the rest of their history. So it goes. When it was found that there was a separate island barely off the shore where Campbell River now sits, it was named after Quadra, and the Brit was given the bigger one. Still, off the coast of British Columbia there are a lot of islands named after Spanish people. British Columbia school children have no idea who these people were.

Vancouver and Quadra had met fourteen years earlier at Friendly Cove, when Vancouver was the youngest gentleman on Cook's last voyage. Now on August 28, 1792, the *Discovery* and the *Chatham* sailed into Friendly Cove, to meet the Don. Vancouver fired thirteen guns and was saluted in like kind from the brig *Activa*.

"Damn, these Mamathni are always so noisy," said one Nootka fisherman.

"They also seem to be unreliable marksmen," said the other Nootka fisherman.

But the Spanish proceeded with their extravagant welcome. The British put on their best clothes. The Spanish brought out the best silverware and wine. The party lasted all day and most of the night. In the darkness there was a twenty-one-gun salute to the monarchs of Britain and Spain.

"*Mi casa es su casa*," said Don Juan Francisco de la Bodega y Quadra.

Vancouver was polite. But he had to find a way of conveying the thought that Quadra's graciousness was accepted while the idea that it was the Spaniard's house in the first place did not fit into British plans.

In the following days the two commanders grew to like each other as no other representatives of their respective empires could have been expected to. Their negotiations were conducted with formality and congeniality. It was a remarkable week, probably the most remarkable week in the history of British Columbia. George Vancouver was the greatest navigator of all time, and Quadra was a success story beyond parallel in his empire. The Spanish did not promote their colonials easily, but the Peru-born Quadra was commander-in-chief of the naval forces in San Blas, responsible for everything in the Pacific from Panama northward. He knew the waters of the coast up to Alaska as well as any person on the globe. He had entered latitudes that no other Spanish-speaking sailor

Captain George Vancouver was the greatest European explorer of the Pacific.

would dare. For twenty years he had been making expeditions that, in his reading of the rules, made this coast Spanish. As far as he was concerned, it was not right for him to concede anything at all. He could see nothing wrong in Martínez's seizing of Meares's ships and buildings. San Miguel was the northern outpost of Spanish domains.

Vancouver was somewhat taken aback by this argument. He courteously pointed out that these matters had been settled in London and Madrid two years ago. His mandate was to go to Nootka and go through the formalities of receiving the port and its buildings. Spanish property did not extend north of San Francisco Bay. Any Spanish settlement between there and here was to be a free port, and neither Spanish nor British ships were to be denied access.

"My house is your house," he told the Spanish commander.

Although they had differing views on the proprietorship of the north Pacific coast, the two captains grew to like one another more and more. Vancouver had never been a man to throw his affection around lightly, and he still felt an itch to be patrolling the Caribbean for French sails, so the affection between the two men must have been something more than natural, a gleam in history.

At the end of September Quadra set sail for Monterey. The two commanders had not settled the political question. Neither would agree to making an official document on terms agreeable to the other. But they had formed a great friendship. They had opted for love over war. They both sent messages back to their capitals, explaining the situation and hoping that the situation could be settled by their successors.

In the middle of October Vancouver set sail for Monterey, where he would rejoin Quadra and enjoy hospitality that would cost as much as a major military skirmish.

Before the century reached its end they would both be dead.

Forts on the River

Scots

Then along came the Scots. One main difference between the United States and Canada is the number of people with Scottish names who have always run things in Canada. Before Louis St. Laurent in 1948, you pretty well had to be Scottish or of Scottish heritage to be prime minister of Canada. Maybe you had to be Scottish to survive in the wilds of northern and western Canada. Hence the North West Company. It was based in Montreal, but it was run by a bunch of Scotchmen in weskits. They were looking for beavers.

The beaver was an unfortunate animal. The same matted fur that enabled him or her to work long days in the water was perfect for making superior felt. In the seventeenth century felt hats, often with preposterously wide brims, became very popular in Europe. All the beavers wanted to do was bite down trees and make dams. But smelly creatures from the Old Man knows where were willing to give the native humans a few farthings to undress the beavers.

In 1670 the Hudson's Bay Company was granted a charter to go and get those beaver pelts. Europe needed hats. The Hudson's Bay Company was not a government, but for the next two hundred years it would seem like one. Its financial backers had a lot of friends who ran things in England and the Empire. It had a governor, and at various times the governor would greatly resemble a government. But the Hudson's Bay Company was private business.

It had the best of both worlds. Here is the territory it claimed a monopoly upon: all the lands that drained into Hudson Bay. That means as far west as the Great Divide. In almost all of that territory there had never been a white man.

For a century or so, the Company was content to set up stations at Hudson Bay itself, and allow Indians and a few others to bring furs to them. But in the late eighteenth century, just as enterprising people were thinking of ways to elbow past the East India Company in the Pacific fur rush, so a bunch of Scots and a bunch of USAmericans dared to compete with the HBC for a continent full of furs. The Scots created the North West Company and shortly thereafter the USAmericans formed the Pacific Fur Company.

But the Scots were the first to penetrate the country west of the Great Divide. They differed from the HBC in two main ways. They did not have a charter from the British government, and hence felt no great responsibility toward it. And they were not content to set up shop and let the business come to them; they sent their agents farther and farther west, setting up fur stations as they went. The Indians still came to them, but they did not have to come so far. And at the turn of the nineteenth century there was not a lot of competition around the westward-flowing rivers.

The North West Company was interested in finding a route by which they could take skins from the Interior to the Pacific Coast, instead of hauling them all the way back to Montreal. Lots of luck, said their Indian guides. Anyone who has travelled off main highways around the province will appreciate the difficulty of trekking up and down rocks-and-tree-strewn mountains while carrying canoes or ninety-pound backpacks. But exploration is exploration; there are times when one keeps going just to prove that one can keep going, putting the reasons for doing so in the back of one's mind.

Alexander Mackenzie was the North West Company's fair-haired boy in 1789. He knew all about Captain Cook's success on the northwest coast, and he was interested in finding a freshwater route to Cook's Inlet. In the spring of 1789, while Estéban José Martínez was sailing north to capture Nootka, Mackenzie's party left Fort Chipewyan at the west end of Lake Athabasca, and headed up the Slave River instead of the Peace, and paddled the great lakes of the north, always hoping to find the much-rumoured westward-flowing river. But from Great Slave Lake he came upon the big river that would later have his name, and though it was supremely navigable, it went north rather than west, and the ocean Mackenzie was to see was the Arctic. He saw a lot of furry animals along the way, but trading vessels were not going to congregate at the mouth of the Mackenzie River.

Mackenzie went back to Britain and studied the stars and the earth and the logs of European sea captains. In 1792 he was ready to try again. This

time he would follow the Unjigah River, or what the whites called the
Peace. Starting in the autumn, he and nine other men fought their way
upstream into the Rockies, until it was time to chop trees and build a winter
post. In May of 1793 they set out again and were soon going downwater, not
exactly west, but certainly toward the sea. Captain Vancouver was on that
sea, fighting storms all the way from the Sandwich Islands. On this return
to the Coast Vancouver landed first at Fitzhugh Sound at the mouth of
Dean Channel at the end of May.

Mackenzie and his men were on the Fraser River, encountering bad water
from time to time. The Indians told them that if they stayed on that river
they called Tacoutch, they would come to Hell's Canyon, which was the
worst news of all. So Mackenzie pulled his much-tested twenty-five-foot
canoe out of the water, put it away carefully, and started hiking toward the
setting sun. The Indians showed them the trail they took when they wanted
to trade for dentalium shells and things made of metal. The country they
went through was not canoe country. But there was an ocean over there,
and they wanted to find out how far they were from it.

It was an arduous hike from the Cariboo to the Coast, but these
Nor'westers were driven by a great challenge. They were Mackenzie, his sec-
ond-in-command, Alexander Mckay, six *voyageurs* from Montreal and two
Indians whose hunting skill supplied most of the fresh meat on the voyage.
Mackenzie, knowing about as much of Native peoples as most businessmen,

*Alexander Mackenzie led the first European expedition to cross Canada to
the Pacific, 1793.*

had thought that they would also be able to act as translators.

Eventually they were met by some Bella Coola people, who took them in their canoes down their river, stopping at various villages for salmon feasts. Soon they arrived in salt water, and paddled out along Dean Channel. There they met some angry coastal Indians who were not happy to see any white people. They had, they said, been recently fired upon by white men who had arrived by sea. Mackenzie had missed meeting George Vancouver by a few weeks.

But he had arrived at the western ocean. It is pretty hard for people living in the age of the wide-body jet to imagine the thrill of looking from a mountainside and spying an inlet after traversing a continent by canoe and foot. The ocean was, as he said in his letter to the king, "much inter spers'd with Island." Mackenzie did not want to leave his bones on the shore of the Pacific, as Balboa had done, and he could see that his customary display of shiny European gewgaws was not going to go down well with warriors who had been exposed to British gunfire. He would turn about and get back to Chipewyan in a month. But before he went he painted the most famous rock in British Columbia. He combined some vermilion and grease and lettered on a big white rock facing the sea:

Alex Mackenzie
from Canada
by land
22d July 1793

Business is business

The people who worked on site for the Hudson's Bay Company and the North West Company had to get used to operating in a cold climate. The colder the climate, the better the furs on the target animals to be found there. So when the first European settlements were made in British Columbia, they were, except for a few places on the Coast, in the snowy parts of the country. Again we will see a difference in conditions between the Indians of the Coast and the Indians of the Interior.

While the arrival of the Europeans and their hunger for pelts would bring some seeming advantages to the Native peoples, iron axes and nails, for example, it would also create some less happy effects. In the St. Lawrence region the various peoples went to war with one another over the fur trade. On the prairies the Native people came to depend more and more on the fur companies for their survival. This latter condition would be seen as well in the Interior of the land west of the Rockies, especially in the far north. But the Coast peoples, blessed as they were by the assets of land and sea, would not have to choose between Nor'westers and famine.

When Captain Cook came to the country there were about 100,000 Native people in the province. By the middle of the nineteenth century, just before the gold rush, there were about 65,000. The fur trade could not have been that good for the indigenous people.

Alexander Mackenzie, disappointed that he had not found a more northerly route to the coast, advised his company and the British government to build a fort at the mouth of the Columbia River, which the USAmerican Robert Gray had named after his ship in 1792, the year before Mackenzie painted his rock. But the British would not have a fort there until they temporarily took Astoria from the USAmerican Pacific Company and renamed it Fort George. They did, however, establish the first post in what would become British Columbia, on the Peace River, east of the Divide. In the first couple of decades in the new century, there would be forts operated by the three companies dotting the rough map from Fort Liard in the north to Fort Walla Walla in the south.

But by the middle of the century there were only six hundred non-Natives living in British Columbia, one for every hundred Natives. Had they wanted to, the Indians could have performed what the people in the Balkans would call an ethnic cleansing in no time at all. The Indians must have had a very tolerant immigration policy.

Thomas Jefferson won the US federal election of 1800. Jefferson, commonly revered as the greatest advocate of democracy, was also an expansionist. He wrote that his country would one day stretch from pole to pole. When he read Mackenzie's story about his trek across the continent, he hired Lewis and Clark to make a similar trip, though over easier country. He told them to establish a USAmerican post at the mouth of the Columbia River, and to stick up a flag. In the winter of 1805-06 Lewis and Clark knocked together some log cabins and stuck the flag up in the rain. But they went back home in the spring. They had established a precedence but no trading post.

There was a lot of country in the west, and no clear decision on who owned it. It was a planet much different from ours. The western forests were a treasure trove, open to anyone. But they were almost impossible to get to.

The North West Company had not crossed the Rockies since Mackenzie's expedition, but when news came that the USAmericans were headed to the Pacific, a meeting was called, and the North West Company ordered Simon Fraser to cross the Divide and start setting up trading posts. They would establish lines of supply and communication that ran from the far west overland to Montreal. There would be no loading on ships in Hudson Bay because the HBC controlled that water. If the North West Company could establish supremacy in the fur trade in the western Interior, and find out whether the Columbia River was safe for navigation, they could make a deal with the traders of the Pacific, loading ships on the Coast rather than canoeing and carrying pelts all the way back across the continent.

When the nations back east started thinking in terms of national borders rather than fur-filled forests, there would be several versions of who owned what. When the USAmericans made the Louisiana Purchase from the Spanish, no one knew quite what was being bought and sold. They all knew that it started at the Mississippi River, but not where it ended. Somewhere in some high mountains, people said.

But for now it was a matter of commercial enterprise. Simon Fraser knew about the USAmericans. His father had been a Loyalist during the War of Independence, and had died in a revolutionary prison. He had come with his mother to Montreal, where he grew up not to be an intellectual giant, but to be highly competitive and adventurous. He was a nearly perfect choice by the North West Company to be their pioneer on the western slope. In 1805 he followed Mackenzie's route up the Peace and down whatever water he could find. He was supposed to find the Columbia, and while he was at it, build some forts.

Fraser was very fond of his mother, who had saved him from the secessionists. She had told him stories of the beauty of the Scotland she had left behind for the New World. When Fraser entered the country west of the Rockies he called it all New Caledonia. The province could have been called that. The term is now used loosely to designate the area north of the Cariboo, with Prince George, perhaps, as its capital.

Fraser's lieutenant, James McDougall, went ahead while Fraser established his supply depot on the Peace. McDougall set up camp on a lake and waited for the rest of the outfit. When Fraser arrived he decided to set up the first fort right there. McDougall had called the water Trout Lake, which has been the name of at least a hundred lakes in British Columbia. Fraser changed its name to Lake McLeod, naming it after a friend. There they built the first structures of Fort McLeod, which would become the first white people's settlement west of the Rockies. It is still there, on Highway 97, though the place is now called McLeod Lake, and in 2005 it will be the first British Columbia town to celebrate its two-hundredth birthday.

The Native people who live in the area will celebrate their 10,500th year.

Company stores

Next spring Fraser came back with John Stuart, found a big lake to the southwest of Fort McLeod, and promptly named it Stuart Lake, next to which they constructed Fort St. James. The Carrier people in the area preferred to call the place Nakasleh, but they were not drawing the maps that went back to Montreal. In fact, friendly as they were, they were a little nervous about the effects of the white people's enterprise. That year the salmon did not come to Stuart Lake. Maybe they were confused by the name change. Fraser sent Stuart southwest again, to a lake full of fish, and there Fort Fraser was built.

North West Company men came west along their trail and manned these forts and moved their furs. In 1807, having established Fort St. James as the centre of operations, Fraser had Fort George built at the conjunction of the Nechako and Fraser rivers. He thought he was at the conjunction of the Nechako and Columbia. Fraser was feeling pretty good. He thought he was on his way to the Pacific coast. He was making strong forts out of handy trees, and the Indians were happy that they no longer had to travel for weeks to get the stuff they wanted from the white men.

The fur company forts in New Caledonia were not built to house soldiers whose job it was to put down Indian uprisings. They were places to collect furs and bale them and store them until it was time to send a long train of packhorses eastward over the mountains. They usually had a square surrounded by poles with points at the top, and a gate that would be closed at the end of every trading day. Trading days were possible every day, but life at the forts could be pretty slow. The men working there were glad to see Indians showing up, not because of the riches that would be accrued by the Company, but because life in a little fort thousands of miles from civilization could be pretty boring.

The forts contained living quarters for the factor and his employees. There would be space for the grain and vegetable garden, and space for the horses to feed and disport themselves. The factor depended on the Indians not only for furs but also for protein, for smoked salmon and fresh meat. The diaries of the Nor'westers often complain of food running out. But they also describe the delight in the small quantities of luxury goods that an arriving brigade from Chipewyan might bring—tobacco or tea or sugar.

In some ways the life at the fur forts might have been like life on the fur ships. There would be a lot of heavy work to do for a while, and then long boring days for a longer while. There would be a commander who wore better clothes and spent a lot of his time writing. There would be plenty of time to develop a hobby, scrimshaw at sea, perhaps, flute-making at the fort. At sea a boy could find a position on a ship, apprenticing himself to the sea. In the forts a lad was employed as gardener and wrangler. These boys looked forward to the days when they might be ship's officers or Company factors.

There was one slight difference. Although in both cases the men were for months and years at a time away from their wives or available mates at home, and although both sailors and landsmen took to themselves aboriginal women when they could, the white men in New Caledonia managed to set up domiciles that resembled family life, whereas a sailor always had a ship to catch. Of course if a Nor'wester had to go back to Montreal or Scotland, he did not take his Native family with him. There was a difference between a fur edge to a Native person's deerskin clothing and an elegant beaver felt hat with an egret feather in it.

So when Simon Fraser set up his string of forts along the waterways west of the Rocky Mountains, he began some serious changes to the population mix of the British Columbia Interior. But he was thinking of enterprise.

Fraser thought that Mackenzie's getting to the coast was a pretty good feat, but he thought that what he was doing was a lot more important to the Company and the world. He said that Mackenzie should have got up earlier in the morning.

White water

Building forts, said the directors of the North West Company, is a very good idea. The forests were full of furry animals, and the Native peoples were good at trapping them, and they were willing to trade them to white people at quite an advantage to the white people. If the white people in the area were Nor'westers, there was sufficient proof that fortune favours industry. *Scots wa hae.*

But there was this great Columbia River, perhaps the last chance to find a navigable waterway to the Pacific. Who knew, as well, how much fur country it might wend its way through. A great river with North West Company forts along its banks was the vision the Company directors in Montreal enjoyed in the fall of 1807.

On May 22, 1808, while the populace of Madrid was rising against their new ruler, Napoleon's brother Joseph, Simon Fraser got into the Nechako

Simon Fraser has more things named after him than any other visitor to British Columbia.

River at Fort St. James and headed downstream. He had four canoes, nineteen *voyageurs*, two Indian guides and two subalterns, his regular lieutenant John Stuart, and Jules Quesnel, after whom a Fraser River settlement would be renamed. In a few days they conducted a little business at Fort George, and then entered the great river, headed south. They managed the first few sets of rapids as Alexander Mackenzie had fifteen years earlier, and were told by perhaps the same Indian people that they would never get their canoes through Hell's Gate.

In quiet moments of paddling they saw tall hoodoos and chimneys of grey rock that looked like earth along the banks. They saw groups of mountain sheep

leaping from ledge to ledge. They saw running horses, and knew that somewhere in the immense past the Spanish had met the indigenous. They saw
Indian men with magic footholds on the rocks, using their long-handled dip
nets to pluck big salmon from the air above the spraying water. When they
went ashore to portage, they stepped on clusters of low cactus and drove the
needles into their own ankles with each step.

But Simon Fraser had himself a river, and he did not want to quit where
Mackenzie had. Like George Vancouver before him, he considered himself
ne plus ultra. He might not get his canoes all the way down this Columbia
River, but he would see it disgorge into the ocean. He passed Mackenzie's
marker, and made it to a village where Lytton now clings to steep dry ground
and experiences the hottest sun in Canada. There the clear green
Thompson River disgorges into the brown Fraser, presenting a colourful display that is described by the narrator in *Hetty Dorval*, the first novel published by the great British Columbia fiction writer Ethel Wilson, as a
"marriage" in which one mate is "overcome" and "lost in the other."

The Salish-speaking Indians at this convergence showed Fraser some
trade goods they claimed came by way of this other river all the way from
the Great Plains. Fraser took the time to name the blue-green river the
Thompson, after his associate who was building forts in the Kootenays.

The Indians who would also come to be called the Thompsons, provided
cedar dugouts, and Fraser's men continued down the sullen river. But the
valley became a series of gorges, swirling white water between high rock
walls. Even portages became impossible, and the Nor'westers had to scramble as best they could with packs on their backs. Then the packs had to be
left behind. The Nor'westers carried only their guns. At Black Canyon and
Hell's Gate they were sorely tempted to leave even these cached among the
rocks, but they did not like the idea of leaving them for the Native men.

If you have seen the gorge at Hell's Gate and the rock cliffs at either side,
you will wonder about the determinedness and sanity of Quebeckers who
would negotiate them with long weapons attached to their bodies. In a
famous piece of understatement, Fraser wrote "We had to pass where no
human being should venture." But in the very stones there was a faint path
upon which people had ventured for centuries. There were slight steps carved
into the rock. There were ladders made from poles and twigs tied with binds,
hundreds of feet above the boiling river. Indians at the top of the cliff lowered
poles so that travellers could grip them and be pulled to the sky. "We saw,"
wrote Fraser, "many graves covered with small stones all over the place."

The Indians negotiated the cliffs with great care, and did their best to
educate the strangers in foreign moccasins. Unlike many later expeditions,
this one passed without fatalities, though many of the *voyageurs* promised
their god that they would perform acts of contrition if they were permitted
to get past these immense rocks and aged twig ladders. They would never

imagine the present-day rafters who scream in enjoyment while riding the white water around which the *voyageurs* picked their way.

Eventually Fraser and Stuart and Quesnel and their entourage arrived at what would become Yale, and took the relatively easy descent to what would be Hope. There the gorge became a wide lush valley, and the river became flat. But the Indians were not as friendly. The Thompsons went back home, and Fraser had to bargain for dugouts with people who had perhaps met white people before. Fraser got his boats, but he was warned that the Cowichan people of the lower river would not be as welcoming as the Interior Shuswap had been.

But the river, at least, was friendly. The Company men could almost relax as they floated toward the sea. They were impressed by the high white volcano they saw to their left, and the "cedars five fathoms in circumference." They were excited to find that they were in tidal waters, and apprehensive upon seeing the gestures made by the local people who espied them from the shore. Eventually they came to the village of Musqueam, a large community on the estuary, within sight of the Vancouver Island arête. The large buildings and carvings were impressive, but the place was strangely underpopulated. There were old people and young mothers with small children. Fraser's Shuswap guide informed the white men that everyone else was back in the forest discussing the question of whether to kill these visitors or sell them to the Kwakiutl.

Fraser did not wait to meet any warriors. He took his readings. He had suspected for some time that he was on the wrong river. Now he knew that this one met the sea at about forty-nine degrees north, while the Columbia was three degrees to the south. He thought about going down and looking at the ocean, but reasoned that there might be hundreds of armed men between Musqueam and the mouth of the unnamed river. His third disappointment, of course, was that Mackenzie had guessed right—whatever river this was, it was not the way to the sea for canoes piled high with furs. Furthermore, the country downstream from Fort George did not look all that good for business. The Indians of the lower valley were too hostile, and the country between there and the northern forts was too hot and bare to support many fur-bearing critters.

Now, thrice disappointed, Fraser had to face the gorge again. Perhaps he would have been a little cheered had he known that his friend David Thompson, returning a favour, would name that powerful and unmanageable river after him.

Mr. Slow and Steady

The men of the North West Company kept getting rivers named after them, but what they wanted was a canoe route to the Pacific Ocean. In the first decade of the nineteenth century it became clear that the Columbia would be their last chance. The question was how to get to the mouth of the Columbia.

David Thompson was Welsh rather than Scottish, and should have been a poet. His prose is certainly far better than anything we have been left by the other North West explorers. He is called the Mapmaker because he was the first white man to make quite accurate charts of the Interior. He was a careful naturalist, and has left us beautiful descriptions of the terrain, plant life, animals, weather, people and rivers of the Kootenay-Columbia country. He was also on good terms with the Kootenay Indians, some of whom he had met when they crossed the Great Divide to Rocky Mountain House in 1806.

Thompson developed his skills as a surveyor and trader while a young man with the Hudson's Bay Company. Now he was a devout family man working for the North West Company, and he had a commission to explore the waterways west of the Rockies and south of Fraser's territory. He took his wife and children with him, fought his way up the Columbia River to Toby Creek, and supervised the building of Kootenae House, the first fort in the south. It was a good thing that Thompson was known to the Kootenay people, to whom he had given gifts and offered protection from the dangerous Peigans in his days on the other side of the mountains. When Thompson's party reached the site of their fort, they were nearly starving. Edible animals were hard to find, and the Nor'westers were not great fishers. Fortunately they were found by Kootenays before they were found by Peigans, and managed to survive in that high beautiful landscape. Eventually the Peigans did arrive, eager to clout their regular Kootenay victims and chase the traders as well, but by this time Thompson had himself a fort. He wintered there and waited for the spring of 1808.

In the meantime, he wrote about the glaciers and the rivers and "an Animal of the Tiger species" his men had killed while unsuccessfully looking for deer. David Thompson wanted to follow the Columbia River to its mouth, but he was not Simon Fraser; he was not in a great hurry. He had heard the rumours about the USAmericans and their designs on the mouth of the Columbia, but he liked to take his time. All through 1808 and 1809 he mapped the Kootenays and the area to the south, building more forts in what would become Montana, Idaho and Washington.

Get down the Columbia River and make a fort at its mouth, said the North West Company. I will, I will, said Thompson, but I have a few more forts to set up here. You should see this country. You should hear the snowmelt rushing down these mountainsides, you should see the thousands of waterfalls, taking everything with them except the bigger rocks. The larches are a hundred and fifty feet tall.

But John Jacob Astor was sending ships into the Pacific. Lewis and Clark had gone home a couple of years ago, and Lewis had already become a governor and an assassination victim. In the US Congress the parties were debating whether to declare war on Britain. No one knew whose territory the land between the Columbia and the Fraser was, and eventually there would be politicians who saw beyond fur-trading routes. Native people were not considered residents. They were natural resources.

In 1810 Thompson was at Lake Superior on his way to Montreal when he received the most direct order yet: get your boats into the Columbia River and stay in it until you get to the mouth. Lewis and Clark were long gone and Astor's men were not there yet. The Columbia could be the greatest prize in the whole northwest. Thompson turned around and headed back to the Kootenays. Before going to the ocean, however, he had a few things to tidy up, a few more notebooks to fill. He visited Fort Salish and his new fort at Spokane, and then went to Kettle Falls, the most important Native fishing spot in the region.

Every year when the salmon came to Kettle Falls, Indian peoples from all directions met there to work and pray and hold sports meets, and gamble and tell each other the news. Traditional pecking orders and ceremonies were faithfully observed. The Salishan peoples depended on the salmon for their continued lives, and they knew that there were years when the salmon did not arrive in sufficient numbers, and they knew why. The invisible world used the shining fish to tell the people their fate and their future. The writer Mourning Dove tells us at length of the procedure at Kettle Falls. For instance:

> It was strictly against the rules during fishing season for anyone to take water from above the falls or otherwise pollute the area.... Women could never throw any salmon entrails in or near the river, where the odor might carry to the fish.... Women had their sweat lodges about a half-mile below the falls and used them only in the evening after the spearing had stopped.

Many of the rules were about what women should not do. In preparing the winter's food, the women had to get up earlier in the morning, and work continually. The men got to do the brave climbing and spearing and boasting. But anyone who has been to a family gathering or a big agricultural exhibition knows that women and men like to get away from their normal domestic situations and find companionship with their own sex. It is a wonderful arrangement that sustains the tribe and the marriage.

The fishing site is beautiful and spectacular. When the various bands arrived in Chokecherry Month the cliffs at Kettle Falls were the site of the largest community in the Interior. Similar conventions took place at other locations, usually at waterfalls, where a river becomes narrow and the fish closer together. For the Okanagan people an important one was Okanagan Falls, where the salmon tried to get into Skaha Lake. In the second half of the twentieth century some white engineers dynamited the falls and made a calm little dam. The USAmericans have built so many dams on the Columbia that the salmon have turned away in disgust.

When Thompson and his nine hungry men from back east arrived at Kettle Falls in the summer of 1811, he was a few days too late to see the rites for the beginning of the fishery, and too early to see the crest of the harvest. The Native history says that the people were generous to the Nor'westers, while Thompson's narrative says that because they could not get enough salmon from the Indians they had to kill and eat one of the horses. One morning a *voyageur* carelessly tossed a gnawed horse bone into the river. Sure enough, the salmon stopped coming, and did not return till long after a Native fisherman had dived into the river and retrieved the bone. Thompson the poet was impressed by the event, and Thompson the naturalist appreciated the fact that the salmon priest ensured that many fish be allowed to proceed up the river to spawn.

There are not many trees around Kettle Falls. Thompson and his men from Quebec had to assemble a canoe from driftwood for the rest of his journey. He left his horses in the care of the local people and proceeded toward Lewis and Clark's turnaround point. In that extremely hot dry country full of sagebrush and rattlesnakes they encountered a lot of green rivers that ran into theirs. Where the Snake met the Columbia, Thompson got out and took up the appropriate posture, and claimed all the region for Britain.

A local fellow with a steel fishing knife told him that there were USAmericans at the mouth of the river.

John Jacob Astor

When David Thompson and his Nor'westers arrived at the end of the Columbia River on July 15, 1811, they found four small buildings on the south bank, their logs still sporting a few green needles. This was Fort Astoria, and the USAmericans had been there for four months. John Jacob Astor from Waldorf, Germany, was the first great USAmerican mogul. He had already sewn up the fur trade further south. He had made a lot of good deals with Indians in English territory around the Great Lakes. He was a major player in Asia. He would go on to make the first fortune as a slum landlord in Manhattan. In 1811 he planned to sew up the northwest and establish a global fur monopoly. He had the mouth of the Columbia, the long-searched-for river of the west. His American Fur Company could just about wrap it up.

Before going it alone to the Coast, Astor had proposed a partnership with the North West Company, but the Montrealers pooh-poohed the idea of the giant organization making a deal with a German upstart from New York. Instead, they ordered David Thompson to get down the river and beat the American Fur Company to the goal. When Thompson and his nine men finally arrived, they were treated in a friendly fashion by the winners. Thompson enjoyed the company and wrote about the beautiful spot where the mighty river opened into the salt water. He had no inkling that by getting there a few months late he had helped the US government in its territorial claims later in the century.

After a week, Thompson decided to head back upriver to check things at his forts, and was accompanied by a few of Astor's men, who were going to scout locations for some inland forts of their own. Thompson's AFC companion on this sojourn was a Scot named David Stuart. David Stuart was the cousin of Fraser's cohort John Stuart, who has left his name on Stuart Lake in New Caledonia. After parting from Thompson's party, David Stuart went north, building a cabin at the confluence of the Columbia and the Okanogan rivers, that would become Fort Okanogan and later just Okanogan, Washington, and then following the Okanogan River northward through the loveliest valley in the western world. His cousin John went southward from New Caledonia, until he too arrived in the Okanagan Valley, and found a convenient pack trail to the Columbia River. Neither of them had anything to do with the fact that today the loveliest valley in the western world is spelled differently by the two countries that share it. In fact, in the fur-traders' records it is spelled every which way. There is a legend that the Spanish conquistadores once rode north through this valley in their shining armour, but so far no spelling of Okanagan has been turned up in the enormous pile of handwritten records in Madrid.

On his way northward David Stuart passed through arid land dotted with greasewood and sagebrush and small ponderosa pines with space between them. He looked at a chain of lakes joined by the river, while his horses stepped past cactuses and rattlesnakes and scorpions. Heat waves shimmered in the air. Reaching the north end of the valley, he struck off overland to the northwest, and arrived at the conjunction of the two Thompson rivers. There he found the biggest Indian population any fur trader had ever seen at one place, at least two thousand people calling themselves Secwepemc. White people settled for "Shuswap." Their place they called something the whites would later hear as "Kamloops," although the first traders tried all kinds of English versions, such as "Cumcloups."

Stuart found a people who were amazingly hospitable. They were eager to trade beaver pelts for just about anything, and they went to all lengths to make sure that Stuart and his employees had a lot to eat, and they instructed the southerners on all aspects of Native life along the Thompson River. Then winter arrived. Stuart was surprised to find that the country that was so hot and dry in the summer could be frozen solid in the winter. The

Shuswap people showed him how to wait it out until February in their pit houses. The guests ate as well as their hosts all winter, but they were not invited to the Winter Dances.

Meanwhile Stuart's companion Alexander Ross had remained with his little dog for the winter in the cabin called Fort Okanogan. He thought he had heard the last of David Stuart. But Stuart did return, and when he did he was loaded down with beaver skins. His eyes were bigger than the star-spangled flag over the "fort," and he had stories to tell about Indians who would love to see more of the American Fur Company.

So in May Ross loaded a string of horses with gewgaws to trade with the Shuswaps and went up the Okanagan Valley to Kamloops. He had a hell of a good time, gathering a mountain of furs and giving as little as he could for them. He was proud of the fact that he could trade five leaves of tobacco for one beaver skin. The Shuswaps gathered around and bought all the USAmerican gewgaws they could, establishing a pattern that continues today in the British Columbia Interior. The last thing that Ross had left was a yard of white cotton. He got five beaver skins for it.

When Ross got back to Fort Okanogan, he told Stuart to get back up there as fast as he could and establish a trading post in a mercantile paradise. Thus was Fort Kamloops started, the first USAmerican franchise operation in what would become British Columbia territory.

The War of 1812–14

But Astor's trading post on the Thompson River would not last long. In fact its site is today unknown, although it would be safe to say that it was at the mouth of the North Thompson. In the fall of 1812 the Nor'westers arrived and built a rival post. The Shuswap people could not believe their good luck. The North West Company had a few years of experience in the area to the north and the east, and knew how to maximize their business. They traded firearms and steel traps, and the future of the beaver population was doomed.

The American Fur Company had to lose the competition on the Thompson because Astoria was dependent on the sea for transport of supplies and furs, while the North West Company, though eager for the Pacific access, had an established overland route to Montreal.

The European powers were, as usual, at war, and the young United States was caught in the middle. The British navy supplied its crews by the employment of press gangs, and the press gangs were not meticulous about nationality. They would raid USAmerican ships and seize sailors who had deserted the Royal Navy, and while they were there they would grab some USAmerican citizens. This activity did not sit well with USAmericans who were proud of their recent War of Independence. Napoleon's forces grabbed

USAmerican ships that they suspected of trading with the British. The British Government demanded that USAmerican ships register with Britain before attempting any trade with France. In the United States the politicians from the south wanted war with Britain, but businessmen and farmers in New England wanted peace and trade with Britain and Canada. It was beginning to look as if there might be secession in the United States.

Eventually the Hawks prevailed, and in 1812 the United States declared war. They figured that though their navy was no match for the British, they could make a lightning raid on Canada, and either hold it or make a deal. As it turned out, the British, Canadians and Indians clobbered the USAmerican land forces, and the USAmerican navy won a series of fluke battles. It would be a stand-off. The USAmericans would again pound their chests and gear up for expansion in the west. But before that was to happen, the peace had to be negotiated at Ghent. In the meantime the large British navy blockaded USAmerican ports along all its coastlines. John Jacob Astor's ships were becalmed or militarized for a couple of years.

Consequently, the American Fur Company abandoned its post at Kamloops, and the North West Company would enjoy a monopoly there until 1821. As a matter of fact, Fort Astoria itself fell out of USAmerican hands for a while. The reasons were both economic and military. The North West Company and its little semi-private army under the command of Donald McTavish arrived first at Spokane and then at Astoria in the spring of 1813.

There's a war on, he told the USAmericans there.

That may explain why we haven't been getting our supplies, said the USAmericans.

That was part of the reason. Another was that an Astor ship, the *Tonquin*, had visited Clayoquot Sound, where white people had been doing business for years. Someone on the *Tonquin* insulted a Native politician he should have listened to, and the locals massacred everyone they could catch and took the ship. The next day there was a big explosion and bodies floated in the salt chuck. Two other ships destined for Fort Astoria never showed up.

So when the North West Company offered the American Fur Company a pile of dollars for its forts in the northwest, and the furs that were stockpiled in them, the USAmericans agreed. If this deal had been made a year or so earlier, when David Thompson was supposed to have been at the river mouth, the U.S.-Canadian border might have been at the Columbia River. Still, if a naval idiot named William Black had not swaggered to the fort with his pistol and his shiny boots, the place might at least have been given a chance to become the port at the end of a British Columbia.

Captain Black was in command of a sloop with the apt name *Raccoon*. He was escorting a British merchant ship, but there was a war on, and he was looking for some gallant action against the country that had stood up against his king. So when he arrived at the river mouth on November 30, 1813, he was appalled to see the Union Jack fluttering from the flagpole of the fort. At the fort he found members of the North West Company chatting and joking and toping with members of the American Fur Company, most of whom had once worked for the North West Company. Black stayed for supper, and went back aboard his sloop, where he thought about the situation for five days. By December 5th, he had made his decision. He would attack and capture the USAmerican fort, but first he had to get rid of that Union Jack.

This was going to be one of the strangest campaigns in the war of 1812-14.

On December 5, Captain Black made his move. He sent the marines ashore. He distributed weapons to the *voyageurs*. He had the Union Jack lowered. He seized the Stars and Stripes from the amused Astorians, and ran it up the flagpole. British gunbarrels bristled. Captain Black had the USAmerican flag pulled down, and up went the Union Jack again. He made a short loud speech proclaiming his success in wresting the fort from the enemy and claiming the country in the name of his sovereign. He smashed a bottle of fortified wine.

He announced that from this day the former Fort Astoria would be known as Fort George.

The Nor'westers told him that they already had a Fort George up north.

The men of the American Fur Company were thinking about how they could get back to Missouri with the bills of exchange.

The Clatsop Indians who watched all this theatre compared anthropological notes with one another. It was to their advantage to understand the folkways of the white men.

The spirit of competition

The War of 1812-14 was ended at the Treaty of Ghent, and the occupying powers of the North American continent set about the long process of fixing borders. The US Congress became highly interested in substituting political boundaries in the place of commercial agreements. On the prairies it was convenient to make a straight line on the map. It was not all that convenient for the majority of people who lived there, but it was convenient for the white people. West of the Rockies the North West Company set up a new command called Columbia, and set about trying to penetrate the Asian trade. But according to the Treaty of Ghent, all places wrested by force had to be returned to their former owners.

The North West Company purchased Fort George from the American Fur Company, said the British contingent at the drawn-out meetings.

No, said the USAmerican contingent. Captain Black took Astoria by force of arms.

Well, you have a point there, said the timid British contingent.

So in 1818 the Stars and Stripes was again fluttering from the flagpole on the south bank of the Columbia mouth. But John Jacob Astor was busy buying property in Manhattan. The North West Company took care of business from the 42nd parallel north. It was agreed, though, that in the far west, the adversaries would have equal opportunity to set up stations and do business. The agreement echoed the one between Britain and Spain after Nootka.

Now Washington bought Florida from the Spanish, and along with it all the rights to Spanish claims along the west coast. The Russians were back, claiming trading rights along the far northern coast. The East India Company was not being cooperative, and the Nor'westers never did see the immense profits they had envisaged in the Asian trade. Back east the Hudson's Bay Company stepped up the competition, and started looking seriously at the market west of the Rockies. This competition began to involve firearms. If the North West Company and the Hudson's Bay Company had been political rather than commercial constituencies, their activities regarding each other would have been called a civil war. Along the Pacific edge the Boston Clippers swarmed, snapping up business the Montreal company was not outfitted to do. And the Indians were demanding higher and higher prices for their furs.

All these eventualities came to mean that the North West Company was overextended. In New Caledonia the factors became farmers to supply their own food, and they spent a lot of the winter looking at snow. At the mouth of the Columbia they sat in the rain and consumed the luxuries brought around the Horn by more and more sails. Asia was heard from less often. The white fur dealers on the western edge of the continent were a long way from Montreal, and the Company was going broke.

In 1818 the Hudson's Bay Company decided that its name was no restriction to its enterprise, and established its first trading post in the Peace country. The directors had New Caledonia in mind. Fur trading was getting expensive for them, too, but they were a hundred-and-fifty-year-old company. When some disgruntled minority stockholders from the North West Company came calling with suggestions about a merger, they listened. In 1821 the North West Company of Montreal was swallowed by the Hudson's Bay Company of London. The technicalities did not change things for the Scots in fur country. They kept their jobs. They kept using their NWC currency until HBC tokens came into the country west of the Rockies.

So old nations and young were signing treaties in Europe. Old companies and young were inking agreements of merger. White men were meeting across tables and putting their names to papers that would be delivered to the important cities near the Atlantic Ocean.

No one even thought of proposing a document with the majority of the human beings who lived in the valleys and coastal villages of the large expanse of land that would be called by an adjective indicating northern Europe and a noun indicating a southern European.

But there were ways in which fur traders interacted with the Native population. The *voyageurs* included lots of Iroquois who came west for the Montreal company. Some of them stayed and acquired property and families among the local bands. Between the Pacific Coast and the prairies there had been trade routes for centuries, but now the trade was specialized: the only goods the white people wanted were the skins of furry animals. The white people traded goods that made it easier to acquire these skins. When the Hudson's Bay Company lost its political control, the white people brought their priests, who encouraged Indians to change their religion and learn to live in agricultural communities near churches.

The factors with Scottish names and the working men with French names began to give their names to women and children. Bearded men from northern Britain had to live a long way from their homes, for long lonesome periods of time. Whether they had wives in Britain or not, they went about acquiring the only women they could find. The procedure had been going on for more than a hundred years, on all parts of the globe where white men were spreading their commerce into lands populated by people of darker skin. If a Company factor were to return to Britain or Montreal, he would probably leave his new family to fend for themselves in New Caledonia. Sometimes he would sire a half-dozen halfbreed children, and then be transferred to another post, where he would start another family with a younger wife. Later in the nineteenth century there were white men who had two families growing up, one white and one semi-Native.

These Indian wives experienced a variety of fates in a country that would become filled with boys and girls of mixed race. Some of them were just abandoned. Some settled down to long marriages with ex-Company men who decided to go into cattle ranching. Some went back to their original communities and lived as well as they could with the mixture of resentment and family they found there. Some, like centenarian Grannie McLean of Kamloops, became famous but never wealthy.

The men who acquired them to do heavy domestic work and satisfy their sexual appetites were of various kinds, too. Sometimes they tried their damnedest to make a way in white society for them. Often they would see their accidental children as forest animals that did not merit much in the way of fatherly responsibility. A lot of halfbreed children grew up with no schooling. Not overly welcome in the Indian community, and not totally recognized in the white community, they got whatever employment they could find at the bottom of the social ladder. They began doing these jobs while very young. They did not receive any schooling except for the Native lore taught by their mothers, who were now themselves outside their former communities.

The coming of the Hudson's Bay Company was not good news for the Native population of fur country. With competition gone, the prices paid for skins would drop. And when the old company took over from the North West Company, its white employees were told that they could forget about trying to get their dark children into English society.

In British Columbia they were called halfbreeds or Indians or nouns preceded by unpleasant participles. The recognition given the Métis people on the prairies was never offered to the children of the HBC.

Simpson's monopoly

When the Hudson's Bay Company acquired the assets and employees of the North West Company in 1821, they won a great battle for monopoly and a great deal of leverage with the British government. They now had no competition in the whole western part of an immense continent. For a good part of the nineteenth century they would prevail in any contest of wills between the House of Commons and the Board of Governors. They would control not only fur but all other trade, from blankets to boats. In 1821 they appointed a governor of their great empire and made him the most powerful man in the western half of North America. This was George Simpson, an aggressive little fellow who would have a fort named for him on the Coast, just south of Russian America.

Simpson enjoyed the monopoly and he welcomed the challenge, as businessmen like to say. The first thing he did was to streamline, to rationalize assets and structures, as they would say in a later time. In other words, he closed redundant forts and released as many employees as he could. If a former North West Company post was paying for itself he kept it; if it was making a living for Native people but encouraging them to look for higher prices because there was another buyer down the river, he closed them. He inveighed against "wasteful extravagance" in the Columbia department. He admonished his factors for developing rich tastes, that is dining on comestibles from Europe rather than chewing salmon from the nearby river.

Simpson, who had made his reputation in the frozen north, was eager to visit his new empire, and to impress its workers with his energy. He was in his late thirties and well focused. In 1824 he assembled a team and pushed them hard, and made the trek from York Factory on Hudson Bay to Fort George at the Columbia's mouth in eighty days, three weeks faster than the trip had ever been made before. And this was with visits to Company forts along the way.

It had been six years since the nominal return of the fort to the USA. George Simpson had a strong feeling that eventually some USAmericans, perhaps in uniform, would stand there on the south bank of the Columbia River and look northward. It was true that there was no national sovereignty over the country north of the river, not yet. But there might be in the future, and the US government might not be as easy to control as Whitehall. Simpson had to have a fort on the north side of the river. But he could not bear the idea of having two forts within easy reach of each other. It looked too much like competition. He went inland, to the spot where the river would last be navigable by ship, and built Fort Vancouver, across from the site where Portland, Oregon, would grow. Fort Vancouver was to be the headquarters of the Columbia department.

Simpson, meanwhile, wintered at Fort George. But he could not stand the sight of Hudson's Bay employees hanging around the post, whittling cedar objects and reading Milton. So in November of 1824 he despatched a large crew, headed by Chief Trader James McMillan, to find and explore the lower reaches of the Fraser River. Despite everything he had heard, he thought there was a chance that the Fraser could be navigable, at least in most parts. Travelling up the coast and into a big river is not a leisurely activity in the winter months, but Simpson was made of stern stuff, and he expected his men to be tough and ambitious as well.

In fact working for the fur companies was a hard and dangerous job. On all the cliffsides and rapids of the huge country that would become British Columbia, there were hundreds of ways to get killed or at least maimed. There were no bone doctors in the Kootenay canyons. If you were a *voyageur* in deerskin shoes, you might end face down in an unnamed lake somewhere north of Fort St. James. You could get drowned, frozen, buried under a rock-slide, killed by a bear or a human being, poisoned, burned, or struck deathly ill by a Tsimshian curse.

Rowing a boat in eight-foot waves, with icy rain in your face, could be considered part of the job. Mr. Simpson was the most powerful man west of York Factory. You spit salt water and rowed. You dragged heavy boats across miles of the mud you were making.

McMillan and his men found little rivers and a way to drag their boats between them, until they found one that took them all the way to the big muddy. A Lower Canadian named Jean Baptiste Proveau recognized the river, because he had been with Fraser on the way down it. Now the HBC men travelled upstream for a few days, and McMillan used his store of Interior Salish words to chat with some nearly friendly Natives. A week before Christmas the newcomers turned around and headed for the river mouth. McMillan would get a river island named after him, right where the first capital of the future colony would be. Further downstream they stopped at a little island in Annacis Channel, just downstream from the site of New Westminster. There they carved the initials HBC into a tall cedar tree. That was a message that this was forever British territory.

Then they floated down the river, and some of them became, as far as any-one knows, the first white men to look at the mouth of the Fraser River, or as the Spanish had called it, the Rio Blanco, or as the indigenous people had called it, Sta:lo Prole. These forty men sat in their boats, soaked with rain water, shivering in the December wind, dreaming of the luxury of Fort George, savouring their triumph.

North of Forty-Nine

"The Government is a perfect farce though the Governor is a wonderfully clever man among the Indians, he does not seem up to governing white people at all."
—Lt. *Charles William Wilson, August 1858*

Fort Langley

The Hudson's Bay Company had managed to get a monopoly in the inland fur trade, but there was still a lot of troublesome competition on the Coast. Yankee schooners sailed freely from island to headland, offering lower prices on their stuff. In 1825 the English and Americans agreed with the Russians that the latter would stay north of 54°40', and the others would ply their trade south of that line.

The HBC decided to build forts with access to the sea. In the summer of 1827 the Company's schooner *Cadboro* pushed its way up the Fraser. High trees offered a lot of accessible timber. Over it all a snowy volcano reminded the newcomers that the land to the east was often alarmingly vertical. Here the Company's horses were lifted by slings to the earth.

The men worked long hard hours, worn down by their diet of fish. The Cowichan people did not volunteer to help. They did not like the look of things when the strange buildings went up. They did not understand what was meant by clearing of the land, but they had a premonition that the disappearance of trees might mean a similar fate for other things. The Cowichans did not attack the intruders, but they lit a few fires in the woods nearby, to show that fire was possible.

When Fort Langley was christened in November, it featured two bastions made of eight-inch logs, with artillery installed. It was supposed to supersede

Fort Vancouver as a supply and collection base. After decades and decades of rain the bastions would eventually begin to crumble, but white people with a sentimental sense of history would try to restore them in the middle of the twentieth century. There would be no sign of the large wooden structures of Musqueam village.

Impressing the Indians was high on Simpson's list of priorities. In his visits to posts in New Caledonia he went in for parades with curried horses and bright blue uniforms, and lots of salutes from artillery and sidearms. His forts were taking on the look of permanent communities. Cattle grazed the native grasses. Sawmills and forges and flour mills were erected. Some of the officers brought their white wives and children to live in the New World. Fields of grain grew up around large blackened stumps. Wooden duckwalks stretched across the mud. François Noel Annance, a halfbreed clerk with McMillan's group, could often be seen studying Tacitus and Plato.

The Indians insisted on being businessmen, not employees. All over the globe the British had found it convenient to impress native peoples as servants, as porters of supplies and servers of tea. In India and Africa and Polynesia, this system had worked pretty well. But the Iroquois men who paddled HBC canoes along the country's waterways were not servants. They were courageous artisans. They might work hard, but they did not do shit work. The Brits found that if they wanted servants and menial labourers, they had to import them. This they did, with people from the Sandwich Islands, Hawaiians, known in North America as Kanakas.

Kanaka is just the Hawaiian word for person. Not all the Kanakas would be from Hawaii—they might be brought on board any sailing vessel that travelled between the South Seas and the Pacific northwest. Often they were not quite volunteers. When the sugar plantations of Australia needed cheap labour, boatloads of Kanakas would be seduced or kidnapped from their islands and brought to the Queensland interior, where they lived virtually as slaves. In New Caledonia and Columbia the Kanakas began a long tradition during which Asians would be imported to do the dirty jobs for which not enough Canadians could be found. The Canadian Pacific Railway would provide a lot of those dirty jobs.

Here is what James McMillan wrote to John McLeod of Fort Kamloops about the Indians around Fort Langley: "The winter here this year is very severe and would not be thought too mild even at your own quarter. I don't know if this is always the case or not. In such cold our naked Indians cannot go about in search of skins, were they so inclined, but they are very lazy and independent, as the sea and river supply their wants plentifully." In other words, they were not Scottish. Note that McMillan found independence as reprehensible as laziness. First in the Company's list of strategies was a monopoly; second was the making of the Indian trappers' dependency.

Fort Simpson

Concerned about the Russian competition, and unwilling to give up his dream of a river from New Caledonia to the sea, Simpson decided to build a fort at the mouth of the Nass River, at the Russian border. It was christened Fort Simpson in 1831, and moved to higher ground a little later. Two years later Fort McLoughlin was established midway between the Nass and the Fraser, near Bella Bella. In the same year, Simpson's supernumerary John McLoughlin built Fort Nisqualli down south in Puget Sound. Thus was the Hudson's Bay Company prepared to stake its claim to the Pacific trade, no matter how hard it might be to transport furs and blankets and firearms down the rivers to the ocean.

But the USAmericans were dumping products at low rates, and the Indians were playing the merchants against one another. The HBC had to meet the Yankee prices, and haggle with the Natives. At one point in the 1840s the exchange rate reached one pelt to one blanket. The Company operated in the red. The absorbing of the North West Company had not resulted in monopoly, and the East India Company was being refractory about their markets in Asia, so diversification had to be put forward to better times.

The Yankees were seen as a greater threat than the Russians, so McLoughlin tried to make a deal with the Russians to freeze the Bostonians out. But the Russians did not like the British any more than the Yankees. The Yankees might have the shortest supply route. The Yankees might be selling liquor and firearms to the Indians, while the HBC had a strict policy against such quick-money strategies. But the HBC was a rival European power, and they had forts that were getting closer and closer to Sitka.

In fact McLoughlin was persuaded by some of his northerners that it would be a good idea to have a post on the Stikine River mouth, at the eastern boundary of the Russian claim. The only trouble was that to get there, and to supply such a post, trading ships would have to negotiate complex channels that might have Russians in them. In fact, when an HBC vessel, the *Dryad*, went for the Stikine early in 1834, it discovered a little Russian fort that had been built quickly a few months before in the constant winter rain. In addition the English discovered a gunboat of the Russian persuasion.

The British traders did not like to have guns pointed at them. They became patriotic. They sent a message to the British Foreign Office, announcing the challenge from the Russian brutes, and asking for British gunships. No gunships, said the Foreign Office. All right, then, what about some financial compensation for loss of business? It had worked for John Meares half a century before. But Fort Stikine (and the further north Fort Taku) would have to be put on hold until 1840, when the Russians agreed to lease the land to their neighbours.

It was an expensive western edge for the Company, but the Company was old and large, and led by stubborn men. The bars at the bottom of the Columbia River often destroyed ships that had come all the way from England to make life a little easier on the northwest coast. The Yankees came out with a new line of bright red blankets that made the HBC blankets look dull. The Company directors in London were reluctant to approve Simpson's request for lots of ships to enter into a non-fur trade, to carry fish and lumber, for example. It would be a little while until the HBC store was the most prominent emporium in towns that would spring up all over British Columbia.

What was to become British Columbia was, then, formed over decades of paradox for the first half of the nineteenth century: the canyons and rivers and dangerous channels made transportation of trade goods extremely difficult; but trade was the only important purpose for the newcomers. The Europeans were surprisingly slow in making political claims. The only agriculture was in the small fields around fur-trading posts. Permanent settlement and colonization were far from anyone's mind. At the middle of the century there were only six hundred non-Natives in the area, and many of them were Hawaiians, eastern Métis and the people the French Canadians called Iroquois.

British Columbia did not see the "Indian wars" common to the USAmerican "opening up" of the west. When it came time to misappropriate Native lands, the descendants of the newcomers did it with Indian reserves rather than army rifles.

In a sense the hairy fur traders were just another tribe, a smelly new customer for ancient traders, especially along the Coast. When they arrived on the west side of the Rockies they found out that they had to use trade routes that had been used by the indigenous peoples for centuries. There were footpaths in the stone over Hell's Gate. Most of the sailing ships they came on were higher but not much longer than Haida canoes. The Indians of the Interior were experienced commercial travellers on the western prairie. The Indians of the coast travelled north and south and far up the fjords and rivers. When they had skirmishes among themselves, they were usually trade skirmishes.

The newcomers benefited by their entry into ancient trading patterns, and consciously imitated them or extended them, bringing sea shells into the Interior or obsidian to the Coast. Their own trading paths followed the intertribal ones, and would do so until the present. The brigade roads and the railroads and the telegraph and the highways were challenged by the same rugged country. Only with the airplane and the satellite telephone lines did the white people manage something the Indians had not achieved.

The Beaver

Events that would become the skeleton of history could be small or large, and if you were close to the small, the small could look large. History around the northwest coast of North America could be wrapped around an ugly little steamboat called SS *Beaver*, and wrapped itself in the frazzled edges of the Holy Alliance.

George Simpson was responsible for the *Beaver* and thus the first engine noise and smoke in B.C.'s inlets. Sailing ships were fine for transporting furs across the oceans to England and its markets, but they were often mired on Columbia's sandbars or whacked to smithereens in the long crooked inlets to the north. When you are under sail in a long crooked inlet, even though you may have the amazingly accurate charts made by George Vancouver, you require perfect winds to negotiate your way past disaster. A vessel driven by steam would solve the problem of inlets. George Simpson asked for a steamship.

SS *Beaver* was built on the Thames by the Green brothers, and the engines were made by Boulton and Watt, the inventors of the Industrial Revolution. In August of 1835, rigged with sail, the ship set out for Cape Horn and Fort Vancouver, where it arrived in March of 1836. There the side-paddles were set up and the engines and boilers connected, and there was funnel smoke over the Columbia River. The *Beaver* was an unbeautiful machine, though made of oak and fitted with mahogany. It was 101 feet long, 2 feet longer than Captain Vancouver's *Discovery*.

HBC man W.H. McNeill became the captain of the *Beaver*, and began its half-century of service along the B.C. Coast. Until the discovery of coal on the islands, it burned wood, making hardly a dent in the forests of the Coast. John McLoughlin, Simpson's man on the Coast, did not like the steamer, but his antipathy was not aesthetic: he thought it was too expensive. It would eat a lot of wood, he said, and thus require a lot of woodcutters. It carried a crew of thirty-one men who had to be paid and fed.

But the *Beaver* did its job well, and Simpson, who was itching to get back to the Pacific to see it, thought he had an edge on the Russians and Yankees. Certainly the Indians all up and down the Coast were greatly impressed to see a boat moving without sails, without human hands on the paddles. For a while they were, like their forebears who had seen Vancouver and Quadra, impressed with the notion that these white people had a connection to the supernatural. Captain McNeill married a Haida woman, thus facilitating trade with those people.

The *Beaver*'s last trip ended on July 26, 1888, when it ran aground on a jumble of rocks off Prospect Point, at the brand new Stanley Park. There were hints in the news stories that her unfortunate end at the age of fifty-four was hurried by a lack of sobriety among the crewmen who were there when the rocks suddenly appeared. For some time, visitors to the park

Wreck of the SS Beaver *at Prospect Point, Vancouver, c. 1891.*

included a view of the tipped-over pioneer in their excursions around the sea walk. It did not look like magic now. It did not look like history yet. It looked like an old tub forlorn on the edge of a brash new city.

The Holy Alliance

Still, the *Beaver* lasted longer and did a lot more work than the Holy Alliance. The Holy Alliance was signed by the Russian, Prussian and Austrian monarchs at the Second Treaty of Paris meeting in 1815, after the final defeat of Napoleon. All the monarchs of Europe would sign except those in Turkey, Britain and the Vatican. The ostensible purpose was to make a European community of Christians, but the real impetus was royal fear caused by the revolutions in France and the Americas. Spain had managed to crush the various uprisings in Latin America, but their colonial troublemakers continued to echo phrases from Danton and Jefferson. The Hapsburgs were continually obliged to put down rebellions in their client states. The Romantic poets of England and Germany were not the favourite reading of Francis I or Frederick William II.

The Holy Alliance was not all that holy, and never amounted to much as an alliance, but in the United States it looked like the makings of not only an entrenched monarchical conservatism, but also an invitation to the Spanish Crown to reassert itself in the western hemisphere. The USAmerican government was having enough trouble with recalcitrant

Indians, who did not always like moving westward, and the English, who were not ready to hand over the northern forests of the continent. Washington did not need a strong adversary from the south. There were Indian lands *and* Spanish lands to be acquired somehow in the south and west. The USAmericans could not always be as lucky as they were when they pulled off the Louisiana Purchase of 1803.

Still, Washington had to balance its rhetoric about liberty with its appetite for land. The Latin Americans who had fought for the independence of their countries asked their revolutionary model for recognition, but the USA held off giving it because they were hoping to negotiate a purchase of the Floridas from Spain. They had managed to nibble at the territory in question. They bankrolled a little revolution at Baton Rouge in 1810, and hung onto the area. They snaffled Mobile in the War of 1812 and just stayed there. Andrew Jackson killed lots of Indians on the Spanish side of the border.

Finally, in 1819, Spain saw the obvious future and sold the Floridas to the US for five million dollars. As with USAmerican foreign aid in later years, the USAmericans managed to insist that the money be used to pay USAmerican property owners. President Monroe's reasoning was that USAmerican citizens had suffered damage to their property and businesses as a result of the European wars in the area, and the Spanish had to recompense them. As a side bar to the sale agreement, Washington agreed that Texas was irrevocably Spanish, and Madrid said that the USA was free to take its claims on the Pacific coast north of California.

Thus the USAmericans would use the details of a forced real-estate deal with the Spanish in one corner of North America to found their claims of land in the opposite corner, where the British thought that their exploration gave them proprietorship. The Native peoples along the Mississippi and Fraser rivers were not invited to the Adams-Onis treaty of 1819.

The Monroe Doctrine and manifest destiny

When a country thinks that it is the instrument of destiny, its neighbours are in trouble. Anyone can think of some horrible examples from the twentieth century. In the nineteenth century the USA looked at its successes and saw itself as the instrument of destiny. In New England the Puritans had an odd tenet of faith declaring that there were people who were the "elect." They were chosen ahead of time to make it into Heaven, and felt that they had to strive for great worldly success to indicate to their neighbours that they were the chosen ones. The whole country began to see itself as the "elect" among nations, and viewed its independence as a sure sign. Thomas Jefferson, the great democrat, said that the USA was going to show the advance of history to the rest of the world, and in the process expand to fill up the western hemisphere, establishing democracy "from pole to pole." People in the USA began to call their country "America." Their great bard Walt Whitman declared that after the US had gathered in places such as California and New Mexico, Canada and Cuba would gladly join the Union. President Wilson would say that the US, after watching three years of World War I, would go "over there" and save the world for democracy. According to US movies and state fair speeches, the USAmericans, after watching World War II for three years, went to Europe and Asia and won the war. Whenever two US sports teams play a championship game, it results in a "World's Champion."

As soon as the US had finished buying the Floridas from Spain, Washington began to recognize the independent countries of Latin America. The rhetoric said that this was done because of high principles, liberty and so on. But the American Revolution was fought about business, and the US government, without a king or state religion, has from the beginning operated on behalf of business. Latin America was seen to be a large trading area. While waiting to see whether they could add the new Latin American countries to their Union, the USAmericans envisaged a profitable adventure southward that would make them the pre-eminent economic force in North America as well.

And they would go it alone. The British asked the US to join in an association that would face up to the Holy Alliance and demand that no European country help Spain in any attempt to win back its Latin American colonies. But the US was looking ahead. Despite the lessons of the War of 1812-14, the USAmericans had an eye on the north as well as the south. In his annual message at the end of 1823, President Monroe articulated the Monroe Doctrine, the official position of the United States concerning the hemisphere.

The Monroe Doctrine stated that the US would consider any attempt by European powers to change things in the new hemisphere a hostile act. The implication was that war would result. The US reasoned that as it would not be interested in establishing colonies in Europe, or overthrowing any government there, so the Europeans should not establish colonies in the Americas nor try to interfere in their governments. This is our turf, said Monroe, and we will defend it. In 1823 the US was not militarily capable of patrolling the whole hemisphere. But the US leadership felt confident that Britain's navy, patrolling the Atlantic, would also be interested in keeping the Spanish and any other Europeans away from the "US sphere of influence."

But while the British were eager to keep the Spanish away, they were not all that happy about the Monroe Doctrine. They saw the implications for the trading area of the northwest, for the area being called "the Oregon country." Sure enough, US citizens were dribbling into the country north of California, and into the land north of the Columbia River. The British wondered what would happen, for instance, if there were gold or silver discovered in New Caledonia or Columbia. They were nervous about the fact that in song and poetry the United States was as often called "Columbia" as Britain was called "Albion." They knew the power of myth. Meanwhile, as soon as Mexico declared its independence in 1821, US Americans began gathering up their slaves and moving in, grabbing land and getting ready to show the Spanish-speaking people that "America" was chosen by the Deity to prevail in North America. By 1824 Mexico had become a federal republic. Twenty-one years later the US annexed Texas. The USAmericans were on their way to the Pacific coast, and pessimists saw them continuing west from there. "Passage to more than India," wrote Walt Whitman.

More and more in public USAmerican speech one could hear the term "Manifest Destiny." It was coined by the bluff John L. O'Sullivan in his magazine modestly titled *United States Magazine and Democratic Review* in the summer of 1845 to envisage "the fulfillment of our manifest destiny to overspread the continent allotted by Providence." Providence, presumably, had no interest in the cares of people called Cheyenne or Lakota or Kwakiutl. Pretty soon congressmen and military officers and businessmen were shouting the phrase while they grabbed Texas, occupied the Oregon Territory and invaded Mexico.

A few years before O'Sullivan's bombast, the Hudson's Bay Company saw the threat of USAmerican migration into the Columbia River area, and began looking for a new headquarters for the region. They knew that as farmers arrived and settled, fur trading would disappear. Fort Vancouver could be kept in operation for a while, as a political statement, but a new fort would have to be built further north, in a place accessible by ship but handy to the factors who were gathering pelts in the Interior. George Simpson sent instructions to John McLoughlin at Fort Vancouver, and McLoughlin sent his assistant James Douglas to have a look around the southern end of Vancouver's Island for a suitable harbour.

Douglas found a satisfactory bay, and hired some of the Songhee people who lived there to start building the new HBC fort. Thus in 1843 appeared Fort Victoria, named after the young queen in her sixth year on the throne. In a few years the town that grew up around it would be filled with USAmericans.

James Douglas

In his years as governor of the colony of Vancouver's Island, and governor of British Columbia, James Douglas kept his wife, Amelia, later Lady Douglas, at home. Amelia Douglas did not circulate in what passed for Victoria's society. It was not simply that Mrs. Douglas was shy. The problem was that she was half-Cree. In earlier days, while Douglas was a young HBC trader in New Caledonia, his wife's parentage was not a problem. But Victoria in colonial days was not Fort St. James in fur-trading days. Even while her husband was posted in Fort Vancouver in the thirties, Amelia Douglas was snubbed by the preacher and his wife.

Race is one of the most interesting topics in British Columbia history.

When European traders spent their young adult lives in lands half a world from home, it was common that the heterosexuals among them sought female solace and servitude among the only available women. Here is how James Douglas described the situation in one of his letters: "There is indeed no living with comfort in this country until a person has forgot the great world and has his tastes and character formed on the current standard of the stage." His father, a Scottish merchant in British Guiana, apparently felt the same way. He "formed an alliance with" a Creole woman there, and with her had three children, James being born in 1803. It used to be rumoured around Victoria that Douglas's mother was a "mulatto," but historians such as W. Kaye Lamb and Margaret A. Ormsby have gone out of their way to claim that she was not a mulatto but rather a Creole. The term "Creole" meant different things in different parts of the Caribbean. Generally it meant native-born. In Louisiana it usually meant part-French or part-Spanish. Along the northern coast of South America it was likely to mean part-African. In the early days of the British colonies on the west coast of North America, there were numerous important men with Caribbean backgrounds, and an easy influx of African genes into the pool.

Douglas went to school in Scotland and joined the North West Company when he was sixteen years old. Six years later, in 1825, he was a young clerk with the Hudson's Bay Company in New Caledonia. He had a large appetite for everything including success, a big ego, and a body to go with it. All contemporary accounts make much of his huge frame and energy. Even as an old politician with his hair combed sideways to hide his bald spot, he was an imposing physical specimen, as they used to say. As a twenty-two-year-old clerk he was soft-spoken and obedient, punctilious with all things demanded of him by the Company and God. He spent nearly every waking moment learning things and filing them in his memory. To others he appeared mild and cool. But every once in a while this giant blew his top, and it was not a good idea to be the target of his wrath.

William Connolly was the chief factor of New Caledonia. He was very happy with young Douglas, and saw to his smooth promotion through the ranks at his headquarters in remote Fort St. James. In 1828, at the age of twenty-five, James Douglas married sixteen-year-old Amelia, the rather fair daughter of Connolly and his Indian wife from the prairies. Nine years later he would have the marriage solemnized in the Church of England. The Douglases would remain married for a long time and produce thirteen multiracial children, some of whom lived long enough to enter the societies of

Victoria and Britain. As a nineteenth-century British colonial, though, Douglas advised his daughters to be white when they went to school in England.

In New Caledonia Douglas exhibited an odd racial behaviour that was far from uncommon among the Company's administrators. A good number of them married Indian women and killed Indian men. Traders such as Donald McLean, for instance, even boasted of his exploits in death-dealing, while fathering a dozen halfbreed children. While it is usually said that the Canadian fur traders lived in peace while USAmericans were slaughtering Indians, there was always a good deal of tension in wild forest country where the isolated whites were outnumbered by more than a hundred to one. There had been some "incidents," such as that in 1823.

In that year there had been a murder at Fort George, about which many lies were told in the histories that followed. What is consistent in all the stories is the fact that there was no "Indian uprising" involved, that the events were played out between individual whites and Natives. In August 1823, J. Murray Yale, the presiding commandant of Fort George, took a party to Fort St. James on business, leaving Fort George to be cared for by two Quebeckers and two Carrier men. One night the two Carriers left the fort, and in it, two dead men. Supporters of the position that Indians are always looking for an opportunity to make "treacherous attacks," reported that a man named Tzil-na-o-lay persuaded his friend to kill the two white men in their sleep and loot the fort. The motive was supposed to be resentment about some disciplining the "thieving murderers" had received at the hands of the newly powerful Quebeckers.

Another version of the story, and one that would not be inconsistent with other events that marked the era, has it that the killing resulted from interracial sexual jealousy. Some Indian chiefs or elders saw the liaisons of their daughters and the leaders among the white newcomers as good business practice. But there were also wives and potential wives selected from the local communities by lower-ranking Company men. It is not difficult, even without knowing the Native ethos, to imagine the feelings of Native men who saw their women being taken unceremoniously by intruders. It is more than possible that Tzil-na-o-lay killed a man who had in some manner had sex with a woman that the Carrier man thought to be his.

But men such as James Douglas had unbending attitudes toward crimes such as murder, especially murder of Company men. Five years after the killing, he heard that Tzil-na-o-lay was living in a house not far from Fort St. James, where Douglas was now chief trader and temporarily in command. This house was the home of an important chief named Kwah. Kwah had for a long time been indispensable to the HBC men of New Caledonia. He had once saved Simon Fraser and his crew from starvation. He was now the purveyor of salmon to the forts, and a shrewd merchant whose importance merited special treatment from the white establishment. He considered himself at the very least the equal of George Simpson, and in fact could have overrun all the forts in the region had he not deemed their presence beneficial to him and his people. So exalted was he among the latter that his house was considered by them a sanctuary. Large and vengeful James Douglas had no awe of non-Christian spirituality. When he heard that Kwah was out of town and that the fugitive was in the building he went in after him.

There was likely a struggle, probably some insults. Tzil-na-o-lay never went to a fort for justice. He was beaten to death in the sanctuary. When Kwah returned to the village, he was highly disturbed by the heathenism of the white men. He was bound to take action against his customer Douglas, not for revenge but as a protector of his world as it lay in the eye of the spiritual world. Kwah prayed and consulted his trusted aides, and planned his response. As a result the Stuart Lake band captured Fort St. James. The huge James Douglas was pinned to a table, a warrior holding his chief's special blade over the trader's heart.

Then teenaged Amelia Douglas saved her husband's life. She spoke up sharply, a halfbreed woman mediating between the Indians and the Scottish. She tossed presents to the angry warriors. She called on the other women to

help her, grabbing trade goods and domestic items and thrusting them upon the Carrier men. Leave my husband be, and take these offerings to your village, she said in all the languages she knew.

But the Indian men were there for spiritual reasons, not for stuff. They were not angry and vengeful because Douglas had killed Tzil-na-o-lay. They were there because he had broken into a shrine in order to do it. Luckily for James Douglas and the Hudson's Bay Company and all the newcomers in what they called New Caledonia, Kwah was both a great chief and a diplomatic businessman. He told his man to put the knife down. He said that Mrs. Douglas's gifts were proper reparation for the white men's crime. His group was filled with adrenaline. After all, they had successfully taken a Hudson's Bay

Sir James Douglas, the only man to govern the Hudson's Bay Company and a Crown colony simultaneously.

fort. But with the proper protocol, they took the reparation and left the buildings.

After the place was back in Company hands, it was time for the white men to say something about their own laws. Kwah was banned from the fort for half a year. It was hoped that this episode, and some other recent violent clashes between Indians and fur traders, would prove to be the exception. No one wanted the constant killings that were going on where the army of the USA was in charge of racial relations.

But the Stuart Lake Indians, and others among the Carriers, could not easily accept the huge trader with the cold eyes and occasional outbursts of temper. When Douglas made his visits to their villages on business, there were always some villagers who looked at him with hatred, and when he had departed there were often verbal threats made against his safety. On one occasion there was a standoff and nearly a clash between Douglas's little party and a larger group of loud young men. Rumours reached Fort St. James that as long as the big man remained in New Caledonia there was danger of mayhem. Douglas's father-in-law decided to ask Governor Simpson to have the ambitious young man transferred to the headquarters of the Columbia territory. James Douglas became the accountant at Fort Vancouver in 1830.

Wagon trains

After seeing the establishment of Fort Victoria in 1843, Douglas returned to Fort Vancouver for the next six years. Fort Vancouver was becoming not just a trading post and administration centre, but an agricultural community along the shore of the wide Columbia. There were more and more cows, and more and more acres of grain; and the family of James Douglas grew, while Douglas grew even more in size and in stature within the Company. While immigration from the eastern US was threatening the future of fur and Crown, Douglas was thinking about *his* future. Even while the USAmericans could be heard hollering "Fifty-four forty or fight!" Douglas was keeping his black boots shining and the sixteen brass buttons on his frock coat untarnished. He had no notion that when he was an old man he would remember as his fondest times the days when he built his campfire on the frozen snow high in the Jasper Pass.

In 1843 the people of the Hudson's Bay forts in the so-called Oregon Territory were filling a role that had once been filled by the Native peoples when the fur traders first arrived. There were more and more USAmericans coming by wagon to the land that was called a new paradise in eastern newspapers. John McLoughlin and others saved the sodbusters from poverty and expiration by giving them HBC supplies on credit. But there were more and more of them. There were also more and more Jesuit priests and Methodist ministers. There were USAmerican warships along the coast, assessing the strength of the HBC forts in expectation of another USAmerican war of expansion. The US Senate declared the "Oregon Territory" to be USAmerican property. George Simpson encouraged some prairie people to move west and settle near Fort Vancouver, but McLoughlin, who was becoming less and less friendly with Simpson, and more and more drawn toward the USAmericans, encouraged them to mix amicably with the determined pioneers. McLoughlin would later take USAmerican citizenship.

Things became hotter in 1844 because there was a US presidential election. In the US, men who want to be president often promise their voters a war. The Democrats in 1844 nominated James Polk and promised "fifty-four forty or fight," that the US would take all of the country to the Russian border by either diplomacy or war, or the first followed by the second. The process had worked with the Spanish. Polk was elected by a landslide. The Hudson's Bay Company sent more and more messages to the British government. The mountain passes and river routes were filled with spies.

Eventually the British navy gathered a few ships around the mouth of Juan de Fuca Strait. The US navy was in the Pacific, though some of its ships were designated for the expected territorial war with Mexico. If the Yankees could not get the earth from pole to pole, they were going at least to go for the ground from coast to coast, and then spread north and south. McLoughlin, who was born in Canada, was persuaded that the United States was the army of democracy. Simpson wanted to keep everything in the Columbia territory British. Douglas was with Simpson, but he was prepared to see the voracious US settlers take everything south of the Columbia.

The 49th parallel

Jf the US had not decided that it could not wage war against both Mexico and Britain, the Treaty of Washington might not have been signed by the nation that called itself "Columbia" in song.

US territorial claims were based on their deal with the Spanish, which ceded to the US all former Spanish claims north of the 42nd parallel. British claims were based on the establishment of their exploration and forts. The USAmericans' position was made by families that were bringing their wagons along the Oregon Trail. The British position was taken by the oldest private fur company in the world. There were no constants. The clearest decision would have been made by war. But the Pacific northwest was still a long way to go for a war, especially if the opponents had to prepare for wars elsewhere.

The 1790 Nootka Convention was, if anything, vague, declaring that the Spanish and British were to share the territory and not to claim suzerainty over any part of it. Luckily for the future province of British Columbia, the US did not find out until too late that there was a further deal at Nootka in 1795 that said specifically that Vancouver's Island was to be shared by the two crowns.

In 1842 the Ashburton-Webster Treaty had fixed a border to separate British and USAmerican territory as far west as the Rocky Mountains, the prairies being divided at the 49th parallel. But in bumpier country to the east, the boundary had had to snake around geographical and social realities. There were no more prairies west of the Rockies. The Hudson's Bay Company lived by rivers and inlets, and saw the Columbia as their river. The USAmericans wanted everything, and thought that fate wanted them to get everything. They were looking at a Russian-US border at 54°40', and many of them were looking farther north than that.

But that could wait for the future. Making an agreement now and finding a way around it later seemed to be working in Texas. Meanwhile, the Hudson's Bay Company was undergoing conflict in its western management. Simpson the patriot finally won his battle with McLoughlin, whom he blamed for the growing power of the USAmericans in the Oregon country. As of January 1, 1846, McLoughlin took his suggested retirement, and was replaced by a triumvirate that included James Douglas.

But the Company would not be a signatory to any boundary treaty. National politics was ready to step in where business interests had prevailed. On June 15, 1846, the Oregon Boundary Treaty was signed, by which agreement the border was drawn along the 49th parallel straight across several mountain chains, until it reached the ocean, then bisected the Strait of Juan de Fuca, leaving the entirety of Vancouver's Island in British hands. Small islands lay on either side of the line. The last little peninsula on the mainland, Point Roberts, projected slightly below the 49th parallel, and remained USAmerican. Eventually it would become a community of Canadians living with a USAmerican post office.

James Douglas was relieved. He was surprised that the British managed to retain the whole of Vancouver's Island and resist Yankee pressure on the mainland. According to the treaty the HBC was not the English government, and retained its right to trade south of the border. The USAmerican population was growing much faster than the British in the northwest. The boundary was at least a political reality that might come in handy when the USAmericans started coming in as they did in Texas.

So far the USAmericans had not managed to get either 54°40 or a fight.

Retiring to Victoria
With the new international boundary at the 49th parallel, the Columbia River looked as if it were slipping away from the Hudson's Bay Company.

The USAmericans started raising customs houses and tariff rates, and despite the provisions of the Washington Treaty, the HBC began to be worried about the future of their brigade trail to Fort Vancouver. With US hegemony in the Oregon country and east of it, Indian wars began to break out, and massacres threatened the peace that had always been good for business. The last shipment of New Caledonia furs travelled the brigade trail down the Okanagan Valley to the Columbia in 1847. James Douglas had to face higher costs, and he had to reassess Simpson's old dream of the Fraser. All he knew was that they would not come by boat through the canyon.

Peter Skene Ogden was told that he had better find a way to get his furs to Fort Langley and Fort Victoria. Fort Kamloops was turned into a great staging area, and every horse Ogden could get his hands on became transportation, some of it not completely broken to the pack saddle. The brigades tried the west side of the Fraser. They tried the east side. They went overland to the Coquihalla. Skittish horses with huge packs fell down the rock faces into the white gorge. Wranglers longed for the gentle trail along Lake Okanagan. But in 1848 the Company had opened Fort Hope. From there down, the river relaxed and widened. Fort Langley had been burned down by some unhappy Natives eight years before, but now it was relocated, reopened and becoming the centre of agriculture. There were horses and men to feed, and the 49th parallel was a bone's throw to the south. The men of the fort showed the local Indians how to milk cows and plough rich valley soil.

Farming was expanded around Fort Victoria at the same time, though there was no rich river soil. What soil there was could be found in pockets between the island's vertebrae of rock. But there were visiting ships to provide. There was supposed to be a new population coming, to people the land and establish the idea that the USAmericans should not consider it annexable. But James Douglas was not much interested in settlers. He had a fur empire to manage. He had Russian and USAmerican ships to provision. He had his own vessels to keep afloat. The farmers of Vancouver Island could hardly keep up. The Indians learned how to thresh wheat.

But in 1849 a new kind of customer began to arrive. Wild-eyed gold amateurs from San Francisco showed up with extravagant stories of the great California Gold Rush. When they departed southward with their supplies, they were followed by fur-trade workers who liked the idea of harvesting nuggets better than sweating for Hudson's Bay Company scrip. Almost all the experienced French-Canadian workers headed south with El Dorado in their eyes. Douglas had to appeal for more Kanakas to do the wage labour at his forts.

He also had to face the fact that the Columbia wasn't his any more. USAmericans and angry Indians threatened his loneliest forts. His ships fell apart on the river bars. In 1859 the HBC's trading licence was due to expire.

A message came from London: move your operations from Fort Vancouver to Fort Victoria. Build more bastions on the Island. Conquer the Fraser.

The fur trade was not what it used to be, either. More and more it became clear to Douglas and his superiors that the Hudson's Bay Company had to diversify, to become a huge general trading company, with fur as its symbol. Ships in the Pacific were becoming interested in lumber and salmon, for instance. When Douglas moved his assets from Fort Vancouver to Fort Victoria, they included a significant poke of gold. Indians from up the Island had told interesting stories of black stone that could be burned, and Douglas's men began to find coal close to navigable ports. The *Beaver* was refitted for coal, and a new market was envisaged. Still, Douglas was not keen on immigrants. He saw ships at Victoria's harbour.

Now the government of Great Britain saw coal and timber, USAmerican settlement and Indian wars, gold and Empire. There were wars in Parliament, too, but the Colonial Office knew about recent history, about "Manifest Destiny." It was decided in London that some sort of British government was required on Vancouver's Island. Vancouver's Island would become the first British colony west of Upper Canada.

The Company and Earl Grey, secretary of state for the colonies, made a deal. Vancouver's Island would be British territory, but leased to the HBC for seven pounds a year. The Company would have to meet certain conditions, the first among them to be the encouragement of settlement by people from Britain, its foreign holdings and Ireland. Everyone knew that fur traders did not think highly of dirt farmers, and James Douglas, for all his diplomacy, could not hide the fact that settlement was not high on his list of priorities. But according to the deal, the *de facto* government of the colony would continue to be the diversified Hudson's Bay Company. They would be the suppliers and customers of the settlers who were to populate the island on land purchased from the Native bands.

However, the formal appearance of Imperial rule would be observed. This would include a British governor. In 1849 the negotiations between London and Fort Victoria resulted in the choice of Richard Blanshard. Blanshard was a thirty-two-year-old lawyer. Douglas was a legend who had faced the knife of Chief Kwah. Blanshard didn't have a chance.

He took the governor's job without pay. He thought that when he came to the end of the world he was going to have 150 acres of land and a governor's mansion. On March 11, 1850, he stepped ashore at Fort Victoria, and before a formal turnout of just about the whole population, read aloud the presentation of his commission. The high beaver hat on top of James Douglas's head made the giant loom ominously on that pleasant spring day.

But there was no mansion. There was no land grant. There wasn't even a room for Governor Blanshard. He had to live aboard the ship he had arrived on, the HMS *Driver*. He had no salary and no prospects. He was the first governor of a British colony on the eastern edge of the Pacific, but he had to twiddle his thumbs. For the next few months he went through the motions of a Queen's representative. He visited the coal deposits up north. He reviewed the dressed-up sailors on the *Driver*. He spoke incomprehensible words to the Indians, who were now for the first time living on British soil.

But the officers of the Hudson's Bay Company ran a closed society. Before 1850 was out, Blanshard wrote his letter of resignation. It took almost a year before he heard back from London. In 1851 he headed back home, to a career that may have promised little but promised it in civilization. The Colonial Office then bowed to *realpolitik* and made James Douglas his successor. The new deal said that he would govern the colony for the British Crown while retaining his directorship of the HBC's monopoly. There were some people who did not like the implications of that decision.

A little bit of olde England

Through the early fifties, despite the smallness of the outpost population, Douglas saw the south tip of Vancouver's Island turning into a nineteenth-century community. The sound of the first sawmills pierced the forest. The steamship *Beaver* chugged between islands. A settler had arrived in 1849. This was a blustery military man named Captain W. Colquhoun Grant, who came with enormous quantities of equipment, and eight workers. He waved his sword at the Indians, and challenged them in broad Scottish vowels. He unloaded horse carriages in a country with no roads. He built a sawmill and started a farm in Sooke, just far enough up the way from the fort to be in the wilderness. Grant tried and tried, and Douglas, sensitive about his lack of success in gathering settlers, tried to help him. But there were wars to join, swords to wave. Grant went to the Crimean War, and then to the Indian Mutiny. He never came back. But before he went, he scattered the seeds of Scottish gorse and broom all over the bottom end of Vancouver's Island, where they grow today.

The colony's first school had begun before Blanshard arrived. It was a boarding school for the children of the Company's men. The teachers were Mr. and Mrs. Robert John Staines, a self-important and very strict couple. Staines had got himself ordained before coming out, and acted as chaplain as well as headmaster. The Staineses, with their liveried manservant, were snobs, and did not hide their shock at the rudimentary nature of this colonial capital, nor their contempt for the mixture of race in some of their charges. The latter had boards to sleep upon, bread and treacle for meals, and quantities of rote to learn. From the boys' rat-infested attic dormitory, they could spy on the bachelors' quarters below them, where noble feasts of oysters, sweetmeats and brandy were consumed by happily childless men. They would not have a proper schoolhouse for a few years, nor a church to pray in until 1856.

But Staines made the best of things. He began acquiring real estate, and started a pig farm. He became the unofficial leader of all those people who were not happy with the way that Douglas and his Company ran things in this British land. He was the first leader of the opposition in Victoria. Governor Douglas was not worried. The Colony was not growing as fast as the settlements below the border, where land was free, but by the time of the first census at the end of 1854, there were 774 "white" people in the colony, 232 of them in Victoria.

The first doctor arrived in 1850. This was Dr. J. S. Helmcken, who helped his political cause by marrying one of Douglas's daughters. When the Crimean War broke out, and the British brought it to the Pacific by attacking Russia's old fur posts on the Kamchatka peninsula, Douglas persuaded the British navy that they could use a naval base with hospital facilities at Esquimalt harbour. Helmcken got a small facility there, and began the long relationship between Victoria and the navy. Like most professionals arrived from England, though, the good doctor diversified. He not only started acquiring land, but also jumped into politics when the opportunity presented itself. Staines and other non-Company men had written so many complaining letters to London that the Colonial Office ordered more government on Vancouver's Island. So Douglas called an election for a seven-member House of Assembly. Any white man with a good parcel of land could vote, and the colony had the first little Parliament in the west. Dr. Helmcken was the Speaker of the House. The members debated and reported to their constituencies. But Governor Douglas had a veto over any law they might enact. He was the boss of the Hudson's Bay Company, the oldest private corporation in the world.

He also managed to extend his powers of government when he thought it necessary. In 1851 visiting Indians showed him some gold they had found sticking out of the ground on Queen Charlotte island. Douglas did not want news of this find getting out, especially to the crazed hordes in California. He sent a secret message to London, and the Charlottes were put under the control of the Colony. A few years later some Natives on the mainland arrived with gold they had lifted off the sandbars on the Fraser River. This time Douglas just widened the responsibilities of the HBC on the mainland, and crossed his huge fingers in hope that he could keep the USAmericans in the dark. That just went to show how much he knew about gold.

Slowly, slowly, Victoria started to look a little like England. The climate was the best in all British North America, and the colonists were doing their best to domesticate a place that kept their boots covered with mud. They planted English garden flowers to compete with the wild varieties. They became obsessed with flowers. Victoria would become the city of gardens. People were very serious about drinking tea. They liked to drink tea in the wan sunlight, surrounded by flowers. No one was going to dump bales of tea in Victoria's harbour.

The authorities in Britain were trying to make a society different from the USAmerican one. The free land in Oregon was available to anyone who could get there. The British did not want US-style democracy, riff-raff from the eastern cities or immigrants from just anywhere in Europe. Land would cost one pound an acre, and the minimum purchase was twenty acres. The squires that immigrated would be forced to bring a certain number of workers for each batch of acreage over that. The idea was that gentlemen would create granges and receive the vote, establishing fine families and employing sufficient numbers of the underclasses to ensure a future labour pool. It all sounded a little like the beginning of the US nation, without the high-sounding constitution.

Making the neighbourhood safe

Of course any attempt at civilization had to include the rule of British law, or at least the appearance of such rule. As long as the Company had been the only representative of Europe in the woods of the Pacific slope, punishment and retaliation were just about the same thing—the exercise of power and control against the forces of misrule and otherness. Of course, punishment was enacted upon the Native peoples more often than it was exercised on whites. So too the exercise of the rule of law.

During the early years of the Vancouver's Island colony, the newcomers ran into some trouble with the various Native bands of the Island, sometimes stumbling into a fracas that had started as an intertribal disputation. On occasion some friendly Indians would attempt to tell some whites to be wary of the approaching Haida, for instance, and the whites, chronically frightened of wild savages, would attack the messengers. Other times the whites would not understand that the Native culture had a non-European attitude toward petty theft. What the Natives might see as a manifestation of humour, the Scots would see as an infernal offence to their entire system of order.

So while most relations between Natives and whites were cooperative and mutually beneficial if not wholly convivial, there were always incidents, and there was a semi-conscious fear of these forest people whom the Creator had for some unknown reason allowed to develop weapons and a point of view. But now that Douglas had the British Crown looking over his shoulder, he could not just burst into someone's house and kill him. He had to administer the law and then kill him.

In November of 1852 a Company shepherd was found dead in front of his cabin. Somehow Douglas's investigators found out that the perpetrators were two young Native men, one of them the son of an important Nanaimo chief. With the assistance of the Royal Navy, Douglas laid siege to the Native village two months later, and captured his two suspects. This is where the rule of law was introduced. Douglas described the outcome in one of his reports to the Colonial Office: "The two Indians now being in custody, they were brought to trial, and found guilty of wilful murder, by a Jury composed of the officers present. They were sentenced to be hanged by the neck until dead, and the execution took place in the presence of the whole Nanaimo tribe, the same appearing to make a deep impression on their minds."

It was a procedure to be followed often in the second half of the nineteenth century, on both the Island and the mainland. The bringers of the rule of law liked to perform their hangings in front of the dragooned Indian populace. If it was not possible to assemble a jury of the accused person's peers, it was at least thought effective to draft his relatives as witnesses to his logical end. From time to time Governor Douglas was to report to the Colonial Office the logical end of a Native who was guilty of murder or "maiming with intent to murder." Usually the trial had been convened on the spot, the jury made up of the officers who had been successful in observing the felon's capture.

Douglas was well aware of the race wars being waged in Washington Territory, and was determined to see orderly British justice prevail north of the border. He hoped that the Natives would see the difference between an armed raid and a hanging.

Unreal estate

But murder and assault were not the only subjects of law. Real estate was another. Here too, the newcomers were persuaded that their ideas on land ownership were logical and just, and that the Indian paradigm was either chaotic or non-existent. The British were spreading their sense of order in several aboriginal lands around the globe, and formulating arguments that would be used in any dispute over ground that they thought to be arable. Their argument went this way: (1) the Native peoples should have British rules about the relationship between individuals and land; (2) the Native peoples should be allowed occupancy but not ownership. In the colony of Vancouver's Island, it was decided to honour Indian claims to their villages and any surrounding ground upon which they had practised European-style agriculture. Communal gathering of wild food did not fit any mode of British jurisprudence. Neither, of course, did any savage notion of a spiritual relationship with the land and the wildlife on it.

But everyone knew that competition for land will cause friction, and strong competition will result in warfare. Douglas set about "buying" farmland from Indian leaders, and signed eleven treaties with the Indians in the

Native village, Queen Charlotte Islands, 1881.

area around Fort Victoria. The treaties were couched in language developed in Britain, and made no gesture toward the Native world-view. They said that the Natives could stay in their villages, and fish and hunt as long as they did not do these things on white property. They also received some Hudson's Bay blankets and buttoned jackets. Some of the Victorian ladies were fainting at the sight of nearly naked Indian men. Douglas also had the Royal Navy as a backup. In the future it might be necessary to think again about land that had been assigned to the Songhee Indians. For instance, what if their little reserve was the perfect site for an impressive Legislative Building?

But tough as he was, Douglas also knew that good relations with the Indians were necessary in order to avoid the slaughter and lawlessness he saw in the history being made by the rabble south of the border. In fact his ability to maintain that difference was one of the main reasons for the Colonial Office's agreement to let the Hudson's Bay Company run things on the Pacific slope and the Island. The Indians should be gradually accustomed to their new situation, while peaceably doing business with the Company store. The US threat to HBC monopoly was also the main reason that Douglas welcomed British law and British military on his turf and in his waterways.

And now in the late fifties he saw a new reason to be worried. The news that the Haida had found some gold on the Charlottes made its way south, and some miners from California were bringing their boats north. The

Haida, long accustomed to trading their resources with Europeans, were not going to put up with white people poaching on their islands. They drove the USAmericans off, in one case seizing one of their ships. Douglas had to do some talking with Chief Edenshaw to save the interlopers' lives. He saw that USAmericans with gold in their eyes were not likely to listen to stories of the proud and fierce Haida.

Similar incidents were taking place on the mainland, especially along the Fraser and Thompson rivers. Gold had been trickling to the Coast, and Douglas had been doing his best to keep the trade secret. He sent messages to London in language so latinate and poetical that loutish adventurers from south of the line would not understand it if they somehow managed to come across it. The Hudson's Bay Company had a long successful history of trading with the Native peoples. They hoped that what had worked for fur would work for gold. He instructed his factors to let the Natives do the gold-gathering, to maintain business as usual. And the semi-secret trade was growing. In the spring of 1858 Kamloops Chief Trader Donald McLean acquired 130 ounces of gold in less than three weeks, some of it from Indians and some from a Scottish prospector. McLean would go on to cause his employers and others a lot of trouble, but this little bonanza might have been the beginning of the worst.

It is unlikely that anyone has ever kept gold deposits a secret for longer than it takes an unshaven old coot to buy a round for the house. But the administrators at Fort Victoria made a strange mistake. They sent the gold they had bought from their various Indian clients to San Francisco to be minted. San Francisco was filled with unshaven old coots with big ears. Before the summer of 1858 was out, there would be thirty thousand of them clambering all over the fur country of New Caledonia.

Law and someone's idea of order

Perhaps the British government might have entered HBC territory earlier if there had been some Indian uprisings, or if the Indian land had been more promising for agricultural purposes, or if the Indians were known to work with gold rather than cedar and obsidian. Perhaps, like the Spanish and then the USAmericans, the British might have militarized their explorations and settlements. But the North West Company and the Hudson's Bay Company were interested in the Indians as suppliers, not as targets. Not that the Company was humanitarian, particularly—it was just that the accountants in London would rather count pelts than coup.

But the field officers of the HBC were no angels. Men who were tough enough to survive the ice and insects and rock-cliffs of the tangled frontier were often rough in their human relations. Though most of the Natives they found west of the Divide were hospitable, some, such as the Chilcotin, were not eager to become servants or imitators of the intruders. Others, seeing their hospitality met by stern Scotch-English demeanour, came to resent the imposition of European frontier law on their daily life.

And history often forgets that there are individuals whose actions are not wholly representative of the groups to which they adhere. Most of the criminal events that crossed ethnic lines in New Caledonia, for instance, were the result of individual actions and reactions. Unfortunately, a Carrier man who steals firewood, for instance, would be called a "thieving Savage," with the implication that the phrase was redundant. A Company trader who is perceived as a cheater of his Indian supplier might be considered to have corporate motives rather than personal ones. His victims might not know that he was putting aside a skin from time to time with a retirement home in old Blighty as his dream.

There was no shortage of "justice" in the country. Often an Indian criminal who had stolen from the whites, or injured one, would be punished by his own leaders, or given over to European procedures. It was not common practice for the Company to hand over to the Natives a white man who had killed a Native. In later days the trying and punishment of Indian wrongdoers would be taken on by the Indians, the Company, the church and the colonial or provincial government.

But there were no large-scale wars—only a limited massacre from time to time, such as a fatal incident at Fort St. John in 1823 and the explosion of the *Tonquin* at Clayoquot Sound in 1811. Fur traders lived a dangerous life.

West of Kamloops there is a beautiful valley called Deadman. If you leave the Trans Canada and enter the valley, it does not look much different from the rest of the sagebrush country for a while. But if you continue up its seventy kilometres or so, against the flow of Deadman Creek, sometimes called Deadman's River, you will see just about every kind of topology available in the central Interior. You will see gravel and cactuses, the gentle country of the Deadman Indian Reserve, green hayfields, ruined orchards and long-abandoned wooden flumes, castle-like hoodoos with stone caps, petrified wood cliffsides, forests and trout lakes, old mining holes, a sudden high plateau spotted with birch trees and small Douglas firs, and finally the spectacular Deadman Falls, which, if you are on foot now, breaks the silence of the high country with its whisper and then roar of water falling fifteen stories to the rocks below. This is perhaps the loveliest place in the Thompson Valley system, and there is not a motel or burger joint within an hour and a half of driving.

This falls and creek and valley got their name after an event of 1815. Alexander Ross, the North West Company man in charge of Fort Kamloops, was away quite often, especially during lulls in the fur-packing season. Sometimes he left the famous chief Nicola in charge of the fort, sometimes a French-Canadian clerk named Charette. On one occasion M. Charette and an Indian companion were riding in the valley in question, and discussing the question of where to camp for the night. So goes the story upon which history has a very loose grip. Perhaps the Company man favoured a scenic spot beside Snohoosh Lake. Perhaps the Shuswap man knew something the French-Canadian didn't know. Perhaps Charette called him ignorant and superstitious. In any case, Charette lost the argument when the other man inserted a knife into him and ended his life. That's what they say. What they say is not often history, but history should pay attention.

In any case, geography has paid attention. We do not know for certain what the creek's name was in Shuswap in 1700, but after 1815 it was called Rivière des Défunts by some Nor'westers, Knife River by some Anglos in the area, and then by the time of the gold rush, Deadman Creek by just about everyone. Nowadays the village near the end of the creek is lived in by the Deadman band of the Shuswap people.

Chief Nicola

The aforementioned Chief Nicola was a very important trader in the first days of white fur business on the Thompson. He, too, has a lake and a valley named after him. His name was Hwistesmexquen, and he was chief of chiefs among the Okanagan people who lived in Shuswap country just south of Fort Kamloops. The French-speaking North West people always gave their Native associates European names, so they called Hwistesmexquen by the Greek name Nicholas, perhaps knowing that the name means victorious among men. Chief Nicola welcomed the traders and encouraged his people to trade with them. He was often at the fort, and went on trading expeditions with the Nor'westers, and after the merger, with the Hudson's Bay men.

In 1823 Chief Nicola gathered a party of Okanagans and Shuswaps and rode west into the country of the Lillooets. The previous winter his father, Pelkamulox, known to the whites as Chief Piette, had been murdered by some Lillooets while he was riding with a Hudson's Bay Company trading expedition. Nicola and his followers rode west to the Fraser River and killed as many Lillooets as his father's spirit required. This was the only Indian war ever to take place in what the white people called historical times, though the plateau echoed with stories of great battles in the past.

In later years an old HBC man named John Tod got a lot of free drinks and newspaper coverage telling wild stories of Indian massacres and musket wars. He apparently got a lot of them out of USAmerican penny-dreadfuls. Tod got a mountain north of Kamloops named after him, perhaps a fitting geographical feature to commemorate his endless narratives.

Chief Nicola was a nearly mythical figure, who enjoyed power from before the first fur-trading fort of 1811, until his death a year after the beginning of the great gold rush of 1858. Although the young fur traders of later years did not give the old man the respect he had received from the earlier newcomers, a lot of gold-hungry foreigners owed their lives to the old chief who calmed the warriors who were not patient with the greedy panners.

Sam Black

Jn earlier days Chief Nicola enjoyed ceremonial dealings with the Company men, making gifts of good valley land, wearing tunics and learning to grow ground crops. One of his closest associates was Samuel Black, a highly competent and highly controversial explorer who became chief factor of the Columbia district but lived near Kamloops. Black had been a Nor'wester and an implacable foe of the HBC. He had considered the competition between companies a kind of far western war, and was apt to capture Hudson's Bay explorers or rough them up. George Simpson called him "Black the outlaw of villainous celebrity."

But in 1823 Black was permitted to work for the Hudson's Bay Company, in whose employ he did not give any sign of refining his behaviour. Simpson had him assigned to the far north, to make scientific observations and scout the trading possibilities around the Finlay River. Apparently Black showed great courage and scientific intelligence up there, so Simpson sent him, by way of reward, to the far south, there to command dusty Fort Walla Walla for five years. Simpson might have kept his old foe in isolation forever, had he not needed an intelligent chief trader at Kamloops.

Black made the most of his semi-exile and bided his time. His chance came when another hothead threatened the stability of Fort Kamloops. In 1830 the chief trader there was filled with anger and shame because his wife had run off with a Native man. Fearing inter-racial violence, the Company transferred the distraught husband and gave Black the job. Black made the most of his chance, getting married and starting a family, proving as good a chief trader as he had been a bushwhacker. He may have been happy, but he was no more placid. The locals found out early that they should not cross him, and when his old associates visited they kept him calm. He was on good terms with his old friend Peter Ogden, who was now in charge of New Caledonia. But anger and violence had a way of sticking to him, and he was no respecter of authority or fame. Once in 1833, for example, he hosted a visit by David Douglas, the renowned Scottish botanist.

Douglas had been a child prodigy in the plant world. He was in charge of the North American collection for the Horticultural Society of London. He gathered plants all across Canada, and climbed mountains never before climbed. He introduced 254 North American plants to Europe. He had 50 species named after him, including the Douglas fir, which would be the mainstay of British Columbia's industry. He would fall into a Hawaiian bullock pit and die just before his thirty-sixth birthday, the most famous botanist in the world. Sam Black didn't care. He offered David Douglas a drink and a bed in Kamloops. They had a few more drinks, and began discussing their travels in the New World.

Douglas offered his opinion of the Hudson's Bay Company personnel. He said there wasn't one of them worth more than the beaver skins they collected.

Chief Trader Black offered him a duel at sun-up on the bank of the Thompson River.

Mister Douglas left in the middle of the night.

In 1837 Black was advanced to the position of Chief Factor of the Columbia district, but he loved his home by the Thompson. He would manage the south by horseback. He had found the place he wanted to put down roots in. He liked the two rivers and the nearby mountains and the rolling brown hills and the big lake. He was a very good fur trader, and the Company, despite George Simpson's acrimonious memory, was willing to accommodate Sam Black. Black also got on well with the Indians. He was an old trail partner with Chief Nicola.

If he had just been able to control his temper. If he had just remembered all the years of pleasant business he had done with Pacamoos, known to the fur people as Chief Tranquille. For decades Chief Tranquille had been as important as Chief Nicola in keeping peace in the country. But one day early in 1841 Sam Black had a disagreement with his old associate and started hollering at him, slamming a door behind his back. Soon after this incident, Chief Tranquille died at his camp at Pavilion, and his widow believed that Black's venomous words had killed her husband. She sent her nephew Kiskiwskin to visit the post. The young man was carrying a handgun which he had purchased for a bale of animal skins. He sat in the reception hall of the post for a while, and then shot Sam Black dead.

There was a big funeral. Chief Nicola made the oration. The Hudson's Bay Company stopped all trading temporarily. They were afraid of an Indian uprising. But the Native leaders, including the amazing Lolo, known as St. Paul, kept things calm. Eventually a party of whites and Natives captured Kiskiwskin, but reported that the man had drowned near the west end of Kamloops Lake.

Donald McLean

Black's murder caused some shuffling of Company officers. Among the moves was the transfer of Donald McLean to Fort Alexandria, where he would become the temporary boss at that post on the upper Fraser, south of Fort George. McLean was born at Tobermory, Scotland, into a clan noted for its fierce warriors. He had been working for the Company since 1833, and before his posting to Fort Alexandria, he had put in time among the

Flatheads and Colvilles south of the 49th parallel. He was famous for marrying Indians and killing them. He often told people in letters that the best way to apply law to Natives was to hang them first and try them later. He received a lot of nicknames from HBC people and Indian bands, and was disliked on both sides. But he was an efficient and loyal trader, and rose steadily in the ranks. He was moved around the New Caledonia district for several years, and in December of 1848 he returned to Fort Alexandria as its commander.

One of his first challenges there was to do something about the murder of a French-Cree halfbreed named Alexis Belanger. Belanger had lived a scoundrel's life, and was often fired and rehired by the Company as a transporter of furs and supplies. In November of 1848 he happened to be in a boat that was carrying furs from Stuart Lake to Fort Alexandria, and he got in the way of a musket ball fired by a man named Tlhelh. Tlhelh was a young man from the Quesnel band whose wife had died, and who thought that she would still be alive if it were not for the white men. He had decided to take his revenge against a white man, and when he saw Belanger in a Hudson's Bay Company boat, he thought that Belanger was close enough. His choice was ironic, as Belanger was a notorious wife-beater. Tlhelh fired his erratic old musket several times before managing to put a ball into Belanger's chest. The victim was taken to Fort Alexandria, where he died a week later.

Belanger was not a man to be proud of, but he had been, between drinking bouts and disappearances, a useful worker, and useful workers were not easy to come by. The Hudson's Bay Company decided that justice had to be done. They were not, however, thinking of a trial. Chief Trader Donald Manson at Fort St. James gave his Alexandria man, Donald McLean, the job of finding and executing Tlhelh. It was a logical choice. McLean was fond of calling Indians "black savages" and the like. In January of 1849 McLean took a sizeable posse and rode to the Indian village at Quesnellemouth.

Tlhelh was not there. In fact the place was nearly deserted. McLean and his sixteen men rode in and found an old man, the Quesnellemouth chief, with his daughter and her baby. McLean was not as big as James Douglas, but he had the same attitude toward the homes of Indians. He barged in and confronted the old man. Where is Tlhelh, he demanded. The old man said that Tlhelh was gone. Well, then, this day you will be Tlhelh, said McLean, and started shooting. He emptied two handguns at the spry old "black savage" and missed him. Infuriated, he got his musket and blasted the man away. The other intruders were shooting, too, and in the raid a bullet shattered the head of the infant and severely wounded its mother. Her husband, who had been working nearby, came running to protect his family, and was shot dead. There was one other Indian in the village. He barricaded himself inside his house. McLean went after him too, but this man had a weapon, and McLean desisted when this lone survivor shot back at the whites.

For a year Donald McLean stewed about his failure to catch Tlhelh. He had a lot of other work to do, so he tried every means he knew in order to put an end to the Belanger episode. He threatened the Indians, offering to eradicate anyone who shielded the escapee. Eventually he found some people, the Nazkhos, who said that they would find Tlhelh in exchange for a hundred skins. Bring the "rascal's" head, and you shall have your pelts, said the man from Mull. And eventually they did. McLean was a businessman. In 1853 he was promoted to Chief Trader, and in 1855 he was awarded the post at Fort Kamloops.

The Chilcotin

Samuel Black and Donald McLean were not the only HBC men with bad tempers. From time to time a fur trader would write a letter to his superior or associate and vent his frustrations by advocating the complete eradication of a certain band of Natives. Sometimes the methods of the US army and volunteers would be suggested for the northern forests west of the Rockies. But the Hudson's Bay Company was not after land, so the Indians were not rivals. They were necessary partners. There were a few white trappers in the bush, but they were living a dangerous life. The Indians might resent that competition, but they liked dealing with the men in the forts. The Indians were all the time becoming more difficult in their bargaining, especially on the Coast, but they were not likely to overrun a fort and massacre the inhabitants.

Except for the Chilcotin. Try as they might, the fur traders (and later the gold boys and the railroad people) could not bring the Chilcotin around. When the Hudson's Bay Company built a fort in Chilcotin country, the Chilcotins told them they were wasting their time. The Chilcotins were not interested in European clothes. They had no women to sell. They wore wolf-skins on their backs and rings in their noses. They could shoot an arrow through a hole their enemies did not know was there. They told the Hudson's Bay Company to get out of their fort, because they wanted to burn it down. The Shuswap people and Thompson people told the Scottish people to leave the Chilcotins alone. Whatever you do, they said, do not try to put a road through their country.

But for the most part the Hudson's Bay forts were not Fort Apache. There were no John Waynes or Geronimos. There were murders from time to time. There were white sea captains and fort commanders who liked to fire off cannon to impress the Natives. There were intertribal skirmishes that spilled over onto Company property if one of the sides was on Company property. But the holocaust for the Native peoples would not really start until the coming of the gold miners and the smallpox, the railroad and the reserve system, the ranchers and the Christian churches.

Colony Full of Gold

"It is vain, puffed up, tyrannical, corrupt, short-witted,
conceited mummies and numbskulls that fear the press
and strive to gag it."
—Amor de Cosmos, 1858

The gold trail

In 1858 the US army was riding all over Washington Territory, killing Indians and driving them off their lands. At the same time, rumours of gold were drifting southward and eastward. The gold miners who started working the valleys of Idaho and eastern Washington were nervous about Indians, and not being fur traders, did not think of them as possible trading partners. These were USAmericans, and they carried guns. When they followed the brigade trail north through the Okanagan, or walked up the Columbia into the Kootenays, they did not know that they had crossed into British territory. They were gold-trail boys, not big readers. They were the advance riders of Manifest Destiny. Some day there would be so many of them they would settle down and ask the US Congress and army to annex this place. It had worked in Texas.

Gold-trail boys marched into the Thompson Valley from the south and the east, the southerners bringing guns and whiskey. But most of the invaders came by sea, some from Puget Sound, some from Hawaii and China, most of them from the devastated gold fields of California. Two-thirds of them, or about 20,000, came by way of Fort Victoria, that tiny flowered settlement of three hundred tea-drinkers. It was just about noon on a spring Sunday, April 25, 1858, that the USAmerican steamer *Commodore* landed in Victoria harbour. This was the first boatload of foreign gold-seekers, Yankees and Brits and just about every kind of European.

There were thirty-five African-Americans from California, where repressive race laws had recently been passed. In March of 1857 the US Supreme Court, with its majority of southern judges, had decided the Dred Scott case, saying that slaves were property and that the US Constitution protected property along with other individual rights. So the federal government of the US could not exclude slavery from any of its territories. But California, because of the two billion dollars' worth of gold, had become a state in 1850, after the US army had wrested it from the Californios who had declared an independent republic. Though there were those who wanted to make it into two states, one slaver and the other "free," it was not affected by the Missouri Compromise of 1850. California was to stay loyal to the North in the coming Civil War. But there were a lot of southerners and other anti-blacks in California politics. The price for remaining on the liberal side of the Mason-Dixon line was a series of oppressive laws against African-Americans. Some of them lit out for the territories. When the news of gold arrived, some of them headed to New Caledonia, wherever that was.

When the first prospectors arrived in Victoria, they found no ship to take them to the mainland, and they were in no mood to wait for one. They knew that there were going to be thousands of pick-axe men behind them. They bought used canoes from the Songhees. They found rowboats. They hammered rafts together and loaded their sourdough supplies on them and set out for the mainland. A lot of them made it. When they got to the mouth of the Fraser their troubles began. The lower Fraser is braided with currents and eddies, and is full of floating trees. Still, a lot of them made it. They squatted on the sand bars upstream from Hope and swished their pans. They shouted at one another in many languages. They whispered *or* and *gold* and *oro* and *guld* and the names of their deity.

As the gold walkers streamed through, Victoria was converted from a tiny British enclave to a roaring camp town. Tents went up and were soon followed by wooden buildings, erected by US businessmen to accommodate US money. In the first six weeks of the gold rush 225 buildings went up. Victoria was becoming the Sacramento of the new bonanza. Sacramento became the capital of California because it grew up fast and supplied the wild-eyed newcomers on the rivers. San Francisco boomed because ships could dock in its large bay, and rich prospectors could pay for a bath and a bar-girl. Victoria in 1858 was on its way to becoming the northern outpost of San Francisco and the new Sacramento.

Land prices shot up by 3000 per cent, and the prime properties were being sold by the Hudson's Bay Company. James Douglas was tempted to turn up his nose at the scent of riff-raff from the south, but he was a Company man. He saw the US steamships taking over the business on the Strait of Juan de Fuca. He knew that as incredible prices were being posted and amazing fortunes were being made, the USAmericans were coming more and more to consider this an extension of their own gold rush. But Douglas had the Royal Navy and his police force captained by Augustus Pemberton. He plugged his nose and watched his town grow. He had never been very good at finding immigrants, and now here they were, substantial merchants and enterprising hoteliers. Of course there were also some who looked like ne'er-do-wells. Business is business, not philosophy.

Besides, a good semblance of the British class system would be kept in place by the professionals. Young lawyers and engineers arrived from the Old Country, and immediately set about being superior. They made jokes about the giant fur trader, old "Square Toes," but they married his daughters as fast as they could. They set up a caste system in which British gentlemen were at the top, rich US businessmen were in the middle, and miners and workers at the bottom. Traces of colour and aboriginalness or southernness of European origin made for a woof in the weft. The governor's halfbreed daughters made for complex manners among the snobbish young swains.

Meanwhile the USAmericans were also expanding their business empires into the heart of the mainland. Ranchers in Oregon and Washington reopened the brigade road through the Okanagan to Kamloops, bringing steaks and whiskey for the gold panners and sluice-jockeys. They made a formidable and aggressive competition for the Hudson's Bay store, bringing items the Company could not supply, and hauling away valuable bags of dust.

And where USAmerican trade goods go the US flag follows. Douglas was not entirely serene. He knew how fragile treaties and boundary lines were if the USAmericans were on the other side of them. Across the Pacific in 1858 the British, with help from the French, were busy forcing the Chinese emperor to open his country to their traders. Douglas did not describe himself as a politician, but he knew the relationship between money and guns.

In April of 1858 he heard that there were USAmerican boats going up the Fraser River for purposes of trade. In May, entangling his roles as boss of the HBC's operations and governor and vice-admiral of the island colony, he issued a proclamation warning that in two weeks' time he would begin seizing and condemning all "ships, boats and vessels, together with the goods laden on board found in Fraser's River, or in any of the bays, rivers, or creeks of the said British possessions on the northwest coast of America, not having a license from the Hudson's Bay Company." Dangerous words. The United States hawks had won the California gold fields when they went to war against Mexico.

Colony

Meanwhile, Douglas was writing letters to London, urging that his actions be officially backed by the creation of a new colony on the mainland.

Otherwise the ruffians from the south would haul all the gold out of the country and leave nothing but discarded whiskey bottles in their wake. Or they would fly the star-spangled banner over every tent and log cabin along the sides of New Caledonia's great rivers. Or the US army would pursue escaping Indians across the 49th parallel, and might not be overly discriminating when it came to targets on the British side. These are the arguments the governor made to the Colonial Office. As an HBC man, he was concerned with the Company's ability to control the gold business. On the first day of 1858, he had issued a proclamation that all gold mines along the rivers belonged to the Crown, and that miners had to purchase licences in Victoria for twenty-one shillings a month. Now he needed actual law and visible police.

And the gold fields kept getting bigger. The news eventually filtered through to London that there might be gold along every river from the boundary northward, and there might be unlimited supplies of gold panners. The Colonial Office, busy as hell with events in India, and their battle to weaken the East India Company, nevertheless found the time to consider matters in the northwest. Lord Stanley left his post as Colonial Secretary to handle the India question in Parliament, and was replaced by Sir Edward Bulwer-Lytton, the fanciful novelist who would get his name attached to the town situated at the joining of the two great gold rivers. In fact Douglas himself saw to it that the HBC's Fort Dallas was renamed for the secretary.

Douglas was proving to be as good a politician as he had been a pelt collector. Bulwer-Lytton did not like the Hudson's Bay Company any more than Stanley had liked the East India Company. He did not like the Company's monopoly and he did not like its director. He had spent some time in Washington. When he came to setting up direct British rule on the Pacific slope, it was not so much to thwart US aggression as it was to curb the Hudson's Bay Company's power. Bulwer-Lytton was adept at making enemies, especially among the better poets and novelists, but an expert at making political allies. He rebuked Douglas for banning US traders, pointing out that the HBC was licensed only to have a monopoly of the fur trade with the Indians. But he also saw to it that Queen Victoria acquired a new colony. In fact the Queen was given the honour of naming it.

She and her advisers decided that New Caledonia might be confused with the French Islands off the coast of Australia. So they chose to call the colony British Columbia. That way it would not be confused with any other geo-political area, perhaps. In all likelihood the emphasis was to be on the adjective, the warning to be understood by any ambitious politicians or military types to the south.

On August 2, 1858, an act was proclaimed, and a colony created. It described British Columbia as the land bordered by the US to the south, the main chain of the Rocky Mountains to the east, the Simpson and Peace rivers to the north, and the Pacific Ocean to the west. It would include the Queen Charlottes but not Vancouver's Island. Five years later the tricky business of the north coast would be taken care of with a new act, making the 60th parallel and the Russian panhandle the new borders of the colony.

James Douglas was to be the governor of this colony, too, but this time he had to give up his position with the Hudson's Bay Company. He did not, however, have to give up the private lands he had acquired while managing the Company's business. Douglas, with a gaggle of important men from Victoria, sailed up the Fraser River to Fort Langley, walked through the mud to the main hall, and at that temporary capital on November 19, 1858, he was sworn in by his new chief magistrate as the first governor. The loyal *Beaver* fired an eighteen-gun salute. The HBC standard came down and was replaced by the British flag. All through the ceremony it rained and rained. Several of our historians have pointed out that the birth of British Columbia took place in typical British Columbia weather. That is a kind of Coast chauvinism that would for the life of the colony and the province establish resentment in the Interior, whose extractable riches brought the attention of the Colonial Office around to making a British Columbia.

The gazetteer

A new colony apparently filled with riches and beset by neighbours needed institutions and able men to establish those institutions. For instance, law, civil engineering, police and the press. From Britain to British Columbia came Matthew Baillie Begbie, Colonel Richard Moody and Chartres Brew, and to Victoria came Amor de Cosmos.

De Cosmos came first. He arrived with the early gold hunters from California, where he had worked as a photographer. Born in Nova Scotia in 1825, he started with the name Bill Smith. He told his associates and readers that he took the strange new name because he had dedicated his life to the betterment of mankind. Perhaps he considered for a while changing it to Amor de Chaos. But there were persistent rumours that he changed it for the same reason that he had left California, whatever that might be. If the rumours had anything to do with facts, this might have been the first time that anyone had ever changed his name

One of British Columbia's colourful premiers, Amor de Cosmos used to be Bill Smith.

from Smith to elude pursuit.

In any case, he arrived in Victoria to find a boom town served by a USAmerican newspaper called *The Victoria Gazette*. De Cosmos decided to create a newspaper that would fight both the encroachment of US interests *and* the excesses of the Hudson's Bay Company. He gave it the pointed name *The British Colonist*, and ran the first number on December 11, 1858. It would prove to be a thorn in Douglas's ample side. De Cosmos began making alliances with the Assembly members who were enemies of Douglas's HBC faction. He was never invited to tea by the hoity-toity circle. He attacked Douglas in the first number of his newspaper, and a week later he started calling the governor's inner circle names. He minced no colloquialisms in his accusations of "toadyism and consanguinity." Douglas was annoyed, and in the coming years he expressed happiness whenever de Cosmos met some political setback. But he was confident that no upstart from the Maritimes would ever rise very high on the West Coast political stepladder. He was the first of many to make that mistake.

The hanging judge

Nowadays US tourists crossing the border in their huge motor homes are alarmed to hear that they have to leave their pistols and assault rifles behind when they enter British Columbia. Judge Matthew Baillie Begbie set that policy when he took the job offered him by the new colonies. He was the son of a Scottish gentleman and officer, a graduate of Cambridge University, and a young lawyer in London with good connections. At the age of thirty-nine he was offered the job in Victoria and the gold fields, and he accepted it. He soon made it known that he would suffer no nonsense from the Hudson's Bay Company or its ex-officers in the colonies' administration. He was as tall as James Douglas, and ready to face him down if the need arose. He was a dandy with a terrific Victorian beard, shiny boots and a great wardrobe. He loved his magistrate's outfit, flashing the red cloth and white fur as he walked. He peppered his talk with French and Italian phrases. He loved it when someone dared him or threatened his life. He played tennis like an avenging god, and smiled sardonically at the young women who had the vapours in front of him.

And he would acquire the sobriquet, "The Hanging Judge."

Well, English law hanged people in the mid-nineteenth century. Judge Begbie presided over a country filled with wild men who had easy access to liquor and a taste for yellow dust. In his first thirteen years he sentenced thirty-eight men to be hanged, and twenty-seven of them were strung up. Four of them were white men. One was Chinese. The other twenty-two were Indians. Indians had a hard time finding good lawyers in those days.

It was never, as far as we know, that Begbie had anything against Indians.

In fact he often went to war with various governments because of their repressive policies against them. After British Columbia entered Confederation, for example, he pronounced on and decided against the federal prohibition of the potlatch, until the feds found a way to write specific new anti-Begbie laws. He was the nineteenth-century Romantic English ideal, the fair-minded, logical, objective voice of abstract law. Well, maybe not the ideal; but certainly the personification of the books. He could not be bribed and he could not be stroked. He flicked dust off his ermine and sat bone straight on a box in a tent beside the Nechako River and listened to the case for the prosecution. When he rode a horse or a mule over the rocks pretending to be a brigade road, his long legs nearly reached the ground. If someone was going to take a shot at him from behind a boulder, he had better shoot straight.

Sir Matthew Baillie Begbie, "The Hanging Judge," c. 1859.

He did not hate Indians, but he was a lot less than fond of USAmericans. He met a lot of them while spending half his year travelling to every white settlement in the huge land. He was not about to see his new bailiwick turned into the wild west, nor would he hide from Yankee weapons. In sentencing a USAmerican rowdy to three years for mayhem, he said, "We have a law which prohibits the use of bowie knives, pistols or other offensive weapons, and in those countries over which the British flag flies there is no necessity for carrying or using offensive weapons." His voice was filled with a superior irony whenever he addressed Yankee ruffians in whatever building had become for that day a courtroom. Once an accused man complained that he had not received good enough representation. Begbie replied, "Very well, I will send up your case for a new trial—by your maker." He was a card, sometimes.

Once he was sitting on the upper verandah in a gold-rush hotel, when he heard two men below him plotting his demise. He went back into his room and retrieved a receptacle of unpleasant water, which he emptied over the conspirators' heads. He may have been a Cambridge man, but he knew how to handle himself in bonanza country.

Thinking big

Lieutenant Colonel Richard Clement Moody may not have been as dashing or as colourful as de Cosmos and Begbie, but he laid extravagant plans for the colonies, and he also knew a good thing when he saw it. He did not stay in the colonies for the rest of his life, as the others did, and when he went home five years after British Columbia was launched, he had acquired three thousand acres of what he knew to be prime land. He spent the last twenty-three years of his life in England as a rich man, not the first gent to grab it and run to more comfortable digs.

Moody had been governor in what the British called the Falkland Islands in the 1840s, a time when the Crown was finally exerting its claim and power there against the newly independent Argentina as well as the Monroe Doctrine. After that he had a position in Malta. At the age of forty-five he was summoned to British Columbia, where he was handed three positions: Commander of the British Columbia Detachment, Royal Engineers, Chief Commissioner of Lands and Works, and Lieutenant-Governor of the colony. Lesser men might have been daunted by the responsibilities, but Richard Moody had an ego as big as all outdoors, and we are talking here of British Columbia outdoors.

The Royal Engineers were not a massive armed force; the detachment would seem to have looked pretty puny compared to the many thousands of gold-fiends pouring across the border, and the rampaging US army just across the line. They numbered 172, and they had two jobs. They were soldiers, but they had to survey the Colony, prepare townsites and build roads. Sometimes the roads were trails, sometimes highways. But these were not the only military in the vulnerable British lands. Bulwer-Lytton decided that the Island colony needed a defence as well. He would direct 160 naval marines from Hong Kong to Esquimalt in early 1859. They did not know that all but a few officers and NCOs would soon be sweating in the bush on the mainland, creating Moody's dream city.

Moody was a man of grandiose schemes, and he cultivated a flair. Thus it was that he arrived in Victoria on December 25, 1858, just in time for the governor's Christmas dinner. Back in England he had pored over maps of the new colony, and created in his mind a series of strategic towns along the Fraser River, complete with squares and statues and dramatic hillside vistas, wide high streets, colonnades and impressive military edifices. People had warned him about the hard-headed Douglas, but he thought that his double expertise would win the governor to his vision. Douglas spoke to his chief engineer diplomatically, at first, informing him that the imperial government was not extravagant in its financial support, that London thought that paying a governor and funding a small defence force was the extent of its duty to the colonies. But Moody saw gold dust coming down the river, and drew bigger and more fanciful pictures. He and Douglas would never get along very well. Eventually Douglas would utter proclamations without consulting his lieutenant-governor.

Chartres Brew was the first police chief to complain to Victoria that he did not have enough officers to do the job. Brew was an Irishman, and he persuaded Douglas that he needed 150 Royal Irish Constables to police the gold fields. Douglas agreed, and petitioned the Imperial Office. The Imperial Office said that he could have fifteen. It appeared that no one at the Imperial Office had ever spent any time at a gold rush in wild Indian country. Like his friend Begbie, Brew spent half his time riding from mining camp to mining camp, as the gold seekers moved ever northward. When the cash-strapped governor appointed him Chief Gold Commissioner as well as the top cop, he made him the centre of just about all dealings between the thirty thousand bonanza-hunters and the British government. He was sentencing the big awkward man to an early grave, which he entered in 1870 at Barkerville.

Somehow the understaffed Chartres Brew, along with his trail-buddy Begbie, managed to persuade the USAmericans that places such as Barkerville were not Dodge City. There were no picturesque gunfights on the dusty main streets of the British Columbia wild west. The corrals in the Cariboo were OK.

The Pig War?

If you were living in a country close to the United States in the nineteenth century, or within reach of the US navy and air force in the twentieth century, there was a good chance that you would be invaded by the US. The USAmericans liked phrases such as "Remember the Maine" or "Remember the Alamo" or "Remember Pearl Harbor." Usually their wars were started by alleged attacks on one of their warships, whether up a Mexican River, in a Cuban harbour, in Hawaii or off the Tonkin Gulf. The Pig War was started after an alleged attack on a USAmerican pig on an island in the Gulf of Juan de Fuca.

British North America lived with the threat of USAmerican ambitions from 1774 onward. Benedict Arnold tried to invade Quebec City in 1775, and free the French-Canadians from the British yoke, before he was chased back home. In 1814 they tried again, and were slaughtered in the dark at Lundy's Lane, while Niagara Falls continued to fall. Again they went home. But now in 1859, off the coast of the Pacific northwest, no one knew quite who was at home. Certainly a porker was not expected to know what nationality he might be.

The 49th parallel had been a simple line to draw. The edges of Vancouver Island, which stretch below the 49th parallel are varied only by the tides. But between the mainland and Victoria there are a lot of smaller islands, the crests of underwater mountains. Almost all of them are farther north than Victoria. In 1858 the farmers and loggers on these islands knew more about their local geography than they knew about the peculiar line drawn at the Oregon Boundary Treaty in 1846. The closest of these islands to Victoria is San Juan. The biggest concern on the island was a Hudson's Bay Company farm, but there were a few farmers on the eastern half of the island who considered themselves US citizens. The Pig War could have been the Sheep War. In 1855 a US sheriff had seized thirty sheep from the HBC farm, claiming them as restitution for unpaid taxes. British and US farmers were not on good terms. Flags flew higher and higher on the two sides of the little island.

Then one day in the early summer of 1859 a British pig got through Lyman Cutler's fence. Cutler was a USAmerican who had failed to find gold on the Fraser River, and retreated to San Juan Island to try farming. He plunked down his shack and fence in the middle of the HBC's sheep farm. When the HBC pig walked through the ramshackle fence, Lyman Cutler did what all good USAmericans do when they are being threatened by intruders; he got out his rifle and shot the foreigner dead.

Governor Douglas, the old Hudson's Bay nabob, was infuriated. He was not particularly sentimental about a murdered porker, but he was of the opinion that San Juan Island was on the Canadian side of the international channel, and he did not like USAmericans squatting on Company land and firing bullets in English territory. He gave a ready ear to the Queen's citizens on the island. But the USAmericans on the island were also appealing to their patriots on the mainland. The letters on both sides reached higher and higher offices. The US position was perhaps that the unnamed pig had been an advance scout. In Washington there were senators who believed that San Juan Island was a US possession, and that the question of Vancouver Island should be addressed as soon as San Juan was safely under the Stars and Stripes. As one solon put it, Vancouver Island was as important to US interests in the west as the other island, Cuba, was in the east. Ominous words, indeed.

On July 27, sixty US infantry men, under the command of Captain George Pickett, stormed the beach of San Juan Island. He was sent there by General W.S. Harney, commander of the Oregon military district. These were not cautious men; they were ready to defend the Great Republic against any perceived threat. Some commentators noticed that they were both southerners, and suggested that they might have been looking for an international war in the north in order to stave off the looming civil war. If that was more than conjecture, it did not work; George Pickett was to become a famous general in the Confederate Army.

Now James Douglas called up his troops. He ordered a shipload of marines to sail down the Fraser, and commanded Captain G.P. Hornby to land on San Juan. In Victoria the House of Assembly echoed with loud defences of the Empire. The city buzzed with excitement. As a major portion of its populace was from the United States, there must have been a complicated atmosphere in the little capital. However, Hornby was a cool man. He did not land troops, but only anchored off San Juan. He sent calm messages to Douglas. While the US infantry dug in, Hornby rested at anchor. Then his boss, Admiral R.L. Baynes, arrived in his flagship. Baynes offered his opinion that it would be silly to get into another war with the US over a little island and its livestock. There were also doves at the governor's ear. Armed conflict was averted, at least for a while.

Eventually the US State Department told the British ambassador in Washington that the president was embarrassed by Pickett's invasion. Perhaps the impending civil war had something to do with developments, after all. The commander-in-chief of the US armed forces travelled personally to Puget Sound, where the Hudson's Bay Company still had operations, and conferred with Governor Douglas. They agreed to a joint occupancy of little San Juan until the matter could be settled by international arbitration. The next year Douglas sent troops to the island, and for the next dozen years, the British marines and the US artillery lived across the isle from one another in tents and a few outbuildings. The war now entered its decorative phase. Social convenors in Victoria and on the US mainland began to stage competitive parties on San Juan, escalating the pageantry and firing fusillades of invitations into the enemy camp.

Finally, in late 1872, Kaiser William the First, appointed as head of the arbitration panel, awarded the island to the United States, and the British Columbia troops came home. One can only hope that the end of the siege was celebrated with a gala pork barbecue.

Moody's dream

The new colony needed a capital city that would make sense in terms of trade and defence. Governor Douglas, assuming that the Colony was for all intents and purposes a continuation of the Company, obviously favoured the site of the original Fort Langley, now renamed Derby after the British prime minister. In the fall of 1858 Douglas had snaffled the area for the government, forestalling freebooting speculators. He had it surveyed and divided into lots, and ordered surveyor Joseph Despard Pemberton to hold a public auction in Victoria. It was a great success: even his adversary Amor de Cosmos snapped up some property at Derby. Meanwhile the governor prepared plans for public buildings and ordered the construction of military barracks.

But Moody had his plans too, and they were not all scenic. He saw that it was a short walk from the US border to the flat ground at the bend of the Fraser. He was cognizant of recent US history, and looked around for a hillside. He liked the idea of a hillside from which British guns could aim southward. Just a little downriver from Derby he found a spot on the north bank that rose nicely. This, he said, would be the new capital. Douglas, who had been on this side of the world far longer than his land commissioner, chafed somewhat, but he had his instructions from London. On St. Valentine's Day of 1859 he acceded to Moody's plan, and named the new site Queensborough.

Now the investors who had purchased lots at Derby were incensed. They had been expecting huge profits out of getting in at the start of an era, and now they saw a plot. The old HBC man had hoodwinked them. Amor de Cosmos strained his wit through his pique. Eventually the government allowed the investors to trade their plots at Derby for down payments for plots on the sloping land of Queensborough. They were in no way mollified when the Queen's office instructed Douglas to rename the future city New Westminster.

Meanwhile, the clash of views between Moody and Douglas continued. Moody was taking his time and scheming magnificent terraces and vistas. Douglas reminded him that he had a hillside covered with timber and close to Salish villages. The site was thick with enormous cedars and hemlocks, many of them twenty-five stories high. The dense underbrush was filled with thorns. It became an expensive undertaking to clear this sloping land, and for years it would remain an unsightly tangle of fallen trees, snags and mud. It did not resemble old Westminster.

And a capital needs its approaches. New Westminster was not Rome, though it was as hilly, but it had a pretty good access to the sea. Now it became important to build trails and roads in the other directions, especially toward the great resources of the Interior and the north. The Royal Engineers could not handle the work alone. Civilian road-makers were contracted. The Royal Marines who had been summoned from China to protect the new colony were set to sawing down trees. Britain sent more surveyors, including Edgar Dewdney, who with a poetry-writing confederate named Walter Moberly, would create the Dewdney Trail, the first road between Fort Hope and the south Okanagan. Dewdney was a wine fancier who later held many prestigious positions with provincial and dominion administrations. As lieutenant-governor of the North-West Territories in the eighties, he would sip his chablis while Louis Riel spoke hot words on the prairie.

But roads had to take second place to the building of the new capital. New Westminster became a pain in the neck for Governor Douglas. It was invaded by businessmen with gold in their eyes, and they started the long British Columbia tradition of reviling Victoria. Douglas incorporated the City of New Westminster in July of 1860, and the businessmen grabbed spots on the municipal council. Douglas was feeling the demands of the gold grabbers up north to make access to the Coast more likely, and now the new city on the lower mainland was clamouring for thinly stretched funds and personnel. The old Company man began to make his disdain for entrepreneurs known in the letters he sent to associates in Britain and conversations he had in Victoria. Words came back at him when John Robson, editor of the New Westminster *British Columbian*, wrote editorials and columns full of boosterism for his city's developers and excoriating the governor and his friends. James Douglas longed for the days when he could give orders to fur haulers and bust down doors in Indian villages.

Meanwhile he made Victoria a free port, and ensured that all deep-sea shipping stopped there. The banks and major marketing emporia would be in Victoria, the *de facto* capital of both colonies.

Native life in the gold era

Now the Native peoples of British Columbia and Vancouver Island had more than their doors to worry about. In 1859 the Thompson fishermen took up their traditional posts and waited in vain for the salmon run. Hardly a fish came by. They were not being punished by the appropriate spirits. They had prepared their equipment properly, and they had not violated any taboos. They were living in peace with all the cousins who had gathered at the forks of the rivers. But the salmon did not come. White fishermen had stretched a net across the Fraser downstream. Commerce had come to the water. It would get worse every year, as white fish business saw another gold rush in the rivers. The Native peoples of the Interior and the Coast were salmon people. The yearly salmon run was their life, literally, and the basis of their religion. When the first white fur traders had trudged into the forests in the one hundred and tenth century of aboriginal dwelling, they had often relied on the gift of Indian salmon to stay alive so far from their North Atlantic home. Now in the nineteenth century of the Christian period, the whites were looking at the pink flesh in the water as a money-making proposition, and making jokes about "Indian-givers."

Settlers and businessmen often stated their opinion that the land was empty or insufficiently used by hunters and fishers. The law and the police and the church said that the Native people had no real concept of justice and order and religion. As late as 1994 the British Columbia poet Robert Bringhurst reported this encounter with an "educator" in Britain:

> Years ago, on a visit to England, I was introduced to a recently retired head of a prestigious girls' school. The discussion turned to the subject of language, as postmodern discussions always seem to do. I made some reference, I guess, to Navajo or Haida or Ojibwa. "What are those?" she asked, and I said they were Native American languages. This terminology wasn't entirely clear to her, and I eventually explained that they were languages spoken by what she might call Red Indians. "Oh!" she said. "Did they have languages?"

During the "settlement" of the Pacific slope, the British newcomers' reports and letters and books portrayed the first peoples as frightening and savage and ignorant, as their worst biblical and imperial dreams come true. Here are some of the words and phrases normally used to characterize the creatures they taught to call themselves Indians:

Treacherous. Murderous. Superstitious. Lazy. Dirty. Cannibals. Savages. Cowards. Indecent.

The whites, some casual, some regardful of themselves as experts, ranked the Natives according to geography. The northern Indians of the Coast were more dangerous than the southerners. The Indians of the Interior were higher on the scale of humanity than those of the coast. Phrenologists offered their scientific judgements. Skin-colour esthetes made comparisons. A nineteenth-century anthropological opinion held that the Coastal Indians were Mongolian in background while the Interior hunters were ancient Europeans.

Not that it mattered. A common learned pronouncement had it that there was a kind of proto-Darwinian principle at work: the Indians were a disappearing race (there was some seeming evidence of this notion, especially during medical crises), and would be replaced by the incoming Europeans, just as nature rotated its crops.

The fur trade had given the Natives someone new to trade with and gadgets to make their lives a little more efficient, but the gold boom was another story. The sheer numbers of whites from the south and east meant that Indian suppliers had to deal with support goods, not the primary item. And there were lots of whites who were looking to get rich by supplying the miners with white people's necessities, such as booze and sex and tobacco. The Englishmen's colony got larger and larger as more sourdoughs squatted beside rivers and built flumes down hillsides. The missionaries and schoolteachers and planters followed them, and trees turned into walls and roofs. The cow became a common sight in the Fraser Valley, and then showed up in the Interior. By the early 1860s there were sawmills at Burrard Inlet and up the Fraser as far as Yale.

In 1864 the telegraph reached the Pacific coast. The Indians would never recover from the telegraph.

Rock Creek

Amateur gold miners are like amateur gamblers, in that they dream of a quick lucky hit that will soon have them in silk trousers. But veteran gold miners are unlike professional gamblers, in that they have to get used to looking for thirty cents in a muddy pan and sleeping in a tent pitched on ground scraped free of snow. All over the southern Interior of British Columbia in the late fifties, there were amateur and veteran gold miners crouched over creeks, doing simple arithmetic. Gold was found in the Similkameen River late in 1859, and soon afterward at Rock Creek, just north of the border and just east of the Okanagan Valley. By the summer of 1860 the Rock Creek strike was beginning to look like a precarious bonanza.

As usual Governor Douglas was concerned about US ruffians. He urged the Fraser River boys to go to the Boundary country and set stakes. Then he decided to ride the newly finished Dewdney Trail himself. When he got to Rock Creek in September he found a town with twenty buildings and five hundred human beings from Canada and the US and Europe. He announced a meeting at which he would address the locals. No one wanted to hear the politician from the Island. His supernumeraries talked up the meeting, which was rescheduled to take place at night in the saloon, and eventually the miners attended and listened without rudeness. Douglas told them that he was impressed with their industry and lawfulness, and advised them that they were subject to British law, though the boundary was a short walk away. He told them that this law included the concept of duties on imported goods. Then he appointed Captain William Cox as the local gold commissioner and border supervisor. When Douglas rode back to his capitals, he was pretty happy about the progress of civilization in the gold fields of his colony.

Captain Cox was not a stickler for London-style jurisprudence. When two disputations miners vied for the same piece of dirt he had them run a foot race to decide the claim. When a young Englishman was caught stealing from a flume, he was sentenced to five minutes of gathering his stuff, and ten minutes of getting out of town, which included settling his debts. On a more serious note, Cox reported the lynching of an Indian man who had apparently killed a French miner. Fifty miners had ridden into Washington Territory to retrieve the man and persuade the Okanogan Indians to hand him over. Then they hanged him from a pine tree. Captain Cox, government gold man and border guard, wrote that he did not see the hanging, therefore could do nothing about it.

Like other gold towns along the border, Rock Creek blossomed for a year or so, and then settled into village life as the news of the Cariboo rush spread southward. For the first half of the 1860s the miners left their sluices and rode north. Others rode through. The bartenders and whores sighed and packed their valises again.

Captain Cox was an invention by Governor Douglas. In the free-wheeling United States there was no such thing as a gold magistrate. Douglas got many of his ideas from the gold acts passed in Australia and New Zealand, and applied them in his government's Gold Fields Act of 1859. But the notion of gold commissioners was his. As he saw the influx of miners to more and more areas of his mainland colony, and as he saw that London would not provide him with as many policemen as he might have wanted to have, he began to appoint young Englishmen and Anglo-Irish to oversee operations at all the new mining sites. These fellows would see that the miners held proper licences and registered their claims, and that there was no skulduggery among the local mining boards. They were also made magistrates and justices of the peace; they had to settle disputes and impose fines. They had a lot of other jobs as well, being land commissioners and Indian agents and tax collectors and jailers. Most of them also took advantage of their placements to open businesses in their spare time.

When the Cariboo Gold Rush began, these eclectic men had a lot to do.

Cariboo Yellow

In 1860 some miners along the upper Fraser decided to hike up the creeks and over the hills eastward, and check out the metal. Down on the banks of the Fraser, the gold boys had grown used to finding enough flecks to make a profit, but now these altitude adventurers were noticing that the farther they went up, the heavier the shiny stuff was getting. They were looking at nuggets instead of flakes. They thought about secrecy. Prospectors who find gold always think about secrecy. It never works.

For one thing, once you get up into the hills you have to start digging for the good stuff. The best stuff was deep in the stony ground. The miners had to sink shafts, and it takes money to sink shafts. To get money to sink shafts you have to get backers or form partnerships. News leaks out and down and south. Your operation is no longer a pan and a mule and some dried food. You need people to build engineering works out of tree trunks and metal parts. You need suppliers and roads for the suppliers to travel. Eventually you need the government.

The first big strike in the Cariboo was made in late fall 1860 by four veteran gold seekers, Doc Keithley, George Weaver, Benjamin McDonald and John Rose. They soon had their names attached to creeks and temporary residences. They thought about secrecy, but they knew better. That winter they were surrounded by tents and lean-tos covered with snow. When the snow melted in the spring, all kinds of strangers were hammering together sluices and water-wheels.

Now began the British Columbia tradition of resource towns that would appear suddenly between the mountains, soon to disappear as the inhabitants looked elsewhere for the glitter. Keithley and his partners were responsible for the beginning of the first two, where Keithley Creek fell into Cariboo Lake, and then a little north at Antler Creek. People who had known each other in California gold camps nodded to each other across the Cariboo mud. Grocers, hardware men, tavern-keepers, barbers, whores, gamblers, photographers, masseurs, men of God, all started converging. Trees

were hacked down and converted into walls and roofs. There were a lot of
people who wanted gold dust and nuggets before they got a chance to head
down the arduous paths to the Coast. There were people who dreamed of
taking the yellow across the line before the Queen's government could
count it. A man named Patterson picked seventy-three ounces of gold
chunks out of the shallow ground in one day. Douglas was hiring gold commissioners as fast as he could.

Starting in 1858, Douglas had made deals between government and the
mining business to make two roads northward. One would go from the north
end of Harrison Lake, where a little town called Douglas was founded,
toward Lillooet, stitching the country from lake to lake. The work began
quickly, and slowed as it proceeded northward. New companies replaced old
ones as the route became more difficult. Bridges had to be constructed.
Freight rates had to be settled. Eventually the mule road eight feet wide had
to be made into a wagon road twelve feet wide. By 1862 wagons could travel
from Douglas to Lillooet, and inns were established along the route. But
meanwhile the bars of the Fraser Canyon had started giving up their gold,
and Douglas, always beset by a cash shortfall, made deals with the avid packers to create a mule road up the Yale-Spuzzum-Lytton route. The Royal
Engineers blasted their way through a mountain at Yale. By early 1861, mule
trains were stepping along the vertiginous left bank of the Fraser from Yale
to Quesnel Forks at a rate of fifteen miles a day, at a toll rate of a dollar a
pound. From there to Antler, the stuff was carried by Indians for forty cents
a pound.

In 1862 the camels arrived. An adventurous packer named Frank
Laumeister brought twenty-one camels to the Douglas-Lillooet trail in 1862.
The theory was that, unlike mules, they would subsist on sagebrush, and go
for a week without water, and carry twice the load. But camels are made for
walking on sand, not rock or mud. Mules and horses and North American
human beings do not like the odour and habits of camels, however. After a
year of packing supplies into the Cariboo, the camels were led over to the
Thompson River valley and let loose to roam the grasslands. Once in a
while a rancher would grab a few and try to make money from them, either
as ranch animals or entertainment. Halfway through the twentieth century,
people in the Interior stopped claiming to have seen the Arabian beasts on
the skyline.

The Cariboo Road

Governor Douglas knew that gold rushes were temporary. He was concerned
that a government might provide services to a population that would disappear in a year. But the Cariboo Gold Rush was making news all over the
world. Douglas saw it as the catalyst for opening the Interior of his huge

colony for a future that might not be filled with USAmericans. He dreamed of another road now, a wagon road four hundred miles long, through country that he knew from personal experience to be the most obdurate in the world.

In May of 1862 he ordered Captain John Marshall Grant of the Royal Engineers to start blasting his way north from Yale. He wanted a road that was eighteen feet wide. All year long the reports of new gold strikes all over the Interior came in, and all year the sappers blew away rock face and built cribbing out of British Columbia trees, including the tough larch that had been known for decades as the Douglas fir. Tough men who had not done as well as they had hoped in their search for gold had no trouble finding work on the Cariboo Road.

People took pride in looking forward to the Number One road. It became an amazing and scary engineering feat. Sometimes the scratch on the side of the cliff face was so high that the river was a ribbon of silver seen by anyone who was brave enough to go to the edge and look down; at other times it was a fast threat a few feet from wagon wheels. At Spuzzum the colony's first suspension bridge was completed in 1863 at a cost of $45,000. Douglas did not hurry to supply his accounts to London. In 1865, after his first structure had been swept away by the river, Thomas Spence completed a bridge to replace Cook's ferry. Late in the fall of that year the last segment of the road was finished when the workmen reached Barkerville.

Now the trains of very heavy wagons could haul goods all the way to the gold fields without depending on ferries and Native carriers. Prices could double or triple from New Westminster to Barkerville. But the governor had his road, and it would be travelled by six-horse passenger coaches as well as the long mule wagons and ox wagons. It would also be travelled by judges and governors.

Barkerville

The instant communities of gold-rush British Columbia were usually called the biggest something west of somewhere. In the middle of the 1860s Barkerville, the most famous of the Cariboo gold towns, was called the biggest town west of Chicago. The overwhelmingly male population boasted that if Barkerville was allowed to include the neighbouring Williams Creek towns of Richfield and Camerontown, it would claim 30,000 "citizens." This at a time when Victoria had about 6,000 inhabitants.

Of course, gold seekers have been known to exaggerate, especially when there were reporters or tapmen in the vicinity. There was no census, and there were a lot of people around who did not particularly want to be counted anyway. A more probable estimate would be ten or twelve thousand.

Most of the buildings in Barkerville were elevated. The hillsides were stripped of their trees, and the valley-bottom received the resultant liquid earth. But those buildings included banks and restaurants and churches, all made of new sawn lumber. They included barbershops, the most famous one operated by the legendary W.D. Moses, the first African-American entrepreneur-inventor of the British Columbia north. There were hotels and well-appointed saloons complete with all the amenities desired by a leisure-bound digger with a poke. There were bakeries run by Germans and laundries run by Chinese men. There were well-stocked grocery shops and smithies. There were butcher shops offering beef and mutton supplied by the new ranches of the Thompson Valley. There were ladies of the night, and day.

There was a weekly newspaper called the *Cariboo Sentinel* (early B.C. papers liked to be thought of as sentinels). There was the famous Theatre Royal for high-class shows featuring ladies from California. There was a swell lending library, and eventually there was even a poet-in-residence, the redoubtable James Anderson, who published in the *Sentinel* and out-of-town papers, and who would bring out the colony's first original book of verses in 1868.

In short, Barkerville, though a long way north of nice weather, featured all the rough elegance of any bonanza town south of the border. But there was one prominent feature of the western US cities that it did not experience. There were no epic gunfights on the muddy main street of Barkerville or at the Wake-Up-Jake Saloon. In nearby Richfield there was an impressive courthouse and a handy jail. Matthew Begbie was British law, and the constables

People liked to be photographed at the windlass at Billy Barker's claim, 1868.

of Chartres Brew kept a lid on the moilers and drinkers from the south. Barkerville did roar for a decade, as they say, even after a drunk burned it down for a while in 1868, but one did not often hear pistols in the night.

Barkerville was named after Billy Barker. He was a lad from Cornwall who had jumped his whaling ship in Victoria and headed for the hills in 1858. He became a world-famous success and then a local character, and finally a tourist attraction. When he and his partners arrived at Williams Creek they were determined men. They dug and dug. The ground was obdurate but they were obstinate. They sank a shaft fifty feet into the ground. Then they dug a couple more feet and found shining bedrock.

They cursed and blessed and wounded the earth and hauled up six hundred thousand dollars in gold. A hundred and twenty-five years later that strike would have been worth thirty million dollars. There would be even richer holes at the Aurora mine and the Caledonia mine, but Billy got the capital city of the Cariboo rush named after him. He attracted journalists and nameless men with muddy boots and sob stories. He attracted a woman, they say, with a better head for figures than Billy had. Billy Barker was what they call a millionaire these days, but he spent the last two decades of his life wandering around the Cariboo, telling tales and looking for another chance. There he often ran into Cariboo Cameron, after whom Camerontown had been named. He had left Williams Creek the richest man in British Columbia. Cameron had gone back east, investing in lots of enterprises that fell into other people's hands. Now he was back in northern British Columbia. He and Billy told each other a lot of lies as their beards grew white.

In 1863, the biggest year of the Cariboo rush, there were six million dollars worth of gold taken out of the old Indian ground. More than three million were reported to Governor Douglas's gold commissioners.

Overland to Canada

"If they trespass on white settlers punish them severely. A few lessons would soon enable them to form a correct estimation of their own inferiority, and settle the Indian title too."
—Amor de Cosmos, 1863

Catherine Schubert

Overall, the period of the early sixties, what with gold miners and rebellious Indians and squabbling politicians, was pretty turbulent. Settlement was not happening as fast as Douglas had hoped, and gold miners go where the yellow is. The colonies were going to go broke unless some people arrived to stay, and money stopped going out of the country so fast. Oftentimes a place is said to be rich if there are lots of natural resources, but if those resources are extractable from nature and can be turned to wealth elsewhere, the place is one day going to be dotted with ghost towns. Governor Douglas was interested in family values. But in the early sixties there were only 1,750 European women in the two colonies, and most of them were clustered in the southern part of Vancouver's Island.

Douglas must have been encouraged by the example of Catherine Schubert.

In 1862 a group of 220 Canadians made their various ways by railroad and steamboat and stagecoach to Fort Garry, at the eastern edge of the prairies. For a hundred dollars each, they bought shares in provisions and rentals, and climbed aboard a hundred Red River carts, and made their way to Fort Edmonton. Some of them jumped ship there, but 125 of them then set out across the Rockies, driving horses and cows in front of them. Eventually they found out how much they could be punished when old trails disappeared and were replaced by goat paths. They freed the horses and turned the cows into jerked beef. Then they formed two groups to float down the Fraser and North Thompson rivers. They were headed for the Cariboo, of course. They were the Overlanders. They went through terrible hardships, and some of them did not make it all the way. One man woke in the morning to find that the rushes he had been sleeping on all night were the cover for a grave containing Indians who had died of smallpox. But eventually the living remains of the two groups converged in Kamloops nearly starved, their clothes in rags, and began one of the great myths of that city. Among them was the wife of Francis Augustus Schubert.

Catherine Schubert saw friends drowned in fast water. She saw Indian villages destroyed by smallpox. She saw her three small children with terror in their eyes. And she was pregnant.

She was supposed to be settled well before the new baby was born, but the real mountains and waterfalls of British Columbia were not the dream the Schuberts had dreamed in Ontario. The trip took longer than anyone had promised. In the last week of her journey Catherine refused all offers of a stopover. She was the only woman in her group. She said she wanted to reach a settlement, and she wanted another woman in whatever delivery room she could find.

All through October of 1862 the rafts straggled into Kamloops. Finally, the raft with the sorry-looking Schubert family fetched up at the convergence of the Thompson rivers. The next day the Schuberts numbered six. Catherine had succeeded in finding a midwife. The midwife was a Shuswap woman with her people's good heart, and the delivery room was in the Kamloops Indian village. The baby, Rose Schubert, was the first white baby born on the mainland colony, and the first hands to touch her were Native.

Fifteen years later Catherine Schubert became matron of the Cache Creek boarding school, while her husband started their farm in Spallumcheen, where they began to live in their own house in 1883.

After Douglas

Soon after its first white daughter was born, British Columbia's white father left his office. The British government was unhappy with the enormous expenses James Douglas was piling up in his seemingly quixotic attempts to open the Interior. The newspapers were suggesting vigorously that he should be more hospitable to democratic reforms. Amor de Cosmos, who would later become the second premier of the province of British Columbia, sniped at him from the *Colonist* on the Island, and John Robson, who would become the ninth premier of the province of British Columbia, took pot shots at him from the *British Columbian* on the mainland. But Douglas employed a strategy that would be mimicked by the Social Credit government a century later: he spent a borrowed fortune on roads to the north and east, and did not notice the advice he was tendered by spokesmen for governmental reform. He started his gold roads and policed them with riflemen on horses. And he paid off the contractors.

All through 1862 he called in the favours he had been owed as business leader and politician, and the lobbying started in London. In 1863 the tall Scot was knighted, and his halfbreed wife, whom he had kept out of the light as often as possible, became Lady Douglas. A few months later, in early 1864, he opened the first legislative session of the mainland council, and then, sixty years after his birth in British Guiana, he retired as the governor of both colonies. Or he was retired: Britain was planning a new kind of government for its west coast holdings, one that would less resemble the structure of the old Hudson's Bay Company.

Retiring in spring, Douglas took a long holiday in Europe, his first sight of that continent since his childhood. He did not take Lady Douglas with him. When Sir James returned to Victoria he came to a big comfortable house within sight of the harbour, where the Hudson's Bay fort had been torn down and the strange new parliament building erected on the south shore.

The Ladies

Meanwhile Catherine Schubert was being joined by other new white mothers in the colonies. In 1862 the city of Victoria was booming. There was money everywhere that aggressive white people set their boots. There was gold in the hills. There were shiny roofs in Victoria and along the mainland rivers. But there were not many unmarried British women. Fortunately for the intrepid bachelors of the colonies, there was an unmarried British woman named Angela Burdett Coutts, a rich orphan in England, who organized some of her friends, and conceived of the idea for the bride ships. They set about finding healthy young women who would be willing to embark for places such as Sydney and Victoria, there to find work as domestics, and eventually to attract swains who wanted to start families. Governor Douglas was delighted. Nothing like this had ever been offered to the fur traders.

The eligible spinsters who managed to make it past the provisioning stops at places such as San Francisco, began arriving in Victoria right after that city's charter had been granted. The first load of sixty arrived with their very serious matron at Esquimalt, and were soon followed by others. Some of them were proposed to by young men before they even got a chance to take up their duties as servants in the new mansions in the capital. By the time that Douglas took his tour of Europe, little Rose Schubert was joined by a sprinkling of white babies across the map, even while the First Nations people were burying their children in smallpox graves.

New governors

Douglas went into retirement while the USAmericans were acting out the final bloody year of their war between north and south, so he felt an easing of pressure from the expansionists on the other side of the frail international boundary. The Colonial Office in London sought to ensure that no successor would have the power the fur giant had wielded, and assigned separate governors to the colonies; Arthur Kennedy would be the Island's third governor, and Frederick Seymour would be the mainland's second governor.

Seymour would have the more difficult job, of course. His first great challenge was the Chilcotin War. His first great opportunity was a series of new gold strikes along Wild Horse Creek in the Kootenay region. These strikes, like the ones at Rock Creek, were just above the USAmerican border, and a lot of the digging and drinking was done by USAmericans. Seymour continued the method of his predecessor, ordering the Dewdney Trail punched eastward. While he was at it, he sank a lot more borrowed money into improving Douglas's roads into the Cariboo.

Meanwhile Seymour did some fancy work with the mechanisms of government. He dissolved Douglas's council before the end of its term at New Westminster, and replaced it with elected members. This action was not immediately appreciated by London, but tended to mollify local citizens who were pushing for reform. It also fed their pride; their little frontier colony was being run in a fashion that resembled that of the longer established colonies back east. Eventually London would scrutinize the work done by Seymour's council and approve.

But British Columbia's financial problems continued to grow. It was an enormous land mass, after all, and the Washington and Idaho diggers kept abandoning depleting mines and moving northward. Seymour knew that he had to keep building roads to keep the gold from draining southward. Now the Kootenay miners found big deposits in the Big Bend country of the Columbia. Seymour built wagon roads, but miners jumped the border anyway. Government revenues were not meeting expenses, and in the comfortable offices of England, they did not like the numbers. Private banks in the colony were failing or languishing. Small-time miners had trouble getting loans to build their mountain operations.

Arthur Kennedy had troubles on the Island colony that were both financial and political. He had no Indian wars, and he did not have a porous border to police, but he had Amor de Cosmos and his friends to encounter. Kennedy was an elegant Irishman with administrative experience first in his starving homeland and then as governor in two African colonies and the huge Western Australia. But this was the first time he had had to work with an elected assembly. The assembly was made up primarily of men from the Victoria area who saw government as an arm of business, especially their own. Kennedy was disliked by these men because of his two characterological facets: he had a genuine concern for the economic well-being of the colony as a whole, and he liked to live in high style. He spent public money looking for natural resources up-island, and he spent public money on fancy meals and the purchase of a $40,000 castle for his residence. Castles were to play a role in the changing face of rocky Victoria. So were bars. In 1865 their were eighty-five saloons, some of them very eclectic in their wares, to serve a population of 6,000 citizens, many of them non-drinkers.

Seeing the pelf going across saloon bars, and desirous of finding funds to develop roads and public services in Nanaimo and the Comox Valley, Kennedy imposed the colony's first income tax, on any yearly intake of more than £150. In early 1866 the assembly voted to remove the income tax along with real-estate tax and reduce the price of liquor licences. Kennedy could not resist noticing that several of the members who had voted to dump the taxes were themselves businessmen who were behind in payments of their own. The battle between administration and legislature continued until 1867. The assembly reduced the governor's salary. The governor tried to have the assembly forbidden to pass money laws. The Colonial Office restricted its comments to stern messages about frugality. In far London the feeling was that Victoria would one day soon see the wisdom of applying for amalgamation with the mainland.

In 1864 the governments of the eastern colonies had convened a conference in Charlottetown, to discuss the question of forming a union. It was supposed to be about Maritime union, but Canada had asked and received permission to attend. The colonies agreed to meet later in the year at the Quebec Conference, where plans for a confederated British North America were devised. Three years later the BNA Act would be passed in London. Word of these developments filled the west coast newspapers and hung in the air in the public and commercial buildings of Victoria and New Westminster.

Now Amor de Cosmos found a new way to vex Governor Kennedy, he thought. In January of 1865 he introduced some bills that would lead to petitioning for the joining of the two colonies. Opposition came from some merchants who feared that Victoria harbour would lose its privilege as a free port. Some pro-unionists such as William Tolmie saw amalgamation as a prelude to joining the eastern colonies. Governor Kennedy, hoping to vex Amor de Cosmos and the Vancouver's Island Assembly, endorsed the union. Over in New Westminster, Governor Seymour angrily defied the idea, seeing an ambition in Victoria to re-exert control over his vast domain. He wrote many despatches to London stating his opposition. In Victoria, Amor de Cosmos resigned and ran for re-election on an amalgamation ticket. He was re-elected, and the nervous merchants saw that their best hope was to favour the union on condition that their port remain free.

But in London there was a government that was falling apart. The dying administration pushed through the act joining the two colonies. Seymour's letters home had done their job. On November 19, 1866, the Act of Union was proclaimed, making New Westminster the capital of the new colony, with Seymour as its first governor, and Victoria declared a port under its administration. The Island was given eight seats in the new legislature, and the mainland would retain its fifteen. Arthur Kennedy happily packed his bags for England.

The Chilcotin War

During the 1860s all roads led to Williams Creek. Road-builders felt as warm toward the Cariboo country as any liquor salesman or lady of the long night. Governor Douglas, eager to find a road that might be shorter than the Fraser Canyon route, and perhaps more importantly, safe from US interference, had for years been thinking about the deep fjords on the coast. The idea was that ships might be met at the head of an inlet such as Howe Sound by wagons that could travel a road only half as long as the Fraser Trail. But the governor's appointees always came back with stories about towering mountains that separated the ocean from the flatter territory inland.

Then along came a recent English immigrant, Alfred Waddington, whom some people regarded as an optimist and others a lunatic. Waddington was bluff and well-dressed, and persuaded a group of financiers in Victoria that he could build a road from the head of Bute Inlet, over a huge mountain that would be named after him, and into easy country.

Waddington was a typical European visionary: he could not see any Indian land anywhere. A hundred years earlier British law had declared that the original nations of North America were owners of all the territory lying westward of the Atlantic watershed. The idea was that white settlement was not supposed to occur unless the original occupants of the lands had agreed to proffered treaties. Across the prairies the whites had made some pretty advantageous treaties indeed. West of the Rockies the newcomers had been after fur, so land treaties had not been a high priority. During the gold rush the white people had been in too much of a hurry to dicker with the Indians. Douglas had signed several treaties with the peoples of Vancouver's Island, but they did not often ensure that the aboriginal people could relax. One symbolic incident occurred at Nanaimo, when the Brits needed a cricket pitch for their Sunday recreation, and the only flat land they could find was on Indian property. The Nanaimo band was not even invited to tea.

So the Chilcotin nation was leery about Waddington's surveyors. Waddington had his financial backing, so it was not hard for him to get a charter from the government. He was supposed to build a road from Bute Inlet to the Quesnel River. The business-minded people of Victoria acted the way they had when New Westminster was invented; they started buying plots of land at Bute Inlet and up the Homathko River, named after the local people. But the work crews and supply packers soon found out that they were not going to be welcomed by all the indigenous folk.

The Chilcotin men had long given other Native groups cause to worry, and they were probably the most worrisome Indians for whites who knew anything about the country. Unlike other bands they were reluctant to wear European clothes and listen to European religion. They had fierce moustaches and long hair. They wore wolfskins and paint, and metal rings in their noses. They raided Salish territory and took slaves. Their land west of the gold trails had not been penetrated by their enemies, and they felt as if it was still theirs. They were very good at weapons, and when white traders offered weapons they never traded land for them. So when Waddington's crews started up the Homathko, the Chilcotins did not ask them to feel at home.

There were incidents such as stirred apprehension in Britishers who had read colonial pulp fiction. Now on April 29th of 1864, Tim Smith became the first casualty of the Chilcotin War. It was not much of a war, if we compare it to the civil war that had been going on in the United States for three years. More than 600,000 soldiers would die in that war, and a president because of it. Tim Smith was a ferryman on the Homathko, and died at the hands of a few Chilcotin wolf men. A day later, in the biggest battle of the Chilcotin War, thirteen more road-builders would die in their camp up the river. In the days that followed, the Native warriors attacked other whites farther inland. When they attacked a settler named William Manning near Puntzi Lake, they killed the man and broke his ploughs and other farming implements to pieces and left them scattered on the ground. It was a procedure they favoured, and a sign of their intentions. It should have said something about land claims to those whites who shouted about "savage renegades" and the like.

But newspaper men and historians like to make points about the causes of wars. A painter who was recording the expedition said that Waddington's men were quick to supply the Natives with weapons, but refused any requests for food. The Indians were so hungry, he said, that they fought with the camp dogs for bones and bacon rind. Waddington himself gave the opinion that the Chilcotins were seeking revenge for the introduction of smallpox. Judge Begbie held the opinion that there were Indians who considered the land theirs.

Smallpox

Colonists take their flags and their viruses with them. Smallpox was deadlier than alcohol and gunpowder for the indigenous peoples of the Americas. In 1780 a sailor introduced it to the Tlingit and Haida, and nearly destroyed those nations. In 1836 one-third of the Tsimshian around Fort Simpson perished. It came to the lower Columbia River during the fur trade, too, and by the 1840s it was making its way through the Indian communities of Washington and Idaho. It came north to British Columbia again during the gold rush. In 1750 there were 90,000 Native people in what was to become B.C. In 1850 there were 60,000. In 1870 there were 25,000.

On March 18th, the Victoria *Colonist* told the people of the capital that their rumours were true—a USAmerican miner was in hospital with small-pox. Two weeks later doctors began to vaccinate all the white people in town. But some of them already had the disease, and it was showing up, with dire results, among the Native population of the Island's south end. An iso-lation hospital was added to the city's building boom, but Indians were not invited. There was panic in the boom town. The *Colonist* declared that the Indians should be chased out of town, and it was not long before the editor-ial was replaced by a proclamation. The May 29 ruling was that all Indians, including wives of whites, had to go to Ogden Point, as far as possible south-west of the harbour. The ruling was not airtight—Mrs. Douglas stayed behind her lace curtains. But white men with uniforms and weapons drove almost all the Natives to their new home. Others were given the job of burning down the evacuated houses.

A week later there were fifteen living Indians at Ogden Point. There were a lot more dead. There were none vaccinated. Others had refused to stay on their rocky promontory, and circled Victoria on their way north. They did not know that they were taking the white miner's virus with them. No one had told them how the terrible skin eruptions passed from person to person. It was not long before smallpox was introduced to the Nootka and Kwakiutl, and carried across the water to the Bella Coola and Chilcotin.

Whites had travelling to do, too. There were no restrictions placed on miners who wanted to leave Victoria and head for the Cariboo. All along the Fraser and the Thompson and the Columbia there were gold dusters sneez-ing and coughing and killing Native people. Along the Douglas Trail and the Dewdney Trail invisible death arrived. By the end of June 1862 there were 200 dead at Harrison Lake, and 175 dead at Lillooet. Whole villages died. The living were so weakened by the disease that they did not have the strength to bury the dead, and had to leave them where they lay. The sur-vivors died while fleeing the infected villages, or carried the virus to others. The famous Overlanders, gold seekers who came from the prairies and down the North Thompson River to Kamloops, were starving on their rafts. When they sighted an Indian camp, they landed, dreaming of food. But they found a community deserted by everyone but the dead lying in the sun.

Practical-minded settlers and politicians quietly welcomed the thinning of the Native population and the defeatism among the weakened survivors. The dying of elders and chiefs would cause havoc in the aboriginal political and cultural systems, leaving the remainder to drift toward a lowly place in the succeeding order. Merchants looked forward to safer pack trains and less competition for land.

Among the Bella Coola and Chilcotin people the ravages of the disease were most horrible. Visitors kept finding villages stinking with putrefaction, or skulls and clothing left behind by wolves. Indians with mutilated faces died at doorways. Two businessmen named Jim Taylor and Angus McLeod saw an opportunity rather than a disaster in the situation. They gathered blankets from the corpses of people who had walked or been carried into the woods, and carried them inland, where they sold them to Chilcotin people. Smallpox can stay alive in woven cloth for a year and a half.

Around the province there were a few lucky Natives. No government officials ever started a vaccination program among the Native people, but a few individuals tried. On the Island and along the mainland coast, a few churchmen carried their own needles and tried to find Indians who had not yet caught the disease. In Kamloops the Hudson's Bay factor allowed some of the Natives to be treated. But for a year the smallpox would ride the cells of unfortunate travellers along the Coast and up the rivers of the two colonies.

Klatsassin

The road from Bute Inlet was very expensive, and funds were eaten up quickly. The terrain was really too difficult, demanding dozens of switch-backs up and over Mount Waddington, and too many bridges and steep hill-sides. Things were also very tough for the Chilcotins, whose country was now being entered by survey crews with their iron tools. In the spring of 1864 the previous year's salmon were all gone, and the oolichans were not running yet. The survivors of the smallpox epidemic were weak and starving and angry. Even the fierce Chilcotin found it difficult to hunt in such conditions. Their alternate source of food was the Waddington expedition.

When they asked for food as compensation for the whites' penetration of their land, they were rebuffed. When they managed to steal some reparations they were threatened. When they looked for work, they had their names taken as possible thieves. The whites also scoffed at the notion that for the Natives the taking of their names was also theft.

There were a lot of things about the Chilcotin that the whites, who tended to see all Natives as the same integers in their colonial plans, did not take heed of. One was the special esteem that Chilcotin warriors were held in. These warriors were not hereditary leaders, and were not even necessarily popular. But a successful warrior was accorded great respect and an unquestioning following. During the time of the Waddington expedition the most highly respected warrior was a man with blue eyes and no moustache. This was Klatsassin. It was he who had fired a musket ball through the head of the ferryman Tim Smith. He and his men carried away Smith's food and left his equipment in a mess.

Klatsassin was a hawk. He and other warriors had never allowed any other nation to make inroads on Chilcotin land. Now the whites from the ocean were cutting trees. He decided that all the whites on Chilcotin land had to be killed. They had offered nothing but insults and a few underpaid jobs to starving Indians. Klatsassin talked to his warriors and to the Chilcotin labourers. He found the camp where the surveyors were blazing trees, and talked to the Native workers there. He asked the white men for some food. The white men said that they had orders not to give away food to lazy heathens. That night the Indians played a drum and danced and put paint on their faces. The surveyors were nervous, but they did not know a lot about Chilcotin entertainment.

It was Chilcotin warrior custom to attack the enemy in the early morning, before wakefulness. The last morning of April was very noisy around the tents occupied by sleeping Norwegians and Danes and others. First there were the war whoops, then the discharging of muskets, and the sounds of knives and hatchets against bone. The Indians cut the tent ropes, and stabbed and hacked the surveyors through the collapsed canvas. The Indian women and children watched while Klatsassin's men fought for their country. As the sun was making its way between spruce needles, the warriors finished their work. Now most of these enemies were dead under canvas or on the ground outside.

Later the site would be called Murderers' Bar. Nine whites died there, and three managed to escape down the creek to civilization. Klatsassin, encouraged by his success, carried his war uphill, where he despatched four more foreign workers. In the following days, the Chilcotin warriors carried their campaign inland, gathering troops as they went. Among their actions was a four-day battle with riders in a pack train on the Bella Coola trail.

A bad dream was coming true for the politicians and businessmen of the young colony. The brand new governor, Frederick Seymour, saw his country beginning to look like the United States. He and his predecessor had always been alarmed by the sheer number of USAmericans in the British Columbia gold fields. Now there was gunfire in the bush. Seymour went to James Douglas for advice. Douglas told him to put the affair into the hands of his trusted appointees Chartres Brew and William George Cox. Brew would lead the coastal force from Bute Inlet, and Cox would head the posse from the Cariboo.

But Brew's forces found it no easier to penetrate the country than the surveyors had. He had to return to New Westminster and head for the heart of Chilcotin country overland. Meanwhile a small contingent made up largely of marines guided by friendly Natives, entered the country from Bella Coola and had some success in killing Chilcotin men and destroying their villages. Cox brought a force of forty men, most of them USAmericans with an unfriendly attitude toward Indians, from Alexandria, and met twenty-seven men under the leadership of former HBC man Donald McLean at Soda Creek. This little army rode west to Tatla Lake. There they were joined by Brew and the governor and the coastal force of police and marines. The governor said that he was there to protect innocent Indians from the USAmericans. Donald McLean knew a lot about Indians. He had spies in the Chilcotin country. Since his HBC days he had become the first rancher around Hat Creek, and the owner of a roadhouse that serviced packers headed for the gold at Williams Creek. McLean told Cox that he would take care of Klatsassin and his fellows.

But this was to be Donald McLean's last experience with Indians. On July 17, 1864, while General Sherman was marching on Atlanta, McLean went out to reconnoitre above Tatla Lake. He had heard that a group of Chilcotins had been sighted up there. Sighting what he thought was a blind behind which his quarry would be hidden, McLean aimed his rifle at it. But there was another weapon aimed right at him from behind. McLean had fallen for a ruse designed by a Chilcotin warrior named Anukatlk. In a second he was lying dead, face down, his iron breastplate beneath him. His wife Sophia was pregnant with their last son at Hat Creek. McLean would not live to see the fifteen years of that boy's life.

A disagreement

The whole summer became drudgery, as the representatives of colonial justice searched the wide country for roving Chilcotin warriors. The Indians were weakened by the pox and starvation. With men attacking whites and fleeing gunmen, the Chilcotin fishery was not properly attended that summer. In the following winter, with the uprising staunched, there was not enough salmon for the Chilcotin women and children.

Meanwhile the white settlers and prospectors of the area between the coast and the Cariboo were calling for the extermination of the Chilcotins, for military action that would work faster than disease and land-grabs. But Seymour was jealous of his reputation as a protector of Indian rights. Judge Begbie redoubled his efforts to prevent US-style vigilantism. But Cox stayed true to his pragmatic method, as had been observed in Rock Creek and elsewhere. Without authority from the capital, he let it be known among the weary Natives in the Chilcotin country that he was offering an opportunity for talks. He sent the rebel leaders a gift of tobacco. Persuaded that he was protected by a truce, Klatsassin led his men into Cox's trap.

To show his faith, Klatsassin arrived on the morning of August 15 among the tents of Fort Chilcotin. He brought with him seven of his army, along with their families. They carried no weapons. The hungry Natives sat down in a row before Cox. Then, through an interpreter, the Klatsassin said that they had brought some captured animals, gold and money, as a signal of their readiness for negotiations. He explained that they would have brought more horses and mules, but that his people had been obliged to eat them. He pointed out that if Cox were to go to the site of the first great battle in his campaign he would see that the surveyors' equipment was still there. We do not want the invaders' machines, he said, and we do not want to till the soil. We want to be left alone to the way of life that was our ancestors'.

You do not understand, said Cox. You are under arrest. Behind the seated Indians stood a lot of white volunteers, complete with firearms. You are charged with serious crimes against the Crown. You are murderers.

We are warriors, said Klatsassin. We are speaking here not of crimes but of war. We are prepared to negotiate a truce and an end to the war.

In the name of the Queen, I am placing you under arrest, said Cox. You are my prisoners.

Cox saw to it that the eight men were bound and heavily guarded while he had a stockade built. Then he imprisoned them. A week later he took the prisoners to Alexandria. The families trailed after them. The prisoners were taken by steamer to Quesnellemouth, where they were shackled and placed inside a log jail. The jail was surrounded by white men with guns.

At the end of September Judge Begbie arrived. He knew enough about Native life to understand that the Chilcotins would have interpretations of the events that would differ sharply from British views. But he was also a rationalist, and saw his role as the bringer of a new order to the land. Begbie was agonized, but he knew that he had a future to take care of. He conducted the trial and tried to explain the whites' system to the prisoners. Finally he condemned five of the warriors to be hanged. After the sentence he went to visit the manacled men and asked them why they had surrendered. Klatsassin explained hunger. He said that the gift of tobacco was in his eyes a guarantee of safety and an implication of peace. In his letter to the governor, Begbie said that Klatsassin was the most intelligent and noble Indian he had met. He told the governor that he did not envy him his final decision regarding the possibility of clemency. On the one hand, even the newspapers had been unhappy about Cox's tactics; on the other, a message had to be sent to the surviving aborigines.

In the morning of October 26, Klatsassin and his four companions were hanged on a single scaffold at Quesnellemouth. This spectacular event was watched by a crowd of Indians, most of them Carrier, who had been encouraged to attend. It was a normal educative move on the part of the colony's keepers of the law.

Alfred Waddington never gave up his fixation on Bute Inlet. In a few years he would be in Ottawa, trying to persuade the Canadian government to run a railroad across the continent to his little settlement at the bottom of the Homathko River. But he did not live to see that fancy come true. In an end that would appear to some people to be ironic and others to be the hand of a spirit, Waddington caught smallpox in Ottawa, and died there in 1872.

Canada?

Governor Seymour was in England, bragging about the riches in his colony, while in Victoria ex-governor Douglas was bemoaning the union. Miners were departing the gold fields of Williams Creek, the Kootenays and the Big Bend, which had acquired the nickname, the "Big Bust." The new gold town of Seymour on Shuswap Lake was a ghost town before it was built. When Seymour came back to New Westminster to assume his expanded role, his unified colony was almost a million and a half dollars in debt.

In London there were a lot of politicians and bankers who wondered how long Britain should bother pouring money into British Columbia. In Moscow there was a lot of sympathy for the idea of cutting Russia's losses in Alaska. In Washington, now that the Civil War was over and great fortunes had been made in various quarters, there was a lot of talk about the resumption of US expansion. While the British and Russians might have been looking at the Pacific northwest in terms of financial drainage, the USAmericans were thinking of the region in terms of strategy. They saw that the British had over the centuries turned the Atlantic into their Mediterranean; now it was time to envision the Pacific as a US sea. Through the sixties the US secretary of state, William Henry Seward, had been trying to work a deal. At the end of the Civil War there were some voices in Washington that insisted that while they were at it the USAmericans should reopen their claims for the whole shebang, claiming British Columbia as war reparations for British interference in their national war.

Canadianists on the west coast reminded London that Alaska was for sale, and urged the British government to put in a bid. We don't need any more expenses in that far part of the world, said the government. But there is probably a lot of gold up there, said the British Columbians. Mr. Seymour's claims about gold do not seem to be panning out these days, said the British government. [Expletive deleted], said the subjects on the coast.

On March 29, 1867, the British North America Act, confederating Nova Scotia, New Brunswick and the Canadas, was given royal assent. The next day, Russia sold Alaska to the United States.

In New Westminster Governor Seymour was drinking a lot. Rumour had it that the first prime minister of the new confederation tipped a few, too. But Seymour was beset by enemies who were encouraged by his apparent physical decline. It was bruited about that he suffered from dysentery picked up in his earlier postings, and that alcohol was not a good cure for tropical diseases. A notable defeat for the governor came when Dr. Helmcken, urged on by the retired but resentful Douglas, introduced a motion in the legislature that

Victoria be made the capital of the combined colony. Seymour argued that Douglas had built New Westminster and that the strategic city was meant all along to be the seat of government. The vote went thirteen to eight in Victoria's favour.

Meanwhile, the USAmericans were building a railroad across their country, to link New York and San Francisco. British Columbians who felt encased between Washington and Alaska saw unhappy implications in that enterprise, especially when the news came that another railroad was going to be stretched across the northern states.

The people of British Columbia (or rather the white businessmen and politicians of British Columbia) now faced their famous choice among three prospects. They could go on as they now were, as a British colony hoping for a little more independence and a lot more economic assistance. They could look across the high mountains and wide prairies, and petition for membership in the new confederation. Or they could throw up their hands and agree that the US destiny was indeed manifest.

The USAmericans had a big army at the end of the Civil War, and railroad czars had made a killing building trains to supply their troops in that dramatic historical conflict. Washington saw a robust and profitable future. Their biggest poet Walt Whitman assumed that Cuba and Canada would hurry to the welcoming arms of the republic. And "what I assume you shall assume," he sang. There may not have been a lot of poetry-readers among the businessmen of Victoria, but there were a lot of USAmericans. The US consul sent despatches to Washington, advising that things were looking good. More and more, the United States seemed to be a lot closer to Victoria than Canada was. At the end of the twentieth century only the methods would be changed—citizens of the Okanagan Valley, for example, would be using satellite dishes to watch US television, abjuring the cable companies that offered Canadian channels; and a tourist scouting the drugstores and supermarkets for the most prominent Canadian magazines would return to his automobile empty-handed.

The British in the colony looked on the two new alternatives with distaste. They were not fond of the USAmerican option, because they saw their jobs disappearing to a rabble of business-oriented democrats. They looked down at the recently arrived Canadians as the families that had emigrated to the Canadas, lower-class folk who had crossed the Atlantic not to establish Imperial Order but to hack out a living they could not achieve in Britain. The notion that they might rise to political power was revolting to some poobahs.

But the nationalists had some powerful champions. Even before the unification of the two colonies, Dr. Tolmie had risen in the assembly of Vancouver's Island and spoken out for the dream of confederation, suggesting that the west coast might be a logical member of the Maritime union they were edging toward back east. In May of 1867, Amor de Cosmos got a resolution passed in the combined legislature, calling upon Governor Seymour to start in motion a petition to the new government back east. Seymour was not a big fan of the idea. He was running his last colony, and he was eating well. Like Douglas before him, he did not feel much like doing anything suggested by the obstreperous Nova Scotian de Cosmos.

So de Cosmos and his associates, among them John Robson and R.W.W. Carrall, representative from the Cariboo, formed a group called the Confederation League. Shortly after the official transfer of the capital to Victoria confirmed a significant defeat for Seymour, the League held its first big meeting at Yale, in September of 1868. The USAmericans and the snooty Brits in Victoria were alarmed to see the number of prominent men who attended the convention. One could not blame citizens on either side for seeing the Yale convention as an omen. As soon as the meetings broke up, Barkerville, the nugget of the mainland, went up in flames. In less than a month, Government Street, the business centre of the Island, burned to the ground.

Coast to coast

John A. Macdonald, the prime minister of the new confederation, was already acting as if British Columbia were part of his domain. The prospect of the colony's dropping into the republic's poke filled him with dismay. For their part, the USAmericans, fond of remembering their war of independence, and resentful about British sympathy for the south in their civil war, wanted to do everything they could to prevent the threat of a British corridor from ocean to ocean. They liked the idea of Alaska as the other half of the nutcracker.

Macdonald did not think much of Governor Seymour—drinks too much, has not built a railroad, gets pushed around by foreigners with property. The Canadian prime minister wrote a letter to the imperial government, suggesting that Seymour be recalled and replaced by Anthony Musgrave, who was in his last days as governor of the colony of Newfoundland, and was a fervent supporter of confederation for the North American colonies. Seymour knew nothing of these machinations. He was at the north coast of his colony, making a personal appearance. Having shown his leadership in the field during the Chilcotin War, he now purposed to demonstrate his ability as a conciliator between warring Native groups. He had from time to time had success in settling small disputes between Natives, and no doubt enjoyed his role, contrasting it to his failure to settle animosities between the white factions in his own house.

So here he was in May of 1869, up the coast again. At Nass River he calmed things between the Tsimshians and their nearby antagonists, made a speech, mimed some Indian gestures, and set sail for the Queen Charlottes. At Skidegate in early June he settled a squabble that he attributed to Yankee whiskey traders, then made his course for another dispute at Bella Coola. But he could hardly make it aboard his ship, *Sparrowhawk*, for the southward trip. His old dysentery, plus the medication he favoured, laid him in his shipboard bed, and the vessel bypassed Bella Coola, proceeding instead to Victoria, carrying the deceased body of the governor. In Victoria Seymour was given a magnificent funeral. Sir James Douglas was the tallest of the pallbearers who carried his bier from Christ Church Cathedral.

In Ottawa, John A. Macdonald drank a toast to the departed governor, and ordered that a cable be sent, announcing that British Columbia's new governor was to be Anthony Musgrave. There were those on the west coast who wondered about the legality of the announcement: how was it that the prime minister of Canada seemed to be in charge of their political disposition? It was a feeling that would never go away in British Columbia. Of course Macdonald was acting with the approval of the Empire, but some Brits and some USAmericans in Victoria did not like the look of things. Canadianists in the colony, however, welcomed the advent of the confederation man. They saw in his appointment a new view in London. Maybe the tea-drinking clique in Victoria would give way to native sons, and maybe the Yanks would be held at bay. More important: maybe the change would mean better economic times in British Columbia. The arrival of Musgrave coincided with the amazing rebuilding of Barkerville.

But in San Francisco, trains were arriving with goods from New York and New Orleans. James Douglas's wagon road to Rock Creek was set into perspective. When Governor Musgrave travelled westward across the continent, he did it on the Union Pacific, thence sailing to Vancouver Island.

Victoria to Ottawa

Musgrave had once been personal secretary to Seymour in Antigua. He knew how to get along with people. In sending him to Victoria, Macdonald and the Colonial Office thought about that ability as much as they thought about Musgrave's espousal of confederation. The opposing sides in British Columbia found him affable and reasonable, and gave him more leeway than they had offered to his predecessor. In return he listened to their positions, the pro-US people, the British clique and the Canadianists, from the hotheads such as de Cosmos, to the gradualists such as John Helmcken. When he reported to Ottawa and London, he informed them that there was support for British North America, but it would cost money and a railway link to the east. A wagon road would be useful, too. The Crown colony satraps would have to be offered pleasant pensions. There would have to be cash grants for private enterprisers. If Victoria would never again be a free port, Ottawa had better make tracks across the land. And the journalists would insist that the legislature of the new province would have to get rid of its appointed positions in favour of fully representational government.

In Ottawa a lot of people who were administering a new country said that they could not afford distant British Columbia. Other people in London told them to listen to Mr. Musgrave. Send your negotiators, said Ottawa. Musgrave sent Dr. Helmcken, Joseph Trutch and his wife, and Dr. Carrall. The *Colonist* sent its fiery democratist editor Henry Seelye, with instructions to get there first and soften up the opposition. In May of 1870 the British Columbia negotiators sailed to Victoria on the *Active*, did some sightseeing and shopping in San Francisco, and boarded a sumptuous first-class carriage on the Central Pacific, for an instructive train ride across the United States.

John Robson and Amor de Cosmos, the champions of legislative reform, knew that there was a message in the fact that they were not chosen for the delegation. The three men and one woman on board the USAmerican train were not radicals. In fact Dr. Helmcken was a noted opponent of new-fangled USAmerican ideas such as responsible and representative government. The people on the train were not pleased by the fact that Seelye the newspaper man would get to Ottawa before them, and use his reportorial privilege as a way to represent the democrats on the west coast.

It is worth noting that there was no election or plebiscite on the matter of applying for union with Canada. If there was going to be representative government, it would wait till later. And the First Nations people now circled by the boundaries of the British colony were not consulted as to their preference. Very few of them knew that in a year's time they would become wards of an unimaginable organization in a place with a name that sounded Algonquian.

Confederation men

Anthony Musgrave the confederation man made himself popular quickly. He had seen service in the West Indies, and so joined an unofficial club of Caribbean veterans in the Victoria establishment. One of his sisters married one of Commissioner Trutch's brothers. And he did not come on as a governor from the Old Country. He was born a colonial child, and spent his boyhood in the western hemisphere. British Columbia's attorney general, Henry Pering Pellew Crease, who himself had been a boy in British Guiana, and whose mother had African blood, welcomed his new boss, referring to him occasionally as a "Creole." It was almost as if Musgrave were gathering votes. He promptly married a prominent USAmerican woman.

Meanwhile, forces outside the colony continued to eat up the north Pacific. Russia may have sold Alaska, but Russians were pouring into China. The USAmericans had forced open the bays of Japan, and were sending flotillas of trading ships to the Far East. In the South Pacific the French were consolidating their hegemony. Britain also had concerns closer to home: Bismarck's Second Reich would be the greatest power in Europe by 1871. In London there was a lot of sentiment for letting the distant colony go. There was also an imperial feeling for securing a Canada that would face the Pacific.

For a short while Crease and others in Victoria fancied a fourth alternative for their colony: an independent country. It would be a pretty big country. The thought died early.

So white British Columbians were eager to hear about the negotiations in Ottawa during 1870. The governor received reports from Helmcken, Carrall and Trutch. They usually arrived after Seelye's despatches to his newspaper, detailing his success at advocating representative democracy. The *Colonist* of Wednesday, July 20, 1870, however, appeared two days after Helmcken's return from Ottawa. The paper ran an article called "The Terms of Union." Seelye explained that while the delegates at the meetings had not been authorized to make the terms public, a journalist from the Toronto *Star* had them "on authority." This process would in the next century be called "a leak."

Businessmen and politicians in Victoria would be pleased to read the terms. Ottawa was going to assume the new province's debt. Annual grants would support the legislature, and the governor and all federal agencies would be financed by Canada. Unnecessary officials of the current administration would receive hefty pensions. There would be a modern dock built in Esquimalt, and regular steamers plying the sea between there and San Francisco. There would be a hundred-million-dollar railroad built between the coast and Ontario. All officials would be accountable and representative. There would be six members of parliament and three senators, two-thirds the numbers requested by Helmcken.

"The remaining terms," wrote Seelye, "are unimportant. They refer to the extension of the postal service, the erection of a Hospital, a Lunatic Asylum, and a Penitentiary, Protection of the Fisheries, aid to Immigration, the election of Senators, the formal admission of the colony in to the Union, the defense of the colony and aid to the volunteer force." If these matters were considered unimportant, one might assume, the debt and the railroad must have been very big items indeed.

As it turned out, the terms were slightly different, but the main points were as reported. Victorians saw the railroad and the nationalization of the debt as great triumphs. But just as the British government had in recent times come to favour moves that the west coasters later thought they were wresting, so in this case, the Dominion government was already thinking of the necessity for a railroad into the west. For one thing, the building of an intercolonial railway was one of the terms of the 1867 Constitution Act. For another, Louis Riel had formed a government of Red River in 1869, just when Canada was thinking of gathering the eastern prairies to its union. Who knew when he or his friends might try something like that again, further west? A railroad would be as useful to federal forces there as it had been to US Union forces going south earlier in the decade.

Now Ottawa was telling Victoria that the USAmerican method would be followed: the railroad would be built from both ends toward the Continental Divide. This way we could have our own golden spike, and workers and contractors in British Columbia would benefit from the activity.

"Will this iron horse be running on tracks across Indian lands?" asked several Native spokesmen in British Columbia and the Northwest Territory.

There is no such thing, they were told.

According to the terms of union, the railroad would be built by 1881. Intelligent people pointed out that a Canadian transcontinental railroad, almost 2,000 kilometres longer than the US one, would be a fantastic expense for a country of 3.5 million citizens. Political people were more abundant in the House of Commons than were intelligent ones. Thank goodness for that, we say now.

So Mr. Trutch showed his hosts in Ottawa a map of the future province, running his finger down the Thompson and Fraser rivers and explaining how easy it would be to run a railroad down these gentle waterways. Simon Fraser and David Thompson held their sides and tried not to burst into laughter up there in explorer heaven. But the federal delegates smiled, and promised to begin the railroad in two years. They promised to spend a million dollars a year on British Columbia's part of the project. They said that the locomotives would be rolling into town at the end of the decade. All British Columbia had to do was grant a strip of land twenty miles to each side of the tracks to the railroad, and Ottawa would even recompense the province $100,000 a year forever.

In November of 1870 there was an election in British Columbia, and supporters of confederation were returned in every riding. On January 5, 1871, the legislative council met and to a man approved the terms of union. The council did not fete the governor's delegates to Ottawa; but Ottawa showed its happiness with the arrangement. Robert Carrall would be appointed to the Senate, and Joseph Trutch would be appointed as the new province's first lieutenant-governor. Meanwhile John Helmcken would resume his place as the most successful doctor in British Columbia, and Henry Seelye his as the most influential journalist.

So British Columbia was now part of Canada. As the gold petered out in the Interior, a lot of the USAmericans and other foreigners went back south of the line, where the railroads were bringing postwar prosperity to the western United States. In the province it was time to replace tents and shacks with stone buildings, to replace rambunctious US-style saloons with opera houses, to raise big families in a place as much like the memory of Britain as possible.

But this was part of the British Empire, after all, and in its colonial nature, the new province resembled other outposts of London's hegemony more than it did the home country. The indigenous people, though their population had been cut to 25,000, still outnumbered the newcomers. The next biggest group was, indeed, British, but most of them were men. What white females there were were married or children—except for the upstairs ladies in the saloons of Victoria and Barkerville. Middle-class women were expected to be in charge of respectable Victorian homes. Farm women were expected to toil in the fields and the kitchens. They were also kept busy giving birth to new Canadians. In the 1870s, especially on ranches or other worksites far from the big towns, half those new Canadians would not be expected to reach adulthood. The more children a wife had, the more likely the farm or the home were to stay in family hands.

But one of the girl babies born in Victoria in 1871 was Emily Carr.

Government men

None of those women would be able to vote. For one thing, until 1876 only property-holders were allowed to vote, and even were a woman to somehow become a property-owner, she would not fulfil the requirements for suffrage. Susan B. Anthony gave a talk about democracy in Victoria in 1871, but the Brits in town pointed out that she was a USAmerican with radical ideas. In 1874 a provincial bill was passed to exclude Indians and Chinese specifically from the franchise. In 1876 a provincial bill was passed to establish "full" male suffrage. This meant that if you were a white man over twenty-one, and a British subject who had resided in British Columbia for a year, and had not moved lately, you could vote in provincial elections. If you were an Indian man with land extending as far as the eye could see, you could forget it. If you were a Chinese gold panner, you might as well stay at the creek on election day. If you were a woman and the strongest human being at your cattle ranch, you might tell your husband how to vote, but there were likely chores that needed your attention.

Ottawa was a long way away by US train, so the most successful businessmen and the most ardent politicos in the west coast province were too busy to become members of parliament. That job was left for men who did not have anything better to do. There were no memorable MPs from B.C. People in the province would always be more interested in their provincial politicians than in their federal ones. It would be well over a century before they would send a prime minister to Ottawa, and when that prime minister first tried to be elected to that job, she would lose her seat. In the early days, the successful businessmen and ardent politicos vied for chairs in the new "fully-representative" provincial legislature. Amor de Cosmos and John

Robson were MLAs. But the honour of being British Columbia's first premier fell to an Irish lawyer from Australia who had just recently made his first step into politics, John McCreight. A little over a year later he lost a vote of non-confidence, and resigned his premiership. An obscure lake was named after him. He was not really suited to be premier of British Columbia, to hold down the job that would go so often to men who would look good wearing big red putty noses. As his biographer Patricia Johnson put it: "He stood for discipline in an era of self-expression, and for principle rather than personality." McCreight would become a supreme court judge, and then retire to the south coast of England.

In its first thirty-two years British Columbia would have fifteen premiers. The successor to McCreight certainly knew a thing or two about self-expression and personality. This was Mr. Amor de Cosmos. Mr. Amor de Cosmos liked a noisy room, and was not loath to create the noise himself. He was the first B.C. political leader to be born in Canada, and his vision of confederation did not allow for interference from the Crown. He chased Lieutenant-Governor Trutch out of his cabinet meetings because he saw Trutch as the representative of the Brits in Victoria. No lieutenant-governor has tried to sit in on the affairs of government since that time.

Everyone knew everyone. When an election was called, perhaps five thousand votes would be tabulated. The fifteen cabinets chosen by the aforesaid fifteen premiers were made up of familiar men who got older with the century and consolidated their power and influence. In those thirty-two years only forty men were members of cabinet in B.C. In the last third of the nineteenth century the legislature was an old-boys' club. When a man was asked to be premier, he would choose a cabinet that expressed his particular interests. There might be party politics in the rest of Canada, and the nonentities who went to Ottawa to represent B.C. interests might be elected from party slates, but Victoria was wrapped up just about as tightly as it had been by the Hudson's Bay Company.

The Spike at Last

"The opening by us first of a North Pacific Railroad seals
the destiny of British possessions west of the 91st meridian.
Annexation will be but a question of time."
—US Senate, 1869

Our home on Native land

In all the negotiations that led to British Columbia's entry into
Confederation, no one ever asked the people who formed a majority of
the area's population how they liked the idea. In the debate leading up to
union the First Nations were not a hot topic. Someone proposed a bill that
would protect the interests of the Native people at Confederation. It was
defeated twenty to one. Then someone proposed a bill that would see to it
that Canadian treatment of Indians replaced the colonial system. The legislators would not even consider voting on that one. When the negotiators
went to Ottawa to present British Columbia's case, they were not carrying
any ideas about a place for Natives in the new democracy. It was only as a
consequence of Ottawa's initiative that there was an Indian clause in the
Act. It was the thirteenth of fourteen clauses, coming right after the one
about creating a new dock in Esquimalt. Its terms did not promise a bright
new day for the original human beings of the new province:

> The charge of the Indians, and the trusteeship and management of
> the lands reserved for their use and benefit, shall be assumed by the
> Dominion Government, and a policy as liberal as that hitherto pur-
> sued by the British Columbia Government shall be continued by
> the Dominion Government after the union.

Gee whizz, a Native fisher dipping his net into the part of the creek that did not go through someone's ranch might have said, as liberal as that?

> To carry out such a policy, tracts of land of such an extent as it has hitherto been the practice of the British Columbia Government to appropriate for that purpose, shall from time to time be conveyed by the Local Government to the Dominion Government in trust for the use and benefit of the Indians, on application of the Dominion Government; and in case of disagreement between the two Governments respecting the quantity of such tracts of land to be so granted, the matter shall be referred for the decision of the Secretary of State for the Colonies.

There was, one might have noticed, no mention of the "treaties" being offered and signed in other parts of British North America. Here in British Columbia, the Haida and the Okanagan and the Tsimshian and the Carrier would have to depend on the largesse of those newcomers who used to say that they just wanted the fur off the animals, but who now showed a deep interest in the ground under their feet. "A policy as liberal as that hitherto pursued by the British Columbia Government" was an astute political phrase. It was like smoke between the fingers. It was like a horse on a raft.

The first Indian "reserves" came about in a disorganized fashion. An eastern Indian who had once worked for the Hudson's Bay Company, J. Baptiste Lolo, popularly known as St. Paul, had occupied the abandoned fort north of the Thompson when Fort Kamloops was moved to the south side. Eventually his settlement would be looked on by the whites as a reserve. Magistrate Cox was soon given the task of defining the term and assigning the lands in question. Things were easier in other parts of British North America, where whites had "purchased" land from Native "owners" or forced treaties after wars with the aborigines. Some Indians on Vancouver Island sold plots to the white administration, but in most of the new province there would be no treaties or bills of sale, and no "treaty Indians." The reserve system would start on dubious legal principles.

In any case, Magistrate Cox had been charged in the early sixties with setting aside Indian reserve land in the ranch country along the Thompson River. He used somewhat vague terms in doing so, and as the economy changed more and more from fur to cattle, he faced the prospect of more and more white immigration, so the vagueness came in handy. Reserves were made smaller, and sometimes moved, because certain Indian lands looked as if they would make good ranch country. The same white people who figured that the Indians would become extinct, went around saying that the Indians were not using the land that had been set aside for them. They thought, or pretended to think, that land was not being used unless it was being cultivated. This despite the fact that ranchers grazed a lot more land than they broke.

The first man to start a ranch on land pre-empted for that purpose had been Donald McLean, former HBC man, who set up his 160 acres beside the Cariboo road at Hat Creek in 1860. He was followed by a few others and then a trickle and then a stream of ranchers, who had a gold rush to feed. By 1870 most of the good bottom land in the Kamloops region was sewn up. Around that time the provincial government was persuaded that ranchers east of the Cascades needed more than 160 acres, so their pre-emptions were doubled, to 320 acres a family. Then Crown land was leased, and the bigger ranchers started to graze cattle on permits. The more successful ranchers, of course, also bought up the pre-emptions of those who could not make the grade.

Meanwhile the Native peoples were being allotted 10 acres per family. This number does not seem all that liberal when compared with the 80 acres allotted to a Native family by the Canadian government where it prevailed. Soon after confederation the province agreed to a doubling of the figure. Any Indian family ought to be able to survive on 20 acres, as long as they did not pursue traditional Native economies of hunting and gathering, and as long as they did not expect to go into ranching, for which white people needed 320 acres a family.

In 1872 the first Indian commissioner was appointed. This was Dr. Israel W. Powell, a friend of John A. Macdonald and a former running mate of Amor de Cosmos. He was a Canadian. He had operated on Governor Musgrave's broken leg. He was going to make a lot of money in Vancouver real estate. He would be the first chancellor of the first university in the province. On a boat trip up the coast in 1881 he would get a lake and river named after him. Dr. Powell was exemplary of the kind of energetic busybody the new province needed to get it on the track to civilization. Over his years on the Coast he would be in charge of the ministries responsible for education, medicine and Indian affairs. He held military rank in the reserves. He made house calls.

Indian Commissioner Powell was always overworked, and he revelled in the condition. Now he was in charge of Indian welfare over the immense province. He was also supposed to gather Native artefacts for the National Museum. Up and down the huge valleys he would have to ride, sometimes stopping to have a chat with Judge Begbie. Dr. Powell was no patrician. He was, though, the first McGill medical school graduate to operate in B.C. And he was the closest thing to a gentleman that smalltown Ontario could produce. Now he tried to run the Indian Affairs ministry from Victoria, while he continued his medical practice. In 1873 he recommended that the Indian family's allotment east of the Cascades be doubled to forty acres because they were engaged in the raising of horses and cattle.

The newspapers were not campaigning for any such thing. They were warning about Indian uprisings every time news came of unrest. How did Attorney General George A. Walkem respond to Dr. Powell's suggestion? He said that the Indian reserves were "in some cases enormous, and in all cases sufficient." They needed cutting back. Especially because the Indians were a doomed race and immigration was not going to stop in the near future, especially with the railroad coming.

The First Nations people, especially those in the southern half of the province, must have felt that their disappearance was a distinct possibility. First the Scotsmen came and thinned out the fur-bearing animals. Then the ranchers came and put cattle spreads where game used to come to water. When an Indian mentioned that he was having a hard time raising a family on disappearing game in shrinking territory, the occupying forces told him to step into the nineteenth century—settle down and take up farming. But do it on little pieces of the land that whites did not want—yet. And while we're here, we would like to take those reed bowls back to Ottawa, to preserve the Native way of life in a museum.

Once our land is all gone, we will not exist, thought the Native people. Once those people cease to exist we will no longer have to bother ourselves with the Indian land question, thought the white government men and businessmen.

Still, the Indians were there for the meantime, and someone had to deal with them, either out of whatever conscience exists in colonial space, or out of fear for another Chilcotin War. In 1874 the federal government saw how busy Dr. Powell was, and decided that British Columbia needed two Indian commissioners, one to send directives from Victoria and oversee coastal matters, the other to be headquartered in New Westminster to take charge of mainland policies. This time the federal appointment must have persuaded the Native peoples that the white man was indeed a mystery never to be understood by rational folk. Ottawa chose for the mainland superintendent one James Lenihan, a businessman in Toronto. Lenihan must have had relatives in power; he knew nothing about Indians and nothing about British Columbia. Furthermore, he was a mental defective, according to all reports of the time. Indians walked out of meetings shaking their heads. During the 1870s the Thompson valley was a tense area in race relations. Every time James Lenihan went into a meeting with Native spokesmen he inadvertently insulted them by saying the wrong thing. The Indians resorted to public ridicule of the Toronto man.

Such was the state of Indian affairs in British Columbia in the 1870s.

Waitin' for the train

The transcontinental train was the greatest threat to the Native people. The government of Canada and the government of British Columbia had agreed to give a wide swath of land to the private company building the line. The men building the track would cut across animal migration paths and dump rock into salmon runs. A thousand immigrants a year were coming into the province, looking for jobs in the surveys being run eastward from the coast. Surveyors and railroad workers were going to demand red meat, and that would mean more white-owned cows, which in turn would need more range grass. When the railroad was completed the trains would be used to transport cows to markets east and west, and the cattle business would spread in every direction.

The future looked like a locomotive.

And if these white men could build a train track from the coast to the prairies, they must be persistent and powerful.

Looked at from a distance, the topographical map of the province seemed as forbidding to rail man as it was to fur collector. Seen up close, it might be even more forbidding. There were surveyors making lines from various starting points, including Bute Inlet, where the Chilcotin War had started. Surveyors felt merciless thorns in their eyes. They fell down shale embankments. Insects made their fingers swell. Obdurate bushes clung to rocky scarps. Money fell into windy canyons. The only way one could do the work these labourers and engineers were doing was to forget the long-range hopes, and bend your head to the weather and land surface of that day. Sweat and curse and see the same ridge you were looking at yesterday.

Amor de Railroad

Anyone who went to school in western Canada knows how important the railroad was to our huge country. If you went to school in British Columbia in the middle of the twentieth century, there were two things you heard about in Canadian history. One was the organization of New France before the Plains of Abraham. The other was Confederation. In British Columbia Confederation was another word for railroad.

In the 1870s it became clearer and clearer to British Columbians that the railroad was going to take longer than ten years. Apparently there were Herculian battles going on in Ottawa about funding and engineers and Conservative majorities. In the province there were surveyors running through money and crawling through bush. Sir John A. Macdonald was still a good friend, but Sir John A. would not live forever, and some people began to think that that was how long it would take to see the tracks. The tracks were supposed to end and begin in Esquimalt, wherefrom ships would carry Canadian goods to the world.

Then during the election campaign of 1872 Sir John A. got drunk a lot, and while he was drunk he accepted a lot of campaign funding that he should have refused. This campaign funding came from the people who were expected to get the contract to build the transcontinental railroad. In Ottawa this turn of events was called the Pacific Scandal, and the Pacific Scandal was in the newspapers a lot. Sir John A. Macdonald and his government had to resign in 1873. This was not good news for Amor de Cosmos and the other Canadianists in Victoria. The second prime minister of Canada was Alexander Mackenzie, Liberal. His oratory in the House of Commons had not been restrained. He called Macdonald many colourful names, and denounced his railroad plans as the financial enslavement of Canadians. He loved the Pacific Scandal. He never had anything nice to say about British Columbia. He said that British Columbians were a small bunch of eccentric and lazy people who did not exhibit Canadian (read Scottish) values of thrift and stick-to-it-ness. There is much of that sentiment expressed at power breakfasts in downtown Toronto to this day.

In any case, Alexander Mackenzie was no Alexander Mackenzie. In 1793 the explorer had been the first Scotsman to cross the challenging country to view the Pacific. He said that he had blazed the path to "the markets of the four quarters of the globe." Now eighty years later this ersatz Mackenzie was saying that the enterprise was not worth it, that the whole province of British Columbia was an impassable maelstrom of nature with a negligible population. Of the deal that promised a railroad for union, the new prime minister said in a speech in Sarnia, it was "a bargain made to be broken." What an interesting concept to be promulgated by a nation's chief administrator!

British Columbians were forming opinions of easterners that would remain for some time, too. They wanted their railroad, and they kept showing people the Terms of Union. When Amor de Cosmos suggested a compromise, some alteration in the rail guarantee in exchange for money to get the Esquimalt dry dock built, he spelled the end of his short premiership. A crowd of politicians and drinkers marched on the legislature, shouting rude verses and waving a noose. Amor de Cosmos hid out in a back room. Pistol-toting men swarmed into the hall, sprawled in seats and commenced to make crude noises. They demanded that the speaker recognize them as the new people's government. The normal legislators had fled the hall. Two days later they returned and passed a resolution forbidding any change in article eleven, the railroad promise. Not long after that a resolution was entered to call for an end to political moonlighting—no man would be allowed to sit in both the provincial legislature and the Dominion House of Commons. Amor de Cosmos gave up his premiership and his Victoria seat, and decided to be the great spokesman for British Columbia in Ottawa. He was replaced in the premier's chair by the attorney general, George A. Walkem, who would represent the Cariboo and the forces who called themselves the

Terms of Union Preservation League. One should remember that British Columbia was run by a small group of men who formed various temporary alliances from time to time. Most of them became somewhat wealthy in the meantime.

Prime Minister Mackenzie and the Liberals had the misfortune of arriving at power just when Canadian economies began a nosedive. Fear swept through banks and governments and the confederation business. Consequently, Mackenzie's administration was seen as timid and feckless, especially from a west coast perspective. His predecessor cut down on his drinking and began to organize a network of powerbrokers who were unhappy with continentalism, and wanted to keep Canada British. They advocated higher tariffs where there had been reciprocity for twenty years. The Liberals would be stuck with their favouring of free trade, and victims of their reluctance to try great Canadian initiatives.

For the election of 1878, the City of Victoria was proud to provide a highly symbolic constituency for their champion, John A. Macdonald. James Douglas, their great founder, had died the year before, and flags had sagged at half-mast. Now the great new Islander Macdonald would win the election and remain prime minister for the rest of his life.

Carnarvon

There had been a third interested party to the Terms of Union. Victoria and Ottawa were both still tied to London. In 1874 the bad words that were exchanged between Walkem and Mackenzie needed some sort of referee, or at least an ear that could profess indifference while promising financial support. This ear would belong to Lord Carnarvon, the colonial secretary. Carnarvon had been for some time wound into the histories of the province and the country. In 1858, for instance, he had persuaded his fellow lords to approve the British Columbia Act, and in 1867 he had brought the British North America Act into parliament. In July of 1874 he offered to mediate the argument between Walkem and Mackenzie. The first rule would be that the disputants would agree beforehand to accept the colonial secretary's decision. Walkem hesitated, thinking that Carnarvon might favour the confederation he had helped create. Mackenzie demurred, assuming that Carnarvon would throw his weight behind the province he had had a hand in manufacturing. Mackenzie had been advised that Walkem would not last much longer as premier of B.C. Walkem, meanwhile, was expecting Mackenzie to fall from power.

The men in Ottawa and the men in Victoria called each other names. This was called post-confederation politics.

Eventually Carnarvon's terms were accepted by both sides, and they went to London to lobby the lord and his advisers. When Carnarvon's decision came down, it seemed to offer assurances to Victoria and breathing space to Ottawa. It became, in effect, a more cautious replacement for article eleven of the Terms of Union. The date for the completion of the CPR was pushed back to the last day of 1890, more than sixteen years away. But the Dominion government would begin immediately on the building of the segment running between Esquimalt and Nanaimo. On the mainland the surveyors would be vigorously traversing the country, and a wagon road would be built along the future rail line, from the territorial border, across B.C. to the sea. As soon as the surveys were finished, the Dominion government would spend at least two million dollars a year on construction.

Businessmen and politicians in Victoria grumbled in public and winked at each other in their panelled rooms.

The bill to bankroll the Island's E&N Railroad got through the House of Commons in Ottawa, but it was defeated in the Senate.

Businessmen and politicians in Victoria were incensed. They suspected that Mackenzie had rigged the senate vote. The prime minister would be able to shrug his shoulders and claim that he had tried. Voices in Victoria enunciated the word "separation" more than ever. Confederation would not look very good if it began to fall apart after seven years. The governor-general, Lord Dufferin, came to the Coast in the spring of 1876, via a USAmerican train, to show the flag and assure the malcontents. When he debarked in Victoria, he saw an arch sporting the words "Carnarvon Terms Or Separation" over the street. Smiling, he ordered his carriage to take another route to his vice-regal quarters. He smiled all the time that he was in the province. British Columbians did settle down. Later they would name streets and hotels after Dufferin as well as Carnarvon.

Back east the newspapers had a lot of fun with the noisy and overweening west coast citizens. Newspapers and magazines published political cartoons that portrayed the federal government as patient suitor to a petulant creature representing British Columbia. Almost always this latter was portrayed as a spoiled young woman. Easterners were being taught that the railroad was a bribe or an overly expensive bauble demanded by a self-occupied debutant.

This image would be perpetuated by the Newfoundland-Ontario poet E.J. Pratt, in his short comic epic poem, *Towards the Last Spike*, published in 1952, three years after the poet's home province had joined Confederation. Pratt's famous poem is subtitled "A verse-panorama of the struggle to build the first Canadian transcontinental from the time of the proposed terms of union with British Columbia (1870) to the hammering of the last spike in the Eagle Pass (1885)." Pratt probably did not imagine that British Columbians might think about them as "terms of union with the Dominion of Canada." (In 1995, another Ontario poet published an article about "three highways that cross British Columbia." In this poet's mind the highways start at their eastern parts and come to an end at salt water; he probably did not imagine that most British Columbians might think that they start in the Pacific and climb eastward.) In a section of the poem called "Threats of Secession," Pratt portrays the woman as no longer in the flush of youth, as doubting the sincerity of her betrothed:

> The Lady's face was flushed. Thirteen years now
> Since that engagement ring adorned her finger!
> Adorned? Betrayed. She often took it off
> And flung it angrily upon the dresser,
> Then took excursions with her sailor-lover.
> Had that man with a throat like Ottawa,
> That tailored suitor in a cut-away,
> Presumed compliance on her part? High time
> To snub him for delay—for was not time
> The marrow of agreement? At the mirror
> She tried to cream a wrinkle from her forehead,
> Toyed with the ring, replaced it and removed it,
> Harder, she thought, to get it on and off—

The sexual imagery runs all through Pratt's poem. The railroad men, politicians or engineers, are heroic males, many of them Scottish. The two greatest geographical challenges to the track are the Laurentian Shield, portrayed here as a giant female dragon, and the huge mountains west of the prairies, which are attacked with dynamite and huge drills, the heroic men boring holes into the resisting rock.

The soul trade

The shameful British Columbia reserve system was not the only means by which the whites controlled the Native peoples of British Columbia while they were waiting for them to disappear. The introductions of pestilent diseases and land practices were not the only ways to keep their numbers down and disrupt their ancestral spiritual and economic practices. There were also the churches. The vast area of British Columbia had been marked off for the harvesting of souls since the Oblate priests had followed the fur traders into New Caledonia at mid-century. The first priests to observe the opportunity for converts were those who had accompanied Spanish explorers in the 1790s. Some Protestant missionaries had had a look around in the 1820s. But it was not till after mid-century that the vast area was divvied up among the Catholics, the Anglicans and the Methodists. There was, by the time the Province had entered Confederation, a gentlemen's agreement that the three big religions would not poach on each other's spheres of interest.

During the fur-trading days, some Anglican missionaries had been attached to the Company's forts. These men were ill-disposed to conditions suggested by the frontier, and most often more zealous than accommodating. They had two dreadful conditions to overcome: most of the workers at the forts and in the forests were Catholics, and most of the people in the area were savages. Their problems were especially tangled when these Catholic men (and some of their Anglican superiors) lived in un-Christian relationships with heathen women, often producing unbaptizable children. Perhaps the most voluble of these agitated men of God was the ironically named Reverend Herbert Beaver, who attempted to ply his vocation at Fort Vancouver in the late 1830s. Beaver was always complaining about his poor accommodations, and sending letters back to HBC headquarters excoriating the immorality of its representatives of all ranks. He even went after Chief Factor McLoughlin and his Native wife, whom Beaver referred to as a "kept Mistress" of "notoriously loose character." The fur traders usually put up with a lot from the evangelical soul-savers, but Beaver pushed McLoughlin a little too far; one day he said something particularly illiberal to the chief factor in the fort square, and McLoughlin pounded the stuffing out of him. Beaver never did get around to saving any Indian souls and, like many of the Anglican and Protestant churchmen, saw himself as a valiant warrior against iniquity on all sides, including the behaviour of James Douglas.

About the time that Beaver left Fort Vancouver (1838), the Catholic priests sent out from Quebec arrived, and began to set up shop wherever the Company men were doing business. Priests went all through New Caledonia, into the Kootenays and up the Salish coast. They started baptizing heathens and using sign language and visual aids to teach the Catechism as best they could. Some of the Native people had seen their symbols before, as the French-Canadian workers had made crosses for them out of sticks, and pointed toward the firmament, where the One God looked down. But for most of the Natives the new rituals were just like any other European innovations, something to be wary of, or something to choose from and adapt as additions to their own economies and spiritual practices.

But when the fur traders were replaced by the settlers, the religious life of the Indians was in for a change. All the fur traders had wanted from the Indians were peace and pelts. But the new whites were different. They were going to stay, and they were going to use the land for their purposes. Any Native people who wanted to stay around were going to have to change the way they lived. They were going to have to try to understand and learn a new culture, which entailed agriculture and Christianity. Both these things would require a change in language.

The purveyors of the new religion were not here, as the fur traders had been, to make deals. They were here to save the Indians from their iniquitous and inefficient way of life. The savages would have to learn European languages, clothing, family life and farming, as well as God's own design. The missionaries expected to be thanked. They were here to "improve" the unlucky heathens, by bringing to them not only the light of God but the benefit of a superior culture and economy. But if any of them were going to survive, they were going to survive as darker parts of civilization.

The Reverend Mr. Duncan

In the 1850s, as towns and ranches took hold during the gold rush, the Europeans found their missions beginning to work. In 1857 William Duncan, the most famous and successful of the Anglican missionaries, arrived in Victoria and prepared for his mission among the Indians around Fort Simpson. In 1858 the Oblates set up their headquarters in Esquimalt and began to send priests through the Interior. In 1859 the Methodists arrived. It is no historical accident that the men of God started hammering up their buildings just as the forest land became the new Crown colony.

We have heaps of material written by the Christian soldiers about the depraved aborigines. They wrote journals and letters and speeches. They were writing the battle reports of their war on darkness. Sometimes they would find some quality to admire among the Native people, and that makes sense—who would bother trying to provide uplift to a people incapable of benefiting from it? But their letters and journals are filled with words such as "iniquity," "revolting," "depravity," "evil" and so on. They were unhappy about the drunkenness they found, about violence and vengefulness, and about the un-Victorian profligacy of the potlatch, for instance. But they were particularly upset about anything that the Indians considered spiritual, but which the missionaries, perceiving a rival belief system, had to call Satanic.

They never considered forming a reciprocal relationship with the shamans, for instance, as the Company men had done with powerful Native traders. They saw the shamans as their chief adversaries in the soul business, sometimes as the emissaries of the Archfiend. They were especially unhappy during the winters, when the winter ceremonies with their secret magic and dancing and weird music seemed to prove that the Devil made work for idle hands. They did perceive that there was an integral connection between Native ritual and Native economies, as for instance in the marriage pot-latches of the coast. They understood that in order to lift the poor wretches out of their idolatry, they would have to change other aspects of their lives.

First of all this meant building schools as well as churches. At Fort Simpson in 1859, Reverend Duncan built a school for the Tsimshian chil-dren, and began teaching them to read and write in English, to add and sub-tract, to sing English songs. And Anglican Christianity. If Duncan was to lift his charges out of ignorance, he had to make the children think differently from their grandparents. The church had not yet fallen upon the solution of taking the children to another location where they would not hear their parents talking to them in their mother tongue. Duncan did, though, set a kind of example with his village at Metlakatla. Desiring to get his new Christian community away from baleful influences both white and Indian, he gathered his flock at Fort Simpson in 1862 and set up a new-style settlement at the old Tsimshian site. There the church, which was already the school, also became the municipal government. It was a step that would be emulated all over the province, and lead to confrontations between church and legislature in years soon to come.

At Metlakatla Reverend Duncan's administration laid out fifteen rules. The first five would forbid traditional Native practices:

1. To give up Indian devilry.
2. To cease calling in conjurers when sick.
3. To cease gambling.
4. To cease giving away property for display.
5. To cease painting faces.

The next four were aimed at gathering the now unheritaged people into proper Anglican uprightness:

6. To cease drinking intoxicating liquor.
7. To rest on the Sabbath.
8. To attend religious instruction.
9. To send their children to school.

The next five suggested the white people's construction of Indian character:

10. To be cleanly.
11. To be industrious.
12. To be peaceful.
13. To be liberal and honest in trade.
14. To build neat houses.

And the last one introduced an ominous alternative to the potlatch:

15. To pay the village tax.

When smallpox swept up the coast in that year of 1862, it devastated the shamanic societies but almost bypassed Metlakatla. Only five of the villagers died. William Duncan was either lucky or he was the bringer of superior magic into the land. The success of his enterprise was assured, at least until he ran into trouble with his own church. He had a thousand adherents in his little honest village of neat houses. Duncan tried to make a Victorian English coastal town on a northern Pacific inlet. His success was very interesting to his Methodist and Oblate rivals, who in their own ways tried to set up model communities set apart from heathen and white temptations. Metlakatla became a source of pride for Duncan's church, and endured for a couple of decades, and Duncan became a legendary figure on the north coast. But his success did not go unnoticed to himself. Having worked among his people for years, he felt that he knew more than his bishop did about the bringing of Christian life to the savage frontier. He waged an unceasing campaign against the old pagan ways. Thus he decided that in his community Anglicanism would not include the taking of communion. Conflicting views regarding his motivation have always existed. It might be pointed out that Duncan came to the rescue of the northwest before he had finished his priestly training at the Church Missionary Society at Highbury College in London, so there is some question about whether he would have been permitted to administer the rite. In any case, he said that the new converts would confuse Holy Communion with savage cannibalism, and he was not going to allow for any melding of beliefs.

Duncan's rule was almost absolute. In 1863 he had been made a justice of the peace. He became notorious for his refusal to share or delegate power. Junior ecclesiasts found it chafing to work with him, and the Church Missionary Society did not like the idea of a powerful saviour. According to their theory the missionary's main function is to train Native churchmen who can then spread the system among their people. William Duncan was a proud man who loved control. The Indians paid their taxes to him, and he taught them how to be Christians.

Eventually Duncan's dispute with the church would come to an impasse. When after twenty-five years he was challenged by a new bishop to share power and follow direction, Reverend Duncan took nearly a thousand of his subjects and skipped the country, landing on Annette Island south of Ketchican, Alaska, and calling his settlement New Metlakatla. A hundred years later there is still a community there, though the word "New" has been dropped from its name.

Before Duncan and his people crossed the border, new villages partly modelled on Metlakatla were starting up, not only on the north coast, and not only among the Natives who were going to be designated Anglicans. Kincolith, and later New Aiyansh were started by the Anglicans among the Nisga'a people, near the mouth of the Nass River. The Catholics, too, tried to work the coast. For ten years they laboured without success to convert the Kwakiutl at Fort Rupert. Later the Anglicans tried their luck. The Haida people on the Queen Charlottes were easier to work with—they even came to the mainland to ask for a minister. The Catholics had better fortune

down south, on the Sechelt Peninsula, where they had the Indians forget
their usual beachfront architecture and make a European village with a
church in the middle of it, to renounce the potlatch and the spirit dance,
and thrill to the blood and pageant of the Catholic rites. Meanwhile, the
Methodists slid into Fort Simpson, which had been left behind by Duncan's
troupe, and there the remaining Tsimshians sang to the new-time religion.

Valley churches

The three branches of Christianity also found their ways into the Interior.
But just as the Native population was spread more thinly over wider expanses
inland than they were on the Coast, so the church men had to oversee
greater ranges. Most of them, Protestants and Catholics, became circuit riders, administering religion on horseback, the way Begbie administered law.
They also worked as the fur traders had, to make alliances with friendly
chiefs among the various bands they hoped to save. Among the most successful of the Anglican missionaries was Reverend J.B. Good, who built schools
and laid down rules among the Thompson people around Lytton. Because he
had to be on his rounds, he could not keep his eye on his flock at all times, so
he devised a system of social control that would be perfected by the Oblate
priests who worked among the Okanagan and Shuswap peoples.

The system was built around the establishment of a kind of puppet local
government. If it looked as if the people's leaders were going to be
intractable, the missionary would appoint his own chief and subalterns, and
two other groups, sometimes made up of the same men. These would be a
kind of militia, whose job it was to enforce the rules while the missionary was
on the road, and a network of spies who would report bad behaviour when
the missionary was back in town. The Oblate fathers had their first successes
in the Sechelt Peninsula, where in 1871 all the Sechelt Indians underwent
the sacrament of confirmation, and especially in the lower Fraser Valley.
Travel along the lower river was relatively easy now, with a good coach road
and tractable landscape. Headquarters was set up at St. Mary's Mission, near
the present Mission, B.C., and the Coast Salish were prepared for the Roman
Church. Villages were set up on the Anglicans' model to the north, and the
first residential schools were built. Children would live at the schools, where
shamanism and the Salish language were not to be mentioned, where Indian
boys and girls would be taught to be Christians and agricultural workers.

In 1845 and again in 1846, a Jesuit Father named Nobili had made visits
among the Okanagans and Shuswap, but the Oblates, directed from Oregon
by way of Esquimalt, arrived in 1859 and were the first to organize a village
at Okanagan Mission, and put a house of their God in the middle of it. By
the time of Confederation they had churches in various spots in the dry
land, including St. Joseph's Church on the reserve at Kamloops. By 1880

that church would have its first resident priest.

Okanagan Mission, just south of Kelowna, would become the first permanent white settlement in the Okanagan Valley. There Father Pandosy
looked around at the gorgeous country, a lake in the middle of a semi-desert,
and began his work of turning spiritualist hunters and gatherers into God-
fearing farmhands. Hunters and gatherers require a great range of land to
supply their needs, especially when the land is arid. But if Indians are scattered over a vast area of land, it is difficult to inculcate new beliefs in them.
It was bad enough that priests and their mission workers had to be travelling so much of the time; it would be worse if the Indians weren't home
when St. Mary's men came with their ideas.

So the priests combined teaching with control. They set up their spies,
and they introduced the idea of hiring one's labour. The Indian bent over
the potato patch was learning not only Christian humility but also the concept of wages. If while the Fathers were away he happened to speak too
much of some Interior Salish tongue, or ate before prayers in the morning,
the spies might bring up his case, and he would learn that your wages could
disappear as fines payable to the church. Okanagan Mission was a company
town. The climate would be fruitful in more than metaphorical ways,
thought the missionaries. They sent away to Oregon for the seeds that would
one day begin the great orchards that the Okanagan Valley would become
famous for. For this reason the people of Kelowna would call their first cleric
"Apple" Pandosy, and name their main street after him.

Digging out roots

The missionaries, some might say, meant a greater threat to First Nations
culture than the white people looking for commercial resources had. When
the fur collectors had come, they had treated the indigenous people as
traders, as means by which to get beaver pelts to Asia and Europe. The gold
seekers did not invite the Natives to any part of their activity, except as
porters before the roads were passable. But the missionaries were after souls.
James Douglas and his lieutenants might kill Indians who threatened the
Company's hegemony. Drunken USAmericans might shoot unlucky Indians
around the gold camps. Judge Begbie and his agents might hang Indians who
broke the puzzling laws of the occupying forces. But the Anglicans,
Catholics and Methodists wanted to root out the language, the art, the religion and the political and economic structures formulated over a hundred
centuries before the Europeans arrived.

The Natives' responses to the churchmen were varied. Some fiercely
independent peoples, such as the Kwakiutl and the Nisga'a were aloof and
sometimes hostile to the offers of conversion. No matter how well-dressed
and smiling the men at their door, they said no thank you. Other groups

decided to mix and match, adopting Eurochristian features that they liked, while continuing practices from their original religions, or observing Christian forms while remaining true to their parents' beliefs. Some zealots attempted to revive Native spirituality and root out the new growths. Others declared themselves prophets of a new kind of religion formulated out of a syncretization of two religions. Some people were attracted by any holy man who carried magic objects and claimed to have preternatural vision. People who had been introduced to poverty noticed that there was food where there were churches.

As the missionaries became more successful, they became more competitive for flocks. The Protestants, especially, directed more and more of their attention toward the pagans who had fallen under Catholic control. Converting heathens was one thing; trying to save heathens who were also trained in the "idolatry" of the Roman Church was a great challenge.

The missionaries, unlike the fur traders and the gold prospectors, were a part of the settlement movement. In fact, they were probably its advance guard, as far as the Natives were concerned. The preachers and priests were advocates of Victorian civilization, not only their religion. They wanted to turn pre-industrial peoples into Victorians. The missionaries got their greatest victory in the 1884 law banning the potlatch and the spirit dances.

The wires

Boys who grew up as I did in the dry interior of British Columbia remember lots of cowboy movies. A few of them would become popular classics. More of them would star Johnnie Mack Brown or George Montgomery. All of them would be set in a landscape that looked as if it could be a mile outside our home town. One of the most often seen themes was the coming of the telegraph poles. The telegraph poles were standing proof that the west was being prepared for a major change. The poles presaged the coming of the steel tracks. The wide open frontier was being prepared for business. The news was always bad for the Indians. These were some kind of know-it-all eastern engineers and wage-earners and war veterans bringing alarming news into the new world. Telegraph poles were something like fences, only worse. Only better, if you were a businessman in eastern clothes. In the cowboy movies there was always someone up a pole, cutting the telegraph wires.

For Walt Whitman the telegraph wire and cable were lines to the great future he envisaged for humankind, led by the Americano example. For the engineers of the British Empire, they promised another attempt at the Northwest Passage.

"Telegraph" is a late-eighteenth century word compiled of two ancient words. Native American smoke signals were a kind of telegraph. So were the semaphore flags and lights used by naval signalmen. All over Europe eager inventors concocted ingenious methods for sending information from hilltop to hilltop. But when the electromagnet was developed early in the nineteenth century, Samuel Morse and his partner Alfred Vail invented an operator key that could send and interrupt an electric circuit over metallic wires. In 1856 they had a sounding key, and in that year the Western Union Telegraph Company was founded, out of a merger of little companies that had been talking to the railway outfits in the USA. Telemetry saw improvements every year for the rest of the century. Europe was criss-crossed with wires, and so was North America. One of the big prizes would be links from continent to continent. Every business tycoon and brigadeer general dreamed about the laying of telegraph cables under the oceans, especially the Atlantic.

This enormous task was first tried by a US entrepreneur named Cyrus W. Field. He tried and tried. He failed three times, and a lot of private and public money sank to the bottom of the North Atlantic Ocean. People began to agree that it could not be done. Then a USAmerican in San Francisco, Perry M. Collins, looked west, or rather northwest. He saw that the Russians were launched on a huge project to join St. Petersburg to their Pacific coast, possibly including their settlements in Alaska. Meanwhile, the British government was trying to raise the interest and money to link their colonies in North America. A line was planned with a terminus in Fort Langley. Some day Mr. Field or a rival was going to succeed in the Atlantic, and London was interested in a telegraph link to its Pacific northwest.

Perry Collins went to St. Petersburg and made a deal with the Russians for the rights to a line from Siberia to San Francisco. Then he got financial backing from Washington and the Western Union Company, talked persuasively with the folks in British Columbia, and hired his surveyors. If Victoria could not dah-dit-dah with London to the east they would do it westward. C.S. Bulkley, a USAmerican, was assigned the job of designing the route. His name was given to a river valley in northern B.C., along which there were supposed to be poles erected every sixty-three paces. Like so many other transportation and communication dreams in British Columbia, the wires were to be strung up the Fraser River. They would go to Quesnel, then veer left and head for the Skeena. Thence they would go to Alaska, and by underwater cable to Nikolayevsk on the Sea of Okhotsk near both China and Japan.

By the spring of 1865 Western Union had connected San Francisco to New Westminster, just in time to send the news that Abraham Lincoln had been shot. Northward through the Interior a sight familiar to several generations of cowboys and children was created. Crews made of Europeans, Chinese and Indians cut a swath ten yards wide through the wilderness, and soon the wires were shining in the sun. The swath reached Fort Stager where the Kispiox River flows into the Skeena. Then, in 1866, C.W. Field succeeded on his fourth try. British Columbia would signal to London across the Atlantic after all, by way of San Francisco. For the nonce the Pacific cable was abandoned. The town of Telegraph Creek, where the line was supposed to cross the Stikine River, was stuck without the telegraph. Crews left a lot of equipment on the ground up north, where the local Natives proved inventive in adapting it for their purposes.

But the connection was solid as far north as Quesnel. The proposed land link between Ontario and Fort Langley had been dropped when Collins's epic began, so that now the politicians in British Columbia could send Morse code to London, but not to Ottawa. Not until twenty years after Confederation would that happen.

In the early years of the province of British Columbia, the telegraph replaced horseback couriers in matters of provincial business, law and government. There was a key operator in Barkerville. Western Union sank a cable to Victoria. Matsqui was connected to Burrard Inlet. A single wire went up Vancouver Island to Nanaimo, across to Gabriola and Valdez islands and underwater to Point Grey and thus to New Westminster. These lines were owned by the Dominion government, indicating one of the many differences between USAmerican and Canadian thinking (and economics). But in 1886, the Canadian Pacific Railway pried a lot of concessions from Ottawa, and one of them was their purchase of the main telegraphic line from Kamloops to Victoria. After that the railroad was the principal builder of telegraph systems in the province.

Many of the poles snaked their way across Indian reserves.

Chinese

When the telegraph crews edged northwards, their social-political make-up was a little dramatization of history. The sixty white men were surveyors and technicians and sawyers. The twenty Native men were boatmen and carriers, as their older relatives had been for the first Europeans in the country. The thirty-two Chinese men were cooks and laundrymen and polemen, doing the service work and the most dangerous jobs, as their relatives and countrymen would do when the great railroads and hotels were constructed in the coming years.

The fur trade had linked New Caledonia between Europe and Asia, especially China. The Europeans, running ships along the Asian coasts, had early discovered that they could hire Asian people to do hard work for low payment. The gold miners and their employers needed big dinners and cheap laundries because they worked long hours in and under the earth. The railroad had to find a way through perilous places such as the Fraser Canyon, and it became necessary for someone to hang on ropes over the gorge and set dynamite charges. But the whites in the new province began to notice that after the heyday of each new industry, some of the Chinese people did not go back where they had come from. It began to look as if they were going to have another problem on top of the inconvenient Indian population. There were rumours that the Chinese were just the opposite of the Indians—they could make a good living by working hard in very little space, and they did not disappear wholesale when diseases and land speculators showed up.

Chinese people first showed up in Victoria during the sudden immigration from the south in 1858. They came from the gold fields and the cities created by the gold fields in the US. Some of them went to the Cariboo; others stayed in booming Victoria, working as servants in the grand houses and hotels, or as laundrymen in the meaner streets. By the time that British Columbia joined Canada, there were about 2,000 Chinese in the province, almost all of them farmers' children from the countryside around Canton. Ten years later there were 4,000, many of them having arrived not from San Francisco but directly from Hong Kong. It was not long until racist songs and fantasies showed up on the Coast. These people, after all, wore pyjamas and braided hair, spoke an incomprehensible language, and did not seem to drink whiskey. In 1879 Amor de Cosmos (Love of the Whole World, remember) brought a petition signed by 1,500 British Columbians to the House of Commons, requesting that Chinese men be forbidden to work on the railroads.

But in May of 1881, there was a lot of dangerous railroad work to do west of the Rockies, and not enough gandy dancers among the population to get it done. Andrew Onderdonk, the main contractor for the CPR from Yale to Kamloops, brought in 2,000 farmers' sons from mainland China. Four and a half years later, just before the last spike was driven, there were 13,000 men working on the railroad, and around 8,000 of them were Chinese. When the work was over, there was room for only one or two Chinese restaurants and laundries in the smaller towns along the route. A lot of Chinese railroad workers went to see what they could do on the Coast. White people were heard to mention the "Heathen Chinee" and the "Celestial Flood." In 1891, the census showed for the first time a white population of British Columbia higher than the Native population, and the Chinese population of 9,000 made up 9.1 per cent of the whole. A half-century later the Chinese population was 2.3 per cent.

More McLeans

When Donald McLean the fur trader, rancher, innkeeper and Indian killer finally met his end in the Chilcotin War, he left behind two families. He had lived with two (some people say three) Indian wives, leaving them both with children to bring up. His first family had been left alone a dozen years before he died on the ground near Tatla Lake, and there were other children born to Indian women here and there, but his second family, at the new ranch and roadhouse at Hat Creek, was made up of his tall wife Sophia and six children.

The McLean brothers, who terrorized farmers and townsfolk, were trapped and captured in this cabin in 1879.

The widow McLean did not have a chance. For five years the Hudson's Bay Company gave her a tiny pension, but it was not long till the ranch and the roadhouse on the Cariboo road were out of her hands. She managed to get one of the children, Charlie, into the school at Cache Creek for a year or so. But these were halfbreed children. White settlers in old fur country did not think that they were quite real. There had been a lot of halfbreed children in Hudson's Bay Company country. Some of their fathers went back to Scotland or England without them. Some of their fathers died in New Caledonia or took a boat to California. Their mothers had solved some problems for their fathers. Now here were the children, an inconvenience, as the Chinese were to become after the railroad was spiked.

For fifteen years Donald Mclean's fatherless children lived as best they could. Halfbreed boys lived on the interface: they spent some of their time on the Indian reserve, talking and fighting; they roamed around the white people's country, picking up jobs on the ranches. Certain legends grew up around them. They were supposed to be the best riders and the best rifle shots in the Thompson country. They were supposed to be eyeing the white farmers' daughters and wives, looking for their first chance. Every time something went missing, people suggested looking in the saddlebags of the Mclean brothers and their friend Alex Hare.

Archie McLean got his first work on a ranch at the age of nine. His older brothers Charlie and Allen and Hector took him along whenever they were looking for work or trouble. What else could they do with him? And the McLean boys often found the trouble they were looking for. Sometimes they got into fights. Sometimes they might steal a horse or a pistol or a bottle of

Hudson's Bay Company whisky. Johnnie Ussher was the only provincial policeman from Kamloops to Osoyoos, the gold commissioner, the tax collector, the jailer and the government agent. He was also in private business, in partnership with the most powerful businessmen-politicians in Kamloops. Every once in a while Johnnie Ussher would nab a McLean or two and put them in jail. If they did not escape, they would be set loose without formal charges. These were, after all, the sons of a man who had been an important pioneer in the district.

Then came December of 1879. The winter of 1879 was the coldest on record for the white people in the Thompson area. But Allen and Charlie and Archie McLean and Alex Hare were riding. They were youngsters with whisky and guns. They went to Bill Palmer's ranch and stole his favourite animal, a beautiful black stallion. Palmer went riding in the snow and followed tracks right into the boys' camp. Haven't seen him, said one of them, though Palmer could see the horse tied under the fir boughs. He looked around at the guns and perceived that the boys were drinking, and turned around. He rode to Kamloops to report his experience to Johnnie Ussher.

Ussher, thinking here we go again, deputized Palmer, and picked up two more men, John McLeod the rancher and Amni Shumway, a famous tracker, and rode to the McLeans' camp. When they got there, Ussher left his pistol on his saddle, and prepared to talk the juiced-up lads into coming to Kamloops with him. But the boys had become a gang. Alex Hare put a knife into Johnnie Ussher, and someone put a few bullets into John McLeod. Archie McLean finished Ussher with a bullet in the face. Shumway and Palmer and McLeod headed back to Kamloops. They needed a bigger posse with more weapons.

The posse was easy to raise. The alarm spread all through the ranch country and by telegraph to Victoria and Barkerville and Cache Creek. Residual hatreds became cries for justice or revenge. A rumour spread that the McLeans were the beginning of the always-feared "Indian uprising." Meanwhile the McLean gang rode from ranch to ranch, taking away weapons and food. They were drunk and they were blooded. On their rounds they killed a shepherd named James Kelly. Terror swept across the province. Justices of the peace with posses rode from every direction. The military was stirring on the Coast. The US border was sealed. Meanwhile the McLean gang headed for Douglas Lake, above the Nicola Valley. There Allen tried to talk the Indian leaders into joining his new war. He, just as much as the frightened and murderous whites, was interested in a sequel to the Chilcotin uprising that had finished his father.

But the Douglas Lake council said no. The best the outlaws could get was a cabin up the road from the lake. There they went in the middle of a dreadful winter, with their treasure of weapons, some food and not enough water. By their first night there they were under siege. There were a hundred gunmen

Archie McLean was sixteen when he was hanged in New Westminster, January 31, 1881.

outside the cabin, and more on their way. There were people who had had a grudge against the McLean boys for years. There were politicians who represented businessmen and did not like gunplay that looked bad for business. There were friends of Johnnie Ussher.

They put a lot of bullets into the cabin's logs and door. They tried to burn it down with a wagon of smouldering hay. They sent halfbreed emissaries to demand surrender. They waited three days, and they saw sticks protruding between the logs— the fugitives were trying to get a mouthful of snow to allay their thirst. After three days of bullets and three nights of severe cold, the boys surrendered. They came out of the cabin like animated rags. They raised their guns and emptied them into the sky, declaring with this ritual their Indianness in front of a crowd of angry white men. As soon as the guns were empty the whites knocked them to the ground and shackled them, pulling boots and coats off the prisoners.

After a hearing in Kamloops the boys were transported to New Westminster, through a blizzard, through the Fraser Canyon, across the ice of the river, to the Provincial Gaol. They arrived in their cells on Christmas Day, 1879.

There followed two trials beset by legal uncertainties. Newspapermen and Kamloops ranchers wanted an end to the threat of rebellion and anarchy, and they wanted a warning to be posted for any Indians or halfbreeds who might be unhappy enough with history to want a hand in it. On the last day of January in 1881, the four youths were hanged together in the yard overlooking the Fraser. They were not children any more. Allen had turned twenty-five in prison. Charlie and Alex were just about eighteen. Little Archie was already sixteen. Their bodies were chucked into a kind of unofficial graveyard where dead criminals and Chinese people were permitted to be buried. Later it would be cleared of its contents to make space for an elementary school.

While the McLeans and Alex Hare were spending their thirteen months in the Provincial Gaol in New Westminster, Andrew Onderdonk's crews started their work at Yale. Five years after Archie McLean's short body was disposed of, the CPR trains would be coming through Kamloops on their way to the Pacific.

Craigellachie

For nearly a decade the Canadian transcontinental railroad remained a dream, and a headache. In Ottawa, the Opposition leader, Edward Blake, and others led the fight against it on financial terms. In Victoria, the provincial government threatened secession if the Terms of Union were not met. John A. Macdonald mollified the west coasters and looked for holes in Blake's garments. In Victoria there was another squabble. The politician-businessmen there wanted to see the tracks laid on Vancouver Island before anywhere else in British Columbia. But the mainland was to benefit first from the railroad boom. On May 14, 1880, just outside Yale, thirty-one-year-old Onderdonk's first blast of dynamite filled the air with dust. The local storekeepers and outfitters cheered lustily. Times promised to be even better than they had been during the gold rush. And as they had in the gold-rush towns, new hotels and saloons gleamed in the summer sun.

All kinds of businesses took hold in Yale: newspaper, freightyard, lumber company, dentist—and mortician. When Onderdonk imported his two thousand Chinese farmers' sons, he brought them in two ships, crowded belowdecks with the hatches closed against a stormy sea. Unlike George Vancouver's sauerkraut-fed sailors of a century before, the terrified cargo developed scurvy, and by the time they reached Yale, one in ten was dying. The mortician now had a government contract he could hardly keep up to. The populace, as they often did when it came to matters of race, began to panic. There was a common conception that Chinese people carried various plagues wherever they went in numbers. White citizens said that the last thing they wanted was to see a new people coming across an ocean and introducing a deadly infectious disease to the country.

Premier Walkem was not happy about the importation of Chinese workers. He liked to tell people that he knew everybody in British Columbia, thus being qualified to speak of their concerns. How was he supposed to keep up that intimacy if the USAmerican hired by the easterners was going to bring in thousands of workers that a premier could not even tell apart? But before turning to Canton, the recruiters had gathered up every bartender and unemployed roustabout they could find in California. Walkem was not happy about a lot of things, and most of those things had something to do with the Dominion government. For the next two years he would cause Macdonald grief at every turn. He would continually lament that Ottawa was not meeting all the Terms of Union; yet British Columbia enacted provincial legislation that countermanded the Terms, at least in spirit. For instance, British Columbia continued to treat the Native population far more meanly than they were treated by the Dominion government on the prairies.

But in 1882 Macdonald found a way to get Walkem out of his hair. He appointed him to the Supreme Court. Walkem accepted the post, while saying that his departure spelled the beginning of harder times for British

Columbia. He would be replaced by Robert Beaven. In the same year Macdonald had a stroke of luck: there was a federal election, and Amor de Cosmos lost his seat. Now the prime minister might have an unsatisfied province on the coast, but its two snarliest spokesmen were gone from the legislature and the Commons.

The long-time residents of Vancouver Island deliberately collated Island ambitions with provincial ambitions when they were dealing with Ottawa or London. When they were dealing with the mainland of the province, they never let it be forgotten that they had become civilized first, and that the Island colony had always been the doorway to the world. On the mainland, from Burrard Inlet to Kamloops and beyond, local businessmen gloried in the opportunities supplied by the railroad and paid for by governments; they were quite satisfied with a route that was supposed to end at Port Moody, or perhaps at the deeper water further west in the inlet. Island politicians and businessmen kept supporting the notion that the Carnarvon agreement meant that Victoria would be the terminus. Meanwhile Island entrepreneurs Robert and James Dunsmuir pointed out the threat of USAmerican rails on the Island, and proposed that they set up a consortium and build an Island line; they would require land concessions, of course, including most of the coal fields up to Nanaimo, and all the Indian reserve land as well. Robert Dunsmuir had been the Hudson's Bay Company's chief mining engineer, and he knew how to use his knowledge and position. He would become enormously wealthy by sending underpaid Chinese miners into the coal under Nanaimo.

In London the threat of British Columbia separatism was at least a bother. World maps drawn in England shaded the Empire in red, and the satisfying feeling produced by the colour red on coastlines around the globe would be threatened if Canada were to be replaced by something else—likely the USA—on its only territory on the western rim of the Americas. So at the end of the summer in 1882, British Columbia was favoured by a long vice-regal visit. It happened that the governor-general was now the Marquess of Lorne, a stately Scot, and more important, he was married to Queen Victoria's daughter, Princess Louise Caroline Alberta. The Marquess of Lorne liked to touch Canadian history. He named the future province of Alberta after his wife, and composed a long poem to explain why. Then he also gave another of his wife's names to the beautiful lake that would be made visitable by the new railroad. On his trip to the fractious province on the western slope, he hoped to remind people of the benefits of being subjects of the Crown and citizens of the Dominion. He was prepared to drop words into ears.

The city of Victoria went gaga over the visit, especially because of the princess. The city fathers caused big tasteless arches to be erected all over the place. Silly slogans appeared on walls. Decorated bearskins were hung from furriers' windows. Representatives of the Queen were used to this; all over the Empire the locals would show their sophistication by hapless attempts at the cosmopolitan. But the vice-regal couple kept a straight face; and they stayed for three months. Princess Louise tarried in the capital while the governor-general toured the province, dropping words in ears all along the route of the future railroad. He was pursuing cohesiveness and national feeling. After his grand tour he returned to Victoria for a big banquet. It was there that he chose to offer the news that the rails would go through the Kicking Horse Pass, thence to Kamloops and down the Fraser River. He expected cheers. Instead the Islanders told him about how much more important and historical Victoria was than Burrard Inlet. Eventually the Dunsmuirs got a grant of two million acres in exchange for financing the Island railroad.

The saga of the Canadian Pacific Railway has been told countless times in countless forms, including popular histories and satirical poems. Hopeful USAmerican tycoons said that it couldn't be done. The Liberals in the House of Commons said that it couldn't be done. Old sourdough prospectors standing one foot higher than the other in the Rockies and overlooking the Fraser Canyon said that whoever those railroad people were, they were out of their minds. The country of Canada was too young and too lightly populated to pull off such a colossal feat. And every week the job became bigger than anyone had thought it would. Money fell into chasms. The British Columbia government tried to keep the boatloads of Chinese wage-slaves out of the country. Young farmers' sons with dynamite in their back-packs fell into Hell's Gate. On the prairies the Métis people and their Indian allies rose in armed defence of their rights. An interesting warrior named Piapot made a habit of holding up every train that tried to cross Saskatchewan District.

The financial backers, the English and Canadian governments, the executives of the company, and the crew chiefs were aware that they were doing what the USAmericans had already done a few times, but doing it through more difficult terrain. They had to build a spiral tunnel in Rogers Pass. They had to get from Lytton to Yale, a landscape that can still frighten people just riding a train through it. When the Union Pacific Company's westward rail-layers met the crew coming east from the ocean, they had a big "last spike" ceremony. The Canadians decided to do likewise. But unlike their flamboyant neighbours, they did not invest in brass bands and bunting. They did not discharge firearms into the sky. They had a Canadian last spike.

The ceremony occurred in a place that hardly anyone in British Columbia can spell or pronounce. It was November 7, 1885, in the high country between Sicamous and Revelstoke, at the western entrance to Eagle Pass. It was a cold and cloudy day, and there was a skim of snow, with more expected. A special train had come from Montreal, once headquarters of the

North West Fur Company, bearing CPR vice-president William Cornelius Van Horne and a coterie of CP officials, including Sir Sandford Fleming, who was somewhat grumpy because he had wanted the rails to go through the Yellowhead Pass further north. He had resigned from the transcontinental project when it was handed over to private business, but he was still Canada's most famous railroad man.

The regular workmen laid the last rail in place, and handed a regular hammer to an old gent with a beaver hat and a long white beard. This was Donald Alexander Smith, another in the long line of Canadian Scots. He would later become Lord Strathcona, but now he was one of the richest men in the Empire, the largest shareholder in the Hudson's Bay Company and its future governor, a principal shareholder in the Bank of Montreal and its future president, and a prominent Conservative whose financial backing was absolutely necessary to the CPR. Now he was going to drive the last spike. The place would be called Craigellachie, after a high rock in Morayshire, Scotland, where Smith grew up. The train doesn't stop there any more. You have to go by car if you want to see the site.

The most famous photograph in Canadian history shows Donald Smith driving the last spike, or at least holding the hammer in the general area of it. It is apparent from the way that he is holding it that he has not often swung a big hammer. He and Van Horne and Fleming are well and warmly dressed, in overcoats and high hats. They are surrounded by younger and less important men dressed in suits and derby hats. In the background railway employees are craning their necks. There is not a Chinese face to be seen. There are no Shuswap people.

Tap tap, went Smith's hammer. "Well done," said William Cornelius Van Horne, and the Montreal people got back onto the steaming train. Nobody made a speech. It was pretty quiet in Eagle Pass as the train chuffed toward Kamloops and the Coast. As soon as it was out of sight, a gandy dancer picked up a hammer and a spike. "I'm driving the last spike," he declared, and did so. Then another man said "No, sir, *I'm* driving the last spike." Pretty soon there were more last spikes in the tie than you could shake a hammer at.

Port Moody

The following year the first scheduled Canadian passenger train left Montreal for the west coast.

Donald Smith and his well-dressed companions were steaming toward Port Moody, at the head of Burrard Inlet. At Port Moody, British Columbians were doing what they had always done when a town site was chosen for something important. They were climbing over one another to cash in. The town had been surveyed, and merchants paid top prices for their lots. When Smith and the other Montrealers arrived, they were met by a cluster of shops and a crowd of well-wishers with gold in their eyes. This was the official terminus of the iron road, gateway to the Orient and California. There were four hundred thousand customers in San Francisco, millions in China. The CPR directors heard some heartfelt speeches. Hats flew into the air.

The crowd was large and noisy. A shipload of Vancouver Islanders had arrived, dressed to the nines. The New Westminster contingent did their best to look as impressive. A brass band from Victoria blasted the noontime air. An opera company belted out Italian arias. It was July 4, 1886, the anniversary of US Independence, and these Canadians were celebrating the end to reliance on USAmerican transportation. Premier William Smithe, who would tie Walkem's record by remaining premier for four years, was there to deliver the encomium from the province. He was disappointed that John A. Macdonald was not on the train, but he liked the noise and the fancy clothes. These easterners could not help but be impressed.

But Donald Smith and William C. Van Horne were millionaires. They must have noticed that the little tidewater town was almost surrounded by steep hillsides at the end of a big inlet. They must have been looking westward.

Advertisements appeared in Victoria and New Westminster, and found their way up the old gold trail. "FROM THE PACIFIC TO THE ATLANTIC OUR NATIONAL RAILWAY," they proclaimed. "Our Sleeping and Dining Cars are Luxurious and our 1st and 2nd class Coaches Marvels of Comfort," they maintained. They promised unequalled cuisine and "The Grandest Scenery in the World." Perhaps most fetchingly, they declared in large letters: "TIME THROUGH FROM PORT MOODY TO MONTREAL, 137 HOURS." Even if the eastbound train were to be, say, half an hour late reaching Montreal, the idea of getting there in five days must have boggled a few minds, especially of those Victorians who could remember coming by way of the Transisthmian Railway in Panama or even the Cape. Now people in Victoria had but to walk aboard a CP ship that would take them to Port Moody, and their seasickness would be replaced by the grandest scenery in the world. They might even witness a trainjacking by Piapot.

But Smith and Van Horne were looking westward. Not as far westward as Vancouver Island. Just twelve English miles.

Granville and Hastings

When the Coast Salish people lived there, the great inlet was surrounded by immense trees, some of them two hundred and fifty feet tall and weighing more than a million pounds. After the first white sawyers had been there for a while, parts of the shoreline began to look like early New Westminster—

Logging on what is now Georgia Street near Seymour Street, 1886.

broken snags surrounded by mud.

The inlet was probably called Sasamat by the Capilano Indians before the Europeans came. The Spanish called it Boca de Floridablanca, not because of any white blossoms they had seen, but after a Spanish politician. George Vancouver called it Burrard Inlet, after a sailor friend from his days in the Caribbean. When the gold rush began the mines and new towns up the Fraser River needed lumber. The first mills appeared at Yale and on the Island, but by 1865 there were saws screaming on both sides of the Inlet. On the north shore Sewell Moody set up a mill that began to look like a town called Moodyville. On the south shore there was a logging community called Hastings Mill, and a half-mile farther west another called Granville, or in the parlance of the day, Gastown. The amalgamated colony of 1858 recognized the need for building materials and the threat of USAmerican ambitions, and encouraged timber merchants by granting them land and timber rights for hardly any money at all. Soon there were big owners' houses on the hillsides, and ships in the inlet. The USAmericans imposed tall trade barriers, so the wood that did not go to the instant towns in British Columbia was exported to Australia and Latin America.

Amor de Cosmos's old running-mate Dr. Powell owned choice land on the south shore, and so did John Robson, editor of the *British Columbian*, big supporter of Moody, and future premier. David and Isaac Oppenheimer owned most of Hastings Mill, and were intent on ripping down giant cedar trees. Over the southern rise, on the north shore of the Fraser, the McCleery family started the first sizeable farm. (George Woodcock, the great man of letters, who would write many books of British Columbia, spent the last four decades of his life on McCleery Street, overlooking the site.) The legendary "Three Greenhorns," Morton, Brighouse and Hailstone, unhappy with their luck as prospectors, had grabbed a pre-emption in 1862.

When work on the railroad began in the seventies, the sawmills had their biggest boost yet. The timber barons loved Confederation as much as they had loved the USAmericans of the gold rush. Hastings Mill and Gastown became little towns. There were lots of shacks, a feature of the inlet that would remain for a century. There were a few hotels. In the mid-sixties there were nearly a thousand white people living around the water's edge. Every once in a while a brain in the military establishment would entertain the notion that Burrard Inlet was a strategic spot on the map. There were Indian settlements all around the water, of course. Once in a while the men with saws and oxen would arrive and suggest that they move.

Vancouver

The people who were trying to cash in on Port Moody might have seen what was coming. In 1882 the CPR had sent an engineer out to examine the whole inlet. He reported that he was fond of the area around what is now Coal Harbour. The water was wider and deeper, and there was plenty of fairly flat land for docks and railyards. Port Moody was the farthest east that salt water would go, but the water was narrow and shallow. In Montreal and in Victoria sentiment grew for an extension of the line twelve miles west of Port Moody. In 1884 Premier Smithe went to Montreal to talk terms. According to the Terms of Union the Dominion-backed rails were supposed to be flanked by twenty miles of CPR land on either side. When Port Moody was designated the terminus, the land west of there was free from the commitment. The people on the Island would not give up their argument that the terminus was supposed to be Victoria, though. Just in case, the B.C. government held lots of land along the Burrard Inlet shore off the market. When William Van Horne sat down with Smithe in Montreal, he said that he would be willing to punch through another twelve miles of rail in exchange for a big chunk of land. Now Smithe had to tell him that some of that land was already being held by lumber merchants and speculators. Talk to them, suggested Van Horne. Smithe talked to them. The Oppenheimers and the Greenhorns and the rest volunteered to give up a third of their possessions to the railroad. People were washing each other's hands all over the place.

So before the great event at Port Moody, the business was pretty well settled. For years, after the announcement of that terminus, the town had been growing, passing the milltowns in size. But Van Horne came out and had a look at Coal Harbour and English Bay, and liked what he saw, wide, deep water and valuable land. He agreed to move the rail port west. But he did not think that the local names would ring any bells back east. He said that the resulting city would have to be named Vancouver.

Now Port Moody businessmen were not the only enemies of the scheme. Merchants in Victoria, as snobbish as ever toward the mainland, objected to the appropriation of their island's name. They were, of course, resentful that the terminus would not be in Victoria, and they hated the idea of an international port across the strait. Why, the few women over there did not even know how to dress properly or set a table, if there was a table to be set. The landowners of Port Moody went to the courts. The merchants of Victoria tried to mount a boycott of eastern goods.

But the eager inhabitants of the inlet circulated a petition, asking the legislature to ignore the Municipal Act and draft a special charter. The legislature sat, and on April 6, 1886, the City of Vancouver was incorporated. Malcolm MacLean was elected the first mayor. By early summer there were about sixty-five businesses going. Twelve of them were hotels, and ten of them were real-estate offices.

Phoenix

A year and a month after its incorporation, Vancouver saw the first train from the east arrive at Coal Harbour. Three weeks after that the first passenger ship arrived from Asia. But it was not the city it had been before the tracks were laid west of Port Moody. In the meantime one city had been erased and a new one written in its place.

It seems as if every city has had a legendary great fire. Every child used to grow up with the story of Mrs. O'Leary's cow. Book people still mourn the Alexandria library. The city of Seattle markets its great fire of 1889 as a tourist attraction. When I was a boy, my imagination was tweaked by the great fire of Vancouver. The poet Daphne Marlatt, who went to high school in North Vancouver, has written several books in which she immerses herself in the history of the Lower Mainland. *Vancouver Poems* (1972) makes use of eye-witness accounts of the great fire of Sunday, June 13, 1886:

"there was a man, driving horse and wagon, caught on
Carrall Street between Water and Cordova…two iron tires
and some ashes was all that was left…"

                                        of our city, our
city is, "swept clean to the bare black earth," a mess of
charred stumps, molten bell smoke-enveloped &, human
    ashes.

There was no suspicion of the disgruntled deed-owners of Moodyville. This was the risk of living in a frontier town during a boom. It had happened to Barkerville, and it would happen to Grand Forks. For weeks on end the three thousand denizens of Vancouver had seen stumps burning and smelled the thick smoke that was always in the air. These were the conditions of such a life.

Just west of the three-month-old city the railroad workers were burning stumps and slash around English Bay, mindful of the wind coming in off the sea. But the wind quickly became a gale, and flames burned their way through heaps of slash and sped eastward into the heart of the city. Church bells rang out a warning but were soon stilled as the flames consumed the churches. People raced to their homes to save whatever precious things they had brought from across the ocean, and disappeared in the smoke. Human beings were running in every direction. The wind whipped fire quickly into the brush and trees to the south and east. People jumped into their wells and prayed. The luckiest human beings headed for the inlet, where pockets of fresh air saved their lives. They gathered on the wharf until ferries and sailboats and rafts could rescue them, or they stood in the water and breathed the air just above the surface. In half an hour Vancouver was gone.

In the brand-new city no one had thought yet of taking a head count, so no one knows how many people died in the fire. Seven victims were identified, but after the place had cooled, workers went around pinning pieces of paper on little packages of ash and bone, not knowing whether they were dealing with individuals or fragments. When the smoke had thinned and the ashes were still hot under boot soles, hardly any buildings remained standing. The Hastings Mill was still there. A vacant oil refinery gave survivors a place to lay their pallets. A few shacks made a very low skyline on False Creek. It was Sunday afternoon, and the three thousand homeless were split between praying Christians and those who found another way around fate.

But this was a sawmill town. Before sunrise on Monday morning there were teams of oxen hauling wagonloads of lumber along the streets. By daylight there were men standing on smouldering ashes, lifting shining wood to the sky. A day ago there had been eight hundred businesses in the city. By Monday night there were buildings for people to sleep in, by Wednesday night there was a three-storey hotel, and by Thursday there were deals being made in a dozen offices. By the middle of July there were fourteen hotels and hundreds of stores. Moodyville and Hastings Mill were working around the clock with hot saws.

In Victoria the businessmen looked at the amazing rebirth of Vancouver and saw the future. In Port Moody the businessmen pressed on with their legal actions against the new terminus. Meanwhile the Canadian Pacific Railway, like the Hudson's Bay Company before them, had ships in Asian waters, waiting for a deep-sea port in Burrard Inlet. The Port Moody people had succeeded in getting an injunction against the twelve-mile extension, but Van Horne had workers building wharves and preparing a path for the rails. Eventually the injunction was lifted, and Vancouver became Canada's "Terminal City."

Anniversary celebrations seemed to be in the air. A little over a year ago the first eastern locomotive had arrived in Port Moody on the US holiday. Now, on May 23, 1887, the first passenger train, hauled by Engine 374, arrived in Vancouver. It was the eve of Queen Victoria's Golden Jubilee, which was making people dress up and be noisy all around the globe. In Vancouver the entire population, five thousand souls, showed up to meet the train. The locomotive was covered with flowers and garlands. The streets were festooned with great evergreen arches bearing pretentious colonial slogans. Premier Smithe, who had lobbied Ottawa for this great day, did not live to see it. He had been re-elected at the end of 1886, but never sat in the new house in January. He died two months before Engine 374 arrived at Coal Harbour, and was replaced by Alex E.B. Davie, who himself would die in office in two years.

Workers and Coolies

"Étincelant diamant
Vancouver
Où le train blanc de neige et de feux nocturnes fuit l'hiver."
—Guillaume Apollinaire, "Les fenêtres"

Making tracks

In the first years after the rebuilding of Vancouver, the real-estate agents were happier than a gold panner on the upper Fraser. The railroad across British North America had completed a rondure for the British Empire, and the harbour at the bottom of Granville Street was a busy place. Great ships passed through the Lions Gate, and they brought with them mail and freight and immigrants. The real-estate agents met every boat. Big solid buildings went up between the stumps. The first Hotel Vancouver, a big stone pile, opened on Granville Street in May 1887. It was not long before someone thought of starting an opera house. Vancouver became a word in European offices and salons. In a little shop on Cordova Street, someone went to work making miniature totem poles.

> Cette tache blafarde dans les ténèbres humides c'est la gare du Canadian du Grand Tronc
> Et ces halos bleuâtres dans le vent sont les paquebots en partance pour le Klondyke le Japon et les grandes Indes
> Il fait si noir que je puis à peine déchiffrer les inscriptions des rues où je cherche avec une lourde valise un hôtel bon marché
> —Blaise Cendrars, "Vancouver"

187

The Kaslo and Slocan Railway provided some spectacular views, c. 1900.

The province was being reconfigured. A hundred years before, the white people's presence was felt largely in the very middle of the land mass that was now inside political boundaries. Now the whole province would be a financial watershed leading to the boomtown on Burrard Inlet. And transportation would be very important in such a diverse and difficult land. In the southeast part of the province there was to be a new mining boom, not in gold this time, but in metals that were nevertheless precious on a continent that was industrializing at frightening speed—silver, copper, lead, zinc. And coal. As had happened during the gold rush, the new mines in British Columbia were made by outfits who had worked in the US, in Idaho, Montana and Colorado. But a couple of sourdoughs with a donkey cannot extract high-grade lead from Mother Earth. These ores had to be blasted deep in the ground by hardrock miners, and hauled and refined, great heavy loads of rock moved and smelted, separated chemically between heaps of the good stuff and piles of slag. No little pokes of gold dust here. The industry required lots of money to build shafts and run refineries, and a complete transportation system.

The railroads webbing their way around the west, and the telegraph companies that went with them, required lots of metal. And the mines that produced the metals required railroads to move between mine and smelter. The CPR became interested in the Kootenays, and so did the Great Northern, which had hooked Idaho to the rest of the United States in 1883. Both railroads poked branch lines into the Kootenays. Paddlewheelers went up and down the lakes. The population grew, and dozens and dozens of little towns appeared in valleys and on shores, making the Kootenays in the coming years the ghost-town champions of Canada. The biggest mines and smelters and supply centres became the sites of towns and cities that would in years to come influence the patterns of highways and hockey leagues. Greenwood would become the biggest town between Vancouver and civilization, and later the "Smallest City in Canada." Nelson would support a lot of hotels and public buildings constructed of stone that bespoke permanence and stature, and which a hundred years later would make great motion-picture locations. Kimberley was the site of the world-famous Sullivan mine, staked in 1892. The USAmericans made a fortune at Rossland, and built a big smelter at a town they called Trail, named after Trail Creek, which was named after the Dewdney Trail that had been constructed in the 1860s to protect Victoria against the threat of USAmerican inroads. Robber barons don't care much about irony.

Eventually the USAmericans would become dissatisfied by the Trail smelter and sell it to the CPR. The CPR became more and more like the HBC, the only player big enough to extort monopolistic concessions over a whole territory from the governments involved. When the Canadian government wanted the Crowsnest Pass opened up, the CPR demanded interest in the huge coal deposits in the area, in exchange for low freight rates for prairie grain. As in the old days HBC traders parlayed real estate and government posts into fortunes, so now the high-rollers managed to handle both provincial appointments and property that the CPR needed. But most of the population of the new towns was made up of wage-earners, men who might end their lives under tons of rock and collapsed struts put there by cost-cutting owners. These workers, more and more of them immigrants from parts of Europe in which the Queen's English had made no headway, became the typical British Columbians. The prairies were filling up with family farms. In mining and logging and fish-canning British Columbia the family men were wage-earners at arduous jobs, risking their lives and health for family men living in big houses and wearing overcoats with fur on the collars.

Logging and ranching worked in a way similar to that of mining. It helped to have friends in the still small coterie of government men, or to be a government man oneself. It also helped to know what valley a railroad was going to go through. The government was always strapped for money, yet pre-emptions for logging or ranching went for pennies. Before April 7, 1887, the government placed no restrictions on timber "harvested" from Crown lands purchased by big companies. On land bought after that date the companies had to pay a royalty of fifty cents per thousand board feet. Ranchers were paying six cents an acre for grazing land. Chinese mill workers were being paid, as they had been while working on the railroad, a dollar a day. Owners of sawmills were building mansions on high ground in Vancouver. Successful ranchers were looking around for neighbours who wanted to sell out. The word "empire" was taking on an un-British meaning in British Columbia.

Mara

Regular people could be forgiven for confusing the CPR with the government. All along the rail line there were towns promising to become cities, and in those towns there were friends of government who saw interesting ways to make money, extolling the virtues of the free-enterprise system, and taking land grants from Victoria and contracts from the CPR. An example of this kind of hustler is J.A. Mara.

John Andrew Mara had been one of the luckier Overlanders of 1862. Most of the Overlanders who had waded ashore in Kamloops, half-starved and in tatters, struck out north and west, looking for gold or the good chance. J.A. Mara headed for the short-lived gold rush in the Big Bend country. He was no prospector; he was looking for a way to make money off the prospectors. And the government: in the mid-sixties the Boise miners were jumping northward through the Kootenays, and Seymour was going broke trying to catch up to them with roads. Most of the suppliers in the region went under or gave up in despair, but Mara grabbed their customers, and built a successful store and packing business. In the years to come he would have steam paddlers on the Kootenay lakes. In 1871 he used his business connections to become Member of the Provincial Parliament for Kootenay. Nobody liked him much, this big man with the thick black beard and fancy clothes, but everyone saw his rivals and enemies falling aside.

J.A. Mara built a big sawmill on Kamloops Lake, in partnership with an early developer named McIntosh and government agent John Ussher. He started a fleet of steamships to grab most the traffic on Kamloops Lake and Shuswap Lake. Now he had the Kootenays and the Columbia country. He became Member of the Provincial Parliament for Yale. He bought a grand hotel in Kamloops and built a big house overlooking Kamloops. He put pianos in both. He was Speaker of the House in Victoria. In 1887 he ran in the federal election as a Conservative and remained member of parliament for the next nine years.

Not many people liked the biggest developer in town, but people liked the idea of being his partner. People threw business his way because he had connections in Victoria and Ottawa. Even before the Last Spike was driven into a railroad tie just to the east, Kamloops became the third biggest commercial centre in British Columbia. Van Horne and Onderdonk had decided that Mara's freight rates were too high, and built their own steamer on his lake, but it fell into his hands in due time. During the surveying, the men working on the railroad route went to Mara's store, though, even to buy their trousers and gloves. There was a rumour that the MPP had a lot of influence when it came to hiring and firing. Mara and some of his partners, called the New Township Syndicate had bought up a lot of land on the east side. Later Mara was persuaded to sell his portion, including a hotel that would become the CPR depot. He always seemed to know where important and expensive developments were going to happen.

Still, there were people in the area who did not like Mara, and thought it unlikely that they would ever profit from knowing him. Mara's properties had a way of catching fire. While CPR construction was underway in 1884, for instance, fires broke out at Mara's store and his mill, and even his palatial home. Eventually, after Mara had retired to Victoria, the store and the mill would burn to the ground. Well, there were a lot of fires in the dry interior of British Columbia, and most of them were accidental.

Some of the people who did not like Mara were not afraid to say so. One of his rivals was William Fortune, who had built an empire of land and mills and packing on the north side of the river. He had married a powerful Irishwoman named Jane McWha, who helped him build steamers and an orchard and a ranch and a hotel. She did his hiring and firing and signed the cheques. Lady Jane, as she was known to everyone, was only one of the many women who became legends in the region, but she was the one that got under J.A. Mara's skin. One day Lady Jane and Mara were standing at the rail of a steamer that was making its way from Savona to Kamloops, and Mara got into an argument with her. Perhaps he became too personal. Perhaps he said something about his political power. Whatever the issue, Mrs. Fortune did what a lot of people wanted to do: she shoved J.A. Mara overboard into the middle of Kamloops Lake.

The Wild McLean boys had grudges against a lot of white men, but they plain hated J.A. Mara. The white power establishment had always used its network of property and business and government to build fortunes on someone else's land, and the MPP was the most obvious example. When the Wild McLean boys got drunk and made their death threats against their oppressors, they always put Mara at the top of the list. And he knew why. It was because of Annie McLean.

Mary Angela McLean was three years old when her father was killed by a Chilcotin bullet. She was six years younger than Allen and one year older than Charlie. While the fatherless halfbreed boys were growing up, getting whatever temporary hard jobs they could find at white ranches, Annie was a girl. She was Sophia McLean's daughter, but the white people had managed to get the McLean ranch and roadhouse away from Sophia. Annie was a halfbreed girl, growing up in the seventies in Kamloops. She got a job as a chambermaid for J.A. Mara, magnate and magistrate and Member of the Provincial Parliament.

When the teenaged girl became pregnant, she managed to keep working. But when she had her child she lost her job. The Oblate priest registered the light-coloured little baby girl as the daughter of Annie McLean and an unknown father. Wasn't that always the way with these people? But everyone in and around Kamloops knew who the father was. Even Premier

Walkem in Victoria knew who the father was. Annie's brothers knew who the father was, and their friend Alex Hare was in love with Annie. They also knew that Annie could expect nothing from the MPP that she was not, for reasons of age, sex and race, even permitted to vote for. They knew that Mara had nothing to fear from the law. They would give him something to fear from the McLeans.

After William Palmer and Shumway and McLeod rode into town to tell what had happened to John Ussher near Stump Lake, J.A. Mara responded to his civic duty with alacrity and personal alarm. The residents of Kamloops and the people living on ranches were afraid that the killing was the beginning of a rumoured Indian uprising, but Mara had his own reasons for the fear that entered through the well-constructed doors of his mansion on the hillside. He lent his authority to the quick assembling of a big new posse. He appointed special constables faster than anyone had ever seen. He was the protector of public safety.

And after the bedraggled and half-frozen McLean boys were hauled into Kamloops for their preliminary hearing, they had to face a panel of four Justices of the Peace: Senator Clement Cornwall, lord of Ashcroft Manor; John Tait, the old HBC factor, and number two on the McLeans' hit list; John Edwards, who had led the siege at Douglas Lake—and John Andrew Mara. They looked respectable and stern on the bench. All through the hearing and their two trials, the McLean boys and Alex Hare kept Annie's name out of the proceedings.

With the threat of an uprising over, Kamloops and Mara could continue to look forward to prosperity and growth. It would be fifteen years and more till Mara's power would begin to ebb. In 1887 the *Inland Sentinel* crusaded for the town's incorporation. It was time to become something other than a convenient company town. But the big developers liked things the way they were. In 1896 the *Inland Sentinel* was bought by a syndicate of Liberals who had reform in mind and they put the paper at the service of young Hewitt Bostock, an Englishman who had started the *Province* newspaper in Vancouver two years earlier. Bostock took Mara's federal seat away from him. In 1900 J.A. Mara and his wife moved to Victoria, where he had cleverly acquired property, and lived out their lives there.

Cumberland

Cumberland is a small town a few kilometres back into the bush from Courtenay halfway up Vancouver Island. Beside the road just outside Cumberland, near Comox Lake, there is a farmhouse with a pickup truck on which there is a canopy, and the canopy has decals on it, pictures of game birds flying upward. On the lawn near the truck there are several very large white domestic geese with thick beaks, looking for bugs to eat in the wet grass. There is a beagle sitting and watching them, his chin resting on a chopping block.

For almost a hundred years Cumberland was a coal mining town. At first it was simply named Union, not because of its workers, but because James Dunsmuir owned it, and his business was called the Union Coal Company. It was not till 1898 that the place was renamed Cumberland, after the place in England where a lot of the underground workers came from. Dunsmuir had a railroad laid in the bottom of the little valley, and workers' shacks in three rows on the slopes. A few of those shacks, now called cottages, are still there in a town that is now populated by people who don't like to live in cities. The little wooden houses have flower baskets hanging in front of them.

The firehall is on the main street, across from the museum. Down the slope behind the firehall is a vacant lot, and in the wet vacant lot there is a thirty-year-old Mercury automobile partly covered by a blue plastic tarpaulin, and the tarpaulin is strewn with fir needles. Nearby there is a little roof supported by posts, and under the roof a sign sketching the history of Number 6 mine. People who read the sign are standing on a concrete slab that was used to cap the mine in 1917. The sign informs them that from 1874 till 1965 there were 265 miners killed in the mines around Cumberland.

At the museum, visitors can get a map of the mine sites around Cumberland. To get to some of them, they have to drive up meandering forest roads that feature holes filled with rainwater. There are long thin tendrils of moss hanging from the boughs of the fir trees. The forest is doing its best to continue after a century of blasting and hauling away the ancient black fuel from underneath. There is a cairn where one of these dirt roads meets the paved road. It commemorates Number 4 mine, which operated from 1890 to 1935. Number 4 gave up the highest tonnage and the best quality coal in the area. In 1922 and 1923 there were fifty-one miners killed in explosions down in Number 4. The cairn was donated by the British Columbia Federation of Labour on Miners' Memorial Day, June 24, 1989.

A lot of the miners did not come from England. Cumberland had a Chinatown, and a good walk outside of town, a little settlement called "Coontown" by the locals. There are two little buildings there now, and a kind of flattened area not yet taken back by the forest. There is also a cairn. On it are written these words: "This cairn marks the site of the pioneer Black community who lived and worked in the Cumberland area from 1893 until 1960. Donated by Cumberland & District Historical Society."

But Cumberland is not going to be a settled ghost town for long. Already there are big new houses built without taste on ground that has been denuded of trees, for people who work in Courtenay but want to live the bucolic life. The area around the little valley is being devastated, turned ugly by big gravel pits and clear-cuts where fashionable housing developments with pretentious names will be plunked down, soon to be followed by franchise hamburger joints and home-entertainment stores.

Unions

Karl Marx and Friedrich Engels published *The Communist Manifesto* in 1848. *Das Kapital* followed in 1867, with a new edition in 1885. Marx and Engels were internationalists, but in the nineteenth century in Europe the history of the union movement differed in each country. The British labour movement would be the most successful in Europe, seeing socialist politics as their route, and wresting legal accommodations from Gladstone and Disraeli.

In the United States socialism would not become as large a part of workers' lives or the situation of capitalist industry as it was in Europe. As a consequence, the United States became the only industrialized country in which labour did not have a political party to represent its interests.

In British Columbia the beginnings of the labour movement were partly British and partly USAmerican, reflecting the origins of the working population. As the company coal mines of Vancouver Island opened to support the HBC's maritime operations, and later the empire of the Dunsmuirs, experienced coal miners from Scotland, England and Wales were employed, along with a few Chinese. Unfortunately for the owners, the British were also used to working in a unionized environment. Established businessmen-politicians in Victoria opined that these immigrants were not the best sort of new colonials. They preferred the sons and daughters of the soil, the children of farmers, who never considered political power. These sentiments would become policy when Andrew Onderdonk imported his thousands of farmboys from southern China to push steel up the Fraser Canyon.

The first strike happened in 1850 when non-unionized Scottish miners laid down their tools at Fort Rupert, where they were extracting coal for the Hudson's Bay Company. Governor Blanshard himself sailed to oversee the settlement, but it was over by the time he arrived. The first unionized people on Vancouver Island were the bakers, who formed a union in Victoria in 1859. During the following decade other tradesmen would organize—the typographical workers, the shipwrights and other craftsmen. Goldmining along the Fraser did not get organized, because it was done largely by individual panners or small companies of diggers. The gold rush was a type of rampant individual competitiveness. Coal mining at Nanaimo was another story. By the 1870s the huge New Wellington seam was feeding the market in San Francisco, and the new province had a stake in the business.

The Dunsmuirs were experts at blackmailing governments, as they showed in their railroad land-grab, and they were not going to be any less aggressive in their dealings with less privileged people. But the miners they had hired were not the kind to sit around and wait for a better day. Just as later the Chinese youths falling to their death in Hell's Canyon would be factored into the risks of building a national railroad, so miners killed or injured or diseased due to cost-cutting underground were seen by the colliery owners as replaceable resources. The Wellington seam would become the site of acrimonious strikes, despite the efforts of the Dunsmuirs' enforcers. In 1877 there was a particularly bitter work-stoppage that lasted for more than four months, and this time the Dunsmuirs had to call in a favour from the provincial government. There was a Dunsmuir castle with an imposing Scottish name on prime land not far from the legislature. Victoria sent in the militia to intimidate the miners and their families in Nanaimo. It was assumed that James Dunsmuir was one day going to be premier; smart members of the small pool that made up the political cadre of British Columbia wanted to stay on the good side of Dunsmuir in a time when the province was not beleaguered by formal political parties and unions.

When the hardrock companies came into southeast British Columbia, they came largely from the mountain country just south of the line. With them came the men who had been working in their outfits in Idaho and Montana. These were militant, politicized men, tough in body and mind, members of the Western Federation of Miners, created in 1893, who had engaged in the social struggle down there, fierce strikes waged against frontier plutocrats and hired detectives. They would amount to a third of the working population in the Kootenay and Boundary region. The B.C. Trade Union Act would transpire because of the resistance of these weathered men.

But as early as 1886 the Island miners were organizing, too, and making their contribution to the future of labour. That year in Victoria they almost started a party for the provincial election. This was the Workingmen's Protective Association, which actually ran candidates in Nanaimo and the capital. But Robert Dunsmuir ran against their candidate in Nanaimo and got elected. Then he managed to get himself seated on any committee that handled issues that concerned his family income. The miners got a good lesson in British Columbia politics, and continued to work along political lines. They formed the Miners' and Mine-Workers' Protective Association, and began fighting for union status, better safety conditions and shorter hours, taking as their examples the demands and successes of their brothers in Great Britain.

In British Columbia, though, one of labour's major issues was race. In the later years of the nineteenth century in British Columbia race issues meant Chinese workers.

Exclusion

Among people from southern China the popular name for British Columbia was Gold Mountain. The first Chinese to appear came with the California gold rush crowd to Victoria in 1858. While the old fort was being changed into a boom town, the Chinese population became a major feature of the place. People of all sorts exploited each other as much as they could, and nourished racial stereotypes as well as they could manage to. In a few years, when the Cariboo became quieter and the miners headed elsewhere, Victoria looked around and saw that the Chinese were still there. A few were still there in larger towns of the Interior too. Hoity-toity families in Victoria had Chinese cooks and servants, and hotels sent their bedsheets to Chinese laundries. Horny miners went looking for Chinese party houses. Chinatown became both familiar and mysterious.

In the California gold rush of the early fifties, the miners used every method they could think of to try to keep Chinese workers out of the mines, and the politicians responded by campaigning against Chinese immigration and employment. Those Heathen Chinee were willing to work harder for less money, taking jobs away from real USAmericans, men from Europe. As the miners moved north so did the Orientals, and so did resistance against the Orientals. It moved up the Fraser River and into the governing houses of the colonies and eventually the provincial legislature.

But at first there was no law against Chinese miners. There were lots of incidents. When boatloads of Chinese men arrived at Fort Hope, the USAmericans would meet them with threats and something in their hands. But the Chinese presence became part of the gold fields. In Victoria, the first newspaper in the British northwest was called the Victoria *Gazette*. It was owned by Californians, and spoke of their education in matters concerning the Chinese. The *Gazette* informed its readership that the Chinese were a threat to Christian civilization because the men were willing to work in dangerous conditions for low wages and thus degrade the conditions for white labour, and the women were certain to undermine the moral standards of any area they found their way into. Chinese people would threaten the future civilization that newspapers were always envisioning. The Celestials would not be "desirable as permanent settlers in a country peopled by the Caucasian race and governed by civilized enactments. No greater obstacle to the coming of the class of immigrants needed in British Columbia could be devised, than the presence of Chinamen in large numbers throughout the upper mining region of British Columbia" (March 31, 1859). Governor Douglas agreed, but said that on a temporary basis they would be useful as a monetary investment. Amor de Cosmos seconded that opinion a year later in his newspaper.

Mine owners who ran operations that were either too dangerous or marginally profitable to attract white miners were happy to engage the Chinese. But while the newspapers were exposing a threat to religion and morality,

Chinatown in Barkerville, 1925.

the white miners felt a threat to their livelihood. If the marginal owners could hire slave labour, why would the big outfits turn their backs on an easier profit? Indeed, some mine owners carted in Chinese scabs when white miners tried to stage a strike. There would be boatloads of Orientals coming across the Pacific, especially with the anti-immigration movements growing in power in the US and Australia. In short, while there were many kinds of anti-Chinese feelings, the feelings were mixed among those who could make money off them, while among the working whites there was very little pro-Asian feeling at all.

The first organized protest against Chinese immigration, then, was voiced by the first white labour organizers, the US-founded Knights of Labour, who flourished for a few years during the railroad boom. The Knights organized chapters on the Island and around Vancouver and New Westminster, signing up woodworkers, teamsters, miners and others. Their targets were the extraction companies that were getting bigger as they bought out small operations—and the flood of Chinese that were now highly visible in the rising cities and which would become even more visible during the post-railroad depression. The image of the knight was attractive to men who liked to see themselves as somehow valiant in the face of national threats, and also riding above another group they could see as serfs, one supposes. While these knights did not act quite as violently as those other knights in the postwar US, they did, in places such as Vancouver, operate both openly and clandestinely. They announced boycotts of merchants who dealt with Chinese employees or customers. They painted a large black X on the sidewalk in front of any offending business. They easily found allies among newspaper editorialists, and lobbied their politicians. They made scary noises in the dark, and they crowded the dock when a boat full of Cantonese appeared.

And in 1884 the provincial legislature finally responded to the uproar. It passed three anti-Chinese laws. The first forbade further Chinese immigration. The second forbade the purchase of any Crown land by Chinese people. The third imposed an annual ten-dollar poll tax on each Chinese person. But the federal government was far enough away to observe the scene with moral impartiality. The federal government also had a very high stake in the success of the national railroad. A month and a half after the British Columbia legislation, it struck down the law against further immigration. Soon the poll tax was defeated in court. But the law against Chinese land-purchase was retained.

But there were still lots of people who did not want those Godless Chinamen in a "Caucasian" country. They smoked opium. They had no toilets. They worshipped idols. They wore pigtails. They spread horrible diseases. They wanted your daughters. Such stories persist.

The British Columbia legislature once again enacted a ban on Chinese immigration, and once again the Dominion government struck it down. But the feds formed a royal commission on the problem. It recommended that there be a ten-dollar head tax on Chinese, and that immigration be highly selective, weeding out several kinds of undesirables. Ottawa, as so often happens, did not act on the commission's recommendations. But the question was being aired; the possibility of legal discrimination was being seriously discussed. What was not being discussed was the suggestion that Chinese immigrants would have any more success than the Native population in getting to vote. John A. Macdonald's parliament passed a law against it. In his speech during debate, John said that the Chinaman would never have any "British instincts."

West-coast labour was not satisfied. In May 1885, at Harmony Hall (yes, that was the name of the labour temple in Victoria), the Anti-Chinese Union was formed. The ACU soon formed an alliance with the Knights of Labour, and in this way labour organization and Chinese exclusion became entwined in British Columbia. Two months later the ACU was cheered when Ottawa finally passed the Chinese Immigration Act, calling for very limited immigration and a fifty-dollar head tax for any Chinese person who managed to get through the screen. Macdonald had managed to delay such legislation until the Last Spike was in sight.

But when the steel was joined, there was an even larger problem. Now there were thousands of Chinese gandy dancers out of work. Some had enough savings to get back to Canton. Some went to California. Most of the ones who remained got jobs of some sort. A few became cooks and opened restaurants in railroad towns. But a large number came back to the Coast and set up ramshackle camps at Vancouver and Victoria. The response of the white populace was mixed. Some set up soup kitchens. Some stood guard over their chickens and pigs. The ACU and the Knights of Labour called loudly for deportation. Chinese shacks mysteriously burned down near False Creek. Goon squads used sticks of wood to persuade Chinese unemployed to move from Vancouver to New Westminster, where they would meet other knights with sticks of wood. Race relations were not pretty on the coast of British Columbia in the late eighties. Even the Indians were not good friends of the Chinese. Once in a while a church spokesman would suggest that burning Chinese shacks was not a Christian deed.

Apparently the white union activists did not consider another solution to their problem with Chinese competition for jobs—getting the Chinese to join their organizations. Just as nationalism had proven too powerful an obstacle for the European Marxists, so racism diverted the British Columbia workers' energy. As the eighties gave way to the nineties, and white population soared, anti-Chinese venom thinned, though it did not disappear. By the nineties the main thrust of the exclusionary movement was in the hands of the new union movements and the race organizations they formed. The province was still, in its early industrialization, in the hands of the businessmen-politicians; organized labour had little leverage. The nascent union movement reached for any handhold it could see. The threat of alien "slave" labour was most obvious.

Lepers

Another form of Chinese exclusion made an emphatic footnote to late-nineteenth-century racial history on the coast. From the beginning one of the major complaints about the growing Chinese population had to do with sanitation and health. The Europeans, who had managed to introduce plagues among the Indians, were regularly informed that China, along with India, was the plague centre of the world. Common knowledge had it that Chinese people had no concept of sanitation, and that among the immigrants were carriers of dreadful diseases from Asia. Once here, the terrible microbes would race through the cramped, run-down Chinatowns and find their way into the white community. Thus, in the nineties the various municipal governments tried to enact sanitation laws that would change certain practices at Chinese laundries, for instance, or try to restrict the numbers of people living in tenements.

Perhaps the most feared disease among people brought up on the Bible was leprosy. It was thought to be endemic in China, and ferociously communicable. In 1891 a handful of leprosy cases was discovered in Victoria. On an earlier occasion the Chinese merchants had been persuaded to pay a leper's passage back to China, but now they were reluctant to take on the expense in perpetuity. So the municipal and provincial governments relied on the practice found all over the Europeanized world—they set up a leper colony.

D'Arcy Island is one of the many little islands in the Gulf. It was perfect for the uses of the Victoria city fathers. It had no known mineral resources, and no one was interested in trying to farm there. It was too far off Vancouver Island for sick people to swim from. In 1891 the first five Chinese lepers were deposited there, to be joined by two from Vancouver. Over the years more victims were marooned, but the population never got high enough to become a political force. There was no sanitarium; the exiles were expected to wait out their unfortunate days in whatever kind of community they could devise. Rumours that leprosy was difficult to catch did not move the white or Chinese populations in the province. No one could see the little island from the mainland or the legislature. Four times a year a medical officer would arrive with supplies, and some people think that these included gifts of opium. The medical officer would take the census every three months. For obvious reasons, he was the lepers' only contact with the world. As far as we know, none of the lepers wrote a book about their strange life on D'Arcy Island.

Chinatown

In *Vancouver Poems*, Daphne Marlatt notes that the city's Chinatown sits near skid road hotels, where the city had its beginning just before the great fire:

> A Parlour, refuge from the trees
> CPR cleared along Water, Cordova, Hastings & Pender Streets
> "by the bowling-pin method", beer parlour whisper you can hear
> dice clicking nights, on Pender,
>
>   wise on whatever, groggy,
> with mired eyes, they view what seems most foreign:
> circumambulation of cars, sight-seers, the moneyed hysteria
> of night-diners, shoppers for asian curios. Don't see.
> Ducks hung, animals all sorts, coiled forms of living cured
> of that dis-ease
>   he
>   stands in (Heian) old man fishing for,
> off galley shithouse or pier, eyes too small a conflagration....

Feeding frenzy

Until 1903 the premiership of British Columbia, and the power to allocate business advantages, continued to be circulated among a clique of property owners who had got to Vancouver Island when the getting was good. The average reign of a premier continued to be two years. That was enough to ensure the naming of Vancouver streets after Smithe and Davie and Semlin and Dunsmuir and Prior. Parties formed along ideological lines were still a foreign or federal concept. In British Columbia rich men who had known each other for a long time created factions that lasted only as long as particular or local financial interests made them necessary. There was a lot of jockeying for positions, favours offered for future power, compromises that looked advantageous, secret cabals in a small legislature. In the last two decades of the nineteenth century the government of British Columbia resembled the Vancouver Stock Exchange of a century later.

Meanwhile, since the completion of the national railroad and the establishment of the port of Vancouver, big interests had been persuaded that what New Caledonia meant for the Hudson's Bay Company, British Columbia could mean for investors. The hand-loggers, the sourdough prospectors, and the family fish canneries were going to find out what it was like trying to make a living next to big outfits whose owners never walked in the local mud. And if a hand-logger did not have a friend who had a friend in Victoria, he might as well get used to enjoying a marginal life, and forget about replacing the tar-paper on his walls with brick. By the terms of Confederation all the mining, farming and logging land in the province belonged to the provincial version of the Crown, and the men who had the power to disburse such land were often the heads of families that would wind up with large holdings of choice real estate. What a surprise. In other parts of Canada, where the entrepreneurs felt constrained to doing their accumulation in more subtle fashion, British Columbia looked like a chubby dolphin in a shark pool.

Here was the simplest way to acquire a lot of pleasant land: get to know a member of the legislative assembly and make him a promise of some sort; then gather a few names to attach to a plan for a railroad to "open up the province," and argue that the most logical place for a railroad is along a fertile river valley; then pay a few cents an acre for the grazing, mining and logging rights to the land in question. Eventually you will make so much money that one day you might be a member of the legislative assembly. Some day the clique of grey-headed men who had been in Victoria since before 1871 would be gone, and it was a big province.

In these circumstances, it is no wonder that John Robson, the old champion of Confederation, who became premier in 1889, could become known as "Honest John." Robson was sixty-five by the time his turn came. He was no longer the fiery newspaper crusader he had been; in fact he was now, like so many of his contemporaries, a rich man. But unlike his part-time friends in the house, he still had some ideas. Ideas were not a high priority during the post-Craigellachie scramble for spoils. There were only four high schools in the province, and children were not voters. But somehow John Robson retained a sensibility that was bothered by the system of land-grabbing in his bailiwick.

At first his administration continued to give land away to paper railroads as his two predecessors had. William Smithe, the first post-CPR premier, died in March 1887, before he could meet the house. His successor Alex Davie gave $200,000 as well as the usual emoluments to the Shuswap & Okanagan Railway Co., a subsidiary of the CPR. Then he handed 200,000 acres to the Kootenay & Columbia Railway Co. Some of the grants were given to companies that actually built railroads. Like Smithe before him, Davie died in office, and was replaced in 1889 by his minister of finance, Robson. He promptly gave land and cash inducements to several railway companies with ambitious names, such as the Crowsnest Pass and Kootenay. They all collapsed and were taken over by the CPR. That outfit was threatening to take over the domain the way the Hudson's Bay Company had done a century earlier. The difference was that now there was a way for thousands of non-Native people to get into the province—via the railroad. These people would become voters, and some of them would voice their discontent about the sweetheart deals made between MLAs and railroad owners.

Robson's generosity toward the CPR was explained in his mind by his fear of US aggression, especially as it was seen in the Kootenay mining country. It was not a new argument, and it has not disappeared. Some self-styled Canadian nationalists late in the twentieth century would support favours for Canadian plutocrats as a way of defending against the US-based "Internationals." But by the time of the 1890 election, factions were threatening to become political parties, and Robson had to ensure a majority by means more subtle than deal-making with cronies. Some mainlanders, frustrated by the fact that Vancouver Island was still being represented by half the seats in the house, formed a quasi-separatist party called the Independents, and won ten seats of the total of thirty-three. Labour elected two members from Nanaimo. When the 1890 session sat, Robson managed to make associates of half the Independents, but he was forced to see the wisdom of dealing with non-CPR merchants, and supplying some kind of hope for unwealthy citizens.

He began to make less generous land grants, and to look into the reliability of the names signed to new railroad charters. The newspapers, especially those backed by US merchants, were still portraying him as the railroads' bagman. He refused all reserves to the CPR. But the smaller lines he supported failed, and the CPR grabbed up the Kootenay subsidies anyway, another 750,000 acres. The "saloon-keepers" he reviled had more to complain about, and made much of the fact that he lived in Victoria, where it did not take many voters to elect a legislator.

In 1892 Robson responded to all the pressure from mainlanders and merchants and editorialists. He enacted the first restrictions against the sharks in the pool. From now on the railway charters would not include mineral rights, not even the coal that would feed the locomotives if they ever appeared. Water rights would not go automatically to the outfits that purchased or leased land. No one could buy more than a square mile of land surveyed by the Crown. Forest land was differentiated from other land, and restrictions placed on its sale. It looked as if British Columbia would be safe from timber giants in the twentieth century. No longer would tycoons from Vancouver Island be able to sell each other or their friends outside the province vast tracts of natural resources. Robson looked like a reformer, at least when compared with all the Victoria gents since James Douglas.

But he did not go far enough in the eyes of the mainlanders, which meant chiefly the people in Vancouver and the Kootenays. Power in Victoria still remained in the hands of Islanders and MLAs in the Cariboo, a nexus established in the days of fur and gold. When Robson's legislature redistributed seats in the house, the metropolis of Vancouver still felt underrepresented. Even Honest John had a hard time with the ambitions of the junior partner; he knew that the merchants in Vancouver and New Westminster wanted the capital moved to the railhead. He was a pretty old man with the belief that whatever culture existed on the west coast was ensconced in Victoria. If the beer-drinkers across the strait wanted to improve themselves, they should put on shoes and approach the south end of the Island. He had been the minister of education. When he managed to get the University Act passed and all the officials in place, he assumed that the province's first institute of higher learning would be in Victoria. The Independents refused to tug their forelocks, and Premier Robson's university remained a paper dream for twenty-five years.

Still, the old newspaperman remains an understandable mixture of snob and Quixote. His last crusade was perhaps not truly typical, but it ensured that he would take his place among the British Columbia premiers that make people elsewhere shake their heads in puzzled admiration or disbelief. Having cooled the ambitions of pirates on the land, he turned his attention to the ocean. With its enormously long coastline, British Columbia could expect a seagoing industry that would, like its forests and minerals, go on forever. For ten thousand years the Indians had been harvesting salmon. In recent years the Japanese had been hauling silver food from the depths. Robson turned his eyes to Scotland. His plan was to bring thousands of crofters from the Scottish islands to develop British Columbia's deep-sea fisheries. In the summer of 1892 he went to London to explain his vision to the imperial authorities. While there he got his finger slammed in a taxicab door, developed blood poisoning, and perished. He was the third British Columbia premier in a row to die in office.

Boom, bust

The lawyer Alex Davie had preceded Robson in office. Now his brother the lawyer Theodore Davie would succeed Robson. This Davie was also a confirmed Islander. It was during his reign that the domed palace built by architect Francis Rattenbury was commissioned to stand beside Victoria harbour and proclaim for all time that Victoria would remain the seat of government. The restive mainlanders could do little but agitate in anger while the new legislative buildings went up, marble block by marble block. They raised a stink about the expense, of course; the edifice would cost $981,000. But these were boom times. The Victoria clique was looking southward to magnificent structures in California and forward to opulence on the Canadian west coast. Solid lakes of silver were, after all, being discovered in the Kootenays, trainloads of eager people were jumping onto the platform in Vancouver, and high ocean liners were hooting their way around Point Grey.

If, as the Liberal leader back east would say, the twentieth century would belong to Canada, British Columbia was going to be waiting at the CPR station.

Unfortunately, despite the seven-year-old Last Spike, British Columbia was a long way from Ontario, and still dependent on USAmerican investment. In the 1890s the US entered its most conscious period of imperialism, invading and seizing independent Hawaii, and scooping up Spanish islands in the Caribbean, but in 1893 there was a quick recession, and all but the fattest nabobs of the gilded age grabbed their turbans and ran for cover. Consequently the glittering corporations inB.C. had to announce cutbacks and closures. Buildings in Vancouver were left unfinished. Southern orders for raw materials disappeared. The real-estate sharpies put their loud jackets in mothballs. A lot of the hopeful folk who had arrived from back east now decided to try their luck in Washington and Oregon.

Independent loggers came out of the bush and hung around skid road, looking for work that did not exist, trying to put together enough coin to buy a beer at one of the bars that managed to stay open. They joined clerks from bankrupt stores at the church-mission soup kitchens. It snowed all winter. Nature always seems to punish the victims of economics in Canada. The winter of 1893-1894 was even worse than the record-setting winter of 1879-1880, when the McLean boys were led in socks across the frozen Fraser at New Westminster.

Those people that did not die from the diseases that attack the starving held on through that grim winter, living on the hope that naturally visited human beings living next to the silt-formed lower Fraser Valley, the richest agricultural land in Canada. Then in the spring the high snow melted, and the lower Fraser Valley was an inland sea. Dead cows floated on the saline muck, and farm buildings drifted along with them. Farms and bridges disappeared under the Great Flood. The canneries at the river's former mouth broke apart, and rotted salmon was carried inland by the tides. The CPR track above Yale was washed away, so no help could arrive from the east for two months. Refugees poured into Vancouver, and the soup lines grew longer while the soup became thinner. When the waters finally receded and the river course could be seen again, there was no hope of planting 1893 crops in the salty valley. The stink was terrible.

The hard times were going to last for most of the nineties, unless you were the Hudson's Bay Company, or a USAmerican mine near Nelson. Premier Davie responded to the crisis by granting more railroad subsidies, and welcoming all the USAmerican investments he could scare up. Sometimes these two measures were joined, as for instance when the Great Northern Railway was encouraged to poke its lines into money pockets of the province. If Davie had been Governor Douglas, he might have tried to put in a rail line where the Dewdney Trail had fallen into desuetude, and helped Vancouver catch up with the brawny Seattle. But all the new rails ran north and south. Meanwhile the smaller mining and logging and fishing companies were being bought up by big corporations, many of them foreign. When John Turner became premier in 1895, he continued the policies of Davie, but also looked to England for traditional money immigration. He mounted a big advertising campaign to bring Britishers to the Edenic agricultural valleys of the Interior. He encouraged British mining investors who had done well in South Africa. The immigrants continued to pour into the province. Between the census of 1881 and the census of 1911, the population of B.C. was to leap from 50,000 to 392,000. It would become more and more difficult for the old-boy system in Victoria to govern such a place. Most of the new population settled on the mainland, and had never listened to a speech by Amor de Cosmos or William Smithe.

Here they come again

As usual, the economy was revived by hordes of shovel-carriers heading north. In the late summer of 1896 a Canadian prospector found a chunk of gold on a tributary of the Klondike River in Yukon, and a few lucky men there kept it a secret until they arrived with gold all over them in Seattle a year later. Once again variegated galoots started hollering the magic word, and the world headed for the Canadian north. The city of Victoria was used to this sort of thing, and Island outfitters and hotel men welcomed the boat-loads of wild-eyed men and smouldering women who began passing through. But Victoria could not handle this new crowd. The half-built edifices of Vancouver were finished, and music poured out of the saloons. Eldorado left solid traces of gold along Hastings Street. Ships stood in line in the harbour. A hundred thousand amateurs and professionals streamed into the territory, where the Mounted Police had already set up camp. In Victoria and Vancouver, money was thick at the top and trickled down a little, enough to buy children shoes to wear instead of eating. Good times, depending on who you were, were back again, except for poor old New Westminster, where in 1898 a fire destroyed the whole downtown.

But it began to look as if nothing could save the British Columbia legisla-ture. Some politicians, especially those who had experience in Ottawa, were calling themselves Liberals or Conservatives; but ideology had little to do with the groups who tussled for power, cursing one another creatively, shout-ing insanely in the house. The old system of factions that had arisen when everyone knew everyone else, was still there, except that now instead of British lawyers, the powerbrokers were likely to be the performing monkeys of large corporate interests. The old Victoria clique were dying off: Robert Dunsmuir in April 1889, Matthew Begbie in June 1894, Amor de Cosmos in July 1897. It was becoming harder to support the gerrymandering that had been necessary to keep such a high percentage of Island seats in the legisla-ture. By the time of the 1898 election the mainland had twenty-four of the thirty-eight seats in the house.

With so many seats, it was hard for anyone to gather a big enough fac-tion. The '98 election was a mess. Premier Turner could not muster a major-ity, some ridings were unable to finish their count, and protests were being entered nearly everywhere. What followed was one of the most chaotic, tedious and stupid five years of B.C.'s political life—and that is saying some-thing. The lieutenant-governor, Thomas McInnes, had to listen to the expostulations of four men who claimed that they should be premier, and it would not be long until his job too was on the line. Any masochist who desires to read about all the infighting and backstabbing that characterized the years 1898-1903 should consult a book more patient than this. Here is a skimming of the events.

Lieutenant-Governor McInnes didn't even wait for Turner to meet non-confidence in the house. He asked Robert Beaven, the former premier and apparently defeated candidate in this election, to form a ministry. Beaven tried, but got nowhere. Then McInnes asked leader-of-the-opposition Charles Semlin to give it a go. Semlin had only half the supporters enjoyed by Turner. This choice enraged Joe Martin, a conceited Liberal from Manitoba, and Francis Carter-Cotton, a plodding Conservative newspaper-man lately from Britain. Semlin tried to smooth things over by making these two men important cabinet members in his regime. That move was to fail in the comic-opera clashes between the two men over the next year and a half.

Semlin decided to handle the situation by having as few meetings as possible, and sending down legislation that would make the populace like his administration. He managed to get an eight-hour day for mineworkers, but the mine owners ignored it. He passed an Alien Exclusion Act, to keep the Chinese out of the placer creeks, but the USAmericans got their backs up. He ignored McInnes's command to have a session in the fall of 1899, and when the house met in 1900, he became the target of Martin's ire, mainly because he had fired Martin in public the year before. Semlin tried his best to seduce a majority to pass some election reforms, but failed; now McInnes demanded that he step down. The house, despising the interference of the lieutenant-governor more than they reviled the premier, rejected the removal. McInnes puffed himself up and called on the self-congratulating Martin to form a government. The first question Martin faced was a vote of non-confidence. He lost twenty-eight to one.

Everyone was getting mad. McInnes marched on the legislature to shut down the session. He entered to a chorus of catcalls and artificial farts from the public galleries. Before he could begin his speech, the rich and staid James Dunsmuir walked with provincial dignity out of the room, and was followed by just about all the members. Left seated were Joe Martin and the speaker of the house. McInnes went red in the face and then white in the face. Then in his feathers and braid he read his speech to Joe and the speaker, while the people in the galleries grew ever louder with their rude noises and untutored witticisms. Having finished his voice from the Crown, he departed, and Dunsmuir led the members back in. The galleries broke into tumultuous cheers.

Another day in the business of B.C.'s government.

Martin had an impossible task in front of him, which he handled as poorly as he could. First he made a cabinet out of the least-distinguished men he could find. Then he appealed to the new Liberal party of B.C. for backing. The Liberals asked Prime Minister Laurier what they should do. Laurier told Martin to call an election. Knowing that he would lose, Martin decided that he would try to ingratiate himself with the voters first. The election came in three months, and proved once and for all that the people were becoming more powerful than the exclusive club in Victoria. Nobody won. Martin, by far the most intelligent animal in the jungle, was supported by a third of the members. But he was too headstrong to manage a coalition with any other faction, and he needed two more anyway. What the hell is going on out there on the west coast, politicians in Ottawa asked, not for the last time.

Before the new legislature was asked to sit, most of the members had a meeting on the mainland, and passed a resolution that the high-handed lieutenant-governor should be shipped out before they tried to do any of the province's business. The chief draftsman of the paper was Richard McBride, a Conservative Anglophile born in New Westminster less than thirty years before. McInnes wrote a message to Laurier, describing the bunch of yahoos he was trying to civilize. But Laurier, experiencing distaste for the sub-parliamentary goings-on in Victoria over the past few years, decided to yank McInnes. He gave the lieutenant-general's job to one Sir Henry Joly de Lotbinière, whose chief qualification was that he did not know anyone in the province of British Columbia. The Liberal associations of Vancouver and Victoria protested the change. Oh, pipe down, said Laurier.

So there was to be a new lieutenant-governor that nobody knew in the capital where one's career was mainly conducted by making sure that other people knew one. So who was going to be the new premier? All the factions rejected each other's candidates because they were party men. The only man they could find who was too rich to be a party man was old James Dunsmuir. The members decided that they would try him for a year. Dunsmuir became the third British Columbia premier of the last year of the nineteenth century.

British (etc.) Columbians

"It is war now between the Oriental and the Euro-Canadian for possession of British Columbia: the prize region of the whole Pacific."
—Tom MacInnis, 1927

The sporting life

Wherever the Brits went while painting the world's map red, they took their peculiar diet, school system, attire—and sports. They taught the Maoris how to play rugby. They taught the Malays how to play cricket. They taught the Sikhs how to play tennis. They brought soccer to South Africa. But if you look around British Columbia you will not see many First Nations dressed in whites, rolling dark balls over clipped grass. The mountains and canyons of the colony, perhaps, made it difficult to lay out a golf course, though by 1890 they were playing polo among the gopher holes on the benches of the Thompson Valley.

The geographical particulars did, of course, seem like a dream come true for devotees of what many people call outdoor sports. Outdoor sportsmen had to be of the intrepid sort; Italians who were fond of plinking little migratory birds with their shotguns, or British toffs who liked to have Native beaters flush quail for them were not likely to be very happy in the rugged landscape of B.C. But big-game hunters who could climb mountains could get a thrill when they found moose or bear or mountain sheep in their sights. Fishing fanatics in canoes off Vancouver Island or waist-deep in a Kootenay stream could get a real workout from the flesh underwater. Mountain climbers were not as numerous as those found in the Alps, but they did not have to look far for a challenge. Scandinavians looked for places to ski between the trees. The old-money (let us say two generations) gentry of Victoria and the *nouveau-riche* of Vancouver rushed to create impressive yacht clubs and rowing clubs.

The Indians had sports of their own, though white preachers and politicians inveighed against most of them because they looked a lot like gambling, a sin that was not, like booze, introduced by the Europeans. The Salishan people, for instance, often had their sports days in conjunction with intertribal fishing meets. There were contests in lifting, running, shooting and jumping among these peoples who had never been to Olympus. (Horseracing was a passion among them, which made for a small irony; the British, who had brought their devotion to horseracing to just about every other colony, did not do so in this one. By the time of the First World War the race season in British Columbia, under the auspices of the Vancouver Hunt Club, comprised two months of racing, with a two-week interval in the middle.) The Indians played various versions of stick games, accompanied by singing, all over the Interior. The rules were a mystery to white observers, but the latter were made uneasy by the laughter and drumming that accompanied them. In her autobiography, the Salishan writer Mourning Dove describes a wonderful sport engaged in at athletic meets in the plateau country:

> A favorite one of old had pairs of men compete against each other. One player rolled a serviceberry ring along a trench while the other man tried to shoot an arrow through it. The ring was decorated with beads, dyed porcupine quills, or feathers. Sometimes a ten-inch ring had spokes laced to make a center hole two inches in diameter. The trenches were about fifty feet long. The players rolling the ring waited on a slight upgrade, and the shooters formed a line along the trench. The winner was the man whose arrow went through the hoop that matched his bow. If there were several "bull's-eyes," these men competed until the best shot got all the bets. It was an exciting game, accompanied by yells and laughter after each game. All gambling required good sportsmanship. It was shameful for poor losers to grieve. They would get no sympathy. Visitors left either walking because they had lost their ponies or gleefully driving a new herd.

The Native peoples also had field games. In describing the Squamish, for instance, the famous anthropologist Charles Hill-Tout reports seeing a variety of lacrosse called "kekqua," and a kind of football called "tequila." The women played something that looked like badminton, called "tckwie."

Lacrosse was, of course, one Indian game that the white Canadians adopted. In fact, by the turn of the century it was commonly referred to as Canada's national pastime. By the 1880s there were already two professional teams in the province, representing Vancouver and New Westminster, each of which, by 1911, would have won the "World Championship" trophy, the Minto Cup. There were amateur leagues in all the coastal cities, too, and they would vie for the "World Championship" of amateur lacrosse, the Mann Cup. The other national pastime of Canada, ice hockey, was played by only a few desperate easterners, who spent their Sunday mornings climbing into the hills of the Interior and shovelling snow off frozen ponds. They often had to skate around an ice-hugged saskatoon bush to make a run at the opposition goalie.

The English, with their notion that sports were character-building for Englishmen and civilizing for the Empire, got into their costumes and played their games on weekends. Perhaps the most quixotic British sportsmen were the aristocratic rancher brothers from Ashcroft Manor, Henry and Clement Cornwall. In 1868 they imported three foxhounds from the Old Country, hoping to set up the nucleus of a pack that would keep the class system going for all time in cattle country. But they did not import any English foxes. The plan was to substitute the local coyotes. They should have listened to the Shuswap and Thompson people about coyotes and Coyote. For the rest of the century the gentry around Ashcroft and Cache Creek went thundering across the plateau, trying to run coyotes to ground. The foxhounds, bred to yap their way across the Emerald Isle, had to keep stopping to bite cactus spines out of their paws.

Soccer, or what was termed Association Football by its adherents, was the first and most successfully entrenched team sport. It was played informally in just about every community in the Interior, and in the coastal cities there were leagues of all sorts, backed by schools, churches, businesses and British counties of origin. Rugby football also caught on, at least on the coast. In fact it crossed the border, and before the end of the century it was being played in California. The first big intercity match was played between Vancouver and New Westminster. Vancouver won a defensive contest eight to three. Cricket was England's national game, and it was to be expected that the Imperial gents would keep their culture going in British Columbia. But in the late nineteenth century it was not easy to maintain the large and well-groomed pitch, even when cocoa-mats were layed down over the expanse. On the raincoast the native ferns and Oriental bamboo kept poking through. In the Interior the sun burned the grass and the gophers dug their homes. Nevertheless the colonials brought out their deck chairs and sipped their tea and mumbled "noble stroke" while paging through last winter's London newspapers. Tennis was an easier matter, the courts being smaller, and it was played all over the province, often by Anglican church groups.

The grand old game

But while government and society were largely British, the towns built around extraction industries were full of USAmericans. The most widespread and successful team sport in the province was, from the time of Confederation, baseball, the great Canadian game. Despite or because of its heavy load of myth-making, no one knows when baseball started. In the Hall of Fame in Cooperstown, New York, there is an English book from the seventeenth century, and in that book there is an illustration that portrays young men playing "base-ball." In the first half of the nineteenth century various cities in the US east had their parks in which various versions of "town ball" were being played. After the Civil War, USAmericans took out their internecine grudges on the ball field. So much did the game become identified with the US that when A.G. Spalding published its history in 1911, he could apologize for not being a literary person, and then prove it by writing:

> I claim that Base Ball owes its prestige as our National Game to the fact that as no other form of sport it is the exponent of American Courage, Confidence, Combativeness; American Dash, Discipline, Determination; American Energy, Eagerness, Enthusiasm; American Pluck, Persistency, Performance; American Spirit, Sagacity, Success; American Vim, Vigor, Virility.

Well, in British Columbia and elsewhere north of the US, it seemed to be the exponent of Canadian Talent, Toughness, Tenacity.

USAmericans used to be told that George Washington threw a dollar across the Potomac River, US beer is worth drinking and baseball was invented at Cooperstown in 1839. But on King George IV's birthday, June 4, 1838, there was a baseball game at Beachville, Ontario, where the local side took on the visiting team from the township of Zorra. No one had yet uttered the canard that baseball was a US game foisted on Canadians who would rather be playing lacrosse or some such game.

In the US and Canada, there were for some decades various versions of "Town Ball," but by the time of the Civil War, intercity associations had begun to develop, the rules became more standardized, and the organization of the sport developed toward the creation of the National Association in 1871, followed by the National League in 1876, which covered the country between Chicago and Philadelphia. Professional baseball, amateur baseball and university baseball worked their way westward very quickly, and the Northwest League was formed among frontier cities before 1880.

The gold rush brought baseball to the British Columbia Interior, and the beginning of railroad construction made it possible to start intertown leagues. Ball-players from the east, where semi-professional players had already operated in Manitoba in the 1870s, came by rail. Kamloops was then as now a hotbed of baseball, and the first league in the region began with regular games between the Old Towners and the CPR squad. Soon they were contesting for the pennant with teams from Nicola, Ashcroft, Revelstoke and First Crossing, B.C. Most of the travelling was done, of course, by train. In 1888 the provincial tournament was played in Kamloops, and won by the Vancouver representatives. Next year the Kamloops Townies went to the Coast and won the tournament, partly because they had managed to induct some athletic immigrants from Minnesota. I can remember that when the Oliver club was beating the Kamloops Elks in 1952, the Kamloops manager complained about Oliver's USAmerican "imports." So it goes.

When the Klondike gold rush happened, the baseball fields of Yukon were being used twenty-four hours a day in the land of the midnight sun. The opposite happened in Kamloops on New Year's Day of 1889. The winter had been very mild, and whenever the ground was not frozen, people loved to play and watch and bet on baseball. As part of the New Year's Day festivities, there was a baseball game between the traditional rivals, the Old Town and the CPR. The conventional seventh-inning stretch was not necessary this day; the players and fans stopped for refreshments while waiting out an eclipse of the sun.

By the end of the first decade of the twentieth century there were just under a hundred baseball teams in Vancouver, including the professional nine that won the Northwest League Championship. In the towns of the Interior, where there were fewer social diversions, despite travelling girly shows, baseball was if anything even more popular.

Baseball drew big crowds in Kaslo in 1896.

Writing before 1900

In D.H. Lawrence's novel *Lady Chatterley's Lover*, which was for years illegal to read in British Columbia, the randy lady and the ever-ready gameskeeper pause in their sport long enough for the latter to read his mail. On one occasion he gets a letter from a mate of his in British Columbia. His mate has sent him some photographs and papers, and these, too, get Connie Mellors excited. For a while they consider immigrating to the most westward province of a country in which people will not be permitted to read about their decision.

In recent years textbook anthologies of Canadian literature usually commence with accounts written by the explorers, but these are almost always the French and Scottish explorers, seldom anything from the Russians and Spanish. This fact may be due as are many in our national education to the fact that the textbooks are written and manufactured back east. Recently it has also been the fashion to sprinkle the textbooks with a few transcribed First Nations stories. If your bookstore has a Canadian section, it will not likely contain anything written by anyone on Bering's voyages of the early eighteenth century, nor the accounts written by the Franciscan friars Crespi and Peña, who accompanied the Pérez expedition of 1774. If your bookstore has a British Columbia section, you might find Vancouver, and you will almost certainly find Mackenzie and Thompson. What you will find more than anything else are memoirs of cattle ranching in the Cariboo, and the like. There was not a lot of literature in British Columbia in the nineteenth century.

The newspapers liked to run poems, often on the first page. The *Cariboo Sentinel* ran the verses of James Anderson, the "Bard of Barkerville":

> The rough but honest miner, who toils by night and day,
> Seeking for the yellow gold, hid among the clay—
> His head may grow grey, and his face fu' o' care,
> Hunting after gold, with its "castles in the air."

Hubert Howe Bancroft was the first notable and very industrious historian of the North American west, and Volume XXXII of his Works is called *History of British Columbia, 1792-1887*. He collected a lot of manuscripts from early explorers and settlers, and when his work was finished, deposited them in an archive in San Francisco. The stuff he missed is in the B.C. Archives in Victoria, the National Archives in Ottawa, and the University of Washington Library. There are also interesting earlier manuscripts in London and Madrid, of course.

The first white people to write fiction set in the area might be said to be Juan de Fuca and John Meares, who fancified and exaggerated their exploits as seagoing discoverers. They created southerly Northwest Passages, and prepared the way for the "Magical Realist" novelists of the late twentieth century. But most of the books set in British Columbia, while extolling the awesome grandeur of the scenery, and the fearful adventures of those who braved its challenge, were travel adventures or inducements to come and get rich both spiritually and otherwise. Simon Fraser, writing of the Hell's Gate part of his river, admitted his failure as a narrator: "It is so wild that I cannot find words to describe our situation at times." But many successors did try, telling lightly dramatized stories of strange bush characters, or working days on the railroads, or observations of Victoria streets during the gold rush. But while there were poets and novelists at work in Ontario, British Columbia by the end of the nineteenth century had not produced any. Robert Service came to Victoria in 1894, but did not start writing his famous ballads until his bank transferred him to Yukon, where he joined a Kiplingesque literary society. Pauline Johnson came through, eventually, and dropped a poem or two about the mist in the trees. Emily Carr did not start to write her charming books until she was incapable of painting in her later years. It would not be until the first decade of the twentieth century that the first British Columbia novels would people the province of minerals, logs and fish.

The Haida, the Shuswap, the Kootenay and the Kaska had been telling stories for thousands of years, of course. They still don't make it into many anthologies of Canadian literature published in Toronto or Vancouver.

Grainger

While Jack London often shows up in surveys of Canadian literature, and other foreigners sometimes mentioned Canada's west coast in their romances, the first serious novel set in the province is a thin book that is still in print, M. Allerdale Grainger's *Woodsmen of the West*, first published in 1908. Born in London in 1874, Grainger grew up an inquisitive boy and an impetuous young man. He came to work in the wilds of B.C.'s north coast, went to the South African war, went to London to teach Japanese martial arts, and then returned to our coast, learning the logging trades. Here he met the woman of his dreams, but was surprised one day to hear that she had gone to England. He followed her, proposed, and suggested that they take up their married life in British Columbia.

But he did not have the money for the passage. Typically, he wrote a novel about his logging days, and made enough money to buy their passage back to B.C., she in first class, he in steerage. The novel bears this dedication at the beginning: "To My Creditors, AFFECTIONATELY." Grainger was not only impetuous; he was also impatient with bad forestry practices, and eager to tell people how to improve them. In 1910 he got himself appointed as secretary of a Royal Commission on forestry, and in 1912 he was assigned the job of writing the Forestry Act, to attack waste and fraud in the woods. From 1916 to 1919 he was chief forester of the province, and after that a successful private businessman in the trade.

Woodsmen of the West is in the spirit of the realist, documentary or muckraking novels about various industries that were having their effect in the USA. In the first pages of the book Grainger introduces "you" to skid road stores and bars in downtown Vancouver, using the actual names, for instance, of outfitters:

> Leckie calls attention to his logging boots, whose bristling spikes are guaranteed to stay in. Clarke exhibits his Wet Proof Peccary Hogskin gloves, that will save your hands when you work with wire ropes. Dungaree trousers are shown to be copper-riveted at the places where a man strains them in working. Then there are oilskins and blankets and rough suits of frieze for winter wear, and woolen mitts.

At age eighteen I bought my Leckies with screw-calks at that store.

In subsequent chapters Grainger takes "you" up the coast, and keeps providing accurate details of the logger's world that would be the envy of any realist writer in the area, perhaps not matched until Gladys Hindmarch's novel about work on a west-coast freighter, *The Watery Part of the World* (1988). And like its successor, Grainger's book is not just a documentary aimed at people who want to read about logging. It is a well-written fiction that tells of the narrator's gradual involvement with the life of an ambitious logging boss named Carter. The book is a fine portrait of this complex man's character, and a balanced and artistic criticism of rampant individualism and ego. The narrator's moral disapproval of Carter's behaviour is joined with his admiration for the man's energy and grandeur of vision. This is not the typical melodrama that would characterize so many outdoor novels of the young century. Yet the plot leads to suspense and a climax that will entrap any reader who may have been expecting only some nifty information about life in the west-coast logging camps.

On top of all that, Grainger is a subtle humourist. Only 150 pages long, the novel is full of humour, suspense, detail, character and critical thought. Readers often say that they wish that Grainger had needed money more often, so that he might have written more novels rather than the bureaucratic prose he spent so many years at.

Canadian Columbia

In the middle of the nineteenth century Victoria was a long way from Europe, and its chief reason for being was trade, so European politics, other than internal British politics, while commented upon by newspaper columnists, was not a subject close to the hearts of the average worker. When

France and England jumped into the Crimean War to save poor Turkey from the Russian imperialists in 1854, there was no rush to the recruiting stations. There were no recruiting stations. James Douglas did worry. He was afraid that the Russians might sail down from Alaska to attack his capital. In fact he came up with the odd suggestion that an army of Indians be outfitted to defend his colony against attack from the north. The members of his legislature just smiled and said no. Apparently Douglas was not in close touch with his successors at the head of the Hudson's Bay Company. They had entered into an agreement with their counterparts at the Russian-American Company not to engage in any hostilities.

Still, there were French and British warships patrolling the North Pacific, and there was even a preposterous attempt to attack old Petropavlovsk, with results as unsatisfactory as most British campaigns in the Crimea. The war, during its two years, did not endanger the colony, but it changed it somewhat. A militia that might have filled Douglas's drawing room was created. In 1855 Esquimalt was converted into a base for the Royal Navy, which it would remain until 1905, thirty-four years after the British army left Canada. In 1865 it was made home to the North Pacific Squadron of the Royal Navy. The coal fields of Nanaimo became the main fuelling source east of Hong Kong.

Victoria was in love with the Royal Navy. Any wedding or birthday of consequence might expect the RN band to supply classy music. The Pig War standoff of 1859 was the closest the RN ever got to international action. If the US expansionists had not been diverted by their other wars, they could have taken Victoria in a day. But the ladies loved a uniform. When the Russians went after the Turks again in 1877, a lot of people thought that the British would stumble after them again, and now there were Russian ships all up and down the North Pacific. People got jittery in British Columbia, but the Russians weren't interested. In 1898 the USAmericans made a grab for Spanish possessions in the Caribbean and the Pacific but Victoria wasn't Spanish. The band played on.

But when the Boer War began in 1899, British Columbia was connected to eastern Canadian embarkation points by railroad, and there were 105,000 people of British extraction in the province's population of 175,000. Britain had learned from the US revolution that the white colonies and the black colonies had to be handled in two different ways. The black colonies were their burden, places where the local populations had to be Christianized and Civilized. The colonies made up of emigrated Brits had to be given a degree of independent decision-making. South Africa was a special problem, because there had been European colonists there since the Dutch arrived in 1652. When the British took Cape Town in 1806, they started more than a century of conflict with the Boers, while trying to Civilize the

Africans. The Boer War that closed the century and opened the new one was fought over a goal the people of British Columbia knew about—gold. And the brutal Lord Kitchener won the war by controlling the railroads leading into Boer territory.

The British of British Columbia were still the most British people in Canada, and they volunteered to serve the Home Country and the old Queen's last campaign. Victoria had been on the throne since before the Island capital was named, and there were few folks in the province who could remember living under any other monarch. So young men marched through the roisterous streets of Vancouver and mounted the troop train that would pick up patriots at every stop along the line. Flags waved and hats flew into the air. In Ashcroft and Kamloops and every stop along the way, cheering crowds greeted the faces at the carriage windows.

But when the boys from the west coast arrived at their mustering stations they were integrated as part of the Canadian contingent. This fact disappointed some politicians back in British Columbia, but it was also one of the key moments in the transformation of the province. When the survivors of the gruesome war returned home, they were Canadians. Queen Victoria died before the peace treaty was signed. For a long time there would be remittance men trying to run ranches and orchards in the Interior, and people visiting the shoppes in Victoria dressed in tweeds and nurturing their English accents well into the middle of the century, but the truth was that the young did not think of themselves as colonials. Among the people of the English-speaking provinces, British Columbians would remain the least normative. Many would think of themselves as BCers first. But the word "British" in the name of their province would begin to take on its common pronunciation of today—"Bri'sh."

The Klondike and the US industrialists invited by the last Turnerites had put an end to the really hard times of the mid-nineties. Things were looking good. But Premier Dunsmuir was getting tired of fistfights in the halls of the legislature. He hung on long enough to attend the coronation of Edward VII, then resigned, hoping that in his castle he might be able to live his last years in the kind of dignity for which he had been scrounging money all his life. His successor was Edward Prior, the mines minister. Prior loved railroads, and continued the process of giving away land to them, especially the Canadian Northern, which was crossing the country and looking for a route to Victoria. He also liked his own business, E.G. Prior & Co., which managed to win some important government contracts. What's wrong with that, he asked when confronted. He was the last of the old factionalist premiers, and did not know that the new century would demand more subtle fraud artists in his chair.

Lieutenant-Governor Joly de Lotbinière had been a constitutional expert before Laurier sent him to the snakepit. He asked Prior to step down, and assigned young Richard McBride, the opposition leader, to take care of things until the election in October 1903.

McBride

Richard McBride would break the mould of British Columbia premiers in two ways. He would preside for a dozen years instead of two, and he would be the first party man in the chair, leading the provincial Conservatives. In fact he was more an opportunist than a Tory, always knowing which way the wind was blowing, and aware of whether it was carrying the scent of new-cut cedar or animal fertilizer. He was also a charmer. He could stand on a stump and improvise a speech that would have his listeners laughing and cheering, even if he had been encouraging their sworn enemies in a fancy hotel restaurant the day before.

McBride was the sixteenth premier, and the first to be born west of the Rockies. (There would be only two others before Dave Barrett was elected in 1972.) His parents were Irish people who had met in California and moved north. Richard became an Anglophile, ambitious and methodical, but always with a sparkle that people considered his Irish birthright. He was born at the end of 1870, just before B.C. joined Canada, and went to Dalhousie Law School. He was called to the bar in his native New Westminster at the age of twenty-one. He was already making political connections and learning the ways in which a young lawyer can make a lot of money in a frontier economy. He went up to the gold fields of Atlin and in a few years he had saved himself a nice wad of money he extracted from the lawsuits of rival miners.

First he tried federal politics, running for the Conservatives in 1896. He tried to appeal to the fish workers, calling for exclusion of Orientals in the canneries and on the river. But Laurier and his Liberals swept the country in 1896. McBride decided on provincial politics. He won the riding of Dewdney as a Turner man in 1898, and as soon as he got in, turned his oratorical skills and his good looks against Joe Martin, trying to seize the top spot in the opposition. Premier Dunsmuir liked that; he considered his main job in office to be the keeping of unions out of the province and Joe Martin out of the premier's chair. McBride became his minister of mines and frequent dinner guest. The ladies liked him as much as they liked the Royal Navy band.

It was at this time that a shrewd betting man should have put his money on Richard McBride. Although McBride was often all dressed up and smiling at the home of James Dunsmuir, the biggest employer in the province, he somehow managed to convey to the working men that he was sympathetic to them. It was an amazing feat, given the time. The first years of the century were tough ones on the labour scene. There were strikes by miners, fishermen

Premier Richard McBride accepts the transfer of the Songhees Reserve to the province, 1911.

and railroad machinists. There were terrible accidents in the mines, and there were militiamen called out to put down workers' demonstrations. There were widows and manipulated Chinese workers. In 1902, Canada's first Workmen's Compensation Act would be passed in Victoria, but the age of the robber barons was not over.

Meanwhile the province was deep in debt. Its credit rating was dangerously low. Dunsmuir tried to keep his head above water by the tried and true method of granting favours to the railroad lobbyists who dogged his steps while he was treading water. Dunsmuir was aching to put his feet up on one of the imported hassocks at Burleith, his stone sanctuary. McBride had his eyes open. His work as mines minister did not amount to much while the biggest mine owner was his boss. And he did not plan on some kind of loyalty that would see him go down when Dunsmuir retired. In September of 1901 he heard that the premier was going to shuffle his cabinet a little, inviting some of Joe Martin's men into a new coalition. McBride immediately resigned his cabinet post, making a big flourish as he crossed the floor, declaring his high principles, and exhibiting a confidence that would catch the eye of restive MLAs looking to their own future. (Half a century later another opportunistic MLA would copy his strategy and eventually break McBride's record for longevity in the premier's office.)

In 1902 the tall young lawyer with the mane of prematurely grey hair ran for leadership of the provincial Conservatives, but the old walruses blocked his way by supporting poor E.G. Prior, who would try to shuffle Dunsmuir's leftover paperwork, get caught buying his own contracts, and sink into oblivion. Finally, on June 1, 1903, McBride, at the age of thirty-two, became premier of British Columbia. On the next day he announced that the house was going to be run on party lines. Sorry, fellows, he said to his cronies on the Liberal side, this is the twentieth century. He called an election for October, and squeaked in, winning twenty-two of the forty-two seats. The socialists, James Hawthornwaite and Parker Williams, would have to be thrown a sop from time to time during the coming session. Dunsmuir would have had a migraine headache. Joe Martin would have suffered spontaneous combustion. Affable and shrewd Richard McBride was in his element.

McBride had two main problems. The unions were on the march, and the province was broke. McBride had to present himself as a friend of the worker, and a defender of the province against the nasty feds who were taking more money out of the province than they were sending back in. He was lucky with the unions. He managed to placate them by introducing legislation for shorter hours and safer working conditions. The Workmen's Compensation Act had happened just in time, and the premier hinted that the unions could look forward to official recognition.

As to the province's financial position—McBride got lucky. In the first decade of the century the salmon were plentiful enough to walk across the rivermouth on. Big canning companies with British money swam into the province. At the same time, the huge US lumber companies, having chopped down Minnesota, were all over Oregon and Washington, and more than willing to bring their new machinery north, especially after US president Teddy Roosevelt created huge national parks to save USAmerican trees from the sawblades. B.C. trees were still there for the taking. The CPR added engines and hauled longer trains, piled high with lumber and fish.

The province was booming. I did that, said Richard McBride.

The tycoons

The province was experiencing what the United States had experienced in the last years of the nineteenth century. Big business, still headed by rapacious individuals, gobbled up small businesses, used their power to direct the actions of politicians, and fixed prices. The CPR's smelting business in Trail, for example, gathered in the most successful mines around Rossland and elsewhere, and created the Consolidated Mining and Smelting giant that would control the lives of just about everyone in the bottom right quadrant of the province. A USAmerican company headed by Peter Larson and J.H. Bloedel bought up the land that was to become Prince Rupert, thus ensuring that money would pour in from the Grand Trunk Railway, the sawmills and real estate. In 1907 a young man from Ontario, H.R. MacMillan, came to work in the forests, and kept his eyes open. In 1912 he returned to run the B.C. Forest Service. In 1919 he started his own forest company, and set about the process of buying the province. There was gold in them thar pockets.

MacMillan had studied the system. If you can manage to start a logging company, for instance, it is a good idea to have your own sawmills. If you had sawmills, it would be a good idea to own the buildings your sawmill workers lived in, and the stores they bought their groceries from. In fact, why not just own the town? All over British Columbia company towns were being created. If that was not stability, what was? Premier McBride, who would have a company town named after him, paraded as the champion of stability and progress. He told the electorate that these things were brought to them by the introduction of the party system, and more specifically by the Conservative Party of British Columbia.

How did the tycoons manage to snaffle all those resources? McBride had that slim majority in 1903. He needed to strengthen the party and his position at its top. He was, after all, only half the age of its most prominent members. The obvious answer was a thorough patronage system. But where to get the funds for such a system? He knew that some robber baron from New York or London was not going to be a voter, but he knew that dollars and pounds were the quickest way to votes. And what did British Columbia have a lot of? Land. In the years between McBride's first term and his second term, real estate just took off.

If the premier sold the farm, so what? There was another farm right next door. McBride travelled the province, marvelling at its size and the promise of the future. The voters saw the money pouring in. They did not get such a good view of the money heading back home. These were good times. There were jobs galore. Raw exports went east and west and south. Immigrants arrived in droves, hoping to get a piece of the pie, even if some railroad magnate was sitting next to them at the table, holding a big fork in either hand. Real-estate prices went up and up. You had to be quick and rush to buy a corner property in downtown Vancouver. You had to be quick on your bicycle to avoid the noisy motorcar that was coming at you around that corner. You might have a ride through the west end or the southern hills of the city, to look at the giant domed houses going up.

You might read the Vancouver *Province*, a big supporter of the Conservatives and McBride, an enemy of Laurier's Liberals and their plan to let lots more Oriental workers into the country. In the 1907 re-election campaign, McBride went to the tactic he had tried in his first federal race. He announced himself as the protector against Ottawa of "White British Columbia." Race has always been an important factor in B.C. politics. Today it is more important than economic policy to the white voters of the province's rural areas, where right-wing politicos with code language know the colour of people's necks. In the early part of the century you did not have to be quite so subtle. Just before the election of 1907, the Vancouver *Province* ran a story maintaining that Laurier's Grand Trunk Pacific was going to import fifty thousand Japanese navvies to work on the new Ottawa-Pacific link.

McBride, who had been given election funds and a railway car by the CPR, won twenty-six of the forty-two seats.

Wallachin and other dreams

The first decade of the twentieth century was noisy. Machinery pounded and whined in the forest. The sound of hammers pounding new buildings echoed off the cliffs. Ore cars came shrieking on their rails out of holes in Kootenay hillsides. Richard McBride made speeches from hotel verandahs and railroad platforms. If all the sounds could have been put together, they would have made an enormous boom. People on other continents and south of the border were listening.

They were looking, too. One of the principal causes of the rapid population growth was the camera. In 1889 the Scottish Lord and Lady Aberdeen arrived in the North Okanagan Valley, felt the warm air, looked at the established Oblate orchards, and decided that they were in paradise. Lady Aberdeen published a book called *Through Canada With a Kodak*. Then she and her husband bought huge tracts of ranch land in the Kelowna-Vernon area, subdivided, and started selling orchard plots to English gentlemen who had seen her photographs. USAmerican and British publications carried photographs from B.C. that we have all seen in later years: groups of loggers standing in front of mammoth trees they have started to fall, romantic cowboys herding vast seas of cattle, valiant hunters with their rifles smiling while holding up the heads of mountain sheep with gargantuan horns, leisurely picnics beside lovely lakes, noble redskins framed against soaring mountains and decorative wisps of cloud.

They probably did not see a c.1884 photograph you can now see in Robin Fisher's book about Indian-European relationships in the province, *Contact and Conflict*. It shows the whole Native population of Quamichan Village on Vancouver Island, sitting or kneeling on the shore, and behind them, between them and the water, nine English sailors and a white man in a straw hat, all standing or sitting on the prow of a boat. There were lots of such pictures of Indians and whites. In the nineteenth century there were not many photographs of Indians standing beside whites, even fewer on horseback. Another photograph that readers in Manchester would not likely see is the white population at "Stump City" (New Westminster) in the early days, where they lived among the desolation they had made of the cedar forest. Many pictures of pioneer conquerors show former forests that look uncannily like photos of battle scenes in World War I. One wonders how the declining Native community felt when they saw what the newcomers had done to their hillsides.

Brochures that were circulated abroad were the combined work of McBride's government and the big holding companies he had encouraged.

They showed idyllic scenes in just about every corner of the province. Sometimes they had to be fudged a little. French artists were creating the new method of collage, but it had not yet reached the advertisers in B.C. They had to resort to the tactics of more naïve artists, for instance hauling big apples from Kelowna and tying them to some other kind of tree in the Slocan Valley, to suggest Edenic abundance where the land was still plentiful.

Fake it and they will come. The interior of British Columbia is replete with stories of English toffs who arrived with expectations of living the good life that was not quite attainable back home. A good example is the town-site of Wallachin. At the turn of the century there was a little railroad sta-tion surrounded by nothing but sagebrush, cactus and tumbleweed, called Penny's, a little east of Cache Creek. In the summer the sun bleached cow bones on the benches above the Thompson River, and in the winter the snow blew in the wind. In the fall the mud froze and preserved the tracks of horses till the spring. The spring lasted for a day or two, and then the sum-mer hit like a sledge hammer. But in 1907, just a day or two's ride to the southeast the Brits were growing apple trees beside Lake Okanagan. One of the many USAmerican engineers in the area, C.E. Barnes, decided that there were more Brits where they came from, and he envisaged another apple valley beside the CPR mainline.

Barnes was not a crazed victim of sunstroke. He had been up Deadman Creek to the north. He had been to Deadman Lake, and he had been up to Deadman Falls. He knew that if he could get permission, not from the Deadman Indian community who had been moved into the valley to make room for white ranchers further east, but from the province, he could build a dam at the bottom end of Deadman Lake and a flume system that would con-vert the sage flats into a lush land of genteel living. There were British people who longed for the days when England was still a land of bucolic estates, and there were British people who thought that by birthright they were the most intelligent people in the world. Barnes made contact with a gent named the Marquis of Anglesey, who had some investment money at hand.

The British Columbia Horticultural Estate was begun. The dam was built, and a wooden flume made, trestles and all. You should make that out of sea-soned wood, said the locals. You should make it in sections in case a section gets in the way of a rockslide, they said. Oh, we are British, came the answer, we know how to do things. We have brought civilization to the whole world. For a while water made it to the flats, and some of it was used for the town's swimming pool. The town of Wallachin had forty gracious homes with shade trees and high ceilings, a school, a big fancy stone hotel, a com-munity hall and dance floor. The orchards were green against the brown hills, and they were run by officers and NCOs who had retired from the Imperial Army after the crisis in South Africa. People did not go to the hotel in work clothes. They worked very hard and long hours to make a go of their orchards, but they had servants, and they used some of their bench-land to make a polo field. They sent home photographs of proper English families taking tea at outdoor tables in leafy back yards.

Then the call of civilization summoned these gentle folk out of Eden. The First World War needed younger men to kill, and still-British ears heard the call all over the Empire. There were 107 eligible men in Wallachin, and 97 of them signed up and took the train eastward. The local boast was that no other town in the Empire sent such a high proportion of cannon fodder. The young orchards were left in the care of older men, women who had to don their departed husbands' work clothes, and children. They didn't have a chance. When the flume was devastated by a torrential storm, the predic-tion by the locals was proven right. The people left in Wallachin could not repair it, and they could not raise the funds to have it repaired. They worked under the trees, but the trees dried up. When the war was over, many of the men did not come back to the bench. Some of them were dead, and some of them could not face the ordeal of starting over.

Wallachin began to fade away. Roofs fell in. Cowboys came to the hotel in spurs. The railroad platform had fewer and fewer boxes of apples on it. Today a tourist can see the skeletons of unpruned apple trees on the bench, and fallen parts of the sun-bleached flume along the Deadman Creek road. The discouraged Marquis of Anglesey tried to sell his investment to the gov-ernment, with the idea of settling war veterans there. The government instead decided to apply the Veterans Land Act in the south end of the Okanagan, at a new town called Oliver.

Another Brit was luckier. Rudyard Kipling bought a couple of lots in Vancouver in 1899 and sold them at a tidy profit thirty years later, just before the Wall Street crash.

Other Europeans

The British were not the only Europeans to try to remake their home coun-try. Starting in the nineties, for instance, a group of idealistic Norwegians set up a teetotalling community on a fjord near Bella Coola. Soon some Danes tried their luck on the north end of Vancouver Island. The Finns, like the other Scandinavians, looked for places to do their traditional work in relative isolation. They set up a number of colonies, notably at Sointula, between the Danes and the Norwegians. Lots of Italians came to Trail. German groups favoured, as they still do, the Cariboo country.

A special case was that of the Doukhobors. They were a sect that had broken away from the Russian Orthodox Church in the seventeenth cen-tury, primarily on the grounds of their belief that God was a light inside each individual rather than a creator whose route of communication was through the clergy. They were persecuted for two centuries, and then, partly through

Communalists, pacifists, foreign Christians, the Doukhobors made business, labour and governments uneasy.

the activity of Leon Trotsky, able to head for somewhere in the New World, as did the various Anabaptists, such as the Mennonites, Hutterites and Amish. Like them, too, they lived a communal agricultural life.

In 1899 nearly eight thousand of these idealistic Russian peasants settled on communal farms on the Canadian prairie. They were given special considerations by the federal government, their own school system, unusual land registry, and because they were pacifists, freedom from any military duty. Just before Saskatchewan was made into a province in 1905, the federal government decided that it could no longer afford the dispensations, and in 1908 the Doukhobors, 6,000 strong, moved again, this time to British Columbia. They set up sixty-five farms near Castlegar, and another twenty-five around Grand Forks, bringing agriculture to an area that had been largely used for metal extraction. They grew apples and groundcrops, and established a famous jam factory at Brilliant. Like the Hutterites in Alberta, they were feared and ridiculed for their language and clothing and success.

When their leader, Peter the Lordly Verigin, was killed by a mysterious bomb in 1924, their coherence began to dissipate. Eventually the banks and the province would chip away at the dream, and today, while there are still Doukhobors who try to keep the language and religion going, the most obvious sign of their heritage is the wonderful borscht to be had at restaurants between Grand Forks and Castlegar.

Bill Miner

USAmericans, aside from religious groups who had lived in the US for a while, did not come to British Columbia as communities. They tended to represent the USAmerican ideal of accumulative individualism. Some were, of course, resource tycoons with three-piece suits stretched over their "corporations." Some were cranky old prospectors with tobacco-stained moustaches. Then there was Bill Miner.

Bill Miner was not a miner, save in a metaphorical sense. He was famous for three things: his quiet politeness, his ability to escape from prisons and his predilection for robbing stage coaches and trains. He was at one time the most renowned highwayman in the US west. But he was a mystery in other ways. Some of the US police reports said that he was born in Canada. Some popular historians say that he was born in 1843, others in 1847. (For the sake of this story, we will accept the earlier date.) They agree that he was born in or near Bowling Green, Kentucky, and died in a Georgia prison hospital ward in 1913. Before the US Civil War, he was already in the west, working as a cowboy, mule-driver and express rider in Colorado and California. These jobs made him familiar with the routes and cargos of the stagecoaches that were the principal intertown carriers of the day. He decided to become a stagecoach robber.

His first stay in San Quentin prison used up the last of his teenage years, and then some. He spent nearly five years there, in a hell-hole of starvation and torture. When he got out, he went back to perfecting his trade, robbing stages up and down California's valleys. He always used two partners, and spoke quietly and politely to the people at whom he was pointing a handgun. A year later he was back in San Quentin, this time for nine years, broken by a day of freedom after his escape in 1874. He spent a lot of his time in the dungeon or shackled to an Oregon boot. When he got out, he moved his stagecoaching to Colorado, where he was almost caught several times, amazing posses with his ability to vanish from box canyons. But California was calling his soul. He went back there and got captured again. This time he was given twenty-five years in San Quentin, and served twenty.

When he got out it was 1901, he was fifty-eight years old, and there were hardly any stagecoaches left—the country was crawling with railroad tracks. The authorities breathed a sigh of relief. Old Bill had spent more than half his life in the unhealthy confines of San Quentin. He was a museum piece. Fat chance. Trains moved a lot faster than stages, and they had locked doors and more room for guards, but the challenge of the new century just meant that Bill Miner had to consider modern ways, such as dynamite. He headed out of California, though, intent like so many of his countrymen, on the boom in British Columbia. On his way he picked up a couple of partners and conducted a dress rehearsal, robbing a train in Oregon.

When he arrived in B.C. he had a new name, George Edwards. He settled

When notorious train robber Bill Miner was finally captured, photographers rushed to immortalize the event.

on a ranch just north of Princeton, and became a friendly old figure with his white moustache and chin hair. He scouted out the Nicola Valley and the area around Kamloops. He was especially liked by children, who could depend on him for grandfatherly talk and candy. Yep, blue-eyed Uncle George was a colourful old coot, with his stories of the old days in the prospectin' business. He ran a few head of cattle, helped old ladies across the street, even filled in when the preacher was ailing. Everyone liked the old guy with the southern accent and courtly ways.

Old Uncle George chatted with just about everyone, and he got so that he knew just about everything that was happening in range country. He knew, for instance, when gold dust and other valued commodities were being shipped down the line. One night in September of 1904, B.C.'s first train robbery occurred just a few miles outside of Mission. It was conducted by a polite geezer in a broad-brimmed hat, and two younger fellows. They got away with gold and currency and other stuff, and disappeared on foot. A huge search party could not find them. The Victoria *Colonist* opined that this adventure was unlikely to be repeated in Canada, though it might be common across the line. As if to prove the paper's point, there was a train robbery of $30,000 in Ballard, Washington, a suburb of Seattle, just a year later. The methods used by the trio of highjackers were just like the ones in Oregon and B.C. Shortly thereafter Uncle George returned from a prospecting trip and was again seen at the dances around Princeton.

In May of 1906, Uncle George, with his partners Shorty Dunn and Lew Culquhoun, went on a prospecting trip east of Kamloops. They stopped in Kamloops to pick up supplies, including milk and stomach pills for the old gent. The next night there was a train robbery at tiny Ducks station eighteen miles up the line. The group used Miner's usual method, separating the engine from the mail car, and speaking quietly while holding a long pistol. But this robbery went all wrong. Bill wound up collecting fifteen dollars after a search that was long but not thorough enough. Once again the group took off on foot, after a kind word from the old guy. They headed for the US border.

Now the biggest manhunt since the Wild McLeans' siege was mounted. The CPR, the Dominion government and the provincial government posted big rewards for the capture or demise of the fugitives. CPR police, Provincials and the Mounties gathered posses. Indian trackers and bloodhounds were brought in. USAmerican detectives joined the search. Cowboys and prospectors and drunks beat the bushes. It was a rancher and provincial constable, Bill Fernie, who finally found the three prospectors, walking across a clearing a couple of miles from Douglas Lake. He had an amiable chat with them, and then went to call for the Mounties. The Mounties concentrated their search, and because they had a Native tracker with them, finally caught up with the trio at a campfire.

"We're looking for three train robbers," said a Mountie.

"Well, do we look like train robbers?" asked the white-haired man named Edwards.

"Could be," said the Mountie.

Shorty Dunn panicked and ran for the bushes. The Mounties shot him. Bill Miner gave in peaceably. A photographer, Miss M. Spencer, was there to take a picture of the old highwayman sitting in a wagon, surrounded by men on horses. The Douglas Lake country is tough on lawbreakers.

The whole town of Kamloops turned out in the rain to greet the cavalcade. The noble-looking old man in need of a shave asserted for the next few months that he had never heard of this Miner fellow they were looking for. While the trial was being prepared, the newspapers all over the province were jubilant with news. George Edwards's acquaintances through much of the Interior were filled with sympathy and pride. British Columbia was excited to be the scene of such drama, starred in by the great USAmerican Robin Hood. There would be a similar excitement eighty years later when a movie called *The Grey Fox* re-enacted the story. In the first trial the jury would not convict, but after the second trial old Bill Miner was sent to the penitentiary in New Westminster for life.

Just over a year later, the old man was gone. Under a fence and over the wall. Nobody his age should have been able to do it. The warden went into shock and had to be attended to by a doctor. The three younger men who went with Bill were caught, but despite a search that went all over the province for a few years, no one saw Bill in British Columbia again. People saw his "Wanted" poster, though. It offered a paltry $500 reward, and a picture of an old coot in a loud jacket. Here is the description of the varmint:

Age 65 years; 138 pounds; 5 feet 8 1/2 inches; dark complexion; brown eyes; grey hair; slight build; face spotted; tattoo base of left thumb, star and ballet girl right forearm; wrist joint-bones large;

moles centre of breast, 1 under left breast, 1 on right shoulder, 1 on left shoulder-blade; discoloration left buttock; scars on left shin, right leg, inside, at knee, 2 on neck.

There was a reason why the authorities in British Columbia could not find the old man. He was now going by the name of George Anderson, and robbing trains in Georgia. In 1911 he was captured and set to do as hard labour as he could manage in a state prison there, but seven months later he was gone again, through the swamp. He was captured after a gunfight in two weeks, and returned to be fitted with Georgia's traditional ball and chain. Eight months later he was gone again. But the posse was quicker than the oldest train robber in the swamp. Bill Miner was caught again, and chained to a hospital bed till he died in 1913.

In the Kamloops museum, where there are no artefacts attributed to the McLean brothers, you can see Bill Miner's six-gun. You will also see the oft-noted information that the Grey Fox invented that great western phrase, "Hands up!"

People in strange clothes

Meanwhile, the Asian communities of British Columbia were facing their usual obstacles—the preponderance of bachelors in their numbers, resistance by white labour organizations, attempted exclusionary legislation by the provincial government and general bigotry among their white neighbours.

Premier McBride was amazing in his ability to please so many people who had opposing sentiments. He was busy promoting new railroads to web the province, while opposing the cheap Asian labour that the railroad builders wanted to get the job done. Another problem was James Dunsmuir, the huge mine owner and employer of Oriental workers, who was also now the lieutenant-governor. In the spring session of 1907 the provincial government passed yet another anti-Oriental act, called the Natal Act, once again challenging the Dominion government that had disallowed their earlier attempts. But there was another factor now: after Japan had entered the world stage by thumping the Russians in their war, becoming the first Asian nation ever to defeat a European empire, the British Empire had seen their alliance with the Japanese as an opening for vastly expanded trade across the Pacific. The troublemakers in Victoria were a threat to Canada's large part in that trade. The governor-general in Ottawa was incensed. The lieutenant-governor in Victoria reserved the act.

In the province the Chinese problem had been taken care of pretty well by the head tax of 1903. Besides, the Chinese dynasty back in China was having troubles of its own, and had no time to complain. Still, in the year before the Natal Act, 1,500 Chinese had managed to show up at Victoria and Vancouver, cash in hand. A much greater problem was the Japanese, who arrived 8,000 strong, ready to start fishing or whaling. Complicating the scene were 2,000 Sikhs who sailed from India, to be joined by others who had been chased out of Seattle. The Sikhs, called "Hindus" by the Vancouver *Province* and other racist voices, were interested in working in the lumber industry.

The population of Vancouver was only a little over 100,000. That number was large enough to include an interesting organization called the Asiatic Exclusion League, and small enough to inspire the fear this league encouraged. There were rumours that the Pacific Ocean was filled with boatloads of "Hindus" and "Yellow Peril" steaming toward Paradise. The Asiatic Exclusion League decided that they could do what their government seemed incapable of doing. They held a parade to Vancouver city hall, burned an effigy of Dunsmuir, listened to speeches by racists imported from the US, heard patriotic tunes from the band, and drank beer and whisky. Then they headed for Chinatown. There they smashed windows and things while the Chinese stayed out of the way. The rioters continued to what was called Japtown, for more of the same. At first the Japanese stayed as quiet as the Chinese had, but then they remembered the Russo-Japanese War.

For the first time in their lives, the white bullyboys of British Columbia heard the shouted word "*banzai*," and found themselves forced to retreat in the face of a counterassault by energetic men carrying sticks, knives and bottles. On the following day, which happened to be the Christian sabbath, they tried again and again were beaten back. It is not recorded how many of them remembered the Chilcotin problem.

The Dominion government sent a young Liberal politician named William Lyon Mackenzie King out to the coast to investigate the racial events. King managed to cool things between Victoria and Tokyo, and the Japanese, nudged by suggestions regarding Canada's attitude toward trade, volunteered to cut emigration. The Liberals also fixed things so that further Sikh immigration could occur only on ships that sailed directly from India to British Columbia. There were no such ships.

But just before the outbreak of World War I there were two major race incidents in the province. In the winter of 1912-13 there was a real-estate collapse, partly due to the disappearance of foreign capital, and Premier McBride went in the following summer to England to employ the charm that had worked so well on previous trips. While he was gone, the acting premier, Bill Bowser, was obliged to do something about riots that were being conducted in Nanaimo. There the angry whites were burning buildings and attacking citizens because the mine owners were again using Chinese and Japanese workers as strike-breakers in Nanaimo and Cumberland. Bowser sent in a thousand troops and put the area under military control that lasted until the war broke out.

The enemy ship

In May of 1914 a more famous episode was begun. A Japanese ship called the *Komagata Maru* arrived from Hong Kong, carrying 376 people from the Punjab, most of them Sikhs, a people even less docile than the Japanese of 1907. These were people who could claim British citizenship and thus entry to anywhere under the Crown. But Canada claimed a regulation that said they could not enter unless their ship had sailed directly from an Indian port. A few of these "Hindus" were able to make it ashore, but the ship remained moored in Vancouver harbour into the summer. Once in a while immigration officers and police would try to board the *Komagata Maru*, but were repelled by a hail of coal. The whites on shore did not want these strange people in turbans to come ashore and take their jobs and subvert their cherished traditions. But the authorities did not want any repetition of the riots in Japtown. Pressure came from both directions. The would-be immigrants had been organized by a militant Punjabi group who wanted to test Canada's special order-in-council that applied to British Columbia only. The Supreme Court and the government of Prime Minister Robert Borden were battling it out over the legitimacy of the rule.

Meanwhile, food and medicine were running out on board the ship. The Japanese line refused to supply any more. Sikhs in Vancouver could not send any supplies out. The courts were busy all June and July, and the newspapers were lurid as ever. The docks and rooftops and the seawall in Stanley Park were covered with spectators. Finally on July 18 the Dominion government won its case, and ordered the deportation of the Punjabis on the *Empress of India*. But the police could not fight their way aboard the Japanese ship. At last the military was brought in again. This time the HMCS *Rainbow* arrived from its base at Esquimalt and trained its guns on the *Komagata Maru*. The hungry and ailing Sikhs were escorted out of the harbour while the spectators on shore raised a cheer.

The newspapers were printing stories about the possibility of a big war in Europe, but Vancouverites already had a victory over a boatload of British subjects in its own theatre.

Another community heard from, briefly

In 1903 Mrs. Emmeline Pankhurst founded the Suffragette movement in England, which became more and more militant every year, proceeding from vocality to attacks on property, in this way alerting the Houses of Parliament to an issue that had not seemed as urgent as the question of votes for the lower classes. In the United States, the Suffragists, led by women such as Susan B. Anthony and Amelia Bloomer, decided to attack their disenfranchisement state by state. Before 1914 a few western states, led by Idaho and Colorado, were allowing some women to vote in state elections.

In the winter of 1912-1913, the Women's Suffrage Movement of British Columbia circulated a petition and got ten thousand signatures of women who believed that the vote should be extended to their sex. In February seventy of these women presented the petition to Richard McBride. McBride's answer was a jargon-filled message that defended the "public interest" against such an idea. The province's unions, less afraid of women than of Asians, supported women's suffrage, and a Socialist parliamentarian introduced a private member's bill into the house. It did not have a chance.

Women, like other unpowerful groups, would have to wait until after the Great War.

Joe Fortes

For the first quarter of the twentieth century, the most popular man in Vancouver was Joe Fortes. At the end of the century his name could still be easily found, especially in the west end, where he lived and worked. At English Bay there was a Joe Fortes memorial plaque. A few blocks away there was a branch of the public library named for Joe Fortes. A few blocks further there was a toney restaurant named after him.

His real first name was Serafim, or as English speakers liked to spell it, Seraphim. If you go to the City of Vancouver Archives and poke around for an afternoon among old newspapers and speeches and oral histories, you will see that though Fortes may have been the most famous and popular man in town, there was not a lot of consensus about his origins. His age varied according to the whims of his chroniclers. His place of birth was assigned to numerous islands in the Caribbean, and at least once to Spanish Africa. His mother was sometimes referred to as Spanish,

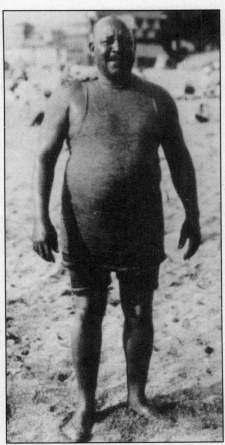

The legendary lifeguard and custodian of English Bay, Serafim "Joe" Fortes.

sometimes as Portuguese. Even his colour was a matter of disagreement, ranging from "ebony" to mahogany." One thing every witness or reporter agreed on was his size. He was a big man with a big voice, and, as everyone pointed out, a big heart.

When Serafim Fortes was a teenager, he became a sailor long enough to get to Liverpool, where he stayed for about six years, working at various jobs and training himself to become the best swimmer in town, which he proved in a race across the Mersey. Then in 1885 he signed on board a ship called the *Robert Kerr* (sometimes referred to as "*Ker*"), which would lose its main mast and flounder into Burrard Inlet. There it would remain. It would be filled a year and a half later by people who had fled the great Vancouver fire of 1886.

In Vancouver in those days there were lots of people with names such as Serafim, but the predominant population would soon start calling them Joe. Joe Fortes picked up a number of jobs in the frontier city, working in sawmills and stock rooms. Eventually he went to work at the Sunnyside Hotel in the middle of town. He was the city's first shoe-shine "boy." He was a porter. His size made him an obvious choice as a bouncer. But it was not long before he became the night-time bartender at the Bodega saloon. Joe was a teetotaller, but he mixed drinks with the best of them in a town full of bars. Unlike some bartenders up the street, he refused to make drinks for men that he thought had had too many, and with his huge smile and imposing frame he did not suffer many challenges to his decision.

But Joe was a swimmer. In the summers he appointed himself custodian of the beach at English Bay. Joe went swimming every day of the year, and drank a little sea water for health reasons. In the summers English Bay was the most popular beach in town, with evergreens on two sides and a wide expanse of sand between them. There Joe became unofficial lifeguard and swimming instructor. He was a special friend of children: the word was that if you were looking for Joe Fortes, you should head to English Bay and look for a cluster of little folk. He taught three generations of Vancouver's children to swim. He was also a custodian, who did not allow anyone to drop litter or open bottles containing liquor. He made sure that men stayed on their own side of the gendered dividing line. In 1900 the city bought him a uniform and a constable's badge and made him official lifeguard and swimming instructor. In his twenty-five years on the job he was officially credited with twenty-nine rescues from drowning. Probably ten times that number really owed their lives to the man who would swim the storm waves to get to capsized boaters.

Joe had a little rowboat that no one would ever steal, and he had a cottage near the beach. When the developers and their friends in the municipal government had a row of cottages destroyed to make way for a new idea, Joe asked for one of them, and it was moved to his bailiwick. He had a lot of visitors, all of whom remarked on its tidiness. These were the people who thought they were doing the right thing when they remarked on the colour of his heart. Even in a newspaper feature of 1961, a columnist remarked that "his colour was black but Joe had a heart of gold." Newspaper columnists dug up the Joe Fortes story every few years, but no one ever wrote about him as well as did Ethel Wilson, who gave him a chapter in her 1949 novel, *The Innocent Traveller*.

When Joe Fortes got pneumonia in January of 1922, his condition was reported in the newspapers. He was sixty years old, and his large body was not going to be in the water next summer. He died on February 4, and his notices were printed in England and the United States. Two days later the Vancouver papers carried eulogies with drawings and pictures. One of them carried an upbeat poem by A.C. Dalton:

'Tis winter yet, though robin sing—
What spring, or late, or soon shall bring,
Joe's cheerful hail, so rollicking
"An' now, an' now, it is the spring"?

When western winds blow strong and hard,
When shattered windows strew the sward,
When tossing billows roar landward,
Our Joe will still be keeping guard!

Yes! whosoe'er shall pass that way
In summer, to himself shall say,
"The folk and children are at play,
And Joe is rowing in the bay!"

There was a big civic funeral at Holy Rosary Cathedral, where Joe had gone every Sunday. The church had never been so tightly packed, and city dignitaries had never been so close to so many people from the other side of town. At the end of the service the organ played "Old Black Joe" very loudly. There was a cortege through the streets whose sidewalks were filled with people of all ages. The hearse was towing Joe Fortes's boat, piled high with flowers. Joe was buried in Mountain View Cemetery, where his grave was to be kept in good condition by the city.

The Joe Fortes memorial plaque was interesting. It would cost five thousand dollars, and the money would be raised by children, under the sponsorship of a service club. The memorial consists of a carved image of Joe with three children. It is attached to a drinking fountain that is low enough for the little folk.

Wars in Europe and B.C.

"All the manliness of the civilized world is due to wars or to the need of being prepared for wars. All the highest qualities of mankind have been developed by wars or the dangers of wars. Our whole civilization is the outgrowth of wars. Without wars, religion would disappear. All the enterprise of the world has grown out of the aggressive, adventurous, and warlike spirit engendered by centuries of wars."
—*Sir William Van Horne, 1910*

Railroad mania

Before an Austrian archduke was shot by someone with an unpronounceable name in Sarajevo, the attention of Englishmen was being diverted to British Columbia, whence came a deluge of advertising for the real-estate opportunities in that green Shangri-la. Towns all over the province were being touted as the new something-or-other. There were supposed to be a dozen railroads or more under charter, and a gross of speculators were holding land along their routes. Places such as historical Fort George were to be the hubs of the twentieth century's future. Seattle investors snagged property for a few dollars and offered the Canadian dream to unsuspecting Brits who could find their way to Paradise. At the 56th degree of latitude, Stewart, for example, tucked between the Cambria Icefield and the Alaska panhandle, recently handed to the USAmericans, was going to be the Pacific end of something called the Canadian North-Eastern Railroad. Englishmen might have been forgiven for wondering whether it was on Baffin Island.

Moderate money men and the opposition, now led by John Oliver, admonished that it was not economically healthy to have sales in real estate leap over such things as mining and logging. McBride dismissed these people as naysayers, and perched in the first motorcar to drive up the old gold-rush road all the way to Fort George, which in 1910 was 103 years old and itching for destiny.

But there really were railroads, and plans for railroads. If you look at highway maps of British Columbia and Alberta today, you will notice that there are a lot more red lines in Alberta than there are in B.C. If you look at a relief map, or the real ground, you will see why. Building an east-west railroad in B.C. is a daunting challenge. But in the first years of the twentieth century the Great Northern had reached Vancouver, the Grand Trunk Pacific had settled matters with Victoria, and was ready to reach for Prince Rupert and the great valleys to the east. McBride prepared for his 1909 election by announcing the Canadian Northern Pacific, which would come down from the Yellowhead Pass all the way to Vancouver. (And, he added, proudly, there would be no Asiatics allowed to so much as touch a shovel.) The Kettle Valley line would make a turn and run right up the Okanagan, using paddlewheelers with tracks on their decks to negotiate the long lake. The Pacific Great Eastern was announced in 1912; it would run from the north shore of Burrard Inlet to Fort George, where it would connect with the Grand Trunk before heading north to Alaska.

McBride shook his mane of silver hair and the gloriole around it and smiled over his imagined kingdom. In the election of 1912 he wiped out the Liberals, and had only two pesky Socialists to contend with in the House.

He didn't notice the numbers of unemployed, many with British accents, who began to show up on Vancouver sidewalks. In 1913 he smiled his way through the celebration for his decade in power, but somewhere in his subconscious he noticed that you could not hear the hammers banging any more. The boom was over. The coal riot and other labour problems held the attention of McBride's lieutenants while he went on one of his jaunts to London to tell the Brits with money that things were looking up in their former colony. Production in the mines of the southeast fell sharply, and companies started going into receivership. The big Dominion Trust Company defaulted, and Vancouver fell into financial collapse. It should have been embarrassing for the government, as 5,000 investors stated their belief that recent legislation had protected them from ruination. Besides, Bill Bowser's law firm represented Dominion Trust. It was quiet at the dock. Half-finished roofs silvered in the rain. McBride threw borrowed provincial money at the railroads.

And he loved a party. In 1914 he was only forty-three years old, but already an elder statesman of Victoria. He loved Edwardian pomp and all the inventions that were making life modern in his world. More and more he was becoming a kind of archduke.

The Empire calls again
Anyone my age, growing up in British Columbia, taking social studies in high school, had to write this essay over and over: "The Causes of the First

World War." I will wager that most of us can't remember what we argued. It was perhaps a great relief for the few of us who managed to get to university to find out that the historians were having problems with that subject too.

If the soldiers in the mud thought about the topic, they probably thought they were protecting their country against the evil designs of those other countries. But the big countries had been able to stay out of war against each other for forty-three years, since the Treaty of Frankfurt ended the Franco-Prussian War, and Alsace-Lorraine was ceded to the German union. The colonial powers of western Europe had somehow managed to keep their overseas competition from breaking out in hostilities on the home continent. The empires did not like each other. The French, especially, were simmering with resentment against the Germanic hegemony in the territory that the Sun King had grabbed in 1681. A lot of the farmers in Alsace had gone to French wine country in North Africa after 1871, but Strasbourg was supposed to be a French city.

But the most volatile rivalry was in eastern Europe. More specifically, the rivalry between the Russian and Austro-Hungarian dynasties was destined to come to flames among the rabid nationalist enmities in the Balkans. The various peoples of the Balkans, with their different versions of God and their different methods of writing their languages, played the alliance game with those giant empires, and what began as a proto-civil war in Sarajevo became a world war when the great seagoing countries of the west entered the fighting. The war really began when Italy conquered Libya, and when in 1912 Bulgaria, Greece and Serbia also declared war on the remnants of the Turkish empire. A year later two of the victors, Greece and Serbia, clients of Russia, turned on Bulgaria, client of Austria. There were few people in Europe who did not know that the big one was coming. The great powers wanted to remain great powers.

In Vancouver, British Columbia, the main news story was the victory of the Canadian navy over the *Komagata Maru*. But the shooting of feather-hatted Archduke Franz Ferdinand did make the papers, including reminiscences of his picturesque hunting trip in the province. It was not long until German troops were heading through Belgium toward France, and at midnight of August 4th, 1914, Britain declared war on Germany. The British Empire heard about that via undersea cables. Canadian men, many of whom had taken some military training at school, flocked to the armouries. By the end of the year the Canadian Expeditionary Force was set at 50,000 men. Six months later it would be three times that number. At first it was going to be a quick war; then it was going to be an unimaginably huge war. Canadian contingents would be part of the British army, and their mortalities would be counted in the British total. There would be more than sixty thousand Canadians in that total. There would be a lot more than that coming home with parts of bodies and minds left in Europe. The survivors would come home to die in the great Spanish influenza epidemic of 1918-19, which unlike the usual outbreaks, attacked the young. Fifty thousand Canadians died of the flu. Gertrude Stein knew what she was talking about when she referred to "the lost generation."

Anyone growing up in a B.C. interior town will have seen the names of some of those young people. Every town has its centrally located cenotaph that declares that their names will not be forgotten by the citizens. The cenotaph in Grand Forks, for instance, has forty-six names on it, and in its early years those names would be read by young men with German poison gas in their bodies. They had mounted the train with the big Union Jack draped over it five years before. The Grand Forks school had four hundred students. When the Canadian government for the first time asked Canadians to lend it money, the people of Grand Forks had made $200,000 worth of Victory Loans.

So the miners and loggers and fishers of British Columbia climbed aboard the trains. Men who had an acquaintance with Premier McBride were made into commissioned officers. The numbers are often cited: the province with a population of about 435,000 sent 55,000 into the armed forces, and more than 43,000 of them served overseas; 6,224 were killed. 13,400 were wounded. Some of them had had British accents; some had not. The Canadian armed forces recruited thousands of Chinese workers, along with many Japanese who would be in internment camps in Canada thirty years later. In Europe the Canadian soldiers would fight alongside a Sikh regiment from Lahore. There would be names on stones all over the province.

As was usual during international wars, the people on the coast got excited about the fact that there were enemy ships in the Pacific. The German navy would not have much of a challenge if it were to head for Victoria or Vancouver or somewhere further north. In 1914 the Canadian navy consisted of the *Rainbow*, whose only test had been a Japanese ship filled with Punjabis. Luckily for Canada, the Pacific north of the equator was patrolled by the Japanese, and south of the equator by the Anzacs. German ships did stop in California, but never made it to British Columbia. But Premier McBride was not taking any chances. Just before the war he had heard about two submarines that were built in Seattle for a Chilean government that was slow coming up with the money. McBride snapped them up for a million dollars out of the provincial treasury. Nervous shore batteries almost opened fire on them when they appeared at Esquimalt. For the first three days of the Great War, there was a British Columbia navy, but the Dominion government took them and reimbursed Victoria. Soon Esquimalt was being visited by Japanese and British warships, and people breathed easier.

But their economy was in worsening trouble. Exports dried up during the war, except for those materials needed for the conflict. Metal prices dropped.

Real estate became a mug's game. Small towns emptied of their workers and then of their businesses. There were railroads but they did not bring in the predicted bonanza. For the first time the whites of the province saw *their* population decrease.

And now it was time for the racists in the province to change their targets. In the years just before the War, Germany and Austria had sent out the message that it was time for patriots to come home and prepare to protect the fatherlands. A few British Columbians did so, and one might assume that those who stayed were more interested in their life in Kelowna or Cumberland than their ancient blood in the Rhine. Still, when war broke out, so did anti-German feelings. Men with clubs marched on German breweries and sawmills and restaurants. The militia and the Mounties rounded up German subjects and plunked them into jails in the Okanagan and on the Island for the duration. Businesses with suspicious names started to change them. Back in Ontario Berlin became Kitchener. Presumably Germansen Lake in British Columbia was remote enough not to be a worry.

Dick's fall

Some people say that Richard McBride never knew what hit him. Others maintain that he knew a lot of things that other people were not supposed to know, and got out before they could find out. Whatever the case, his departure from the political scene in British Columbia was flamboyant, sudden and puzzling. Remember that in the 1912 election he swept the province except for the two Socialist seats. Yet just before Christmas 1915 he resigned his position and headed for his beloved London.

In the first year of the War he was still riding high, despite the economic woes of his fiefdom. Now he was the great military leader, taking over the defence of Canada's west coast. He was the Irish prison warden's son who had risen by his own wit and energy to the throne. He thought that everyone should learn by his example, but he thought that no one could do it as well as he had. He was a forerunner of certain Social Credit premiers to arrive on the scene later in the century.

But in 1915 the province had a debt of ten million dollars. Worse, it had promises of eighty million dollars laid out for the railroads. Unemployed people and failed shop owners did not appreciate the premier's grand vision. They were becoming less enamoured of his long annual jaunts to London, too. His purpose there was to tout B.C.'s opportunities to English investors, and to oversee the building of B.C. House in the British capital, but potato-eaters back home could not help but notice that McBride was wearing expensive clothes at a lot of upper-class functions, and taking quick trips to Paris. The British Columbia government had to rescue the municipalities who could not meet the expenses of their breadlines. Destitute families saw public money being shovelled into rich railroad families' fireboxes, and rethought their enthusiasm for Prince Richard.

Meanwhile, there was a tide of reform sentiment coming westward across the continent. The big strikes just before the war were harbingers of even greater labour unrest. The women who had been scoffed at by McBride in 1913 had not disappeared. Now they wanted not only the vote but also legislation against booze. They were joined by evangelical church groups organized as Christian Endeavour, who called for Temperance and meant prohibition—this in a province that had always been characterized by its prominent saloons. Various businessmen, through their boards of trade, joined in the demand to attack liquor. When Harlan C. Brewster took over as leader of the Liberals, he would champion all the reform movements, and he did not have a head of flowing silver hair.

It did not help that while people were hungry and reformists were pamphleteering, there were scandals and dissent within Conservative ranks. One of McBride's ministers had to resign for selling himself some cheap government assets. It was not 1875 any more—such goings-on would not work during the era of party politics. Accusations arose against many of the government members, and in the fall even McBride had to defend himself against charges of fraud. Meanwhile, he was losing his control of his own associates, even Bowser, who had to hold the levers and dodge the shrapnel while the premier was riding carriages in London. A good example was a sensational pamphlet that showed up in the spring of 1915. It was called *The Crisis in British Columbia*, and written by a prominent accountant who filled the pages with tables and statistics. The message was that the Conservative government had been two things: prodigal and crooked. While it became the favourite reading material in British Columbia, McBride was on one of his sojourns across the Atlantic.

Still, it appears that McBride was beginning to hear the news. The spring sitting of the legislature did not offer much hope to the suffering citizens of the province, and apparently caucus meetings had persuaded the premier that half his members were no longer followers, especially of his railroad dreams, especially of the Pacific Great Eastern. The Vancouver *Sun* published a story stating that Bowser was leading a palace revolt. McBride, having promised an election, put it off. Then he dissolved the house, but gosh darn it, he discovered that the lieutenant-governor neglected to sign the dissolution paper. The government, or rather Bowser, would have to just carry on while McBride took care of things in England.

As a matter of fact, Bowser had been the *de facto* party leader for some time. Unlike McBride, he read books and understood the organization of political thought and of a political party. He did not have McBride's big smile or good looks, and he did not receive nice gifts from big businessmen. He was blunt and direct, and knew how the patronage system worked. He was a professional with a hatchet in his desk drawer. McBride employed him for just that reason. And Bowser was waiting.

He had to wait only until McBride's forty-fifth birthday. On that day, December 15, 1915, McBride left his office, and prepared for his new job as B.C. Agent-General in London, where he would preside at the glorious new building he had been watching grow on Regent Street. The electorate, though they had become disenchanted with the prince, was caught off guard. Why did he quit? Was there some unrevealed scandal only a few insiders knew about? Was Bowser blackmailing him? Was he planning to come back gloriously as federal Conservative leader? His personal finances were in a state similar to that of his province; was there some sort of deal that history should not find out about? Less than two years later McBride died of Bright's disease in London. Had he known he was dying?

Whatever the case, Bowser inherited the premiership and set about appointing his own satraps to manage the recovery of the province and help win the war for the Triple Entente. He would never make it that far.

Alert Bay

While the country was sending Christians to kill Christians in Europe, there was still the war against the Native civilization within the province of British Columbia to be pursued. Alert Bay on Cormorant Island, between the north end of Vancouver Island and the mainland, was the home of some Kwakiutl people who could never find it in themselves to surrender to the Indian Act of 1884. They called their village Yeleese, and there they defied the white church and a long series of Indian agents, building the tallest totem poles in the world. It was the village of Yeleese that prompted Matthew Begbie to challenge the Act, and the Dominion government to tighten the anti-potlatch law. But the Kwakiutl at Alert Bay, named after a British gunship, were not about to surrender.

Today Alert Bay is really important to white people for fishing, logging and foreign tourists. But while the white people in other parts of the province were trying to figure out how to make their economy work, the Kwakiutl on Cormorant Island were still holding potlatches, practising an economy that had worked pretty well for them during the centuries they had been fishing and marrying on the coast. The current Indian agent was not about to settle for a role as adviser; this was a war to extirpate heathen ways. He knew that the Indians were stockpiling masks and costumes and rattles and shiny coppers and the like, waiting for the moment when they could all come together and give them away.

The representative of the Canadian nation gave the Kwakiutl a choice: they could hand over all their Indian stuff to him, or go to jail. The Kwakiutl got ready for a big potlatch. The Indian agent could not get hold of a gunship, given the priority of defence against German destroyers, but he did have some policemen with him, and they did manage to employ a fishing scow in their raid on the beach. Around the financially troubled cannery they came, and established a beachhead. Lots of Indians were arrested and tried at Alert Bay. Twenty-three went to jail. All the beautiful masks and headdresses and coppers were captured and loaded on the scow. They were headed for the National Museum in Ottawa. The Yeleese elders felt souls slipping away.

But the Mounties had not heard the last of the Kwakiutl.

UBC

The University Act had been passed in 1890, and a university chancellor and senate had been announced, but the cities of Vancouver and Victoria were squabbling over everything, and potential freshmen had to head east or south for a while yet, or eventually to scrabble together credits at McGill University, which made some courses available on the west coast. Twenty years later Premier McBride was so popular that he aroused little ire when he stated that the university would be located on the promontory west of Vancouver, Point Grey. In September 1915 the first classes began in some shacks in the CPR's townsite of Fairview on the southern hills of Vancouver. Many men of the first year's class went through the formality of registering and then went straight to an army recruiting office. The construction of a proper stone and ivy campus would have to wait for the good times after the war. When Canadians came home in 1918 and 1919, those shacks were crowded with soldiers who had put off their classroom education in favour of practical geopolitics in the European mud.

But it would be another decade before the imagined Point Grey campus would appear on the forested headland, and it might have been longer if the dissatisfied students in the shacks had not undertaken the Great Trek to Point Grey, a demonstration that has taken on legendary colouration at the university.

The Liberals

Some of the Conservatives thought that there should be a convention to choose a leader after McBride's defection. But his deputy William Bowser just went ahead and announced a new cabinet. He also handpicked a couple of candidates to run in by-elections to fill empty seats in the house. Both of them were defeated by Liberals, the first representatives of their party since 1912. They were harbingers, the first carnivorous birds of a flock that would converge around the body of the Conservative party. One of the new opposition members was Harlan C. Brewster, a man who would manage to give discomfort to "The Little Kaiser," Billy Bowser.

That was the nickname given to the premier by Charles Tupper, a prominent old Tory who had for years been feeling unappreciated by these young whippersnappers. He did not like the smiling McBride, and he so much disliked the frowning Bowser that he went public with his disapproval, displaying for all eyes the rift that was growing in the Tory caucus.

In the spring session Bowser plugged ahead as he always had, methodically, scientifically, logically. He managed to introduce some mild but solid ideas, most prominent among them an improved Workmen's Compensation Board to execute the act of 1902, and an independent Department of Agriculture, a ministry that would attract a lot of attention in the years just after the War. But the Liberals and Socialists in the house, and the dissidents in his own ranks, pestered Bowser all that session and during the summer's campaign for the September election. Accusations of skulduggery, most of them accurate, were flying in all directions. There is a more than good chance that some politicians, civil servants and businessmen maintained fluid notions of the meaning of corruption and the public weal.

Seeing his support weakening in traditional places, Bowser tried to gain some backing among two groups who had been laughed off by McBride. He promised plebiscites on prohibition and women's suffrage, hoping that their champions would drift his way from the Liberals, who had spoken up for them largely to gain their votes. Prohibitionists and suffragists did not want plebiscites; they wanted legislation. Bowser passed a so-called Prohibition Act, which was really a measure to hold a plebiscite in 1917.

In the September 1916 election Bowser just barely held onto his seat. He was joined by eight other Tories. There was one Socialist returned—and thirty-seven Liberals.

A bad time to be premier

What's the use of worrying?
It never was worthwhile....

The Liberals formed their first government during the darkest year of the war. The provincial economy was not yet showing the benefits that would come when thousands of trees would be required to make airplanes and ships. To make matters worse, the new premier, the Baptist salmon cannery millionaire Harlan Carey Brewster, appointed honest ministers and went on record against the patronage system, introducing a Civil Service Commission. Well, he did this after turfing out heaps of Conservative administrators and replacing them with more friendly faces.

He also paid attention to the two referenda: he implemented Bowser's Prohibition Act, and extended the vote to women (of the right race). These measures would be quite unpopular with the returning soldiers, who had voted against both of them from their war-zone polls.

It was a heady experience to sweep the Tories out of office, but it was a bad time to be premier. The cost of living was rising. Wages were stuck at pre-war levels. The Dominion government was trying to bring in a conscription act. And just when orders started coming in for war *matériel* from the west coast, there was a severe manpower shortage. In Europe the enemy was employing new and more horrible weapons. The military hospitals in Vancouver were filling up with shattered young men.

Brewster had made much of his opposition to logrolling, and he had said over and over that he was not going to let the railroads run the province. Unfortunately he had appointed a man named M.A. Macdonald as attorney general. In most of his appointments he had been wiser: four of his ministers would become premiers. But Macdonald had been a focus of the Conservative attack during the election, being accused of accepting big campaign money from US interests. Now he was in trouble for taking $25,000 from the Canadian Northern Railway Company. What was Brewster to do? He had to fire his attorney general. It did not take Brewster long to grow sick of provincial politics.

And rumours spread that he was looking toward federal politics. Prime Minister Borden consulted Brewster on strategy in the forming of the Union government that might pass conscription despite the opposition of Laurier and Quebec, the traditional source of Liberal strength. While Brewster was back east, his agriculture minister with the rural English accent, John Oliver, ran the ship.

Nineteen seventeen started as the very worst year of the war. But the conscription bill passed, and the USAmericans finally got into the fight. Orders for wood and minerals came in, and newly enfranchised women clambered into the workforce. Mines were scraped bare for the war effort, and southeastern towns like Greenwood and Phoenix would never recover. The Boundary country would be left with empty mansions on hillsides overlooking quiet slag heaps.

The miners who built those slag heaps were becoming more and more militant, and more and more socialist. The Industrial Workers of the World, begun in Chicago in 1905, expanded rapidly across the west on both sides of the border. The Wobblies were not tradesmen, and they were not nationalistic; their ranks were filled with unskilled immigrants from eastern and southern Europe. IWW ideology leaned toward syndicalism, and its main political strategy was the big strike. The dream was "One Big Union." The IWW had been pretty well beaten apart by governments and police before the beginning of the war, but there were still lots of Wobblies. In British Columbia the targets of the union movement were the big two: US control of the resource sector, and the cheap Asian labour imported to work in those branch-plant enterprises.

The year 1917 saw many strikes in the province, especially in the coal fields of the Crowsnest Pass, where the federal government had to intervene. Brewster, a champion of conscription, also announced that he was interested in the "conscription of wealth," but he did not have in mind what the syndicalists did. There was a revolution in Russia. The call for socialization of industry was heard more and more often, from Atlin to Fernie. The B.C. Federation of Labour opposed conscription on the grounds that the war was being fought for imperial wealth and power in Europe, and using the last months of young Canadian lives to fight it. Meanwhile McBride's dream, the Pacific Great Eastern Railway, was gobbling up public money and laying a few miles of track in the easiest part of its surveyed route. No wonder Premier Brewster was spending so much time in Ottawa.

Late in 1917 he adjourned the legislature and took the train east to confer with Borden, who had lost Quebec, won the conscription battle, formed his Union government, and was preparing the details of the call-up. Brewster never made it back to Victoria alive. He was taken from the train in Calgary, and died there of pneumonia on March 1, 1918, after little more than a year in office. His caucus met and chose a pig farmer as his successor.

Honest John

The idea was to garner sympathy from the restive working folk. The new premier did not resemble any of his forerunners, but in his way he was as colourful as any de Cosmos or McBride. He was not a popinjay—far from it. He would revel in his nickname "Honest John." His chief asset and working principle, he said, was "common sense." The wives of lieutenant-governors rolled their eyes and took a step backward when they saw him stroll into a room in his baggy tweed trousers and clunky brown boots. He grew up in the English Midlands, and now he raised hogs on the silt of Delta. He had never gone to school much, he seldom spoke a sentence that was grammatically correct, and he wore a cloth cap as a kind of badge. He was a hayseed, all right, and he played the role to perfection. He ate lunch at a greasy spoon so that he could see what he was getting.

He was a hayseed with a head full of politics. He made sure there was a reporter nearby when he made one of his colourful rube remarks. And he was usually talking. When he became premier, he thought of the caucus and civil service as the stock on his farm, and he was big on farm management. His demeanour did not sit well with the more elegant and professional members of his party. But the electorate ate it up. If they did not give his party a clear mandate in the next two elections, their reluctance had more to do with the fractious and suspicious Grits than with "Honest John," whose nickname implied anomaly.

For some reason John Oliver had been Brewster's minister in charge of railroads, and now that he was premier he had to handle the problem of the languishing Pacific Great Eastern Railroad. Its directors had moved their office to Seattle. The tracks rusted in the fog. Oliver complained that he had inherited a white elephant, but people in Prince George (which had changed its name from Fort George in a 1915 civic election) were waiting for the railroad. Oliver decided to go ahead with the PGE, a railroad that was now most famous for the insulting names invented to fit its initials. He decided that the province should take the project out of the hands of the company, and borrow some money to get it moving again. But there was a terrible provincial debt, and as the end of war approached, it did not look as if it would be easy to pay off. Oliver decided that it would not look good to add big numbers to the provincial debt, so he invented something called a contingent liability. No one knew what he was talking about, but it sounded better than another eighteen million dollars in the hole.

W.A.C. Bennett was in New Brunswick and only eighteen years old when this happened. He was not in the habit of reading, so it is unlikely that he caught on to Oliver's idea till years later.

The government did a few more appropriations around the province, and war orders for wood, fish and minerals were picking up. The Russians were fighting each other to see what measure of socialism they would experience, so Oliver the working man kept busy using government funds to keep capitalism working. This process was not without its dangers in such a province: for example, Oliver's minister of finance, John Hart, was made a director of the PGE. In order to protect the big investment, he purchased lots of insurance for the railway—from his own insurance company. Honest John was sick of railroads. He decided that his main interest was in agriculture, a sector that had not captured any government's interest in the way that furs and mines and forests had.

Besides, farmers were honest tillers of the soil. They worked long hours, wore denim pants, and never went on strike.

Ginger Goodwin

Ginger Goodwin, like the McLean brothers, gets scant mention in most history books. Goodwin, a small man with imperfect health, had immigrated from Yorkshire to the coal fields of Vancouver Island, bringing the British colliers' socialist activism with him. He was a very successful organizer, and played an important part in the Cumberland strike of 1913. When the war came, he was declared ineligible for military service for reasons of health. When the Dominion government managed to pass the conscription act, it followed that move with other declarations seeking to control labour. Strikes and management lockouts were banned for the duration of the war.

So were unions affiliated with serious socialist organizations, such as the IWW. This did not sit well with the radical miners of southeast British Columbia. Ginger Goodwin was now in the Kootenays, a thirty-year-old firebrand, organizing the mine and smelter workers. He organized the strike that secured the eight-hour day in Trail. He was an officer in a number of labour organizations, and a target of the nervous owners of mills, mines, smelters and even the shipyards in Vancouver.

Everyone who had heard Ginger Goodwin orate had heard him coughing between sentences. But mysteriously the conscription board found him now fit for the trenches in Europe. Goodwin and the unions mounted two appeals against his reclassification and were quickly rebuffed. Like a lot of men in his situation, Goodwin took to the hills. He hung out in the familiar woods of the Comox Valley, where friends brought him food and told the Pinkerton detectives they had not seen him for years. The forest was full of various kinds of policemen and hired thugs. The authorities did not spend this amount of manpower looking for a draft-dodger; Ginger Goodwin was a local Lenin as far as the magnates and their friends in government were concerned.

Eventually a provincial constable named Dan Campbell got lucky. Campbell set up an ambush and shot the little Yorkshireman to death. It was one of the smelliest incidents of police work of its time, so smelly that Campbell was arraigned for manslaughter, and pleaded self-defence. They must have been holding their noses even in Victoria. The mine owners, probably a smidgeon lighter of pocket, breathed bad-smelling sighs of relief. There was a trial, but it was kept secret; the details have still not been released, and Constable Campbell was acquitted.

On the day of Ginger Goodwin's funeral, August 2, 1918, there was a general strike in Vancouver and all through the mining regions. It was to be a twenty-four-hour shutdown, but businessmen enlisted soldiers to break it up. In Vancouver the soldiers attacked the longshoremen's hall, and forced streetcar drivers to stay in their cars. The provincial constables did not interfere when uniformed men attacked union property. British Columbia continued to become polarized between labour and capital.

Eight decades after his death at the age of thirty-one, Ginger Goodwin remains a hero to working people and their allies in the Comox Valley and elsewhere. If you want to, you can buy a Ginger Goodwin tee-shirt today.

Sophia

There are ships and pieces of ships on the ground under the salt chuck all up and down the northwest coast of North America. Some of the pieces belonged to the CP steamship *Princess Sophie*. On October 23, 1918, during a snowstorm, the ship sailed from Skagway, bound for Vancouver. People in Atlin and Yukon would take the ship south from Skagway on their way back to civilization. This time they did not get out of Lynn Canal. The ship hit Vanderbilt Reef in the storm, and suffered the pounding of high seas for two days while the blizzard attacked. Small craft were thrown around while trying to approach the ship and its terrified passengers. After two days the *Sophia* was torn to pieces, and all 343 people aboard were lost.

Armistice

Premier Oliver was fond of the image of serious men of toil, but he did not much like workers' unions, and he did not much like the complaints of the unemployed. He was a self-made man, and thought everyone should be a self-made man. Give them each a shovel and show them where the dirt is, was his advice. He always used his colourful country language to complain about white-collar layabouts clogging the cities. He did not much like the idea of society women or women in the workforce, especially women in the ranks of the professions or politics. He thought they should all be dressed in gingham, baking pies for their sweating menfolk.

His problems would not be allayed by the peace that broke out in Europe on November 11th. Of course the news of the armistice was greeted with wild joy. When the CPR telegraph brought the news to Vancouver just after midnight, it was spread throughout the city faster than the fire thirty-two years before. The downtown streets were filled with people letting off fireworks and kissing strangers. Every vehicle in the city, including boats in the harbour, shone lights and sounded horns. That afternoon there was a huge parade, bands blaring, soldiers and sailors marching, politicians beaming, widows biting their lips. Things were quieter on the CPR steamship *Princess Alice*, which was approaching Vancouver harbour with a cargo that included seventy-six bodies pulled out of the cold water where the *Princess Sophia* had broken apart on Vanderbilt Reef. In all the towns along all the railroads there were loud celebrations. Some foreign president had announced that this was the last war, and it was over. For a day our citizens were willing to believe it. For a few hours miners and mine owners forgot about each other.

But there was too much that could not be forgotten at the end of 1918. Ghost towns sat where mines had been cleaned out. Soldiers who had been waiting for normal life for years found women and Asians holding jobs while they could not get one. The cost of living was a shock to them: inflation had reached levels no one ever expected to see in a British Empire. The influenza epidemic was reaching its highest horror, and even burials were getting expensive. Things were tough all across Canada, but tougher in British Columbia, as usual. Those returning soldiers felt as if the home fires might have been kept burning, all right, but they wondered what was being consumed in the flames.

All across Canada the labour movement had been getting more and more aggressive since the turn of the century. As one travelled west across the country, one became more and more aware of that. The One Big Union movement was growing especially fast on the prairies and in British Columbia. The Russian Revolution cheered politicized labourers on and frightened the pants off conservative politicians. The great Winnipeg General Strike of May 1919 scared the hell out of every level of government, because of the solidarity it demonstrated. It was started by skilled tradesmen, but was soon joined by the large immigrant population, many of them communists, and by sympathetic preachers from the Protestant churches. Public workers joined the demonstrations. The spectre of totally unified wage-earners hung over Winnipeg and Ottawa and Victoria. At its height, the Winnipeg General Strike had thirty thousand workers marching through the streets, while only essential services were kept going.

There was opposition to the general strike. It was organized by bankers and manufacturers and politicians, and waged in the newspapers, wherein the strike organizers were labelled a small cabal of "alien scum." "God Save the King," added newspapers. The Dominion government read the newspapers. They sent out two important ministers to meet with the "Citizens' Committee" representing the banks, etc. When the strikers asked the ministers whether they would like to hear their side of the story, the ministers said no.

First the Dominion government changed a few national laws having to do with immigration and sedition. Then they sent in the Mounted Police to charge their horses into the marchers' parade. Then they sent in army troops under the War Measures Act to occupy the city. Out-gunned, the workers went back to their lathes and trains. Seven strike leaders were sent to jail on charges of trying to overthrow the government by force. The strike was over on June 26, ending perhaps the most important six weeks in western Canadian history.

There were sympathy strikes across the country. In the marble parliament building of Victoria, this looked like the Bolshevik Revolution come across the ocean. Outside agitators had somehow managed to get the ears of miners in Atlin and Cranbrook. Thus the bankers and mill owners and their friends in Victoria were just about the only people who rued the withdrawal of the Siberian Expeditionary Force in Siberia. In the summer of 1918 Britain, using an excuse involving violence between freed Czechs and freed Germans, the United States and Japan decided to send troops to Vladivostok to side with the White Russians against the Reds. In October, four thousand Canadians, mostly infantry and Mounties, embarked from Vancouver. They were to patrol and sit in Siberia for less than a year, before returning from Canada's least known and least popular military campaign. An intrepid pilot from the Kootenays named Frank Kearns flew a few planes into the Russian soil, but for the most part the Canadians just tried to keep warm through the winter. No one knows how many of them were big fans of the Mensheviks.

Fairview

On a dry bench overlooking the Okanagan River, Fairview was a hot mining town in the last decade of the nineteenth century. Gold was discovered in 1887. The town site was laid out in 1897. Soon it boasted a lot of noisy hotels. The Fairview Hotel, usually called the "Big Tepee," was the biggest hotel in the B.C. Interior. There was the "Fish House," run by John Kearns the Catholic. Hardly any of the hotels in Fairview were called by their proper names. The Golden Gate Hotel was always called the "Bucket of Blood."

In 1902 Fairview suffered the fate of almost all pioneer towns, a fire that took most of the important buildings. The town staggered along, but when nearby Oliver was created to serve the Great War veterans who were becoming orchardists, some of the best remaining homes were carefully hauled down off the benchland to the river valley. In the middle of the century, boys living in Oliver went up the Fairview road and poked around the site, picking up sun-stiffened high-heeled shoes and antique medicine bottles.

Now on an autumn day beside the road that still bends where it did a century before, it is so quiet that you can hear people hitting on the golf course two kilometres away. Now the flats look the way they did before 1887, with brown grass, greasewood, sagebrush and a few willows along a dry creek bed. In mid-October the noise-making insects are gone and the snakes are in their holes. The sun as always shines out of a blue sky, but up here on the benchland it is not summer any more. The apple trees and grape vines down along the valley are still green, but just about all the fruit is in cold storage at the packing houses.

Here there is a little roof of grey weathered shakes protecting a display of sun-faded photographs and an 1895 townsite map of Fairview. On the other side of it is a rusted steel cross imbedded in a worn stone cairn where the Presbyterian church once was. In 1929 that church was hauled away to Okanagan Falls, fifteen miles to the north. If you walk between cactuses away from the road, you will find that the ground is soft in places. The metal-detector hobbyists have been here every year for decades, but you can still find useless objects—dark brown flattened cans, an old bottle that has changed colour, a big rusted bolt, maybe an oven door. You can bend over and break off a piece of green-grey sage and rub it between your thumb and fingers and then smell your hand, reason enough to drive to this quiet place.

Postwar

The period immediately after the First World War looked perilous to those old Victorians who worshipped order based on remnants of the class system. There was an immediate depression to go along with inflation, influenza and revolutionary talk. Premier Oliver looked hard for a lever to tilt things his way, but he was never to get a sweeping majority in the house. Still, managing tricky alliances with non-Conservatives, he was able to hold onto the premier's chair for nine years until his death in 1927, the third-longest reign of any British Columbia premier. He was, they said, lucky. After 1922 the economy began to pick up in his province. The unions, after the defeat of the Winnipeg General Strike, and the attrition in the ranks of the One Big Union, became more and more quiet, until the Depression. Like W.A.C. Bennett after him, John Oliver rode the placid waters of a postwar economy. He smiled as he saw long rail trains of grain cars arriving from the prairies and being loaded into deep-harbour ships, many of which would head for the new Panama Canal.

Oliver could never quite get it into his head that it is not enough to wear unpressed suits and attract the support of the working majority, that politics is a game of dancing with your powerful friends and dodging your powerful enemies. He was never to have an easy time of it in the polls. He was once to lose his own seat and pick up a by-election vote to stay in the house. The PGE was to remain an embarrassment all through his reign. He would have no friends among the educators; in 1922 he actually cut funds for the struggling new university. He reasoned that there were slackers sitting in classrooms when they should be out in a ditch with a shovel.

Most of all, Oliver wanted to be the "Farmer's Friend." While the farmers on the prairies and in Ontario were becoming unified and developing progressive political parties, getting ready to become governments, in British Columbia they were too few and too much diversified to make the United Farmers of British Columbia more than an association looking for better production methods and marketing opportunities. The fruit growers of the Okanagan, for instance, were still mostly Brits who saw themselves as agrarian gentlemen rather than radical pols. Oliver saw the farmer as a man (of course) who was too busy working to start any political trouble, and he looked upon agriculture as the poor cousin of B.C.'s economy. Furthermore, he looked on agriculture as an industry that would not depend on foreign sales or investments, as the extraction industries always had. He had himself turned a marsh into a rich farm by a careful system of draining the wetland and building dikes against its designs to return to its natural form. He thought about doing such a thing with the whole province.

So he started acquiring land. He got the prairies of the Peace River region back from the Dominion government. He bought up the Sumas area and drained the lake and marshes there. He built roads into valleys not served

The Kamloops polo team, made up of ex-British officers who took up farming, 1921.

by rail. He advertised for farmers. It was not long before Mennonites from Russia, like the Doukhobors before them, came to B.C. They started farming the new land in the lower Fraser Valley. But Oliver also saw a solution to the problem facing unemployed war veterans. He was looking at the arid stretch of land south of Penticton in the South Okanagan.

The geologists call this area the Upper Sonora Desert. Salish-speaking people had used it as a place to live in the winter. The Spanish had once ridden north through it, looking for gold. The fur companies had contested it. During the gold rush the roaring town of Fairview had sprawled over a hillside. The logging giants looked around and saw more sagebrush than timber. But the cattle barons liked the brown grass that covered the rock, and the river that flowed south. At one time the richest man in Penticton, Tom Ellis, ran thirty thousand acres of grazing land all the way to the US border. Then a land company with dreams of irrigation bought up most of it, but could never find the money needed to turn it into anything green. They sold it to John Oliver's government. Oliver passed the Veterans' Land Act, formed the South Okanagan Lands Project, and handed the job of creating another Eden to his lands minister, T.D. Pattullo.

There would be no Wallachin disaster here. Pattullo's surveyors mapped out a sturdy and complex system of siphons and concrete irrigation ditches and flumes to irrigate ten-acre plots from McIntyre bluff to the border. The idea was that anyone from British Columbia, especially returned soldiers, could get an orchard plot with 10 per cent down, twenty years to pay it off, a five-hundred-dollar rebate after five years, and a water rate of six dollars an acre. The first auction of lots to provincial citizens took place in 1921. Then the sale was thrown open to anyone. Within a year of irrigation there were cantaloupes and watermelons bulging in the sun while ex-servicemen planted baby trees and lived in shacks they would replace with houses in their spare time in the winters. An interesting local architectural tradition was kept alive and modified. The Okanagan Indians lived in pit houses during the winter. The new people built basement foundations and often lived in them for years before they acquired the time and money to build frame houses on top of them.

The little dam on the Okanagan River at the head of the irrigation project was called the Pattullo Dam. The main town that began to form in the middle of the project under the constant blue sky would be called Oliver. Its motto would be "Where climate and effort bear fruit." My father moved his little family there in 1943.

Public women

John Oliver might have thought that a woman's place was in the pantry, but it was during his career that they started showing up elsewhere. During the war they did "men's work" while the men were overseas doing the Devil's work. After the war they were in the fields and orchards beside their husbands and sons. From the 1916 election onward they were in the voting booth. In 1917 Helen Gregory MacGill was sitting on a judge's bench in juvenile court.

Helen Gregory was born in Hamilton, Ontario, in 1864, and grew up as a daughter of privilege with more than parlours on her mind. She was the first woman to graduate from Trinity College in Toronto, where she got two degrees. She became a reporter, and travelled west, picking up a husband, developing feminist ideas, making a trip to Japan, being widowed, and getting married again, this time to a man named James MacGill. The MacGills set up residence in Vancouver in 1903, and Mrs. MacGill started agitating for women's votes, a proper university and the rights of children. One of the reforms she promoted was the formation of a juvenile court. In 1917 Premier Brewster appointed her as the first female judge in western Canada, and only the third in the whole country. She held that position for twenty-three years, and set a great example. Her daughter and biographer, Elizabeth, became Canada's first aeronautical engineer, designing the air force training plane.

The men in government were not as welcoming to Helena Gutteridge. Gutteridge was nobody's wife until late in life. Born in London in 1879, she came out of the English working class, a labour activist who brought her organizing skills and fervent socialist oratory to British Columbia in 1911, where she became the strongest voice in the B.C. Women's Suffrage League. She became secretary and popular spokesperson for the Vancouver Trades and Labour Council, the most militant of the labour groups. It was Gutteridge who made sure that the unions were ahead of the government in women's issues. During the Depression she would be the first woman on Vancouver City Council, where she sat as a CCF member.

But Brewster and Oliver had to contend with women in their own party, too. The most successful was Mary Ellen Smith. She was born Mary Ellen Spear in 1863, a coal miner's daughter who grew up in northern England, became a school teacher, and married a coal miner. She had been listening to men talking about social politics all her life. She served as the model for a romantic novel about the struggling miners of Britain. In 1891 she and her husband moved to British Columbia, where her husband became an MLA, then a Liberal MP, and then a Liberal MLA. For twenty years Mary Ellen Smith not only shared Ralph Smith's political life, but organized women's groups in Nanaimo and Vancouver. She arrived in Vancouver in 1911, the same year that Helena Gutteridge did, and found that women were ready to listen to ideas about their advancement.

In the legislature and in the House of Commons, Ralph Smith spoke about the enfranchisement of women. More often than not, the idea was treated as a joke. More often than not the men in representative government were a little behind the times. But in the 1916 election, B.C. women won the right to vote, and Ralph Smith was named to the cabinet. A few months later he died, and in 1918 there was a by-election to fill his Vancouver seat. Mary Ellen Smith ran as an Independent and won it. She took the first women's vote, and she got the progressive men's vote, too. She was not a quiet person in Victoria's august chamber. She introduced a Female Minimum Wage Act, and got it passed. It was a bill without much in the way of teeth, but it was in the books, and would be the basis for lots of action later on.

In the 1920 election she ran as a Liberal, and won a huge majority in her riding. How about doing the logical thing and making me a cabinet minister, she suggested to John Oliver. Oliver tried to mollify her with the speaker's chair. Cabinet, she said. So Honest John made her the first female cabinet minister in the British Empire. But she was a minister without portfolio. She put up with being left out of vital activity for a few months, and then quit. She became the *de facto* minister for women's issues, fighting for mothers' pensions, child support from absent fathers, registration for nurses, the establishment of juvenile courts and more. She was re-elected in 1924, and stayed fighting till the Liberals were swept out of office in 1928.

Emily

Meanwhile Miss Emily Carr was travelling to Indian villages and making paintings of totem poles and thick native forest edges. No one in Victoria was looking at them. Carr supported herself by teaching art to middle-class children, and running a boarding-house she had acquired in 1915.

Growing

Through the twenties the province recovered its economic strength, so that from 1924 onward it would set records every year for prosperity. Labour was quiet and productive. The Delta farmer sailed along, managing to handle his enemies among the Conservatives, who kept raising accusations of corruption, and the Vancouver Liberals, who were furious because the premier would not appoint one of them to the cabinet. They steamed inside their broadcloth suits while Oliver made colourful speeches about the iniquities to be found in the cities and the clean dirt honesty to be found in rural individuals.

Oliver could never find himself the electoral landslide that McBride had enjoyed, and he had to win every motion in the house by one or two votes, while looking for a way to attract ballots from the populace. He decided to use McBride's method—flail the feds. Being a champion of the farmers and no friend of the railroads, he fought Ottawa about freight rates. Three times during his reign he went back east and succeeded in having the grain rates reduced. He also tried to persuade the Dominion government to nationalize

Artist Emily Carr working out of her caravan at Esquimalt Lagoon, 1934.

the bothersome PGE, but Ottawa knew better. Then Oliver went after the original gifts to the CPR, demanding a renegotiation of the terms that had given the railroad a wide belt of land along the tracks. Meanwhile he assigned money to road-building within the province, a technique that would be used successfully by W.A.C. Bennett thirty years later. In the 1924 election the voters narrowly defeated a proposal to allow the sale of beer by the glass in hotels. Oliver decided to allow it anyway, calling upon the municipalities to approve.

And Vancouver, now becoming the third biggest city in Canada, *was* a den of iniquity. Perhaps four people over the age of five years did not know that nightclubs and cafes were illegally selling drinks by the glass (or mug or paper cup) in back rooms and late-night hideaways. Waiters sold ice and mixers to customers who did not seem to have anything to pour them into. In the 1920 election there had been a vote for moderation: that is, instead of buying liquor in a drugstore for medicinal reasons, people could buy liquor from government-operated liquor stores. The Conservatives had another opportunity to complain about patronage, of course.

But now the United States decided to go dry. From 1920 to 1933 the great experiment with prohibition, which had grown out of the women's movement and other reform bodies, helped bring good times to British Columbia. Now, though B.C. no longer had its own navy, many of its citizens had boats that managed to elude the US coast guard and to deliver booze from our coast to theirs. Sometimes the liquor was legal in B.C., whether made here or imported. Sometimes it was manufactured in stills along the northern coast, where there were a million places to hide among the trees up the fjords. Vancouver might not have had anyone in the cabinet, but by the end of the twenties it had a lot of millionaires, and many of those millionaires were in the export-import business.

The third-largest city in Canada, and Seattle's great rival on the coast, was also dope city. The common association of Vancouver with narcotics had started in the gold-rush days, when the story was usually about opium-smoking Chinese. Now it was as easy as pie for anyone to shop for all the drugs that in the twenties were a common theme in movies and fiction and popular music.

Perhaps the Roaring Twenties were going on most visibly in Paris and Chicago, but Vancouver, despite its many puritans, made quite a lot of noise.

More and more of that noise was being made by automobile engines. Some of it was being made by airplane engines. In June of 1919 two Royal Air Force pilots, John Alcock and Arthur Whitten-Brown, flew a biplane nonstop from Newfoundland to Ireland. All over the mechanized world pilots were trying to be the first at something. It was a great year for aviation on the west side of Canada, too. Someone flew a plane from Vancouver to Victoria. There was a great to-do made of the first airmail flight to

Seattle. Ernie Hoy flew his frail kite, the Little Red Devil, through the frighteningly turbulent air above and between the Rocky Mountains. During the 1920s the airport became a feature of flat ground near British Columbia cities and towns.

In 1920 there were 18,000 motor vehicle licences in B.C. A decade later there would be 100,000. It was becoming clear that the coming highway system would make an impact as great as the railroad system of the previous century. In 1922 the province decided that drivers had to switch to the right side of the road. Driving on the left might be all right for people who live on islands, but Oliver and his engineers believed that there was going to be a negotiable road link to California where they drove on the right. For a few years many of the automobiles in British Columbia were rigged with complicated devices that enabled the driver, sitting on the right side of his car, to make turn signals outside the left window.

Br'ish Columbia made a lot of adjustments to the powerful influences from the south. In Ottawa a soldier from Loyalist stock, James "Buster" Brown, got himself named director of military operations and intelligence, and drew up a plan called Defence Scheme No. 1, the master plan to be employed in case of a war between the USA and the British Empire. In 1931 the Defence Staff guessed that Canada might not be able to halt a USAmerican invasion, and scrapped the plan. Brown moved to Victoria, ran unsuccessfully for office as a Conservative, and spent the rest of his life there, fulminating against socialism and other terrible threats to good British order.

Meanwhile, Victoria, noticing that it was becoming a residential city while Vancouver (and even places like Prince Rupert) were attracting nearly all the industry, reacted by becoming a haven for old Brits and would-be Brits. Various kinds of "shoppes" sprang up along Government Street. It did not take Victoria businessmen long to realize that looking like a bit of Olde England would look good to tourists from the south.

The Honest John

British Columbia being British Columbia, it would not be long before the party system would have to be roiled up. The farmers' parties that became powerful on the prairies and in Ontario never got far in the mountains, but in the 1924 election John Oliver and his Liberals had to face something called the Provincial Party. The browned-off farmers had lent their support to some Conservatives who hated the idea of William Bowser as their leader, and some Vancouver businessmen who hated Oliver because he was opposed to Vancouverites in his cabinet. In the campaign, Oliver and the Provincials competed with each other to see who could bash Ottawa most often.

The Provincial Party was financed heavily by a millionaire named General Alexander McRae, so they ran him as their leader. McRae had managed to keep himself a good desk job during the war, made a fortune on questionable land deals on the prairies, and piled up a lot of money in traditional B.C. resources, lumber and fish among them. After John Oliver set June 20, 1924 as election day, there transpired the most extravagantly bitter election campaign in the province's history, and that is saying something. When the dust settled and the mud dried on everyone's clothing, it was discovered that the Liberals had squeaked through again, winning twenty-four of the forty-eight seats. The Conservatives got seventeen, Labour got three, and the Provincial Party won only three despite piling up a quarter of the popular vote.

The real indication of the voters' mood was the fact that all three leaders failed to win their ridings. Oliver was dumped in Victoria. Bowser lost the Vancouver seat he had held since just after the turn of the century. And General McRae was knocked out by Mary Ellen Smith. A few months later Oliver parachuted into Nelson and won the by-election there.

Winning another reduction in freight rates, improving roads into the Interior, trying to make people forget the PGE, Oliver muddled through for another three years, while the province caught the edge of the boom times that were being celebrated back east. Some interesting legislation was allowed to get through. Oliver gave the apple growers of the Okanagan a cooperative marketing act. He showed off his great white beard and passed Canada's first old-age pension and started working on a health plan. As Oliver became an old man, he became more progressive, and guided his party slightly to the left. Gone were the mossback remarks of his blustery days.

But his own health was going. His last hurrah was the Liberal convention in the spring of 1927, where he beamed while the band played. It was there that he fashioned a reformist dream—pensions, health plan, even significant aid for higher education. He was cheered at every turn, and easily won reconfirmation of his leadership. After the convention he went away for a well-deserved vacation. Not many people knew that he took his vacation at the Mayo Clinic in Rochester, Minnesota, where he underwent an operation for cancer. When he came back to Victoria in the middle of the summer, he was no longer the big bluff pig farmer, but a frail old man. He told his MLAs to pick a new leader. They said no. He insisted. They compromised, making the minister of finance and education, John Duncan MacLean the leader-designate. A month later, while the Prince of Wales and his brother George were making a gala visit to Victoria, John Oliver lay in bed dying.

John MacLean was pretty well the opposite to Oliver, not that he wasn't honest. He had held all the important cabinet posts. Another of the numerous Maritimers who became B.C. premier, he had been a school principal and a doctor. He was also a conservative Liberal, and thus a little out of step with his party. He favoured the economy over social legislation, extending

Oliver's favours to agriculture and transportation. But he made sure that he gave voice to a sure vote-producer on the coast, passing a resolution against the immigration of Chinese or Japanese people, pointing out that these Orientals were somehow better at making farms and babies than were the Anglo-Saxons whose land this properly was.

In 1928 he was pretty well forced to call an election, and hoped that the good times would keep his Liberals in at least their marginal power. But he forgot that the voters of British Columbia were usually more interested in personalities than in policies and legislative records. His opponent, the smiling Dr. Simon Fraser Tolmie, even had a name that fairly cried out for destiny. He got it from his father, who had been a bigwig in the Hudson's Bay Company. Tolmie was a Tory veteran, and he was also a veterinarian. He had been holding a federal seat for the Victoria Conservatives since 1921. He had no connection with the snarling, suspicious provincial Tories, and he looked like a man of the people. At close to three hundred pounds, he was even bigger than Oliver.

Tolmie was canny, too. He travelled the province by motor car, patting the heads of children and dogs, uttering mottoes rather than speeches, pointing out that he had been born in British Columbia. The doctor didn't have a chance against the veterinarian. The Conservatives swept back in, taking thirty-five seats. Just in time to watch the great stock market crash in New York City.

Percy

In 1928 Vancouver produced a man who could run better than John Oliver whenever a pistol shot was to be heard. This was Percy Williams, who like many others at the beginning of the century suffered rheumatic fever in his childhood, and was left with a damaged heart. A year out of high school the diminutive lad ran a hundred yards in 9.6 seconds, tying the world's record. A year later he represented Canada in the 1928 Olympics in Amsterdam. There, at the age of twenty, he shocked a very fast field by running off with the gold medals in the one hundred metres and the two hundred metres.

The USAmerican promoters knew a good thing when they saw it, and they set up a series of races in the indoor tracks of the major US cities. As such things go in that country, the scenario was supposed to include victories by the USAmerican lads against the Olympic champ. Percy Williams won every race. It would be thirty-two years before Vancouver's Harry Jerome became holder of the world's records in the one-hundred-yard and the one-hundred-metre marks.

Percy Williams died on November 29, 1982, at the age of seventy-four. Harry Jerome died eight days later, at the age of forty-two.

Broken Glass

"Appeals for redress by means of any documentation
bearing the signature of more than one complainant, or
by organized committees combining to make a complaint
are strictly forbidden."
—Relief camp regulations, 1934

Thud

In the late twenties it looked as if peace would become a good bet. The
borders of Germany were set by the Locarno Pact. USAmericans were
investing heavily in European and South American industries. In the US
you could not beat off the stock-buyers with a stick. Well-dressed US presidents promised amazing things in the future. Irving Fisher of Yale University,
the most respected economist in America, said you ain't seen nothing yet, or
words to that effect. In the summer of 1929 Wall Street share prices were
four times what they had been in 1925, and speculators rushed to put imaginary money to work for them. It looked as if you could put all the air you
wanted into the balloon.

Then on Thursday, October 24, 1929, the balloon got away, and bodies
were passing windows on their way down. In a week forty billion US dollars
just disappeared. This was bad news for any country that did a lot of trade
with the United States. The USAmericans stopped lending to foreign countries, and called in the existing loans. Meanwhile they insisted on prompt
payment of war debts. Meanwhile they raised tariffs to enormous heights. In
effect the United States was exporting its economic collapse to the rest of
the world. A year earlier the US had been consuming 40 per cent of the
world's raw materials. Now the producers of those raw materials would be up
against a wall.

263

The two main international effects of the US's self-interest would be unemployment and poverty around the world, and the rise of totalitarian governments, especially in Europe and South America.

Extraction and subtraction

White businessmen and government men had always looked at the colony and province as a vast piggy bank full of furs and trees and minerals. John Oliver had been proud of his road-building that would facilitate trade with the US. He may have championed the man who got his hands dirty at work, but he and John MacLean and Simon Fraser Tolmie liked the look of Wall Street and the big US machines making their noise on B.C. soil.

Between 1921 and 1928 the rate of mineral values doubled, and forestry values rose by 50 per cent. The overall value of production in the province increased by 75 per cent. The *per capita* income was the highest in Canada. The future looked as rosy in Victoria as it did on Wall Street. But B.C.'s happy economy was based on raw materials. Now, after the crash, the former customers had crouched behind their wall. Between 1929 and 1933, the timber, fish and mineral markets collapsed, falling by two-thirds. The value of B.C. production had been ahead of the Canadian average; now it led Canada again—downward.

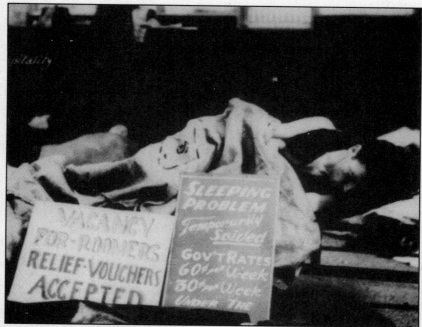

Vancouver's mild climate attracted jobless men from all over western Canada.

But times were hard all over the country, where production value fell by half. And British Columbia had a nice climate. The unemployed poured into the province, mainly to Vancouver. Unemployment was already a huge problem on the Coast because British Columbia had a higher percentage of wage-earners than did other provinces with more self-employed farmers and fishers. In the 1931 census, B.C.'s unemployment rate (leaving out the hidden unemployed who were not counted because of sex or race) was 28 per cent. And it would get worse.

Dr. Tolmie could not have picked a worse time to bring the Conservatives back to power. He had very little money with which to curry favour, and everyone wanted it. The businessmen wanted tax breaks and inducements. The more socially sympathetic, such as school teachers and nurses, wanted aid to the underclass. The unemployed began to look elsewhere for help. One could argue that there was not much that Tolmie and his inexperienced cabinet members could do, and that is what they did. In their first session of 1929 they introduced a minimum wage act for men, but there were many provisions in the act for employers who wanted to get around the act, so that farm workers, maids, part-time workers, the very people who were most in need of protection, were not covered.

Tolmie's caucus was made up of newcomers, of course, and the opposition, led by Duff Pattullo, were veterans of the pit. As usual, the cabinet, including four members from Vancouver, featured incompetents and rich men who had made their fortunes in ways that would not bear a lot of ethical scrutiny. Meanwhile the destitute unemployed were scooped out of Vancouver's streets and dropped into muddy relief camps, where they were idle and underfed. They, along with the employed, whose real wages were falling, began to listen to various left-wing groups, including the Communist party.

In the smaller towns of the Interior and the Island, nearly everyone felt the crush because those towns and those people depended on the raw resources, fruit and logs and coal, that were now going nowhere. School teachers lost their houses. Banks foreclosed on orchards. Bank clerks lost their jobs. There were hobo camps around all the small-town railroad stations. There were beggars and would-be odd jobbers at every kitchen door. In the early thirties the provincial government and the federal government set up work camps all over the province, setting underfed men to fix roads and repair public works. Thin men slept in shacks with leaking roofs. Communist diplomats came by for a chat. The mayors of Vancouver and Victoria were thankful for the rural work camps.

But Vancouver would not escape the wrath of those unfortunates. In 1929 the city had annexed Point Grey and South Vancouver, and was looking eastward for more. It was a big industrial hub, where nearly a quarter of a million people lived under a sky full of chimney soot. Soon after the crash there were thirty thousand unemployed in the streets, and it did not take long for agitators to encourage the agitated. In the early years of the Depression, the police were kept busy breaking up demonstrations and arresting socialists. Then in early 1932 men streamed out of the relief camps of the Interior, forming a great "hunger march" on the city of Vancouver, fending off the attacks of policemen on their way. The demonstrations in Vancouver became larger and more violent. In 1933 the relief camps were placed under control of the federal defence ministry.

Who were these people numbered as "the unemployed"? They were, for the most part, poor white men. Married women were, of course, invisible in their kitchens, as far as the statisticians were concerned. Single, unemployed women were almost completely without hope. When they appealed for help, they were told to get married, or they were told to go into domestic service (which was not a big job market during the Depression), or they were the recipients of lewd hints and gestures regarding their natural resources. When men are concerned with the hardships faced by any other group, they tend to trivialize the hardships faced by women, which are, ironically, redoubled. As for non-whites, the unemployed Chinese were not welcome in the camps, and were meted smaller amounts of aid at the relief offices, while for the Native people the Depression had started a hundred years earlier. Now they could expect no casual work rather than very little.

Dorothy Livesay, a great modernist poet who was born in Manitoba, but whose work ranges Canada and the world, joined the Communist party and wrote for its various publications, while organizing the poor and unemployed in Montreal and then Vancouver. She offers one of the best portraits of a woman struggling through the days of the Depression in her short story "A Cup of Coffee." It tells of a chance meeting in a coffee joint between a destitute mother and the father of her child. Written in the fashion of naturalist fiction of its time, and made up almost totally of inelegant dialogue, it is a slice of desperate life, as the woman, Hilda, refuses to consider Nick's suggestion that she make it easier on herself by giving up the child. At the end of the story Hilda leaves and Nick is left alone at the counter:

"Well, goodbye, Nick. I'll have to fix my face. Get cleaned up. Make the rounds."
"Sure. Goodbye, Hilda."
They shook hands, then she ran out of the cafe.
The waiter brought him his bill. Two bits. That left him thirty-seven cents for the rest of the day.

The tradition of folk verse that existed on the frontier and in the early newspapers of the colony was strong through the hard times, and as always offers a reliable image of the people's feelings during the angry decade. Even today you can dig into the back-room boxes at used-book stores and find thin volumes of poetry written by poets you will never hear about in university literature courses. Take for instance, one E. St. C. Muir, a politicized scribe, whose verses warned of a revolution to come. Here are the last two stanzas of "The Relief Case":

> And you come away embittered,
>   Degraded, and feeling sad.
> You feel like a bum, as you take their crumb,
>   And you've given the last you had.
>
> You have given your all, your self-respect,
>   For a morsel to fill your guts,
> And your weary feet on the city street,
>   Plod on in the same old ruts.

But the most impressive literary work to come out of the Depression years in British Columbia was Irene Baird's novel *Waste Heritage* (1939). Baird was born Irene Todd in England in 1901, and became a newspaperwoman in Vancouver in the thirties before joining the federal civil service. *Waste Heritage* is the second of her four topical novels, and often referred to as a neglected classic. In documentary detail and with a clear eye for characterization, it tells the story of the unemployed, and centres its attention upon the climactic sit-down at the Vancouver post office in 1938, the forced eviction of the demonstrators and the consequent march on Victoria by one thousand radicalized poor. Baird weighs the views of all sides in the struggle, but persuasively exhibits the willingness of government to betray its citizens during a climate of fear. Baird is not a stylist, but she is a serious novelist, and her novels are as important to British Columbia culture as those of her famous contemporaries Ethel Wilson and Sheila Watson.

Another interesting novel about the period is Earle Birney's *Down the Long Table* (1955). Birney is the most famous poet to emerge from British Columbia, and except for the comic war novel *Turvey*, his fiction receives little notice. *Down the Long Table* borrows its stylistic documentary technique from John Dos Passos, and tells the story of life among the Trotskyites during the Depression years.

The "Irish Hero"

The manly art of self-defence also produced a professional off the meaner streets of Vancouver in the early thirties. Jimmy McLarnin was born in Belfast in 1907, and moved with his family to Vancouver three years later. At the age of twelve he took up boxing, as did so many boys in Vancouver's east side. He lied about his age and turned pro at age sixteen, and won nineteen straight fights before reaching the legal age. After having beaten everyone as small as himself in the region, he moved to Los Angeles and then to New York, where he was touted not as a Vancouverite but as another in a line of battling Irish kids.

In 1933, a year when thousands of young men were trying to fight their way out of poverty, Jimmy McLarnin took less than three minutes to knock out the third man to bear the name "Young" Corbett, and won the World Welterweight Championship. (This was well before the time of dozens of weight divisions and champions.) The boxing world and its press loved the "Irish Hero." In the middle thirties the biggest fights were McLarnin's three matches with Barney Ross. Early in 1934 Ross took the crown away from McLarnin. The Vancouver newspapers were disconsolate. Later in the year McLarnin battled back and became the champ again. But in 1935 Ross won the rubber match, and a year later, at twenty-nine, Jimmy McLarnin retired from the ring. In 1950 he was voted Canada's best boxer of the half-century.

Year after year

During the stock-market boom of the late twenties, people thought that the good times would just keep on getting better. The USA had become the major world power and consumer, and seemed to be the exemplar of the new world, just as Walt Whitman, the great poet of progress, had said it would. When the system crashed, people who had seen smaller slumps thought that after a year or so things would pick up, and if there was a lesson to be learnt, the stock traders would have learned it. But then the Depression grew worse as the years went by. Governments, even those that still put their faith in the capitalist dream, began to wonder whether there was anything anyone could do. More and more individuals started listening to Marxist arguments that individualist capitalism had been a phase of history, as temporary as the feudal system and the great religions.

Meanwhile, as the months and years ground on, children started wearing shirts made from sugar sacks. The governments that told citizens to pay taxes did not suggest that they forget it until the end of the ordeal. The school board at Peachland ran out of money, and my father, their employee, taught for a term without a pay-cheque. The union movement, despite left-wing militancy, was flattened while the factories were closing down. Right after the war the non-agricultural workforce had been one-quarter union-ized. In 1934 the figure was 7 per cent, and it would climb only a little until the Second World War opened the factories. But the Liberals and Conservatives could not relax. The CCF would soon be here.

The Kidd Report

The unfortunate Tolmie administration did not know what to do. There they were, trying to sell raw materials to a world that could not buy them. They had the restless poor in unstable enclosures, and they had businessmen demanding a return on their political investments. Tolmie was certainly not going to listen to any advice from the poor. He had tried imposing a 1 per cent income tax on wages, but it aroused enmity from the workers and the chambers of commerce. He decided to call for an investigatory commission. It would be a Tory commission, made up of "non-partisan" (in British Columbia this phrase has always been a code-word for the representatives of business and real estate) gents. It was fronted by five comfortable business-men, and headed by George Kidd.

The Kidd Report would not be binding on the cabinet, of course, but in desperate times the government was inclined to listen to experts who had had success in their own outfits. The commission's chief premise was that competition was a good-sounding word but that business worked better if you could eliminate it. The government wasted a lot of money on party pol-itics, draining funds on such things as patronage and welfare. Taxes were already as high as they could go, especially taxes on businesses. The only direction that could be taken was to cut expenditures drastically, especially in the area of social legislation, and pass expensive administration to the federal government. Funds for education should be cut drastically, conser-vation should be eliminated, minimum wage laws should be repealed, the mentally handicapped should be sterilized, and the only public works should be road-building. And government should be placed in fewer and more effi-cient hands. The lumber baron H.R. MacMillan loved it. He and his fellow nabobs could operate more efficiently with an uneducated peasantry and a government that would be an arm of industry.

It did not take long for the Tolmie administration to find out how unpop-ular the published report would be with the electorate. Most of the Tories probably sympathized with the capitalist dream, but they knew that it would play into the opposition's hands. So they quickly distanced themselves from the recommendations, while maintaining that they were doing everything possible to follow its spirit. But they should never have let the business élite's monster out of the laboratory. Now the people of British Columbia knew how the bosses conceived a society; they knew that it had no place for the social programs and reforms that defined a twentieth-century coun-try. B.C. was more than ever a polarized society. And there was an election coming in 1933.

The CCF

In 1921 the United Farmers of Alberta threw out the Liberals and became the government of that province. Ten years later the party decided that a similar thing might be possible on a national scale. In 1932 there was a convention in Calgary, which was attended by UFA people, a group of academics called the League for Social Reconstruction and a number of Christian socialists who had managed to get elected to the House of Commons. In photographs a quarter of the delegates are seen to be activist women. The Calgary meeting formed a farmer-driven coalition that would call itself the Co-operative Commonwealth Federation. A year later they held a party convention in Saskatchewan, issuing the famous Regina Manifesto, which called for a mixed economy in which vital industries would be nationalized, and for broad social programs, including health insurance, children's allowances and workers' compensation. J.S. Woodsworth, a veteran MP, was elected leader of the party. In the next federal election seven CCF MPs were returned.

The CCF was even more successful than that in the B.C. election of 1933, especially given the fact that farmers had never been a large political force in the province, and there were not that many academics in a place where the university struggled for any government support. The unions were a little quicker to get behind the new party than they were in other parts of Canada, but the unions were neither powerful nor unified in 1933. In the year after the hunger march, the provincial CCF's most powerful assistance probably came from the authors of the Kidd Report.

The CCF advocated a political system that was just the opposite of Kidd's, and they pointed out that neither of the old parties would really carry out reforms that threatened their chief supporters. They were not the only newcomers; William Bowser formed a little party calling itself Non-Partisan, and struggled through the campaign until he died before election day. The CCF became very popular very quickly among rank-and-file victims of the Depression. The Liberals quickly formed a strategy that they would use for the rest of the century; they ran on the claim that they were the only "free enterprise" party that could stave off the socialist threat. Before the election Tolmie had approached Duff Pattullo with the idea of forming a union government on the model tried by Ottawa during the war. Pattullo, seeing Tolmie's offer as a sign of weakness, and being convinced of his own destiny, turned it down. He could take on the new socialist outfit himself. The newspapers joined the anti-CCF battle, making more and more wild assertions about the terrible things the socialists had in mind, such as teaching atheism in the schools and forcing teachers to be socialists.

In the election the CCF got 31 per cent of the popular vote and seven seats. The victorious Liberals got 41 per cent, and thirty-four seats. The Conservatives were just about wiped out. It was a nightmare for the authors of the Kidd Report: the socialists were the official opposition, and the Liberals under the buoyant Duff Pattullo had campaigned on a slogan of "socialized capitalism."

(Three years later, the businessmen in Vancouver would get an even worse shock. The CCF entered civic politics, and took three of the eight aldermanic seats in the 1936 election. The store owners and developers quickly formed a coalition called the Non-Partisan Association in an attempt to hold off the revolution.)

Duff

Haven't you always thought that Pattullo was an Italian name? In fact he was yet another B.C. major domo of Scottish heritage. His father was an Ontario newspaper owner and friend of Mackenzie King. Young Thomas Dufferin went to Dawson City and made money as a broker, then moved to Prince Rupert and got into the land business, becoming mayor while he was at it. In 1916 he got elected to the B.C. legislature, and started building a provincial political base while working hard for Harlan Brewster and John Oliver. The Vancouver Liberals did not like him. They thought he was an outsider and just a little too much concerned with his own natty appearance. He in turn shook hands all over the province, promising to get the party out of Vancouver's grip.

If the people and newspaper reporters of British Columbia thought they had seen swaggering premiers before, the sixty-year-old Pattullo was going to try to make them forget de Cosmos and McBride and Oliver. He revelled in his self-drawn image as a "professional politician." He adored big words and grand pictures. He wrapped his substantial torso in perfect clothes and spouted long series of imaginative epithets with which to excoriate his enemies. Whenever the occasion offered itself, he let it be known that he was B.C.'s version of Franklin Delano Roosevelt (although he always pointed out that he had formed notions of state-regulated capitalism before the US president announced his), and he was interested in a New Deal for his province, which would be called "work and wages." He never tired of predicting a great future, and he was convinced that the government had a key role in its development. He had spent a lot of time reading while he was the leader of the opposition. He read about Italy, for instance, and had a good look at Mussolini's public works programs. He read a book by C.H. Douglas titled *Social Credit*.

Now the province's debt was a towering $165,000,000. The banks were not persuaded that they could live with Pattullo's interventionist ideas. Duff went to the federal government for cooperation. Unfortunately the federal government was R.B. Bennett's Conservatives. In 1935 Mackenzie King became prime minister, and Pattullo called in old family favours. The federal Liberals came through with loans rather than grants. Every once in a while Pattullo tried that old scare word, "separation," but Ottawa had heard that too often from the Pacific coast.

Here is an example of Pattullo's vision, and of the plans he set before the federal government. Somebody found gold in B.C.'s north again. Like premiers before him, Duff dreamed of transportation and migration, and expansion into a huge resource base. He proposed that British Columbia double its size, taking Yukon and the Mackenzie River valley off the Dominion's hands. In exchange the feds would build road links to the north, and take over the vexatious PGE, making it part of the Canadian National Railway. There were those in Ottawa and Victoria and towns north of the sixtieth parallel who were of the opinion that Duff Pattullo was thinking of starting a new country with himself at its head. He had a habit of referring to his province as an empire. He would not be the last legend in his own mind to suggest B.C.'s grabbing of Yukon.

Cartoonists and rival politicians often accused Pattullo of being not a little Roosevelt but a little Mussolini. He played into their hands when early in his regime he forced through a Special Powers Act, which enabled him, were it to become necessary, to suspend the legislature and take "dictatorial" powers. The voices of conservative capitalism, such as the Vancouver *Province*, spoke their alarm. Luckily, the act was never invoked. But Pattullo would never shake his reputation as a provincial *Il Duce*.

But Pattullo was strong enough to get some government control into the economic system, and he offered as much assistance as his cash-strapped department of finance could manage, in both directions. He sent aid to mining companies and fish plants, while raising the minimum wage and setting a forty-eight-hour week. He exempted the working poor from the 1 per cent income tax. He fought the federal government over the income-tax pie. He demanded that the feds pay attention to the fact that the unemployed kept arriving at the west coast. He brazenly announced big public-works projects, promising jobs to workers and contracts to businessmen, and then blackmailing the federal government into showing its concern for the jobless and contractless. His favourite project was a big bridge over the Fraser River at New Westminster. It would be a great job (and debt) provider, while vastly improving highway connections to the US and the north. The Conservatives said that the Liberals were sinking the province into crippling debt. Pattullo's finance minister, John Hart, spent a lot of his time in Ottawa, bragging about B.C.'s future and offering the federal purse a chance to get in on a good thing.

Pattullo was indeed a liberal Liberal, a man who, while believing in the capitalist system, saw the modern necessity for a planned economy. He genuinely sought help for the indigent, even though he eventually took harsh measures against the able-bodied employed, cutting aid to municipalities in an attempt to stem the influx of hobos. He offered free transportation out of the province to forestry workers whose seasonal make-work jobs were finished. He got the RCMP to search boxcars at the Alberta border and chase tramps back toward the prairies. These measures only provoked greater militancy among the migrants, who went straight to Vancouver and mounted demonstrations that often resulted in violence.

A major demonstration had taken place in downtown Vancouver in April of 1935. At the end of 1934 more than a thousand men from the relief camps had made a march on Vancouver, to protest conditions in the camps, where they were earning twenty cents a day clearing brush, being treated by doctors who may not have been totally sympathetic, eating food prepared by people who may not have been professional cooks. In Vancouver their rally was greeted by federal officials who promised that the camps would be looked into. By April nothing had been done. Now 1,700 men from the relief camps, encouraged by the Workers' Unity League, marched on Vancouver with a lot less patience. They picked insects out of their clothes as they marched. This time they announced that they were strikers, and they used Pattullo's phrase, "work and wages." They visited the food wholesalers, and then they chose a target that was central to the city and more than symbolic of the moneyed right, the big Hudson's Bay store. They occupied the store, stomping up and down the aisles. When the police intervened, the angry men, or their political advisers, broke some display cases and pushed over mannequins. Other strikers occupied the city library, where they took advantage of the opportunity to educate readers. When they were forced out of these two buildings, they marched to Victory Square, and sent a delegation to city hall, desiring to speak to the "Non-Partisan" mayor, Gerry McGeer. McGeer had ten of them arrested instead. Then the mayor hied to Victory Square, where some of them had friends' names on the cenotaph, and mumbled the Riot Act while the crowd detailed its complaints in robust voices.

McGeer said that he would see what he could do. He was planning a new city hall on the hill overlooking False Creek. He was thinking of other grand buildings. What do you hear from Victoria, he was asked. He said that Victoria had said they would see what they could do. The hunger strikers waited for two more months, then decided to take their demonstration to Ottawa. McGeer had sent a message to Ottawa, trying to get the feds to take the Communist insurrection seriously. The Communists were the new Chilcotins, but today they were in the Vancouver streets. Now in June the hunger strikers jumped onto east-bound freight train cars, in what would become famous as the On-to-Ottawa Trek. All along the CPR track through British Columbia the trekkers were met by people with baskets of food. More and more hunger strikers climbed aboard, looking forward to explaining things to R.B. Bennett. They had to ride through Alberta, then as now a province with more than its share of right-wing zealots. From Calgary the railroad's telegraph cable went east a lot faster than any freight train, carrying the message that a fearful army of 2,500 revolutionary terrorists, led by European agents, was on its way to wreak a violent overthrow of the Dominion government. If they ever got to Winnipeg, they would be joined by the seasoned Reds who had fomented the general strike.

The hunger strikers were met at Regina by Bennett's decision. The armed police halted the train and started pulling men off the boxcars. The Regina Riot resulted in marvellous headlines across the country. A policeman got killed. Lots of hunger strikers were injured, and a hundred of them and their local sympathizers wound up in jail. R.B. Bennett claimed a victory over outside agitators with strange names, but he could not hold the fort against Mackenzie King and the Liberals, who won the federal election in the fall.

The post office

By 1938 the unemployed and their spokespersons were better organized, and the governments were even more frightened of them. The Workers' Unity League had been disbanded after the Regina Riot, but there were other socialist organizations with other names. Some of the best Canadians were fighting Fascism in Spain. Others were contending with nearly a decade of deprivation at home. It was hard to get assistance from a town that was in receivership.

Duff Pattullo, noting a slight but steady improvement in industrial values and employment, had called and won an election in 1937. He kept the Conservatives and CCF where they were, and laughed at the new Social Credit party that managed to garner a lowly 1 per cent of the vote. But there was still a solid clump of long-unemployed men and women, the figures of Irene Baird's *Waste Heritage*, who were unaffected by the upturn in resource markets, who still looked hopelessly into the empty tin cans they held in front of them on the sidewalks of Vancouver and other towns.

Many of these men were from the prairies, and had not accepted the offer of a free train ride to the dust fields across the mountains. The authorities in the province and the city of Vancouver had always managed some success in their announced plan to stand up to Ottawa and the rest of Canada. On May 10, 1938, the labour minister announced that unemployed men from the prairies would get no more welfare. The new mayor, George Miller, decreed that panhandling, even if done during "tag days," would no longer be allowed in his city. The unemployed panhandlers did not disappear. Instead they formed a surprisingly neat demonstration, dividing themselves into platoons and occupying key buildings in downtown Vancouver. Sixteen hundred men sat down in the art gallery, the post office and the Hotel Georgia. We can't have people occupying the Hotel Georgia, said the aldermen to the mayor, the tourist season goes into high gear in a week or so. On May 21, the city showed up at the hotel with some money, and the three hundred demonstrators evacuated the building, impressing everyone with their near-perfect parade demeanour.

The aldermen and the mayor felt that they could hold off on the other two buildings; tourists did not come to Vancouver to look at art, and the post office was a federal building anyway. At the post office nearly a thousand men occupied themselves and visitors by putting on musical shows and theatrics and indoor sporting events. Sympathetic people brought better food than they had been used to in the relief camps. The provincial authorities did not like the looks of such solidarity. On June 4, Premier Pattullo warned the protesters to get out of the buildings. Come on down and see the show, was the response. Time went by. Toilets did not get as smelly as the authorities might have wished.

A month went by. The sit-in was big news across the country, and that too made the authorities nervous. There were a lot of big post offices in other provinces. Another week went by. Then on June 19, perhaps to celebrate the equinox, the various governments staged a coordinated assault. The commandos struck before dawn, hoping that at 5:00 a.m. the defenders would be at their least wary. The Vancouver police were at the art gallery. The Mounties were at the post office. They gave the defenders a half-hour to emerge, then fired tear-gas into the buildings. At the art gallery there was only a little violence, because young Harold Winch was there. Winch was the son of Ernie Winch, a veteran of the Winnipeg Strike, now an MLA and one of the great figures of the CCF. He asked the protesters to spare the paintings and save the gallery from violence.

But it was a different story at the post office. A fiery leader with the wonderful name Steve Brodie asked his men whether they wanted to surrender this fine morning. The answer was loud and negative. But the Mounties had sneaked in by a back door, and they were wearing bizarre masks and carrying satchels of gas bombs. Soon there was gas slithering along the floor and filling the air. The defenders smashed the plate-glass windows to let the gas escape. There was a terrific noise of human shouting and broken glass and popping gas bombs. As the unemployed emerged from the building, they fell under the clubs of the Mounties. Then the other Mounties on horseback rode into the building and employed their government-issue whips. Everyone was after Brodie. A group of Vancouver policemen were pounding him with their clubs while an RCMP sergeant watched. Finally the Mountie stopped the fun and had Brodie hauled away. While the tears fell down the faces of the fleeing men, windows collapsed at the big Spencer's and Woodward's department stores, normal targets in the class war.

Thirty of the unemployed were injured badly enough to require treatment. Five policemen had to be attended to. Two dozen men were tossed into jail.

The damage came to thirty thousand dollars, which would have been enough to buy a lot of soup with meat in it. The CCF leaders demanded the resignation of the Liberal cabinet. A crowd surrounded the police station and demanded that the prisoners be set free. Duff Pattullo, meeting with solid citizens in Vancouver, said that he had done all that he could.

On Granville's theatre row the newsreels showed pictures of Adolf Hitler saluting long marches of goose-stepping men in shiny leather boots.

Nazis and Nisei

"And I prayed to the God who loves
All the children in his sight
That I might be white."
—Joy Kogawa, from "What I Remember of the Evacuation"

1939

In 1939 it appeared obvious that there was going to be a major war in Europe and elsewhere. That summer the king and queen of Britain made a royal visit to Canada, but when they toured British Columbia, they did not get the automatic acclaim afforded to previous royal visitors. The newspapers and magazines seemed to love them. There were thousands of little school kids out with Union Jacks. But Canada had been Canada since 1914, and British Columbia was not as British as it used to be. The country turned its back on European Jewish refugees, not wanting untraditional immigrants just when the worst of the bad times seemed to be over. British Columbia's Depression years premier, Duff Pattullo, was another kind of isolationist; he kept up the threat of independence in his dealings with Ottawa.

But as the war approached, and in its first year, Pattullo seemed to be out of touch with the feelings of his citizens. He began to lose the loyalty of his cabinet ministers and riding workers. When the Allies declared war on Germany in September, Canada entered a new era. The First World War had made Canada a twentieth-century industrial nation. The Second World War would pull it out of the Depression and prepare it for the boom in the fifties. Unemployed men and others became soldiers. Men and women streamed to the Coast to build ships. The farms of the Interior could not find enough workers. The workers of the Coast could not find enough housing.

When you are fighting or working to defeat other countries in a world war, you have not got the time nor the inclination to fight your own country. You are a Canadian before you are a British Columbian. Duff Pattullo did not grasp that notion. It was not that he failed to support the "Mother Country" in the time of need. But he had built a career on the time-honoured platform of fighting the feds for his province's weal.

At the beginning of 1940 there was a conference called to discuss a royal commission that had been mulling federal-provincial relations for nearly three years. Pattullo figured that Ottawa would take advantage of the patriotism aroused by the new war to push through the centralizing of power. In Ottawa he joined with two oddball premiers, Mitch Hepburn of Ontario and Bible Bill Aberhart of Alberta, in resisting the suggested changes, such as the assigning to Ottawa of personal and corporate income taxes. Because of the intransigence of these three important provinces, the talks were stalled.

If Pattullo thought that he would return to British Columbia as its heroic defender, he had completely misread the mood of the times. He came back to a nest of disapproving hornets. The business community gave him hell for being divisive in a time of international emergency. The CCF came out in favour of the federal commission's suggestions. And within his own party there were people, perhaps led by his lieutenant, Minister of Finance John Hart, who no longer praised him enthusiastically. The Vancouver newspapers attacked the premier for putting politics ahead of Canada, and papers across the country joined in the attack. The only people that seemed to like him were the adherents of the new Social Credit movement, and Pattullo was not exactly thrilled about their support.

But Duff was impressed with his own record; he had always been a one-man show, a man with a perfect crease in his trousers and a quick answer to all questions. There might be murmurs from businessmen and politicians, but the people were with him. He called an election for October 21, 1941, and went stumping. He was in for a surprise. For the first time in history the CCF took a plurality in the popular vote, winning 33 per cent. But because of the fact that most of their votes came in the cities and resource towns, they took only fourteen seats. But the Liberals won only twenty-one, and the Conservatives took twelve. The CCF was the official opposition again, and Pattullo's minority government Liberals would be in no position to slide any legislation through the house.

Things were starting to look like the legislature before the introduction of party politics, back when cliques had to curry favour with each other. The various political leaders started offering their solutions to the impasse, not in their caucuses but through the press. Pat Maitland, head of the Conservatives, suggested a union government to get the province through to the end of the war, which was expected to be pretty soon. Harold Winch immediately announced that the CCF would have no part in such a scheme.

John Hart told the papers that he liked the idea of a Liberal-Conservative coalition, to meet the threat of the socialists. That was that for the old friendship between Hart and Pattullo. But other Liberals sided with Hart, and Pattullo was kept busy firing cabinet ministers and taking over their jobs himself. He portrayed himself to the reporters and to Mackenzie King as a Caesar-like target of a big plot among his old associates and the big petroleum interests. He also portrayed himself as the only saviour of the Liberal party in the west.

Pattullo had always known that the big interests in the cities only tolerated him. He had always been a flash from the north, and rewarded his supporters up there by pushing northern development. If he could not annex Yukon, he could at least try to make sure that there were airports and roads and rails to the frontier. But in the election he had won Prince Rupert by only seventy-eight votes, and now the north turned on him. The legislature was supposed to sit on December 4. On December 2 and 3 the Liberals had a convention, at which was introduced a resolution calling for a coalition. It passed easily, 477 to 312. Pattullo hiked up his toga and got out quick before the knives were visible. On December 8 his hero Franklin D. Roosevelt got the US Congress to enter the war. On December 9, Pattullo resigned his premiership and became a backbencher, where for four years he would talk about the conspiracy to bring him and his party down, until he was defeated by the CCF in Prince Rupert in 1945. He spent the rest of his life in a seaside mansion in Victoria, saying I told you so.

Vancouver Lights

In 1941, Earle Birney, British Columbia's most famous poet, wrote a poem called "Vancouver Lights." The narrator of the poem is looking at the city at night from a north shore mountain. He muses on the short history of settlement there, and shows fear of its ending. Here is the second of the poem's five stanzas:

> Through the feckless years we have come to the time
> when to look on this quilt of lamps is a troubling delight
> Welling from Europe's bog   through Africa flowing
> and Asia   drowning the lonely lumes on the oceans
> tiding up over Halifax   now to this winking
> outpost comes flooding the primal ink

Germany

At the time of the First World War, Canada had more or less joined as part of the British Empire. Mackenzie King made the point, in 1939, that

Canada was entering as a nation coming to the assistance of the Allies after the German invasion of Poland. There was a formalized debate in the Commons, and Canada entered on September 10, more than a week after Britain had declared war. In British Columbia, there were still a lot of people with British accents, and some of these rushed to join the British forces. But for the most part enlistment was a Canadian patriotic action. B.C. was still a long way from Europe, and quite a distance from Ontario, but commercial airplanes were flying across the country, the Toronto *Star Weekly* and the weekend edition of the *Winnipeg Free Press* were to be found in B.C.'s rural mailboxes, and national radio was reaching even into the secluded valleys of the westernmost province.

For more than a year, the war was a European war as far as official Canada was concerned, a development of old European rivalries with the addition of Fascism. Even on the Pacific, the military and industrial workers thought that they were contributing to the defeat of German and Italian ambitions. But the British also had an empire in the Pacific to worry about. All through the thirties the Japanese had been showing off their muscles in the Pacific. The agreement after the First World War, whereby the Japanese had been given a mandate over the islands north of the equator and the other victors over those of the south, became moot when the Anglo-Japanese alliance was killed in 1921 at the Washington Conference, where a comparative quota of Pacific naval shipping was declared: the US and Britain would be allowed equal navies, while Japan would be allowed 60 per cent of the US total. In 1934 the energetic Japanese wanted the ratio to be made equal, and then said to hell with the agreement altogether.

Meanwhile Japan was creating an empire. By 1932 it had grabbed northern China. The United States had earlier created Panama out of a northern part of Colombia in order to clear the way for its hegemony along the canal. Now the Japanese tried to force its new subjects to call themselves Manchurians rather than Chinese. Five years later Japanese forces were invading the rest of the Chinese coast. The British, preoccupied with matters in mainland Europe, sent a small force to show the flag in Hong Kong.

Meanwhile, Canada made some adjustments to its west coast defences at Esquimalt, Point Grey and Prince Rupert. But Europe heated up, and while Canadians watched Hitler's moves, the Japanese began moving into Indochina. Britain asked for a little help in Hong Kong, and Canada sent two battalions of soldiers. These men were trained to parade around a garrison, not to engage in full-out war, and they were severely unequipped. The day after their attack on Pearl Harbor, the Japanese attacked Hong Kong, and from then until Christmas Day the 14,000 defenders, with absolutely no hope of reinforcements, defended the colony against a vastly larger force. The 1,975 Canadians among them were the first from their country to fight in World War II. They fought with hopeless courage, 290 of them being killed during the attack, and another 267 dying in the brutal Japanese prison camps.

US-B.C.

While the Canadians were dying in Hong Kong, the US was declaring war on Japan and the other Axis powers. Small-town boys in British Columbia now learned to draw airplanes with rising suns on them to go along with those with German crosses on them. The coastline of B.C., once placed under the protection of the Royal Navy, was now dependent on the US navy for its defence. The Canadian navy and air force were coordinated with their allies to the south and north. In fact the headquarters for the RCAF Western Command were situated in Alaska. In 1942 the Japanese actually landed troops on a few of the western Aleutian islands. Now the Canadians started to carve out airstrips up the northern path, to build a defence against Japanese expansion and to create a supply line to the Russian allies. The renowned Canadian poet Al Purdy remembered his air force days in the B.C. bush:

> A big eagle circling the sun
> with eyes a golden snare
> looped round the green valley
> snow peaks overhead
> dust blowing across the airfield
> the Skeena sailing past
> railway tracks heading for Rupert
> 48-hour-pass cancelled
> myself stuck there forever
> where even Japs would be welcome
> but they have more sense
> and no woman for miles
> and no woman for centuries
> All this a long time ago:
> I remember grass tickling my chin
> mountains near and high and far away
> axe blows smashing at silence
> Indian canoes on the Skeena
> totem poles and some friends
> nothing is lost

The war was opening up the northern part of the province in other ways. Prince Rupert became a major staging area for Canadian and US ships. Bush pilots would for decades enjoy the facilities left to them. Radio towers stuck up beside pine trees. Survey maps filled shelves in Victoria. An oil pipeline was built from the Mackenzie River to the B.C. coast.

Perhaps the most dramatic development was the Alaska Highway. The US had been talking about this highway for years; having failed to acquire British Columbia, they felt that they could use an international corridor. Now the war had loosened Congress funds, and the work began. The road, all-weather gravel eight metres wide, and almost as high, was cut through forests and mountain ranges at a prodigious pace, averaging thirteen kilometres a day. Eleven thousand US soldiers, a large number of them African-Americans, and sixteen thousand US and Canadian civilians, punched the road, officially termed the Alcan Military Highway, 2,300 kilometres from Dawson Creek to Watson Lake, to Whitehorse, to Fairbanks, in eight months. The US corps of army engineers worked in temperatures that fell below −40 degrees. When big graders broke down, they were buried under the gravel. Many vehicles were parked and left in the bush, where Indian children play among them today.

The US government spent $150 million on the road, which included 133 bridges, and the Canadian government paid $110 million for the airstrips and buildings and communications, vastly improving the telephone system in the north. After the war the Canadian army would take over the Canadian section, which was most of the road, widening it and doing the endless repairs, until 1964, when it was transferred to the federal department of public works. But since 1962 the B.C. department of highways has been spending a lot of money on maintenance. Some of the highway is even paved today. The highway did a lot for Edmonton, from which supplies were despatched, and mitigated the isolation of southwestern Yukon. For decades now the Canadians have been, without success, trying to get the USAmericans to share the considerable expense of keeping a roadlink open between, say, Minneapolis and Fairbanks.

The Yellow Peril

In eastern Canada people were alarmed by the possibility of German U-boats skulking up the St. Lawrence River and lurking just outside Halifax harbour. In British Columbia people were deeply impressed by Pearl Harbor. The national magazines, published as they were back east, tended to treat the Second World War as a battle against Hitler. In British Columbia there was a much stronger sense of the war in all oceans. Air-raid drills became a customary feature of a school child's education. Air-raid sirens were installed and periodically tested in the cities and towns. Black-out curtains appeared on house windows, and air-raid wardens patrolled the streets to see that no light was spilling out. Comic books showed children what the fanatical "Japs" looked like: they had thick glasses and big buck teeth, and were entirely cold-blooded in their service to their emperor.

There were a lot of rumours about the inventiveness of the Japanese war machine. They had bombs that would float across the sea and blow up any boat or pier that got in the way. They had incendiary balloons that would drift eastward on the prevailing winds and start enormous fires in British Columbia's forests. But in reality, the Japanese were a lot more interested in their campaigns in Asia than they were in North America. Pearl Harbor's purpose had been to sink the US fleet, not to gain real estate. But British Columbia did become the first Canadian province to receive foreign hostile fire since the Pig War. In June 1942 a ship called the *Fort Camosun* was torpedoed by a single Japanese submarine. The next night the sub, in all likelihood off the B.C. coast to probe defences and promote fear, performed target practice on the lighthouse at Estevan Point (the first place in B.C. to be given a European name), a weather station on the west coast of Vancouver Island near Nootka.

The submarine lay on the surface three kilometres from shore, and in three-quarters of an hour fired twenty-five shells toward the lighthouse and its little community. The first shells fell short and tore up the beach a little. The light was switched off to make siting more difficult. The next shells went over the target. Men, women and children headed out of the settlement. The Japanese sailors never did land a shot, though a few shell fragments plunked into the side of one building. Eventually the submarine chugged away into the night, and the next morning children scrambled over the site, collecting bits of Japanese metal for war souvenirs. There is a chance that they had once been scrap metal shipped from Vancouver to Japan during the thirties.

Meanwhile, USAmerican and Canadian servicemen stormed ashore at Siska and Attu, the western Aleutian islands, and found that the Japanese invaders had all left.

The fear of enemy attack far outstripped the likelihood, as it turned out, but few people were saying that in the early years of the Pacific War. The First World War had created lots of exciting stories about spies, and the Spanish Civil War had introduced the term "fifth column" to our lexicon. In the months after Pearl Harbor the US and Canadian governments did not need persuading that there were Japanese spies living all up and down the Pacific Coast, from San Diego to Anchorage.

So the whites of British Columbia had a new fear to play upon them, and upon which to play. Anti-Asian sentiment and violence was older than the province in Victoria and Vancouver and New Westminster. It existed in the Interior as well, nowhere more than in the Okanagan Valley. The new town of Oliver had a vigilante committee to keep Chinese and Japanese people out, not even permitting laundries or cafés. In places such as Penticton and Kelowna there were often public meetings at which Board of Trade presidents, veterans' association leaders and ministers of the gospel would give advice on how to make "our town unattractive for the Yellow man," and to exhort the locals to give their support. At the end of such a meeting everyone would sing "God Save the King."

In Vancouver the rumours of a Japanese fifth column had started a few years before Pearl Harbor. Preachers and newspapers reminded each other that Japan was highly militaristic and fanatically imperialistic, and told the public that there were Japanese military officers hiding among the immigrant population on the Fraser River and along Powell Street. But now a saviour rose up against the enemy threat. This was a Vancouver alderman named Halford Wilson. He would be an alderman for a long time, and forgotten very quickly, except by the Japanese-Canadian community and its supporters. In 1938 he tried to get Vancouver city council to place a special limit on the number of business licences for people with Japanese names. He and others said over and over that there was a lot of illegal Japanese immigration and that it posed a threat to white business. But in 1938 it seemed to be more difficult than it had been earlier to get rioters to carry sticks into "Japtown." It was equally hard to move the federal government. Mackenzie King said that he would make a public inquiry into illegal immigration.

Evacuation

Halford had a loudspoken ally in the Commons, though. This was a Conservative MP with a satirist's dream for a name, Capt. Macgregor MacIntosh. Unsatisfied with the government's lukewarm response to west coast anxieties, he actually demanded that all Japanese and Japanese-Canadians be forcibly shipped out of the country. He and Wilson were disappointed when the public inquiry determined that rumours of illegal immigration were grossly exaggerated, and Vancouverites did not seem to care much about the meetings, hearing the xenophobes out and going about their business.

Vancouver city council did their best to restrict Asian business licences, and there were from time to time angry exclusionary speeches made, but anti-Japanese fear got caught up in the swelling of anti-German emotion at the beginning of the war. Alderman Wilson continued his crusade. Ottawa began to feel that he was more of a threat to order than any subversives among the Japanese community. The Department of National Defence was, though, thinking of a contingency plan to intern people with Japanese names in case of a perceived threat from greater Japanese expansionism. Those Japanese had a lot of fishing boats, and they could carry explosives into any harbour in B.C.

The RCMP was on the case, too. They employed their own spies in the Japanese-Canadian world. In fact the RCMP made public statements against

Japanese women, carrying their babies on their backs, work in the fish canneries in Richmond, 1913.

the xenophobes, stating that their investigations indicated that the Japanese community in Canada was more patriotic than average when it came to supporting the war effort, buying more bonds, trying to enlist, supporting the Red Cross. But at the end of 1941 the Japanese-Canadians had two strikes against them: they looked exotic, and people that looked like them had bombed Hawaii and invaded Hong Kong. In the spring of 1941, Alderman Wilson had announced his new strategy—all fishing boats owned by people with Japanese names should be seized. In December, he was delighted. Pearl Harbor was always called a "sneak attack," and now he was eager to point out that there were thousands of potential sneaks living among us.

Immediately after the declaration of war against Japan, the first thirty-eight Japanese citizens were interned. The Japanese fishing fleet was tied up. The Japanese language was made to disappear, as newspapers and after-school schools quietly closed down. Leaders in the Japanese-Canadian community made public avowals of patriotism, but Wilson and MacIntosh spoke a lot louder. People with Japanese names began to lose their jobs, and some shops had their windows broken. The mobs were slowly being aroused, despite attempts from various authorities to calm them down. Panic-driven citizens claimed that they knew about Japs who kept their blinds up during blackouts.

In January 1942 the King government offered a kind of compromise. They would remove all potential enemy aliens, including Germans and

Italians, from key areas, regardless of age or sex. There would also be a pub-lic-works outfit called the Japanese Civilian Corps, for which Japanese-Canadian men could volunteer, easing the threat of their presence on the coast. This was essentially the plan that Premier Hart had been calling for. It would also be a lot less expensive than the wholesale internment that Wilson was calling for. But it did not work. Petitions from white British Columbians, from labour unions, service organizations and lawn-bowling clubs demanded that the Japanese be shipped somewhere else. When Parliament sat on January 22, Howard Green, the distinguished Conservative MP for Vancouver South, led off the demand for expulsion, and he was joined by Liberals from the province. The B.C. attorney general was given the job of representing the coalition government's appeal to the feds for total evacuation. The King government was pinched; King said over and over that he did not want to take any action drastic enough to bring anything terrible down on the necks of Canadians captured by Japanese forces at Hong Kong.

British Columbia's traditional racism was reaching its peak in 1942. Chinese store owners posted signs indicating that they were not Japs. Japanese-Canadians tried the same thing, announcing that they were Canadians. The whites, with few exceptions, were not willing to listen to the distinction. White fishermen were interested in improving their eco-nomic luck. White farmers were tired of being outdone in the strawberry patches. Greed took its place alongside fear.

Finally, on February 27, 1942, the Dominion government announced that all people of Japanese ancestry would be removed from the so-far-undefined "protected" zones. The great evacuation that was to merit one sentence in Margaret Ormsby's standard history of B.C. was begun.

Internment

In the two months that had followed Pearl Harbor the Japanese navy, air force and army had expanded very quickly into Asian and Pacific lands, pretty well crippling the US and British naval fleets. Every day the British Columbia newspapers carried front-page stories of these quick victories, and mentioned that in places such as Singapore and Burma they had been pre-pared by local fifth columns. White people in B.C. added fear to their hos-tility. Who knew what those people with their incomprehensible language were saying to each other? Meanwhile, the Japanese community in B.C. had even more reason to be afraid, surrounded as they were by chronically unfriendly whites. They tried everything they could think of to demonstrate their loyalty to Canada, but all such efforts were received as ruses on the part of the Yellow Peril.

The traditional racism of B.C., complicated as it was by the war, was now joined with the traditional edginess of the relationship between the province and Ottawa. Mackenzie King seemed to be taking forever to act on his promise to remove the hidden enemy. At the same time, various towns in the Interior, especially the Okanagan, announced that they would not allow any evacuees into their neighbourhood.

In the growing hatred and fear, Alderman Wilson's voice was drowned. Now the most prominent spokesman for total relocation was Ian Mackenzie, the prime minister's only cabinet minister from B.C. Now he began to get protests from Interior towns and Southern Alberta regarding the first Japanese-Canadians who had gone east on their own. The feds were being squeezed between those who wanted the "Japs" out and those who did not want the "Japs" in. The only friends that the Japanese-Canadians had were to be found among the CCF and some Christian socialists. While calling for civil rights for Asians, these groups also agreed that the Japanese community should be dispersed through the country, to avoid blood on the streets of Vancouver. It was only after the war that the civil rights movement grew large enough to affect government action, as when Mackenzie King was thwarted in his attempt to deport large numbers of people to Japan against their will.

Meanwhile twenty thousand people of Japanese ancestry, two-thirds of them Canadian citizens (although not allowed to vote), were hauled from farms and out of canneries and off boats, and placed in holding camps in Vancouver, many of them at the Pacific National Exhibition grounds. Their farms and boats and houses were seized and subsequently sold at pitiful prices, often to good friends of someone in government. Before the proceeds were given to the former owners, there were deductions made for their upkeep in the crowded camps. Then, while European Jews were being transported to concentration camps by the German army, Japanese-Canadians were deposited in shack towns or deserted mining towns in the B.C. interior or to beet farms in Alberta, where they might have been able to see the POW camps for German prisoners.

I was living in Greenwood when it became a Japanese-Canadian town. That made life confusing for a boy in grade one. We had blackout curtains on our windows, and we drew pictures of Zeros going down in flames, but I went to a Japanese dentist, and ran around with a tall skinny Japanese kid named Harry.

Meanwhile Muriel Kitagawa, a wonderful second-generation Canadian journalist, was writing letters to the Custodian of Japanese Properties, trying to save her family's property, and trying to explain logic and human sentiment to a less-literate bureaucracy. Here is the conclusion of one of her letters:

Now you understand a little why I must contest the sale to the last bitter ditch, if we are to hold up our heads. You will concede us that, especially as this is the very principle for which the democracies are fighting.

However, if all fails and you are upheld in your purpose, then kindly send us our "proceeds" in one sum that we may personally reinvest it in something solid... Victory Bonds, for instance.

There are still a few personal possessions in our home for which I shall send at once. You would not deny us that, I hope.

"Good" times

During World War II British Columbia bought the return of economic prosperity at the price of dead youths and amputees. Midway through the war, B.C. had the highest *per capita* income in the country and a government that was characterized by dullness and sound financial management. It was also a time of centralized nationalism, and the province finally gave up the gathering of income tax in return for grants from the Ottawa purse. People had more income tax to pay. Gone was the financial drain of the relief camps. War contracts brought full employment and a large infrastructure of manufacturing plants for the shipbuilding and airplane-building industries. Workers swarmed to the Coast from the Interior and from other provinces. By the end of the war there would be a million people in B.C. As a result of the demand for workers, the labour movement became strong again, and although the federal government restricted work stoppages for the interim, it also brought in the right to unionize and mandatory collective bargaining. There were stronger unions across the political spectrum, from the communist-inspired United Fishermen to the gentle groups that made up the Trades and Labour Congress. The teachers formed their federation late in the war while their salaries, sometimes reduced to nothing a decade earlier, began to do away with their image as poor ink-daubed wretches.

The Coalition purred along, though some Conservatives were upset that they had not been able to grab the top jobs, and treated the province as a business that was in the right place at the right time. As soon as the Alaska Highway was in place, a new highway cut across from Prince George to the Alberta border, and would a decent time later be called the Hart Highway. Plans were put in place to turn the old Dewdney Trail into the Hope-Princeton Highway, and a shack town for Japanese-Canadian workers was set into the hills to do the early work. The dusty and icy Big Bend Highway, begun in 1929, had by the early forties made it possible to drive from Golden to Vancouver, shortening a lot of hours and some lives.

In small towns around the province, the local newspapers kept track of native sons and daughters in the war zones. Names were often jotted down on lists that would be added to the cenotaphs after this war. Penticton lost seventy young lives among its eight hundred service people. If we did not suffer another lost generation, we did notice gaps in our neighbours' families and in our school class photographs. One school offered something more than lives to the war; the Vancouver School of Art sent painters to the army, where they became war artists and helped give form to one of the most enduring and interesting periods in the country's art history. Among them was Jack Shadbolt, who has been B.C.'s most successful artist after Emily Carr, whose work had made an immense impression on him since he had seen her big 1930 show in Victoria. Shadbolt had in turn become teacher of young Molly Lamb, who was born in Vancouver in 1922. Lamb married a Polish immigrant painter named Bruno Bobak and joined the army with him, becoming in 1942 the only woman to be commissioned as a war artist. About this time Emily Carr was becoming too weak in health to carry on her prodigious art career, and turned to writing. She would die in the last year of the war, but between 1941 and 1946, our literature was blessed with her four marvellous books, *Klee Wyck* (1941), *The Book of Small* (1942), *The House of All Sorts* (1944) and *Growing Pains* (1946), the last published after her death at her request.

War's end

One should not get the impression, though, that full employment and new highways and rising wages made a transformation in the lives of people all over the province. Weathered outdoor toilets stood in back yards right inside towns such as Oliver and Vanderhoof. Most roads in the Interior were still made of gravel. Wartime rationing meant that children could deem themselves lucky if they got molasses on their porridge. If breadwinners had the money to buy things, those things might not be around to be bought. There was a big disparity between public services in the Interior and at the Coast, and not a little resentment upcountry about the gap. It was not until three or four decades after the war that the difference would be narrowed, at which time people in the Interior began to wish it had not happened. Kelowna, for instance, became by 1990 an automobile-choked shopping mall, a cluster of franchise stores and fast-food joints, where there had once been a paradise by the lake, the smell of apples in the breeze.

In 1945 people in the southern Interior of British Columbia compared their facilities with those across the border in the US west. If they had the gasoline rations to drive to Vancouver, they would travel by Idaho and Washington highways. They listened to California radio stations because, unless they lived close enough to Trail, they could not hear Canadian radio. In the south Okanagan a lot of people were still living in concrete foundations they had not been able to build houses on. USAmericans, though they did not live in mansions, and though they too had rationing, always seemed to have newer cars and cheaper cigarettes. Yet people in the coastal cities had their gripes. Houses crowded with the expanded population were falling apart. The streetcars were creaking and there were not enough of them. Streets had potholes on both sides.

But we were winning the war. Canadian graves lined up in Holland, but boys too young to go to war looked at the newspaper maps every day—the dark parts representing German-held territory became narrower, while more and more of the little Pacific islands had US flags growing out of them.

One day in May the air-raid sirens howled through the air over the cities and towns, and people once again danced in the streets of Vancouver and Courtenay. Young women kissed strangers in uniform. There was no riot like the affair in Halifax, but it was not a day for going to school or getting to bed early. Three months later the mysterious and horrible bombs were dropped on the citizens and prisoners of war in two Japanese cities, irradiating some people who had been B.C. residents a decade earlier, and a week later there was more street dancing. Soon the boys would be home, but they would not be boys now, and samurai swords would join Luger pistols in recroom souvenir collections.

Dad's home

B.C. schoolkids would once in a while ask their parents what the Coalition was. They would hear mention of the Coalition in the classroom, or they would catch sight of a story alongside the funnypapers, and see a big blank abstract adult word: the Coalition. Sometimes parents would do their best to explain, but it was a hard concept for a kid to grasp. The best the kid could do would be to see some sort of analogy with the wartime terms, "the Allies." Then who were the Allies' enemy? The answer would depend upon the parents' political leanings.

In October of 1945 the Coalition government decided that a time of euphoria and emotional exhaustion would be a good time to hold an election. They may have been unnerved a little by Labour's overthrow of Churchill in July. But they did not want to experience the usual fate of governments that hang on for a full five-year term. They need not have worried, as it turned out; though the CCF added four percentage points to their popular vote, they earned only ten seats to thirty-seven for the combined Liberals and Tories. Now it was time for the dull business-as-usual regime to face the domestic demands that would be made by returning veterans and those on the home front that had put their plans on hold for six years. There was a slither of fear throughout the populace that the war had been an economic blip, and that they would slip back into the Depression. Prices, especially for productive land, were heating up while income rose at a slower rate. Parents were doing what it takes to produce families that had not been advisable or possible during the war years. There would be a demand for new schools and hospitals and roads. The Coalition's main job would be to find ways to turn wartime production to peaceful purposes.

The way they chose was to open the province to foreign investment, to allow the big timber and pulp companies to gobble up the little mills or just make them obsolete. In the northeast the oil fields were opened to private business, and there was an oil rush that reminded people of their grandfathers' stories about the gold rush. Returned soldiers and immigrant workers were making demands for housing, and the businessmen who ran the province wanted to meet those demands. The ravaged European countries urgently required commodities they could not yet supply each other. The new giant paper mills in Powell River and elsewhere required huge new supplies of electricity, so dams were constructed, creating lakes where ancient Native villages had been. The woods became very noisy, whether along the unpeopled coast or up the north shore mountains above Burrard Inlet. It was a great time to be a "forest giant," the popular newspaper phrase for a foreign company with big operations in British Columbia. New building materials and the proliferation of newly available gadgets led to a general feeling that B.C. was getting to be quite modern, but the frontier mentality ruled the business of government and the government of business. A third of the voters felt that huge profit-making industries should be nationalized, but a lot of the nabobs of business did not even have official votes in the province—they had other ways of influencing Victoria.

"Development" was the most favoured word in that capital. "Immigration" was another word that often appeared in the same conversations. Now more than ever there was good reason for Europeans to emigrate to Canada. They were most often called displaced persons, or as the nervous citizens of agricultural valleys and company towns said, "DPs." Immediately after the war the British began to arrive, soon followed by the Dutch and Belgians. As soon as a ban was lifted at the end of the decade, the Germans arrived. Scandinavians, traditional immigrants to the forest, kept coming. Unlike Asians, all these northern Europeans were welcomed as logical contributors to "development." If B.C. had been developing rocketry, Werner von Braun might have been asked to set up shop on the high plateau around Merritt. Potential immigrants from southern Europe and western Asia would have to wait a decade or two.

Late forties

J always say that 1948 was the greatest year in the history of civilization. Women's fashions stopped looking military as the New Look appeared. Alan Ladd and Veronica Lake knocked everyone's socks off. Bebop could be heard on the radio, even in the mountain valleys of the B.C. interior. The first World War II novels began to arrive with *The Naked and the Dead*. The

Cleveland Indians and the Boston Braves finally won pennants and played a marvellous World Series. My father and his teacher buddies started building extensions on each other's houses, and we got siding put over the tar-paper on our house. The new high school was assuming shape on the hill, a futuristic L-shaped building with a real gymnasium and a semicircular music room.

But we kids still didn't quite know what the Coalition was. In 1947 Premier Hart announced to the Liberal Association that he was ready to pass the torch to another businessman. Herbert Anscomb, the leader of the Tories, was certain that he was the leading statesman in the province, and he had a cranky disposition. He argued that the Liberals had been treating the Coalition as if it were a Liberal government since the beginning, and that it was time to choose a Tory as premier. He was not at all ambiguous as to the right Tory for the job. The Liberals chose to put him in his place (which turned out to be the finance ministry) by handing the head job to a man who had entered the House in 1945. This was a Victoria-born hardware merchant named Byron Johnson, whose parents had immigrated from Iceland. He had not had time to make enemies, so he won the Liberals' nod over the veteran Liberal pol Gordon Wismer, 475 votes to 467. Who is this guy? a lot of people outside Victoria wondered. They did not know that Johnson had been an early supporter of the Coalition idea, and thus kept the Liberal party in power.

Johnson was really boring. People had trouble remembering his name. But he got the voters used to seeing a hardware-store owner in the premier's chair, a tradition that would be exploited by his successor. A lot of people look back on W.A.C. Bennett as the jingoistic merchant who pushed giant public works into most corners of the big province, but he was really continuing the dreams and methods of the man called "Boss" Johnson. Johnson did not get that nickname because he was some west coast Tweed; he got it from his family nickname "Bjoss" and from his position at the store. Johnson quietly soothed Conservative disaffection by adding Tories to his cabinet. Then he set about turning B.C. into a big store, striving for efficiency, expansion and labour peace.

Johnson understood building supplies, of course, and he watched with approval as the big lumbermen, Bloedel, Crown Zellerbach, H.R. MacMillan and Leon Koerner, brought their European expertise into the "harvesting" of softwoods. Of course the International Woodworkers of America were more than thirty thousand strong, and they could be bad for business if they laid down their saws. The Coalition government in 1947 passed an Industrial Conciliation and Arbitration Act (even Johnson's legislation sounded boring) whereby a government-supervised strike vote could not be held until a long complicated series of conciliation meetings had been conducted. Bad idea. Johnson's MLAs kept their ears open in their ridings, and reminded the Boss that he would be holding an election in a year or two. In 1948, the Act was rewritten in such a way that the MacMillans and Zellerbachs could not stall forever.

The Johnson government did not hesitate to show their impatience with private business if private business failed to show its faith in the big store. People have often noted W.A.C. Bennett's penchant for praising small business while nationalizing great service segments of the economy. Byron Johnson did not strut the way Bennett would, but in 1947 the government showed its impatience with the old B.C. Electric Company, which had concentrated on the money-making market around Vancouver. The B.C. Power Commission was created to see about expanding electricity into the hinterland. There might not be much gold left in them thar hills, but any store needs to satisfy its suppliers before it can satisfy its customers. Johnson's men envisaged a steadily improved system of roads and other communication methods to bring resources to the coastal ports, while showing the low-population ridings of the Interior that Victoria cared about them.

It was for that purpose that Johnson and Anscomb decided to pick up Duff Pattullo's old idea of a hospital insurance plan, hoping to steal a little of the light off the CCF torch. They passed the Social Security and Municipal Aid Tax, the first sales tax in the province. The idea was that the voting public would say "oh boy, the government has found a new kind of tax to help us out, and it is so cheap!" The tax on retail goods was set at 3 per cent, and it excluded items such as groceries, farming machinery, medicines and any restaurant bill that came to less than fifty-one cents. Two of the three cents were to be spent on various welfare plans, including the hospital plan. But citizens also had to pay premiums to keep the plan operative. The idea of public hospital money was not unpopular, but there was a lot of suspicion of the handling of the proceeds, especially in rural areas. People called their tax pennies "Herbies" after the finance minister, and found ways to get around the act. At lunch counters everyone asked for separate checks when they had their pie and coffee.

Still, there was a sense of relief around the province when the feared postwar slump did not materialize. Items were removed from the ration books one by one, and almost every child knew another child whose father had bought a new Ford or Chevrolet. Kids that lived close enough to the US border could go to Oroville or Spokane and buy bubble gum or pegged pants. The Coalition went to the polls in June of 1949 with confidence. The cold war was on, and the Coalition Company Ltd. went to the hustings to tell British Columbians that they had never had it so good, and the Left, from the CCF to their friends the Russians and the Chinese, was their only real danger. All year the big business corporations, many of them US branch plants, had been taking out newspaper and radio advertisements praising venture capitalism and its hope for the future. Chambers of Commerce inveighed against the Red Peril, and announced that business was staying away from Saskatchewan since that province had fallen to the CCF. The word "free" was bandied about a great deal. The Coalition won big, taking thirty-nine seats and reducing the CCF to seven. Neither the Liberals nor the Conservatives could muster as many votes as the CCF could, but both groups were elated by their victory. The government had extended the vote to Native people, and the Natives had elected Frank Calder, a Nisga'a, to the house as a CCF MLA, but the socialist hordes had to be satisfied by their continued one-third of the popular vote.

Pave it, Dam it

"In this little fella, you'll find lots of faults and I'll make lots of mistakes but, with the help of God, I'll do my level best for British Columbia."
—Phil Gaglardi, maiden speech in the legislature, 1953

Korea

As 1949 came to an end, the newspapers were filled with stories and advertisements about the half-century. The sports pages displayed features about the greatest athletes of the half-century. The entertainment sections picked the best movies and musical recordings of the half-century. The half-century was summarized in terms of world events and the growth of British Columbia. Automobile merchants and furniture salesmen offered half-century bargains. A few calm thinkers pointed out in letters to the editors that all this hoopla was a year early, but there was no stopping the enthusiasm of buyers and sellers in the postwar boom.

The term "postwar" was a convenient usage in the twentieth century. Wars in the twentieth century had a way of leading to later wars. By the middle of 1950 Canada was involved in another war, and many of the soldiers and sailors who had experience in Holland or Italy found themselves under fire again. Once again British Columbia found itself a staging area for a Pacific conflict.

World War Two had officially come to an end on a US navy ship in Tokyo harbour. Then Korea, which had been grabbed by Japan in 1910, was occupied by Russian troops in the north and US troops in the south. The Russians quickly set up a Communist Korean government north of the 38th parallel, but in 1947 the new United Nations created a commission to supervise an election in the whole peninsula. The US nominated Canada to act on that commission, and after hesitating, Canada agreed to be one of the seven countries represented. The election never happened; the Russians and North Koreans would not allow the commission to operate in the north. So the US called for a USAmerican-style government in the south. Once again Canada was reluctant, and along with Australia voted against the idea. But the US prevailed, and the cold war had found another flashpoint.

In June 1950 the North Koreans invaded the south, took its capital Seoul, and advanced southward. The Security Council of the UN, where the Soviets were not sitting for the nonce, called for a "police action" to repel the invaders. There were Chinese and Soviet volunteers among the northern forces. Eventually seventeen countries lined up on the side of the United Nations, under the command of the US leaders. Canada put the Royal Canadian Air Force and Canadian Pacific Airlines into the business of flying supplies to the south. The Royal Canadian Army's special force became part of a Commonwealth brigade. But the greatest contribution was made by the Royal Canadian Navy, whose destroyers and submarines carried troops and supplies into and out of the theatre of war, and patrolled or shelled the coastlines.

On the whole, Canadians did not get as excited about this war as they had been about World War II; it was a big war for the USAmericans, who since Nagasaki saw themselves as the protector of the "free world" in the cold war. Canada did send 25,500 soldiers and sailors to Korea, one of the highest contributions *per capita*, and 313 of them were killed, but in the Remembrance Day rites of later years, the Korean veterans would be mentioned only as a kind of footnote to the services committed by the veterans of the two world wars. But the "police action" gave a further boost to the Canadian economy, especially in British Columbia.

End of the Coalition

The Coalition had been formed by the businessmen in order to keep the CCF from becoming the government, and even in the economic good times of the war and the immediate postwar period, it was probably necessary to that purpose. A more adroit way would have been to address the social problems that persuaded voters to lean toward socialism. But the Liberals and Conservatives seemed more interested in the power struggle within their alliance. The Conservatives had long been impatient with the Liberal domination, and the Liberals kept telling themselves that they could go it alone, that the voters more or less considered the Coalition to be another name for their party anyway. In the heat of their moment, the government representatives did not seem to care that the public was listening to their squabbles.

Then one day in 1952 the Conservative leader, Minister of Finance

Anscomb, got the press together and announced the terms of the latest fiscal deal with the federal government. That damned man is acting as if he's the premier, thought the premier, and announced to the press that Anscomb was fired. Who are these people? the people asked themselves. I told you so, said Duff Pattullo on the porch of his Victoria mansion.

Pattullo had said long ago that the socialist-fearing folks of British Columbia would look for a new party if the Liberals allowed the Conservatives to put a drag on their reforms. Pattullo had been proud of his version of the New Deal, and he cautioned that it should not be abandoned with the end of the Depression. He was not the only one to stick a wet finger up and feel the wind direction. A small-town hardware dealer named Cecil Bennett not only sensed the breeze, but also knew a thing or two about making wind himself. He had been sitting as a Conservative member from Okanagan South, and he had often told people that the Coalition should forget its "temporary" nature, cut itself loose from the two old parties, and become a permanent bulwark against the socialist threat. The big boys from the Coast told him that they knew how to run things. In 1951, Bennett crossed the floor of the house (actually he stomped out of the house, but later snaffled a chair in the back row of the CCF area) and sat as an independent. A few discerning pol-watchers were reminded of Amor de Cosmos. Bennett was from the Maritimes too. We haven't seen the last of this guy with the huge smile, they said. In December of 1951 Bennett declared that he had joined the Social Credit League and would sit as a Social Credit member. Now the people had another question to ask. One day around then, I was poking around in cardboard boxes in our dirt cellar, doing some boyhood archaeology and history, and came up with a pamphlet with this title: *What is Social Credit?*

What is Social Credit?

The answer from most people used to be "funny money." Very few people ever tried to find out what the monetary ideas of Social Credit were, and among those who did, very few understood them. Most people scoffed at them without finding out what they were. They were encouraged to do so by bank managers and big investors and anyone who pushed imaginary money around.

Among other things, *Social Credit* was the title of a book published in 1924 by an economist from Cheshire, C.H. Douglas. It was reprinted in 1926, and an enlarged edition came out in 1933, when the Depression was hurting just about everyone but the munitions makers and the banks that made loans to the governments that bought the munitions. It was Major Douglas's eighth book about economics and democracy. In the middle of the boom of 1924, it predicted that a world depression was due to follow.

Social Credit was a clever amalgam of socialism and people's capitalism that would have worked well if it had been applied all over the world at once. Unfortunately, it was an idea that was anathema to the large international banking system. Douglas's ideas, though fascinating, cannot be conveyed in the short space we are allowing them here; but then probably less than 1 per cent of the B.C. voters that marked Social Credit on their ballots had ever heard of Major Douglas, anyway. Douglas's chief argument is quite logical. He says that in regular capitalism the worker can never hope to make as much as he has to spend, because in order to set prices, the company he works for has to factor in two major expenses—the wages he pays to the workers, and the price of materials and bank loans. Douglas says that the disparity between wages and prices can be narrowed by doing something about the banking system. He points out that a major bridge, for instance, costs the government (the taxpayers) more in interest payments than in capital. The banks are allowed to make loans of imaginary money to the government, and receive actual money back from the taxpayers. Thus national debts will continue to climb, and the money that could go to making life better for citizens is delivered to the banks. So profits and bank charges will always be more than the amount of money put into circulation.

Social Credit suggested first that the government would save a lot of the people's money by giving itself rather than the banks the right to lend imaginary money. Now the manufacturers would have only the cost of materials to add to wages in determining its prices. Here the government would take care of the smaller gap between wages and prices by fixing prices and offering compensation to manufacturers to ensure their profits. A national dividend would be distributed to consumers. Of course money would be worth a little less the older it got. But currency is only a token of the community's real wealth. A government freed from crippling debts to the big banks could offer credits instead to the people whose labour produced material wealth.

The ideas of Major Douglas repelled traditional capitalist economists but attracted many adherents in the twenties and thirties, when alternatives to the rampant robber baronism of the nineteenth century were being examined in Russia and Bavaria and elsewhere. The most famous of them all was Ezra Pound, the greatest twentieth-century poet in the English language. In Australia there was an active Social Credit League that maintained a busy printing press and found the ear of politicians in the state of Victoria. Pound saw parallels in the Italy of Mussolini, the ex-socialist journalist who attacked the banks and built great highways to the mountains. In 1932 an Alberta evangelist named William Aberhart took up Social Credit along with Jesus, and used his radio program to urge both on the people of the depressed province. From then on Social Credit would be associated with right-wing Christian fundamentalism in Canada. In 1935 Aberhart's Social Credit party swept to victory at the polls. Aberhart would be followed by another radio preacher, Ernest Manning, and Social Credit would run Alberta until 1971, when a lot of the right-wing vote looked for a little more respectability with the Tories. Over those thirty-six years, the party moved from radical fiscal reform and buckwheat religion toward conventional conservatism, riding on a huge underground lake of oil.

The Alberta Social Credit popularity was fuelled by verbal attacks on the federal government and the eastern banks. Alberta's government with the strange name created provincial credit shops, and as early as 1936 issued some sound-looking currency called "prosperity certificates" with dollar markings on them. In a method approved in his writings by Ezra Pound, the consumer would attach one hundred and four cents worth of accumulated coupons to the certificate, and redeem a dollar, 4 per cent being the traditional number before usury. A few of Ernest Manning's oldest cabinet members toward the end were still diehard Douglasites, but most of his members by then were chiropractors and born-again ranchers with an eye for *laissez-faire* government.

During the 1950s and 1960s there were a few Social Crediters in the legislatures of the other prairie provinces. And there was a national party as early as 1935, when seventeen Social Crediters went to Ottawa, most of them from Alberta. In later years most of the federal MPs would be from British Columbia and Quebec. During John Diefenbaker's minority government in the early 1960s, the Socreds and the NDP shared the balance of power. By 1980 the Socreds had vanished everywhere but British Columbia.

But in British Columbia the party was never a C.H. Douglas organization; it was a W.A.C. Bennett invention.

Wacky Bennett

William Andrew Cecil Bennett was born in 1900 and raised in a small New Brunswick town that has since disappeared. He got the name Cecil after Cecil Rhodes, the business wizard and imperialist who was at the time taken as the model of adventurous individualism. His family had been among those British who took over Acadian lands after the French had been expelled. In later years Bennett would claim to be a United Empire Loyalist, something a little more respectable. His mother taught him to be a devout Presbyterian; the Bible was the source of all wisdom and correctness, and cleanliness was consistent with devotion. His father also served up a lesson; he was a chronically failed businessman and provider, and therefore probably not a good Christian.

Young Cecil's political upbringing was Conservative, and as a child he was hauled by family members to Tory rallies, and instructed on the close relationship between conservatism and Christianity. During the First World War, he dropped out of grade nine and went to work in a hardware store.

Thus on the other side of Canada started the tradition of British Columbia Social Credit premiers and cabinet ministers without high-school diplomas. By 1919 the non-smoking teetotalling lad was working in a hardware store in Edmonton. During the years of exciting union activity, he hustled hard for bonuses and competed for advancement. He remembered cleanliness and dressed in conservative suits. He kept active in church affairs, and as a young adult maintained chastity to go along with sobriety and health, while teaching Sunday school and improving himself with correspondence courses. He avoided the temptations that would divert a soul from religious and economic success, abjuring the aforementioned sins and staying away from art and literature. He was a ready champion of all the corny puritanical success programs that were being invented in the United States in the first part of the century. He associated the uncomplicated with the desirable and successful. He did not hear about irony.

In 1927 he started a partnership in a hardware business in a small town north of Edmonton, and married a chaste young woman. A year later he and his partner bought a second store in another small town. But in 1929 Bennett had a look at the stock-market collapse in New York and sold his share of the business to his unfortunate partner. It was time to leave the province of Alberta and look for somewhere else to create a hardware empire. He left the province about the time that Social Credit entered it. He spent no time pondering the philosophical or historical implications of his decision; it was just good business.

There was no question of going to the big city. Bennett would remain all his life a small-town self-made man, a figure straight out of a novel by Sinclair Lewis (though it is a good bet that he never read one), a champion of the clean air and high morals of the rural life. He settled on Kelowna, at that time a place where one could see through clean water to the pebbles at the bottom of the lake. He started to go around the valley with a smile pasted on his face and homilies offered to one and all. He joined the Chamber of Commerce and every service lodge that seemed useful to his ambition. He bought into a winery but never tasted its products (a good idea at the time, even for non-Puritans). He announced that advertising was the way of the future, and started building a political base. First he tried to get on the board of governors of the new Bank of Canada in 1934, and took his rejection hard. Then he tried for nomination as Conservative candidate for the 1937 election, and was really miffed when the Tories chose instead a parachuted candidate from Vancouver.

But Bennett had ambition, and it was not as a party man. He went back to expanding his hardware business, and bided his time while a Liberal held the seat he wanted. He finally got the nomination in 1941, and won his seat. Now he was a backbencher in the minority segment of a Coalition government. In the following years he looked every direction for advancement.

Sometimes he argued for a new party made out of the Coalition; but when the leadership of the Conservative rump was up for grabs, he grabbed, and was rebuffed by the big-city boys. Neither his party nor the press knew where he was coming from, this white-toothed hustler with his slogans and free apples. But he was always a jump ahead of everyone, even if he did not know where he would land.

In 1948 he decided that he would get nowhere in the Coalition, so he resigned his seat and ran for the Tories in a by-election, for a local seat held by his party for twenty-four years. Unfortunately, Bennett chose to travel the campaign roads in a big shiny Packard during a year when the orchardists were taking a beating from bad weather and insufficient compensation. Despite the fact that John Diefenbaker had led a gaggle of prominent Tories into the riding, Bennett was beaten by the CCF's O.L. Jones. Once again he threw himself into the selling business, refusing to campaign for the man chosen by his party to succeed him in Victoria. In 1949 there was a federal by-election, and Bennett tossed his hat into the ring, but the Tories decided to go with another man against Jones this time. A lot of British Columbians, especially CCF supporters, would later wish that Bennett had been permitted to represent the Yale constituency in Ottawa.

Bennett the Socred

Now Premier Johnson called a provincial election for 1949, and according to Hart's formula for the Coalition deal, there had to be a Tory representing Okanagan South. But Anscomb, wary of the "Loner from Kelowner," did all he could to persuade the incumbent to run again. It did not work; when the day came, W.A.C. Bennett would be back in the legislature. For years he would tell everyone that he was being directed by an authority higher than any politician; God had ordained that he lose his chance at federal politics so that he could become the leader of British Columbia during its glory days.

For a second time, Bennett gathered a group of B-players (Bonner, Bewley, et al.) and challenged Anscomb for the Conservative leadership, and once again Anscomb fought off the challenge, making no secret of his satisfaction at having done so. It appeared as if God were taking his time, perhaps testing his chosen agent. But it appeared to Bennett that he had to do something out of the ordinary to reach his goal. In later years, the anti-socialist politicians of the province would hop from party to party, but in the Coalition years hopping was not an option. In 1950 and 1951 he travelled around the province, telling people that the Coalition was a mess, and suggesting that younger Tories such as himself were the wave of the future. In the house he made vociferous attacks against the Liberals' expensive hospital insurance plan. He and his supporters intimated that the Liberal party were near-socialists, and that the older entrenched Tories were a dead end. All his life,

Bennett's theme would be the people's opposition to "politics," but he was an expert and ruthless politician, a great organizer and opportunist.

Halfway through the century he was fifty years old. He had been defeated all over the political map. Another man in his place might have devoted the remaining years to a hardware empire. In fact some of the older Coalition men said that the outsider was finished. Then on March 15, 1951, the B.C. Hospital Insurance Bill came up for final reading. Bennett rose from his chair and delivered a long diatribe against the Johnson government, at the end of which he announced his dissociation and strode out of the room.

Socred surprise

In its last days the Coalition government made a lot of mistakes, but the most amusing was the Elections Act amendment it passed in preparation for the remarkable 1952 election. The seated Liberals and Conservatives knew that their alliance was in trouble. They sensed that the united CCF was likely to win a minority victory, if not a majority one. In order to forestall such a catastrophe, they designed a complicated preferential ballot to present to the voters in the province. They would be asked to rank the candidates in their riding. Let us say that you are a voter in 1952. If your first choice should finish last, he would be eliminated and your vote would go to your second choice. Then the procedure would be repeated until there was a clear victor. In this way, no candidate could win with a minority of votes. Here is the way it was supposed to work to keep the socialists out: Tory voters would give their second vote to Liberals, and vice versa. CCF voters would give their second choice to the Liberals, of course. It would not matter if the Coalition broke apart; the CCF did not have a chance.

But the best-laid scheme of these mice went agley. On June 12th, the voters marked their complicated ballots, and several weeks later the harried vote-counters had finished their subtracting and adding. Johnson and Anscomb had shot each other in the foot. Angry CCF voters had given their second choices to the Socreds because they wanted to mark the Tories last and the Liberals second-to-last. Most Social Credit voters were from the sticks, and wanted to get back at the big-city lawyers. Many Tory and Liberal voters used this method to punish each other and carry on the bickering that had characterized the Coalition in recent years. When the pile of paper was finally packed away, the province found itself entering a new era. The CCF got 34.3 per cent of the votes and eighteen seats. Social Credit candidates got 30.2 per cent, and nineteen seats. The old parties, in their last hurrah for a while, managed ten seats. Their leaders, Johnson and Anscomb, were both turfed out.

On July 15, those nineteen Socreds got together to choose a leader. They looked around at each other, a gathering of small-town salesmen, preachers and notary publics. There wasn't a lawyer in sight. There were only two people who had any experience in the legislature, and one of them was Tilly Rolston, a Christian lady who had been a Conservative until Bennett had bullied her into running for the moralistic Socreds. She was reportedly dying of cancer, and she was a woman anyway, not a good choice of sex among the Bible-thumpers. Bennett easily won, and on August 1 a perplexed Lieutenant-Governor Clarence Wallace, after consulting every expert he could find, found himself calling on Wacky Bennett to form a minority government. When the new premier made his first public speech, the audience was full of country haircuts, many of them on the heads of an army of Alberta Social Crediters who had roamed the province, slapping backs and bragging about the oiled kingdom east of the Rockies.

Big grin

Social Credit people did not like to be called a party. The others, the political ones, were parties; Social Credit was a movement. It was a crusade. Social Credit meetings started with the singing of "O God our Help in Ages Past," and God was cited often. When some lawyers and other professionals found their way into power with the Socreds, they always looked a little uncomfortable in their company. It was not long before newspaper cartoonists portrayed Socreds with severe puritan suits and affixed halos. Old-fashioned fundamentalism promised sin-free (non-political) government, diligence and a balanced budget. The Bible was a better guide to recovery than was any book by C.H. Douglas. Purity had another side, too, or maybe another part of the same side. Social Credit women were expected to be good wives and homemakers. One would look far to find a dark face among Social Credit gatherings. Dissident Asians or African-Canadians or Native peoples would have to look to the CCF for a voice. Bennett's eccentric public works minister, Phil Gaglardi, was of Italian extraction, but no longer a Catholic—he was a Pentecostal preacher who spoke in slogans and superlatives. In various parts of the world, some Social Crediters had had the unfortunate habit of uttering anti-Semitic remarks. Ezra Pound, of course, had found Jews running the great European banks. It is unlikely that the typical Okanagan Socred was in the habit of reading modernist poetry, but he might have listened to the ominous speeches of the visiting Albertans, or Reverend Ernest Hansell, Bennett's stalking horse, who regularly warned against the machinations of the international bankers that were a "government more powerful than governments," and many prominent Canadians, such as UBC president Norman MacKenzie, who were "traitors or communist dupes." But W.A.C. Bennett made sure that he himself was above such tactics. He aimed his attack against the political machines and their monopolistic business friends at the Coast.

Bennett, with his sense of personal destiny, and the realization that he had to govern with an anti-government caucus, would keep most powers to himself. He knew that he would not be able to operate for long with one seat more than the CCF had. His first job was to attract votes for the next election, and he decided to reach for the low-population ridings of the countryside. His would be a government by outsiders, the revenge of the goodly folk in straw hats.

Still, Bennett did not feel good about appointing high-school dropouts to key cabinet positions. He reached beyond his caucus and persuaded an old ally, young lawyer Robert Bonner, to act as attorney general. He tapped his hardware store's accountant as finance minister. Later he would pry some lesser lights out of their elected seats to make room for these men with higher education.

Sophisticated professionals and resource magnates were throwing up under the magnolia trees in their Shaughnessy gardens, but hinterland board of trade members were rubbing their hands, thinking of the beautiful blacktop they could expect on their highways. But it was a year for a tumultuous house, and it called for the premier to use all his skills of political finagling. Harold Winch, the CCF leader, had been the lieutenant-governor's first choice for the job, and when Winch managed to engineer a defeat of the Socreds on a house vote, he expected the lieutenant-governor to give him a second chance at it. He did not know that Bennett had staged his own defeat in order to dissolve the legislature and go to the hustings again. The bill that failed was a measure to build schools in small towns while holding the line on big-city schools. Winch played into Bennett's hands again by resigning in a huff. He should have looked carefully at the big white teeth of the premier as they shone like a headlamp on the first PGE train to trundle into Prince George.

In the 1953 election campaign, Bennett announced grand plans for opening up the whole province to the coming economic miracle, and he presented his crew of earnest hard-working Christians who had been ganged up on by wicked socialists *and* the minions of the old plutocrats. They shouldn't have called him Wacky when he was so Wily. This time the two old parties managed five seats between them, and the Socreds won twenty-eight seats to the CCF's fourteen. And they had made incursions into Vancouver and Victoria, where the new pattern of British Columbia voting was established—the anti-CCF voters had decided that this strange new party was their only bulwark against the revolution. For the rest of its life the conservative voters would not even think about the meanings of the two words in "Social Credit"—it was just a name for the right.

Now W.A.C. Bennett, the epitome of the travelling salesman, would be seen all over the province, opening highways, stomping on ceremonial shovels, promising the "good life" to his parishioners. He rode the wave of unprecedented business in the banks his movement was supposed to distrust. He continued the Coalition's brave public works, and upped the ante considerably. He dressed up nicely and took credit for the boom in windy speeches that defied grammatical parsing, and his followers loved it. It became a running joke in British Columbia that no one could find a voter who admitted to being a Socred, but Bennett would go on winning election after election. Who wanted change while the roads were becoming as good as those in the US and big dams were bringing power into and out of the remote valleys? The CCF voters in the Kootenays might have to put up with potholes while the voters around Kelowna got a new bridge and a wide jet-black highway, but US money came pouring into the forests. Bennett did not believe in philosophy or even ideology. If there were citizens who asked about social programs, his answer was that government-guided free enterprise, transportation and electrical power would bring prosperity that would reach down to the bank accounts of any honest working man.

Not that the opposition did not find scandals in the B.C. tradition, even among these evangelicals: there were endless gripes about patronage, especially by the MLAs who had friends in small-town main streets. Spiteful grumblers complained that the sons of ministers such as Bennett and Gaglardi were doing very well in business. The most famous case would be Robert Sommers, the first SC minister of lands, forests and mines. As a notorious poker-playing man, Sommers should never have been a Social Credit candidate; and when he got into personal financial trouble he might have had too many drinks and borrowed money from someone attached to the forestry business. The Vancouver newspapers loved the Sommers case. The *Province* was a Conservative paper and the *Sun* believed in the Liberals. The case dragged on for several years, and in 1955 Sommers would be cleared by a commission that was mocked by the papers. In 1956 Bennett asked for Sommers's resignation; he knew that his minister was going to go to court and probably to jail. Eventually Sommers would go to jail, but by then Bennett would have made himself appear a victim of a gambling man. The joke went around that Bennett would retain his halo and grin even if his cabinet turned out to be drug-taking war criminals.

Bennett had a government that had sent expectant representatives from all over the Interior of the province, and he followed the program that had worked so well for previous provincial bosses. In his first few years he spent more on highways than any other government had, including bridges that wowed the locals. He was telling the people in the sticks that it was *their* province. He put on his expensive hat and coat and presented himself as one of *them*, who had made good just as they could if they but followed his dream. He opened up the north, just as his successful forerunners had tried to, and he even reiterated Pattullo's ambition of offering Yukon annexation into the good life. He would push the PGE from North Vancouver to Dawson Creek.

He even disguised federal projects as great provincial feats, and put billboards proclaiming his dream near any public works. He was an ebullient salesman for the province. He asked school students to stop saying "BC" and use the full term, "Bri'sh Columbia," at all times. For a while he tried to get newspapers and officials to call him "Prime Minister" instead of "Premier."

Empire

Like the flamboyant premiers before him, W.A.C. Bennett put the province before the country, though he was not as ready as some to keep up a threat of going it alone. He was nursing his resentment at various personal snubs by the federals, and not at all quick to remember the electoral help he had received from Diefenbaker and the Conservatives. He was an early expert at arranging photo opportunities, especially when he could be captured grinning beside foreign business giants and statesmen and royalty. So when the fifth British Empire Games came to British Columbia in the summer of 1954, the flashbulbs were reflecting off his teeth several times a day as he stood with hair slicked back beside important people from around the world. In eastern Canada the politicians and press shook their heads and went about their business. They were resigned to the fact that that province on the edge would always be full of kooks.

When the British Empire Games opened in July 1954, the scene was the magnificent Empire Stadium on East Hastings Street. The games may have been played by people from English-speaking countries all over the globe, and the home team may have been Canada, but there was no doubt that they were hosted by Social Credit's west-coast province. The hardware man liked the edifice so well that one might have thought he had been the provider of its building materials. There were 33,000 permanent seats, most of them under a roof. At last we were in the big league.

There were several memorable moments in these games. The cameras followed a marathon runner who staggered into the stadium and teetered on the edge of collapse during his lap around the oval. But the high point was the Bannister-Landy showdown.

During the whole of the twentieth century there was a magic phrase in the world of track: the four-minute mile. It was believed by coaches and sportswriters and amateur scientists that that barrier was beyond human capability. The fastest mile ever run was achieved by Sweden's Gunder Hägg in 1945. He had managed it in 4 minutes, 1.3 seconds. And who would manage the stressful event better than an emotionless Swede? But Roger Bannister, the Brit, was a physician. He handled his body as a laboratory specimen, and researched the mile. In May of 1954, at the age of twenty-five, he set up a dual meet at Oxford, and ran with the sole intention of breaking the barrier. He did it in 3 minutes, 59.4 seconds. Now the track world saw a great physical and psychological restriction gone, and predicted that humans would now have an undesignated limit. Sure enough, in very short order, John Landy of Australia broke Bannister's record. So when the Empire Games came up, the only two sub-four-minute men brought a lot of international reporters, many of them outside the sports beat, to East Hastings Street—and there was W.A.C Bennett, waving his homburg to the crowd.

The race produced one of the most famous photographs of the twentieth century. It shows both thin men running through the protests of their agonized bodies down the last few yards of the homestretch. John Landy is taking a quick look over one shoulder—but Dr. Bannister is just starting to pass him on the other side. For the first time in history two men ran under four minutes in one race. The photograph would be transformed into a romantic metal sculpture that would take its place in front of Empire Stadium.

Three weeks later the B.C. Lions (Bennett would upbraid any fool who referred to them as the Vancouver Lions) played their first game at the stadium.

For years the four-team Western Provincial Football Union had been saying no thanks to west-coast overtures for a franchise. But when Vancouver got the games, and the largest stadium in the west was planned, the league saw that profit-sharing dollars would exceed travel expenses and welcomed their new partner. All through 1953 there was a motto being heard through the land: "The Lions Will Roar in Fifty-Four." That prospect was highly unlikely (and in fact the Lions won only one game in their first season), but it was full of the kind of spirit that Premier Bennett understood. Visiting football dignitaries should not have been surprised to receive gifts of bright red B.C. apples.

Big talk

Cece Bennett hardly ever stopped talking but he was not in the conventional way a good orator. For one thing he had a high-pitched raspy voice, which delivered words in short bursts. And with each burst his sentence would veer off in a new direction. He usually spoke in clichés and mottos, and almost always as if he were addressing a small-town chamber of commerce. Reporters wondered whether he talked to his good Socred wife, Audrey, that way. After his death Audrey confided that his ambition had been to become a millionaire by age thirty, and added that she never knew whether he had done so. Perhaps he felt that families should be run the way he ran his cabinet. When the opposition tried to introduce a daily Hansard into the legislature, Bennett would have nothing to do with it.

Though reporters shook their heads while taking notes, they also moved their hands as fast as they could, because the premier made up with speed what he lacked in syntax. He could talk faster than anyone in the house or anyone in front of a microphone, and he gave the impression of great energy; maybe his own confused words could just not keep up with his quick political moves. Developers and businessmen and civic groups scrambled to get in his way. The province had money to give away, and petitioners just had to persuade the premier that they were struggling small-timers with big dreams. Back in the days of Bowser you might have got by by buying influence from the oligarchs; but Bennett was going to procure them piecemeal. You had to move fast to do that. To help raise the cash, his government raised the sales tax that he had excoriated a few years before, to 5 per cent, but softened the blow by excluding some more items from the surcharge.

The self-made premier made a lot of friends among people who had dreams of doing likewise. He was living proof that you did not need a high-school diploma to rise to the top. He did not seem to care or even notice that he was not welcomed as warmly by people who placed a higher premium on education. While keeping business portfolios to himself, he handed the ministry of education to Tilly Rolston, the ex-Tory. Rolston had to respond to the old-fashioned anti-intellectuals that carried the Social Credit ethos of Alberta into the new era in B.C. J.A. Reid, the MLA from just north of Bennett's riding, started the ball rolling by going after the Devil's work in the schools. He said in his first speech to the house that the province's schools were teaching immoral books filled with dangerous socialist ideas, creating dope fiends, prostitutes and juvenile delinquents. His main target was a course called "Effective Living," which had replaced "Health." He said that the course was teaching high-school students all the nasty details of sex. I remember looking forward avidly to "Effective Living," and being disappointed that it was just instruction on how to keep clean and neat, and treat people politely. But the education minister was impressed by the rednecks. She announced that she would see to it that students in her province would learn less from immoral texts and be directed to more useful classes such as agriculture and machine shop.

Away we go

Bennett tried to stay away from the arguments raised by the rednecks, but he managed to help turn the house into the circus it had been before the Conservatives and Liberals had arrived. He gasped and gloated, waving his arms and his voice. He relished those moments when he could reduce the attack on his enemies to the most simple terms. "All the opposition can do is smear, smear, smear," he would shout, "while the government continues to build, build, build." He kept the sessions as short as possible, piling up bills to be rammed through late at night of the last day or two. He was still huffing and puffing while his enemies and his own caucus members were staggering with sleeplessness. He had little fear of the CCFers and Liberals, and little respect for his own backbenchers. He wanted to pave and electrify his way into every corner of his realm.

And he was quick on his feet. He extolled the virtues of "pay-as-you-go" economics (called by his critics "pave-as-you-go"), and claimed that he was erasing the provincial debt. He appeared to be erasing the direct debt, while fiddling with the books so that grants to towns and construction companies would be called expenses figured into the mathematics of future developments, to be balanced against expected profits, etc. Those indirect debts piled up quickly while the premier grinned at dam-openings and the like. Old-time Social Crediters with a whiff of Douglas remaining in their noses complained about this joker who was using their name to drop taxpayers into hidden debt, but it was too late for them. Bennett had his own cadre of opportunists and political hitmen, and no time for ideology. The newspapers made fun of his legerdemain, but every time he called an election the newspapers would come around on the last day of the campaign, urging their readers that Social Credit was the only viable protection against ungodly socialism.

Bennett did not show much respect for the federal government, either. Sometimes federal-provincial meetings would feature an empty chair where B.C. should have been sitting. Other times it would be filled by a junior representative from the province. When Bennett did attend, it would be with the smallest contingent, and he would show little knowledge of national affairs that did not pertain directly to British Columbia's interests. He treated Ottawa the way he treated all his problems. Any questions that were not of a

Premier W.A.C. Bennett rode the first Pacific Great Eastern train into Prince George, August 29, 1956.

practical and monetary nature were uninteresting; Confederation simply offered tools with which he could pry money out of the national capital.

Meanwhile it was boom time and zoom time, all through the fifties. If the B.C. Electric Company was reluctant to take a chance on rural electrification, Bennett would take it over and combine it with the B.C. Power Commission. Of course there would be a spectacular new building towering over Vancouver's downtown. If in 1958 the unions brought trouble to the private island ferry companies, the CPR and Black Ball Ferries, Bennett would build a fleet of government-owned ferries to ply the waters and join new blacktop to new blacktop. If in the early sixties the national government was a little slow in announcing its plans for assistance, the premier would put on a hardhat and announce that British Columbia was going to construct dams on the Columbia River and create giant lakes in the north. If you had a big construction business and you wanted to harvest the dollars, you had better jump now while the jumping is good.

All over the province people laughed and shook their heads, and when Bennett called an election they kept their mouths shut and voted Socred. Gearing up for the 1956 election, Philip Gaglardi, the speeding road minister, paved every riding that was marginal. The new blacktop presented a stage for a genuine B.C. folk hero, one Eugene "Bomber" Lacey. Lacey, who lived in Princeton, was a driver for Greyhound Bus Lines, who irked his employers, terrified his passengers and became a role model for impatient youth when he set completely unofficial records for the fastest bus trips between Princeton and the Coast.

Bennett put an end to the preferential ballot, just in case. He introduced bonuses for pensioners. He almost forced grants on the municipalities. He redrew the electoral map, to the alarmed amusement of his critics, and went to the polls with fifty-two ridings. On election night the grin was a province wide. The Socreds had achieved their highest popular vote yet, at 45.8 per cent, and garnered thirty-nine seats. The CCF held on to ten. Bennett's old party, the Conservatives, were gone for good.

The Mounties

When the B.C. Lions became the doormats of the professional Canadian Football League in 1954, the kind of sports fans who prefer gladiatorial simplicity declared that Vancouver was a one-sport town. But immigrants from the prairies and further east supported the Vancouver Canucks in the high-minor Western Hockey League, which offered competition with teams from Seattle and Winnipeg. For many years the Vancouver Capilanos baseball team had had a franchise in the Single A Northwest League, the third-oldest professional baseball league in existence. But in 1956 the Vancouver Mounties were born.

Phil Gaglardi revelled in his nickname, "Flyin' Phil," and his reputation for fast driving.

The Pacific Coast League had long been a proud organization. With the major leagues concentrated near the east coast of the US, and when the Boston Braves' "western swing" meant stops in Chicago and St. Louis, the PCL ruled California and the Northwest. At one point the teams played 190 games a season, while the major leaguers were playing 154. The league produced national heroes such as Joe DiMaggio, but there were also big stars who were induced to stay on the coast. So confident was the league that for a while they spurned the notion that they were a supplier to the Majors, and changed their designation from AAA to "O", meaning "open" classification. However, in the early fifties there were ominous events that would presage big changes in the PCL. In 1953 the Boston Braves were moved to Milwaukee, in the first franchise shift in the twentieth century. Soon the Brooklyn Dodgers were playing some of their "home" games in New Jersey, and there were rumours that they too would be moving. A couple of years later the Dodgers and the New York Giants would move to California. In 1956 the Oakland Oaks decided to get out of the Bay Area while the getting was good, and in 1957 they were the Vancouver Mounties. Vancouver had joined Montreal and Toronto at the highest rung below the major leagues.

Vancouverites took to the new team early, and in that first year the Mounties, though they were not a power in the league, drew more than 300,000 fans to Capilano Stadium nestled at the foot of Little Mountain. Nat Bailey, who had made his fortune with the chain of drive-in hamburger places called the White Spot, was pleased. He was the principal backer of the team, and reportedly looking forward to a big-league franchise in his city. It soon became a commonplace among sportswriters that Cap Stadium was the most picturesque little ballpark in baseball. In a few years it would be home to the "Million Dollar Infield" when a remarkable quartet of future Baltimore Orioles cavorted there. One year the Mounties performed in red home uniforms, to the dismay of the baseball world, who ridiculed the innovation, but it would not be long until bright colours started showing up on major-league players.

But there were a few built-in handicaps that doomed the Mounties to failure. They never did win a pennant, and football fans who laboured under the illusion that the B.C. Lions were major league were not going to be satisfied by a triple-A team run by a triple-O burger king. The debts piled up, and the crowds got smaller. By 1961 they were down to fewer than 90,000. In other PCL cities, such as Seattle and San Diego, the teams were kept afloat by beer sales, the lifeblood of minor-league clubs. But in Social Credit's British Columbia, there was no likelihood that the Mounties would be able to sell beer. In 1962 the Mounties were gone. In 1965 Nat Bailey talked the league into accepting Vancouver again, but in 1969 fewer than 60,000 fans came out for seventy games.

The sportswriters in Vancouver have never been much interested in baseball for some reason. They write about hockey in the summer and football in the spring. They like the kind of games enjoyed by the panel-van driver. They like to think of their city as big-league. They are interested in huge arenas and sports that get onto television and bring in advertising. When the Mounties left after the 1969 season Denny Boyd claimed that baseball had "died for keeps." But Vancouver was back in the Pacific Coast League in the eighties, and became pennant contenders just about every year. They sold lots of beer in the stands of the Little Mountain park, now renamed Nat Bailey Stadium, and they were renamed the Vancouver Canadians, even wearing uniforms that looked suspiciously like a certain beer-bottle label. They were covered on radio and even appeared on cable television. There were more people talking about a major-league franchise for the city, but the habitués of The Nat hoped against it, not wanting to look at baseball played too far away under a Teflon dome.

Second Narrows

W.A.C. Bennett was not much interested in a little baseball diamond beside a treed hill with lovely sunsets in the fifth inning. He was interested in colossal monuments. Like numerous twentieth-century leaders of right-wing populism, he equated the future with what would come to be called megaprojects. If Nat Bailey would have an intimate jewel of a ballpark named after him, W.A.C. Bennett would have a big new lake in the north named after him. In the 1950s the contractors were pouring concrete and welding steel as fast as the logging giants were ripping down forests. The new highways were filling up with new automobiles, and the automobile culture demanded access. By 1958 the North Shore of Burrard Inlet had too many cars for the slender 1938 Lions Gate Bridge that connected it with Stanley Park. In 1958 Bennett was going to form the B.C. Ferry Crown Corporation, and a highway would soar past North and West Vancouver, along the edge of the mountains to Horseshoe Bay terminal. The people and their automobiles needed a second bridge across the inlet.

For millennia the cascading Lynn River and Seymour River had been making a delta on the north shore and a narrowing of the inlet. When the logging mills were started in the nineteenth century, ferries went into service across this second narrows. When the dream of the PGE railroad was conceived, plans for a bridge were elaborated. During the First World War two complex systems were devised, involving swing-sections and dams and marine locks. In 1925 a rather low rail bridge was actually built, but it required barges to wait for low tide, and eventually a misguided barge brought the span down. In 1929 they tried again, rigging the bridge with a lift-span. Vessels crashed into the bridge from time to time, but caused only temporary delays in rail traffic. The crossing was not wide enough or constant enough for the envisaged parade of cars and trucks, though, and in 1956 the highways ministry had its contractors starting a giant cantilever structure to support a six-lane road to the Upper Levels Highway. The structure would be three kilometres long and high enough to escape barges and oil tankers.

Between 1956 and 1958 four workers were killed in accidents at the site, but the big steel girders took their place on solid concrete pilings. On June 17, 1958, there were little men in hardhats and bright jackets all over the steel. Fifteen seconds later the steel had folded and crashed into the water, sending waves to both shores. Thunder was followed by silence. Little men were trapped in the buckled steel or moving in the quick current underwater. Police boats and civilians gathered round the disaster site. It was an unusually hot June day. Divers began to search for bodies, and rescuers with acetylene torches laboured to free the crushed and the amputated. Dozens of men were thrown into the drink that afternoon, and anyone who made it to shore or a boat had his name checked on the boss's list. The rescue went on for many hours, and the search for bodies continued day after day. On June 27 a diver died in the search in the current of Burrard Inlet. When the bridge would finally be opened in August of 1960, it included a plaque with the names of the twenty-three men who had been killed to create those three kilometres of highway.

The Second Narrows collapse was the blackest mark on the history of the government's massive building projects of the fifties and sixties. Not a few people saw it as a rebuke or at least a warning to those who think that human greatness is won by "challenging" nature. Earle Birney was in town, writing his beautiful and satirical poems about our destruction of the forests and rivers; but advisers to the regime's education minister warned that Earle Birney was one of those communistic atheists who were endangering the minds of our school children.

The Second Narrows disaster came at an ironic time. In 1958 the B.C. government was making a big advertising campaign out of the first of our centennial years. In 1858 James Douglas had presided over the creation of the colony of British Columbia at Fort Langley. In 1960, cars would start whizzing over the new surface of the Second Narrows Bridge, many of them with fading bumper stickers on the back, celebrating a century of progress.

Sheila

While Cece Bennett was getting his picture taken at great ceremonial openings around the province, Sheila Watson was writing the best novel to come out of the province. It was not a grand project in terms of physical size, only 116 pages. And it was prefaced by these words that a book-reading premier or engineer might have paid attention to:

> He doesn't know you can't catch the glory
> on a hook and hold on to it. That when you
> fish for the glory you catch the darkness too.
> That if you hook twice the glory you hook
> twice the fear.

Sheila Watson spent a good portion of the fifties writing *The Double Hook*, and when it was published in 1959, it was immediately recognized as something very important that the literary criticism establishment had trouble understanding. It is an elliptical, poetic, mythical text about extremely real people living in isolation and spiritual deprivation in a hamlet across the Fraser River from the giant Gang Ranch. No résumé could hope to convey the book's story, but in its spare and beautiful language it shows a struggle by impoverished people, perhaps Indian, perhaps Euro-Canadians, to rediscover spiritual values in the lack of material wealth. It is perhaps the ghostly antithesis of the ancient First Nations hunting valley and graves lying under the lake created by the W.A.C. Bennett Dam, which would be completed in 1967.

The Double Hook has been in print almost continuously since its publication. It is not difficult to read, but it is challenging. More than any other Canadian novel, it is loved and referred to by the innovative poets and fiction writers who have arrived on the Canadian scene since 1959.

Flowers and Towers

"No, J am not a lawyer. J am just a blunt businessman."
—W.A.C. Bennett, 1964

Swift as an arrow

W.A.C. Bennett's hocus-pocus retirement of the B.C. debt led to a typical bit of Social Credit show business on August 1, 1959. The miracle election had occurred seven years before, and Bennett had two reasons for picking 1959 as his official year.

In the first place, seven was a magic number in just about anyone's superstition, for instance the peculiar religionists called the British Israelites. Everyone in small-town B.C. seemed to know an older family member or friend's mother who espoused B.I. beliefs, principally that a lost tribe of Israel fetched up in Britain and found its natural level in British nobility, and that the solution to economic troubles can be found in a cryptic reading of the Holy Bible. The British Israelites were not fond of foreigners, though they liked Madame Chang Kai-shek, and were especially unhappy with Jewish bankers. They bought into Major Douglas's theories, and became early supporters of the Social Credit movement. One of their beliefs was that the Bible told them to dissolve all personal debts every seven years.

In the second place, Bennett was planning an election campaign in 1960.

Kelowna had always been fond of its place on the lake, and its civic celebrations always involved the water, which takes on mythic qualities in the arid Okanagan Valley. Each of the Okanagan municipalities holds a big summer festival, and Kelowna's was the oldest of all, a reflection of its British heritage—the Kelowna Regatta. W.A.C. Bennett decided that his show would be a big family affair involving fire and water, the old pagan elements of change. There was a cook-out and a children's choir and a costume contest, and not an open beer bottle in sight. There was good low humour, too. Four lads competed in a swimming race, representing the four parties, and the Social Credit lad won going away—with the assist of an underwater tow-rope.

But the evening event was the highlight. Seventy million dollars' worth of purportedly cancelled bonds had been brought to Kelowna in an armoured car, and piled onto a barge and drenched with gasoline and covered with chicken wire to keep the lake free of paper. At the prepared moment the band struck up joyful but not highbrow music, while the premier and his gladsome cabinet members approached the barge in a launch. The idea was that the premier would shoot a flaming arrow into the hill of bonds, but he could not seem to make the bow work. So he got the launch moved up till he could almost touch the barge, and threw a flaming arrow at the bonds. It bounced off the chicken wire and fizzed into the lake. The night was saved by an RCMP escort who had been kept out of camera range. The Mountie torched the gasoline, and the Kelowna folks on the beach were treated to their ballyhooed "bond fire," while the premier approached the shore as if he were crossing the Rubicon or the Delaware.

In Ottawa the Dominion Bureau of Statistics released the news that British Columbians had the highest *per capita* debt among all provinces.

Dam the rivers, full speed ahead

The year 1960 officially marked the end of the Eisenhower era in the USA and elsewhere. The new president, John F. Kennedy, was touted as young, and described as long-haired, though those adjectives were perhaps relative to the retired Ike. Kennedy was the first Catholic president, and more important, a Democrat in the White House after eight years of smug postwar conservatism. Among the so-called "left" in the US, and throughout the generation that had heard rock-and-roll in their young adulthood, there was a sense that change was coming, and that change would involve sensitivity toward the poor, the Third World and the life of the planet. That Kennedy would turn out to be a war-maker abroad all the while he was a civil-rights strategist in the US south, was a complexity to be discovered later. In 1960 he was a youngish man presiding over a nuclear power, while the rest of the large countries were headed by old gents.

As with most shifts that happen in the USA, young people and more liberal politicians in Canada felt as if things would lean Kennedyward north of the longest undefended border. That is why the thinking citizens of British Columbia felt as if they were living inside a contradiction during the sixties.

In 1963 Lester B. Pearson's Liberals got the country back from the Tories, and soon the colourful Pierre Trudeau would enter the cabinet. A dictator and the USAmerican mob had been kicked out of Cuba. In 1961 Babe Ruth's home-run record would fall, but the Berlin Wall would go up. The Cold War was about to enter its hottest period, but the West would be led by an increasingly new guard. However, in British Columbia the Social Credit monument-building was only through its first phase. In the 1950s W.A.C. Bennett, the latest Roman of them all, had built his mighty roads. Now he was ready to reconfigure the map of British Columbia with aquaducts, or rather big hydroelectric dams.

The big long rivers that had offered hope and delivered danger and disappointment to the fur companies, and then sparkles of metal to the gold seekers, now produced a gleam in the eyes and on the teeth of W.A.C. Caesar. There were cities and factories south of the US border that were hungry for electricity. In British Columbia there was a private monopoly, the venerable B.C. Electric Company, that charged rates much higher than those paid by people in Washington, and refused to undertake costly service to the far corners of the province. The premier put two and two together, and though he might not have known what they added up to, he knew an opportunity for progress and a good fight.

First he decided to knock off the opposition at the polls. He had three trump cards, all having to do with innovative money-handling. Most spectacular was the "retirement of the debt" on that Okanagan night. Most surprising was the "homeowner's grant" that had been a campaign promise in the 1956 election. It was a scheme that resembled original Social Credit notions, while persuading the hardworking family that an anti-socialist state-capitalist government had their dreams in mind. Bennett proclaimed that homeowners made up a protective wall against communism. The municipalities had the unpopular task of taxing their homeowners, and the homeowners filled out applications for rebates from the provincial Socred government. Then the provincial government would shuffle the money back to the municipalities. The aspiring middle class could congratulate themselves for settling into their real estate, while looking on the Social Credit party as the good guys. If there were any union members who owned their own home (that is, had mortgages), they might be weaned away from the CCF.

Now Bennett played his third card, and it proved to be equally popular: the parity bond. The big corporations sold stocks and bonds to raise capital for their operations. The federal government had sold a lot of war bonds in the forties. Bennett decided that he could sell province-backed bonds to raise money for the giant projects he had in mind in the north. The bankers and his civil servants told him that nobody did such a thing. Bennett the old outsider decided to show them that somebody did, too. After all, a debt-free citizenry should be eager to snap up a share of the future. The parity bonds were as safe as money, he said, and more valuable in the long run. This was not exactly Major Douglas's idea of Social Credit, but it was a way of looking elsewhere than to the banks for capital. A bondholder could sell a bond any time before the end of its lifetime for its cash value. If he held it till its maturation, he won a prize and drove over nice fresh blacktop to get to it. Bennett's target was ten million dollars. There were so many customers for the first issue that the government had to cut off sales at thirty-five million dollars. Bankers and civil servants said that it was going to take a lot of money to pay off those bondholders. Bennett said that by then the Columbia and the Peace would be rivers of serious money.

Bennett seemed sometimes to enjoy gloating in front of the opposition, and at other times to let them get under his skin. He really wished that he could get rid of the socialists the way he had got rid of the Tories. He thought that his transformation of the province would ensure Social Credit hegemony forever, even if no one had any idea what the party's name meant. At the least he wanted to get all the seats in the house, and more than 50 per cent of the popular vote. He thought that the 1960 election would get him that majority. "Vote for the Government that gets things done!" was his plain campaign slogan. But for some mysterious reason his percentage went down from forty-six to thirty-nine, and the CCF's rose from twenty-eight to thirty-three. The movement's representation fell seven seats to thirty-two, and the CCF gained six, seating sixteen MLAs. In fact, on election night it looked for a while as if the Socreds were going to be dumped, and only with the late returns of hinterland polls did it prove that they could go on for a while. The mysterious reason was that the CCF had worked hard in the ridings, gathering more union support than ever before, while the premier was dreaming great hydroelectric dreams and not answering telephone calls from his backbenchers.

The message would seem to have been caution and conservativeness. But the premier was Wacky Bennett. This was the man who threw flaming arrows at gasoline, after all. In the sixties they were going to call him that dam Bennett. Back in 1956 he had been carrying on secret talks with the agents of a Stockholm millionaire named Axel Wenner-Gren. In 1957 he had presented an astounding deal with the Swede. Wenner-Gren's outfit was going to be given a contract to develop forty thousand square miles, a tenth of the province, in the northeast. He was going to build a railroad to Yukon (Bennett was still thinking of Greater British Columbia), construct the biggest pulp mill in the country, survey every iota of resources in the reserve that was bigger than some European countries, and build a billion-dollar monorail that would zip along the Rocky Mountain trench at 160 miles an hour.

MLAs from every party sat with their mouths open. The press would make a great hullabaloo. Rumours circulated that Wenner-Gren, the

Electrolux king with large industrial developments around the world, had been involved in some purely pragmatic deals during the war. Bennett had finally blown his top. But there was only an agreement to check the Peace country out, no firm deal. Later in 1957 the Swedes reported that the Peace River could deliver the biggest zap in the world. Bennett called the press together and offered them the big news, the potential for the "greatest hydroelectric project in the world." There he goes again, the reporters thought, as they scribbled. Bennett was waving his short arms and bouncing a little. He claimed that the project would be so immense that it would create a 250-mile lake and change the climate of the continent. He claimed that this day, October 7, 1957, was the greatest day in B.C.'s history. There was an exclamation point after every sentence or sentence fragment.

He had started his famous "Two River Policy." For a long time desultory negotiations had been going on among Ottawa, Washington and Victoria concerning a deal to develop hydroelectric power in the international Columbia River. Bennett wanted things to move faster. Now he had the Peace River and a Scandinavian developer to hold over the negotiators as a threat. B.C. could go it alone. Wait a minute, wait a minute, said certain critics in B.C., noting that Bennett's much-suspicioned old pal Einer Gunderson was made a director of the Wenner-Gren British Columbia Development Company, isn't that some kind of conflict of interests? Oh, smear, smear, smear, shouted Premier Bennett.

Two rivers

During the 1960 campaign one of the CCF planks had been the nationalization of B.C. Electric. Social Credit small-timers dubbed the CCF leader Bob Strachan the "Fidel Castro of British Columbia." Bennett let his underlings scoff at the idea of public electricity while he kept still, the free-enterprise man who thought of government as a business. In August 1961 the premier beamed as the opposition quietly joined him in making the vote to take over the power company unanimous. Wacky like a fox, his reluctant admirers began to say. Canada and the United States had already signed a Columbia River treaty earlier in the year, though wrangling about how to conduct jurisdiction was still holding things up because of an earlier agreement between B.C. and the US. The Aluminum Company of Canada had been building Kitimat and their giant smelting plant with water brought from the dam on the Nechako River a hundred miles to the east. But regarding the Columbia, the Canadian government was not happy about B.C.'s eagerness to export power to the US at a cheap price and no guarantee of Canadian access to it. Eventually Bennett would take advantage of the teeter-totter battle between Diefenbaker and Pearson, and again grin before the cameras at the Peace Arch on the international boundary in September

1964, while President Lyndon Johnson himself handed over a cheque for a quarter of a billion dollars for thirty years' worth of electricity. International financiers said that the Texan had put one over on the man with the Woody Woodpecker voice, but Bennett had the money to build three dams in the Kootenays, where the flooded land had been used only by Indians and left-wing voters, anyway.

The Native people of the southern Interior had always told stories about the mysterious and comical creature Coyote, and the stories reflected the differences in their locale and other conditions. In the second half of the twentieth century one of the new Coyote stories told how Coyote blew up the dams on the Columbia River and restored the ancestral lands to his people. This story was never told in the marble palace in Victoria.

One river down, one to go. But first another election. In 1963 the Socreds gained a seat and upped their popular vote by 2 per cent. Bennett went after the Peace. The B.C. government, with its railroad and ferry business and power company, was now the biggest employer in the country. When asked about the question of massive nationalization by a party that preached free enterprise, W.A.C. Bennett said "Nothing is freer than free." Reporters used their pencils to dig into their ears.

Poetry

At the University of British Columbia in the summer of 1963 there was a celebration of words that would have had the reporters running for their lives if reporters had thought that poets really are the unacknowledged legislators of the world. (Phyllis Webb, who was to become in later years the most respected British Columbia poet among her peers, ran unsuccessfully as a CCF candidate in the 1949 B.C. election, at the age of twenty-two). Vancouver in the early sixties had somehow become one of the nodes of poetic activity on the North American continent. More particularly, Vancouver had become what it would continue to be in the following decades—a centre for avant-garde poetry. Since 1961 a batch of brash young writers had been putting out a monthly poetry "newsletter" called *Tish*, and connecting with the leading experimental poets in the United States, especially in New York and San Francisco. In the summer of 1963 their local guru, an unusual professor at UBC named Warren Tallman, persuaded a gaggle of friends to organize a three-week summer session for credit at the university, plus a highly concentrated schedule of readings and other sessions at the campus and around town. Tallman and friends decided to invite as headliners the most famous USAmerican poets of the postwar revolution: Charles Olson, Robert Creeley, Denise Levertov, Robert Duncan and Allen Ginsberg, who came to Vancouver directly from his famous residency in India and Japan. The sixth headliner was Margaret Avison, whom the contemporary Canadian poets saw as their best exemplar. Many other stars of the contemporary US and Canadian poetry scene arrived, and students and other adherents poured into the city from all over North America and elsewhere. It was an occasion that would become legendary in the annals of avant-garde poetry. It would be such a success that similar gatherings would occur in Buffalo in 1964 and Berkeley in 1965.

Olson and Creeley and Duncan were thought of as the triad at the head of the renowned and vilified Black Mountain "school" of poetry, but in Vancouver the three of them were together for the first time. Olson was at the height of his momentous power; the six-foot-nine man from Gloucester, Mass., was now considered the heir to Ezra Pound and William Carlos Williams as the most influential poet in America. The excitement in the air, indoors and outdoors, was something that would be carried back to every corner of the continent, and the Vancouver Poetry Festival, because of the electrifying talk of its headliners and the thousands of meetings among other poets, illustrious or future, would feed the poetry world for decades to come.

It was a kind of world's fair. In many parts of the US now poets say the word "Vancouver" and they mean summer 1963. The sleepless participants in the festival did not have time to reflect on the fact that this first great gathering was taking place in a province in which the government leader extolled entrepreneurial action at the expense of mere word and thought.

Lust for power

When he took over the hydroelectric power business in the province, W.A.C. Bennett became the only provincial premier whose name was known in USAmerican business circles and the business press. He may have been a little discomfited when the conservative papers mocked or attacked his power grab, but the old hardware man had always looked kindly on advertising, especially free advertising. In his account of the era given to his biographers, he mentioned his conversations with presidents Kennedy and Johnson, and how close he sat to them at banquets. In his fantasy British Columbia was really a country, and his business was to make it an important country.

The 1963 election was a test of his mettle and a threat to his plans for power to the people. For one thing, the CCF had joined with other traditional enemies of right-wing government to become the New Democratic Party. Bennett always called it the "New Depression Party," adding that threat to his usual Red-baiting. But the NDP was buoyant in 1963, and had, in its federal form, become quite a glamorous story in the popular news media. The Liberals, under Ray Perreault, were less of a threat, except that they might take soft free-enterprise votes away from the Socreds. But the biggest problem might be the Supreme Court of British Columbia.

On July 8, the Columbia River Treaty had been nailed. Hooray. Now exactly three weeks later Chief Justice Sherwood Lett brought down a decision that had been pending for nearly two years: he said that the legislation used to nationalize B.C. Electric and create B.C. Hydro was invalid because the company's operations reached outside B.C. Even if the takeover had been constitutionally legal, the new owners would have had to pay an additional twenty-one million dollars. Oops. Bennett got his lawyer Robert Bonner working on that problem on a legal basis, while he mounted an election campaign to handle the public-relations aspect.

It was a lively campaign. In some polls the NDP were touted as winners of a minority victory. The Liberals said they wanted their province back. And now the Conservatives were looking to re-enter the lists. They were going to start with a man who was a B.C. blueblood, if ever there was one. This was the peaceful and dignified Davie Fulton, who had represented Kamloops for the federal Tories for years, and was fingered by some observers as a future prime minister. Stepping into provincial politics may have seemed to his friends in Ottawa a quixotic move, but there was tradition to be considered. Two members of his family two generations back had been premier of B.C., and one generation back his father had been attorney general and his uncle speaker of the house. He was a Rhodes scholar and a war veteran. He was going to bring the Tories back into the province and return dignity to the land.

But he was up against a new kind of politics. They didn't have many small-town hardware hawkers and evangelical shouters in Ottawa. W.A.C. Bennett, the man from New Brunswick, castigated Fulton as an "outsider." He said that Fulton had helped sink the federal Tories and was now going to be the last nail in the coffin of provincial Tories. The hardware man had a hammer. He had an old grudge against the Conservative party that had rebuffed him as leader. He had "Flying Phil" Gaglardi as his man in Kamloops. Kamloops was the hub of the finest highways in British Columbia. Bennett, who usually nestled in Kelowna for election finales, travelled to Kamloops over one of those fine highways. While he was there, he waved his arms and announced to the voters that the B.C. Electric case had been settled, and that the Socred-designed B.C. flag, a gaudy item that looked like a Hawaiian shirt, was now flying over the lofty B.C. Hydro building in downtown Vancouver. Gaglardi beat Davie Fulton, and the Conservatives were gone. They would get two seats in 1972 when a pair of malcontent Socreds ambled across the floor, and one in 1975, but their necks were too white for the voters in the fringe province. Especially in the Interior the folks were not interested in book-reading lawyers. They liked the typical Socred slogans such as "Keep B.C. Moving."

The dismissal of Davie Fulton was symbolic. With his power deal Bennett was announcing to Ottawa that his administration was interested in doing business with the United States, and that Canada could come aboard if it wanted to get a grip on a good thing. He had just won a fifth term, and led a "stable" majority government supported by big business despite his power takeover (it was not a socialist takeover—it would be good for the businesses that saw profits to be made in Bennett's grand future), while Prime Minister Pearson was facing problems with his brand new minority government in Ottawa. It was simple over complicated. Bennett liked to divide the province between those who believed in B.C. and those who did not. He was a patriot lifted above a bunch of left-wingers who had too many ideas and not enough faith. As Phil Gaglardi so eloquently put it, the people of B.C. could look forward to a whole bunch more highways.

Dam it

Bennett said that he was "humbled" by the faith the people had put in him. He said it over and over as he jumped around the province, staging opening ceremonies for the photographers from the Vancouver newspapers that had mocked him before the election. When he got to the Peace country, he heard from the chambers of commerce up there. They said that he was the biggest thing to happen to them since Alexander Mackenzie nearly two centuries earlier. They liked him so much that they held a big feast and told him that they were going to call the huge structure at Portage Mountain the "Bennett Dam." Chances are that he already knew that; and he did not, out of his humility, decline the honour.

In August of 1964 Bennett decided to stage another bond-burning gala, this time in celebration of twelve years of Socred rule. If the number seven had always carried magical portents, the number twelve had from antiquity signified financial and legal reliability. This time he would use railway flares to ignite the barge, perhaps because they had become expendable with the expansion of the highway system. For the site he chose the beach at Kitsilano, with its showboat stage. The Vancouver crowd was not as impressionable as the Kelowna crowd had been. The applause rippled rather than exploding. And there were a few young protesters, one of whom carried a placard suggesting that the premier was a fake. In the early sixties the neighbourhood of Kitsilano had filled up with poets and artists, and would soon be the Canadian centre for the youth revolution, Fourth Avenue a kind of Haight Street, replete with head shops, and the old houses turned into "communes" packed with flower children and acid-freaks. In the mid sixties you could not find any Social Credit people in Kits. At the 1964 bond-burning there were catcalls and US coins hurled toward the stage. W.A.C. Bennett was reminded that his act would always play better as a back-country road show.

Serious stuff, too

In earlier times political life in the province had resembled a comic opera; now in the fifties and sixties it was coming to look and sound more like the music and motion that assail the senses when the clowns are released into the circus tent. But despite the perceptions of journalists back east, there were people west of the Great Divide who pursued serious lives. They might be said to be led by two remarkable composers whose names were largely unknown to either Socreds or hippies in the sixties—Jean Coulthard and Barbara Pentland. But in the fifties and sixties the Canadian Broadcasting Corporation had not yet decided to centralize its operations in Toronto, and the Vancouver production centre made these two great women's works available to the country's more sophisticated ears. (In those days there were even poetry readings on Vancouver CBC.) Coulthard, whose works were to be heard often in the early nineties, was born in Vancouver in 1908, when Earle Birney was five years old. She studied at the Royal College of Music in London, because that is what you did when she was a young composer, and her lifelong interest in vocal music was probably influenced by Ralph Vaughan Williams, her most important teacher. In 1967 her cantata *This Land* was her contribution to Canada's heady centenary celebrations.

A more avant-garde composer was Barbara Pentland, four years younger than Coulthard. She was born in Winnipeg, and like her friend Dorothy Livesay, lit out for the world to learn and practise her art. She studied at the Juilliard School in New York, the Berkshire Center in Massachusetts, and in France and Germany. In early middle age she welcomed the advanced experimental music of Karlheinz Stockhausen, and brought chance, seriality and electronic sounds into serious Canadian music. She was a prolific composer, who pushed the limits of a wide range of forms, even a spectacularly unwelcomed opera about Ogopogo, the legendary monster of Lake Okanagan. She wrote a trilogy of books called *Music of Now*, introducing students to the possibilities of twentieth-century piano music. Like Jean Coulthard she taught at the University of British Columbia's remarkable music faculty, where she was as rigorous with her students as she was with her creations. Pentland is a Canadian genius who worked seven decades in an art that has never received the popular media attention given to our painters and writers.

The west coast was also fortunate enough to be home to three-quarters of the remarkable Adaskins. They were a musical family with origins in Latvia. In fact the eldest brother, violinist Harry Adaskin, was born in Riga in 1901. With his wife, Frances Adaskin, he toured Canada and elsewhere, often premiering Canadian compositions. Their house in Vancouver featured a recital room with facing grand pianos. In 1946 Harry Adaskin founded the music faculty at UBC, and hired its brilliant teachers. He was interested in all the arts, and knew them with an acute insight. When the US poet Jack Spicer gave his three famous Vancouver lectures shortly before his death in 1965, Harry Adaskin was in the responsive audience, and exhibited the best understanding of Spicer's difficult argument. Murray Adaskin, born in Toronto in 1906, was a violinist, conductor and composer who studied with Darius Milhaud, and promoted Canadian music, especially its folk strains, through his various disciplines. He headed the music faculty at the University of Saskatchewan before moving to Victoria. The third brother, cellist John Adaskin, held the fort in Toronto, where he promoted young Canadian composers during his years at the Canadian Broadcasting Corporation, and commissioned them to write material that could be performed by music students.

R. Murray Schafer is arguably Canada's most successful composer, certainly viewed internationally as our most daring innovator. Born in 1933, he worked in England and Austria before returning to Canada. When Simon Fraser University was opened in 1965, it promised to be a radical departure from the usual university scene, and drew Schafer as its first artist-in-residence. SFU was built in grand scale by Vancouver's flamboyant architect Arthur Erickson, on top of Burnaby Mountain, surrounded by trees and higher mountains. Schafer would never be content to create works for chamber music or even small halls. He was drawn by the natural environment and the mythological, even mystical, forces that animated nature and human interaction. In the early seventies he would outfit his music students with custom-built stereo recording devices, and send them out to create the enormous "World Soundscape Project." As a composer, Schafer took the whole planet Earth simultaneously as his instrument and his concert hall. His art and his religion and his politics were not to be winnowed from one another. A lake in the northern Ontario woods might become the sounding board for individual horns to be played across its night-time surface. The horns might be bringing echoes of ancient mythic voices out of the forest, and speaking of industry's air-carried threat to the lake's ancient health. Schafer is also a prolific and complex writer, especially about poets and composers and what can happen to human ears in the classroom, especially when the classroom is the planet.

SFU

W.A.C. Bennett did not have weirdos like R. Murray Schafer in mind when he called for the building of Simon Fraser University. Two of his party's predilections came together to give rise to the structure atop Burnaby Mountain—the desire to erect highly visible monuments of progress and the desire to keep power out of the hands of the lawyers and other intellectuals in Vancouver. In the postwar era, and especially in the fifties, the University of British Columbia was growing fast. The library was second to that of

University of Toronto in size. As the province became something more than a huge bank of primary resources, more and more young people were expected to acquire university degrees and postgraduate degrees. There would soon be thirty or forty thousand students at UBC, where few friends of the Social Credit movement could be located. Now that highways had joined the towns in the hinterland, and dams were bringing jobs to the river country, it was time to bring the rest of the province into the education business. Federal statistics showed that B.C. spent less *per capita* on education than any other province, and was experiencing the highest immigration of any province. W.A.C. Bennett and his men were characterized as anti-intellectuals, but Bennett said that he was in favour of education. In David J. Mitchell's book about him, he is quoted as saying: "I'm in favour of good, clean minds that come from universities." His sons never went to university, but it was not necessary: one was going to be an investor and the other was going to be premier of B.C.

In 1963 Victoria College, the Island's portion of UBC, was given a charter as the University of Victoria, and would soon have a big circular campus among the short trees at Gordon Head. That year the bulldozers were slugging through the mud where trees had been shaved off Burnaby Mountain. In Nelson, the long-standing Jesuit two-year college, which often sent senior students to Gonzaga University in Spokane, was allowed full status as Notre Dame University. The fundamentalists in the Social Credit movement were not excited by its religious orientation, but did like the idea of a private university in the Kootenays. In the coming years Social Credit governments would enable community colleges in most regions of the province. Responding to local sensibilities and expressing the general relationship between Social Credit politicians and education, the colleges would not be for eggheads alone. Some of their students would read literature and physics and then proceed to a university, but many of them would be trained in fashion design or industrial support trades.

But Simon Fraser University was the movement's colossus. Bennett's vision was a big new university somewhere in the lower Fraser Valley, where farmers and fundamentalists elected right-wing MLAs, and where their grateful children would proudly graduate from a local university. The lower Fraser Valley was also going to experience a big population boom, because suburbanites could not find much room to build houses north, west or south of Vancouver. Bennett tapped Gordon Shrum, a go-getter who co-chaired B.C. Hydro, to get an instant university up and running. Shrum, a guy the premier had to love for his preference for action over eloquence, wanted to plunk the future on top of a Burnaby Mountain rather than some cow pasture in the valley, and Bennett, recognizing a kindred spirit, approved. The bulldozers were still chugging when the first classes were conducted in 1965. The plan, despite the relocation, was to call the place simply Fraser

University, but at the last minute a Socred cabinet minister had a vision of the initials that would be emblazoned on campus sweatshirts, and the explorer's first name was added. It did not matter to wags at UBC who dubbed the new rival "Simon Fraser Academy."

The university would feature innovations that were populist. Older students with life experience would be allowed to attend without full prerequisite credits from their earlier education days. SFU would be one of two universities in the country with a trimester system, so that working students could fit their studies into their work schedules. In its first years faculty were encouraged to try out their experimental schemes for pedagogy.

It would also be a place rife with irony. In the late sixties and early seventies it would be the scene of radical student activities. Faculty dining facilities would be "liberated." Washrooms would be degendered. The students would rename the place "Louis Riel University." Some departments would experience schisms that would remain unhealed for years. Some students and a few faculty would wind up behind bars or sent down off the hill. Bennett and Shrum must have tasted something bitter behind their wide grins. In later years the ironies would take another form. The road up to the school would be renamed Gaglardi Way, and students with automobiles would honour the pugnacious little ex-cabinet minister by driving the road at illegal speeds. The central building would be called W.A.C. Bennett Library, and its foyer would feature a big photo of the smiling ex-premier. Fittingly, it is situated at a good remove from the nearest book.

Late sixties

British Columbia became more and more schizophrenic throughout the sixties. The worldwide youth rebellion woke up all sorts of liberation movements associated with the left, but W.A.C. Bennett won elections in 1966 and 1969. In 1966 his grinning face was on the cover of the Canadian edition of *Time* magazine. In 1969 he won his seventh election with the highest popular vote yet—46.8 per cent, and the second-highest number of seats—thirty-eight. It was getting harder and harder to keep up the image of the little guy fighting the socialist hordes and the big-city lawyers at the same time. Many young people voting for the first time could not remember a time when the Socreds were not the government.

Many of them were wearing headbands and tie-dye shirts, and reading underground newspapers, including the *Georgia Strait*, which was begun in 1967 by a group which might be said to represent the "new left," regular socialists, hipsters, dope-smoking poets, environmentalists, rock-and-rollers, anarchist cartoonists and university professors who did not wear neckties. Posters of Che Guevara showed up in shop windows on Fourth Avenue in Vancouver. Draft dodgers from the U.S. introduced the insidious game of slo-pitch softball to Kamloops. In Paris the students were throwing paving stones at the police. The US burned villages in Vietnam and the Russian army's tanks rolled into Prague. The Black Panthers carried rifles in the streets of Oakland, and the Democratic leadership convention in Chicago turned into a police riot as horses chased poets and college students through the parks and streets. In Northern Ireland the civil rights movement was turning into a civil war. African guerrilla forces became part of the cold war, and in China the "Cultural Revolution" was mounted by Chairman Mao to preserve the purity of the original revolution. The PLO was formed to fight for a homeland, and in Quebec small cells of revolutionaries formed to fight against the upsurge of Canadian nationalism that peaked during the 1967 centenary hoopla. In the United States, people with guns were shooting black and white spokesmen for progressive causes. Electric guitars could be heard from San Francisco to Saigon.

In Vancouver a businessman driving across the Burrard Street bridge might see young people with long ponytails and radio earphones leaning on the rail and staring westward at the sun-dappled water. He might think that the anti-establishment crowd was made up of acid-dropping unemployed teenagers with new names borrowed from Hindu mythology. But the Peace & Love & Sandals folk were only one facet of a growing dissent. For nearly two decades the Social Credit government had been rewarding its voters with pavement and concrete and "balanced" budgets. They had been riding on the wide back of postwar good times, and deferring hidden debt to be handled in the even better times to come. In the late sixties the economic situation began to suggest trouble. Also in his late sixties, Bennett decided to keep applying his methods. It seemed to work in 1969, when he went into the election with B.C.'s first billion-dollar budget and got his biggest vote ever. But the year before, he had lost his lawyer. Robert Bonner had never felt at ease among the yokels, and had lost his Point Grey seat in the 1966 election and had to be parachuted. He decided he had a better future as a senior executive with the timber giant MacMillan-Bloedel. On leaving cabinet he gave the warning that Social Credit had depended on a dangerous idea in financing big projects to be paid for by an ever-expanding provincial wealth. He characterized Socred financial planning as a belief in "magic."

Unemployment, especially in the resource areas of the countryside, where Socred votes were a cash crop, was rising steadily. Mining and forestry were becoming highly automated. The big projects that employed construction workers were mainly finished. Foreign investors were not surveying the hinterland for places to drop dollars. The government, though it had reached office to help the little guy, had never paid much attention to development of the small manufacturers, where human hands still outnumbered big machines. Though Bennett's speeches were filled with words about the limitless future, he characteristically channelled money toward old-time resource-extraction. There were people who tried to explain to him in print that the world was changing, that logs and electricity and minerals could not feed and employ an increasing and diversifying population.

And there was an alarming new fact of life. Inflation was suddenly rising even while unemployment was getting worse. This was not supposed to happen. Now labour became aroused again, and in the late sixties and early seventies, a series of strikes occurred, not only among the blue-collar workers, but by teachers and civic workers, and it was becoming clear that these actions had a political edge. More and more the Social Credit movement was targeted as the big guy by people who could not remember when Bennett was the arm-waving outsider. In the boondocks the transformation of the province by the combination of good times and Bennett's road and dam policy began to double back on the premier. The small communities where his speeches found the ears he was looking for began to disappear. Little coastal logging sites disappeared as the timber giants roared through the woods. In the Interior, village grocery stores grew moss on their collapsed roofs while people jumped into their cars and drove over smooth highways to bigger towns to buy the stuff they had seen advertised on TV. Television also killed small-town baseball leagues and northern social clubs. While instant towns had grown up next to aluminum plants and hydroelectric dams, old towns disappeared as people moved to the Coast or Prince George.

The shifting of the B.C. population to the cities aroused a lot of argument about the disparity between ridings. Of course most of the Socreds' representatives came from east and north of Vancouver. Critics pointed out that a Vancouver MLA might need 40,000 votes to get into the house, while a member from Atlin might get away with fewer than two thousand. Bennett's answer was that it was a lot harder job for a rural MLA to represent people over great distances. Citizens in the Interior naturally resisted the arguments of the metropolitan folk, arguing that they needed things the way they were in order to slow down the influence that the city slickers held over their lives. Eventually Bennett did some careful arithmetic and introduced a scheme whereby a few city ridings would elect two representatives. That became one of the factors that would bring about his eventual fall, but not the major one.

Flyin' Phil

W.A.C. Bennett was born in 1900. He was past retirement age when the "Summer of Love" was announced with Nepalese temple bells and psychedelic Volkswagen buses in 1968. He had already passed all records for longevity in Victoria, and among the youth culture longevity was not considered an asset. A lot of their heroes died in their twenties or forties. Greenpeace, the worldwide environmentalist group of the nineties, started in Kitsilano as an anti-A-bomb outfit in 1970, one year after Social Credit's greatest electoral win.

The Socred ship was manned by people who had always been strange, but which were now seen to be old and strange, not only laughable now, but also cynical. Bennett the teetotaller was a ruthless politician, but had always been able to avoid personal scandal. He was not always so lucky with his satraps, and his efforts to keep real power out of their hands was not always enough to keep the party's image clean. He had managed to weather the Sommers storm, but even he must have felt the heat during the Summer of Love. Robert Bonner had left with his unsettling words about "magic" financing. Then there was the Gaglardi problem.

It was not that Gaglardi looked funny and ran off at the mouth, often saying silly things too fast. It was not just that the highways minister kept getting caught and ticketed and losing his driving licence for driving at dangerous speeds on his new roads. He revelled in his nickname, Flyin' Phil. He said publicly that high speed was not a factor in highway safety, despite what the law said. He did not seem to understand the principle of public trust, of the difference, say, between government money and personal money, of the conflict of interest. All through 1968 the NDP complained that Gaglardi had awarded highway access to a private company in which his sons had an interest. Apparently the company's signs were painted not in a private shop but in a government facility. What's wrong with that, asked the minister. The charges went on and on. The government did road work on the Gaglardi ranch. The highway was especially beautified where a Gaglardi motel was situated. Finally it was pointed out that Gaglardi had been flying his family around in his government-owned Lear jet, which he had acquired when his driver's licence was suspended. He could not show that he had sent a family member to Dallas on government business. When Charles de Gaulle made his famous "*Vive le Québec libre!*" speech in Montreal, Gaglardi said that he was planning to take his Lear jet to Paris and divebomb that there palace in Paris or wherever it was.

Bennett asked Gaglardi whether it was true that he had flown his daughter to Texas. Gaglardi said no, it was not true. He could have said that he had flown his daughter-in-law to Texas. When Bennett found out how strict Gaglardi was with the truth, he took over the highways ministry himself. That way he could also be more likely to keep the chirpy little fellow from saying something he should not say about the Treasury Board investigation that was going on concerning the handling of the highways budget. But Gaglardi was more popular with his riding's voters than the brainy Robert Bonner was with his. After the defeat of Social Credit, stumpy Phil Gaglardi would put a cowboy hat on his round head and become mayor of Kamloops. His sons would be owners of a large hotel chain.

Home on Native land

The various popular movements of the late sixties liked to use words such as "liberation" and "free." There was free love and there was free jazz. In the United States a professional basketball player would change his legal name to World B. Free. When the term "women's liberation" was first used, the men in the various liberation movements said don't trivialize our campaigns, but eventually came to see the seriousness of the question. The government of British Columbia could not see anything but a threat to "free" enterprise and good order, even while the advertising world was finding a way to make a dollar from protest.

Supporters of apartheid in South Africa and the US often told Canadian protesters that they ought to leave Durban and Selma alone and go home and do something about the plight of their own depressed minority, if they were so altruistic. Clean up your own back yard, they were told. Yet it would be another decade or so until the crusading white youth would have a good look at the social and political lives of Canadian Native peoples, and that would happen when the anti-war folk turned to look at the war on the environment.

From the beginning of the European arrival, the Native peoples were placed at several disadvantages. They were demoralized, of course, by firearms, whisky and smallpox. But they were defeated by business and politics. For thousands of years the Native peoples had organized themselves along social lines rather than political lines. Family and village were the cohesive factors and the determinant in any ranking system. Religion, or rather spirituality, happened every day. For the white people politics, especially as they related to business and property, took precedence over social matters. The relationship between the individual and anything else would be a major factor in the misunderstandings between Indians and newcomers.

The great engineering feats that had altered the face of B.C.'s Interior during the Social Credit regime had not done anything to improve the lives of Native families and villages. The only ones that had been transformed were those that were now under deep water behind the new dams, or those who had had to move to make way for new highways. British Columbia differed from other provinces in that the Indians had not been induced to make treaties and cede land to the Europeans, except in a small area north of Victoria. Such a situation had not deterred the succeeding white governments from developing the land for their various purposes, or from devising Indian reserves. White governments were able simultaneously to ignore the fact that the Native peoples were diverse of languages and economies, and to take advantage of that disunity. The big construction projects during the first Social Credit regime took place mainly in the Interior, where the bands were not as well off or as well organized as the bands along the Coast.

Leaders in the process of land claims have always been the Nisga'a people of the Nass River on the north coast. The local chiefs formed a unified voice in the late nineteenth century to resist the new province's surveying teams. They told the whites that they could not see the logic in being granted small parts of the land that they had no memory of losing. They told them to go back to Victoria and tell the government there that the Nisga'a people were ready to hear about a treaty, including a generous offer of compensation. They did not hear back. For the next hundred years they would press their case. Their land committee got a promise of a hearing by the British Privy Council, but were later told that they had to go through all the local courts first, which they refused to do. A result of the standoff was that the villages in Nisga'a country formed a lasting confederation that would come to be called the Nisga'a Tribal Council, a congress created by the Natives, not a method of organization laid upon them by any Canadian or B.C. government.

In the 1960s the Nisga'a were ready to take their land claims to court. With lawyer Tom Berger, recently head of the provincial NDP, they fought all the way to the Supreme Court of Canada, where in 1973 they were told that, well, yes, there was such a thing as aboriginal rights, but that, uh, we can't decide whether they can be taken away by some provincial law. In 1973 Tom Berger's party was at last in power in British Columbia, but the Nisga'a Tribal Council could not persuade them to come to the table and negotiate land claims. The Nisga'a Tribal Council did not say OK, we give up. They remained an example for other Native peoples in their efforts to organize and press for negotiations.

Early in the twentieth century the Nisga'a people reached out to other groups in the province and formed a larger alliance called the Allied Tribes. An interested group was the association of Salish-speaking peoples of the Interior, who had a major white supporter in the famous anthropologist J.A. Teit. Other groups were supported by sympathetic clergymen. But ironically, their cause was hurt by other anthropologists and archaeologists who presented the theory that the Indians of the Americas had arrived by way of a land bridge from northern Asia. That gave support to whites who could then claim that the Indians were also immigrants. Of course the Native peoples had their own narratives concerning their antiquity; they said that they had been born from the earth of their continent. According to them, people had used the land bridge all right, but they had passed freely in both directions.

In the twenties the federal government released an opinion that the Indians had not established any title to the land. Aboriginal myths were just the folk tales of an unsophisticated people. The Indian Act was altered to prohibit fundraising for land claims. The Indians should be encouraged to begin entering the majority culture. In the twenties they were permitted to enter the commercial fishing fleet on the coast. Taking their cue from Native fishers in Alaska, the Haida and Tsimshian and Kwakiutl chiefs organized a union called the Native Brotherhood of British Columbia and in the forties a union newspaper called *The Native Voice*. In 1946 the federal government had another look at the Indian Act and explored further ways in which the Native peoples might be integrated into mainstream society. Most B.C. Indian spokespersons welcomed any change that would loosen controls over their lives, but said that the Native peoples had no desire to become non-Indians.

Indian children were allowed to attend regular provincial schools rather than the residential schools, where for a century they had been separated from their families and languages, and often subjected to physical and sexual assaults by the Christian teachers and staff. But it was not easy to be an Indian kid in a white people's school. Not many of them made their way through high school, and those that got that far were generally shunted to non-academic streams, which had been their norm in the residential schools. Still, by the end of the sixties 70 per cent of younger Indian children were in provincial schools.

In 1951 the Indian Act, which seemed always to be undergoing revision, was changed to reduce government control, with the hope that Natives would become more like regular Canadians and less likely to think that they had special historical status. At last they were allowed to go into a beer parlour and drink beer. Now they were permitted to raise money in support of their political activity, including the paying of lawyers. And finally, the Victorian church having lost its great influence, the ban on the potlatch was removed. The peoples of the Coast soon suggested to Ottawa that they would be pleased to see the return of the ceremonial potlatch items taken away from their grandparents.

The industrial boom of the fifties and early sixties did not trickle down to the First Nations communities. Consolidation of primary resource extraction into big companies meant fewer operations in fewer and larger centres. Indian people who were used to working in canneries or sawmills close to their reserves were now farther removed from these jobs. They were caught in a double bind. They were not nomadic people like the prairie and European immigrants who arrived in the province to do manual labour; their social being was tied up with their families and clans. In the second place, even if they wanted to relocate in the cities where the jobs were, they were not allowed by the Indian Act to sell their assets off the reserve. In fact, in many cases they had no clear title to individual real estate or fixed property. During the fishing disputes and land-claim hassles of the nineties, white rivals who felt their livelihood threatened but who did not make a practice of researching their positions would carry placards demanding "One country, one law, regardless of race." One did not see these people, or their parents, displaying such sentiments during the boom years of the fifties and early sixties.

In 1966 Harry Hawthorn, a prominent anthropologist at the University of British Columbia, was assigned to make a federal report on the status of Canadian Indians. His findings did not bring out placards in white villages, but they were shocking to people who were animated by the spirit of social progress in the sixties. Hawthorn found that Native people had to get by on 20 per cent of non-Natives' income. They trailed non-Natives in life expectancy, but far outpaced them in infant mortality, suicide and accidental deaths. They went to jail a lot more, and they suffered alcoholism at a higher rate. They depended a great deal more on welfare. They did not go to university much. The Hawthorn Report said that the federal government should find a way to change that pattern. The government of South Africa said that Canadians should do something to fix up their own back yard.

According to the report, the Native peoples in British Columbia were better off than those in other provinces, but the figures were lifted by the more prosperous Native fishers of the Coast, particularly toward the north. The Beaver people of the northern Interior were just plain poor, and other Interior peoples were not among the beneficiaries of the Socred "miracle."

But the First Nations people were developing leaders outside their traditional clans and villages. Some of them, spiritual leaders especially, would remain unknown to the incurious majority population. Folks living on the Kamloops reserve, for instance, would share respect for elders from distant North American nations of whom white burghers across the river in Kamloops would never have heard. There were also prominent Natives whose names would show up in newspapers and magazines, on radio and television. Frank Calder the Nisga'a CCFer had been elected to the provincial legislature by the Native people of Atlin in 1949. In 1968 the people of Kamloops-Cariboo elected Len Marchand, an Okanagan Liberal, to parliament. He was just the second Native to sit in the Commons, the first being Louis Riel. Pierre Trudeau made Marchand the first Indian cabinet minister when he gave him the ministry of small business and then the ministry of the environment. Marchand would be defeated along with the Liberals in 1979, but would be appointed to the Senate in 1984, where he scored another first.

Another interesting man arose from the same part of B.C. Activist Natives were aware of a tricky situation they found their people to be in: they knew that they needed to form associations with First Nations groups across the country if they hoped to have much effect on the federal scene; at the same time, they knew that integration in the national political structure posed a threat to their peoples' special relationship with the land and the Crown. George Manuel was born in 1921 on the Neskonlith Reserve to a family that would remain prominent for years. Manuel was a remarkable young man who learned a lot more than they could teach him in school, and became the smartest politician in Shuswap country. He was the strongest force in the creation of the National Indian Brotherhood in 1968, and became its second president in 1970. During the early seventies the white authorities had to meet a lot of unusual manifestations of Indian discontent, and had to meet the First Nations in court more than they had been used to. The Department of Indian Affairs grew accustomed to quoting George Manuel when they made decisions.

Manuel found a third way of handling the conflict between national organization and local integrity. He announced the existence of a "Fourth World" that existed within the other three. George Manuel took to travelling around the globe, speaking with aboriginal people on other continents. He consulted with Julius Nyerere, who was trying to organize his new country, Tanzania, as a confederation of tribal communities. He spoke at the United Nations. In 1975 he was the first president of the World Council of Indigenous Peoples. Now when Maori groups come to Victoria, for instance, they are not just there to perform traditional dances to entertain the crowds at the Commonwealth Games.

Native artists

In the late years of the nineteenth century and in the early years of the twentieth century, representatives of the churches and governments had thought nothing of grabbing Indian "artefacts" and depositing them in their homes and museums, the latter also repositories of Indian people's bones. Indian art was often treated as the instruments of pagan superstition, or as sociological data. Europeans (with the exception of a few individuals such as Pablo Picasso and D.H. Lawrence) had a difficult time coming to the notion that African carving and drumming could be described as "art." They were just as slow in British Columbia. But there had always been a few middle-class collectors who bought ceremonial masks for their parlour walls, and in the 1960s we saw the beginning of a change in attitude that would develop to the point at which the art world would embrace Native artists, especially carvers from the Coast, as "ours." The fact that some of those artists would not live lives free of the social ills that ravaged the rest of their community was not often spoken about in polite circles.

Mungo Martin, whose traditional name was Nakapenkim, was born in the late nineteenth century at Fort Rupert, the Hudson's Bay Company coal field on the northern end of Vancouver Island. He was a great artist, a carver, a painter, a singer and a storyteller. He was born into a line of Kwakiutl artists and would be recognized as one of the greatest potlatch chiefs. He made art in defiance of the potlatch ban, and his poles were a source of pride for the Kwakiutl people whose spiritual life had been under attack by the church and the merchants. The University of British Columbia sought his help when he was about sixty, to head their program to restore and renew ceremonial poles. They also asked him to record two hundred songs. The provincial museum then wooed him to lead their restoration program. While he was in Victoria, he carved the tallest pole in existence, and with his failing eyes saw it raised in Beacon Hill Park. He died in Victoria in 1962, at the age of about eighty. His Native students would be the most prominent Kwakiutl carvers in the next decades.

Bill Reid was born in Vancouver in 1920, and seventy years later would be the most famous Haida artist in the world. His mother was Haida and his father was a USAmerican with Scots upbringing. Reid, who became a great storyteller in an untraditional way, recounted his discovery, during his teenage years, of his Haida heritage. Reid studied jewel engraving in Toronto and England, learning to master European methods, and then more and more devoted his art to the imaginative life of his mother's people. His work may be seen in two main forms—exquisitely engraved metal jewellery and amazing monumental sculptures in wood, stone or metals. His breathtaking works, such as "Raven and the First Humans" (it is made of the Coast Indians' sacred cedar and is the centrepiece of UBC's Museum of Anthropology) or "Spirit of Haida Gwaii," which is the centrepiece of the Canadian embassy in Washington, are considered by many people to be the greatest works ever created by a Canadian. His images are not strictly traditional; he transforms ancient stories into stunning metaphors that make any intelligent viewer hanker to know how they got here. Bill Reid won every major award given to an artist by Native people or whites, but would still be seen, a button blanket over his shoulders, his frail body standing in the rain along with Native people protesting the careless destruction of their old forest land by the noisy resource-extraction companies.

In the eighties and nineties there would be a growing number of poets and fiction writers that emerged from the various Native nations around the province. Many of them would honour Mourning Dove, the Okanagan writer who became the first Native woman novelist, and George Clutesi. When Emily Carr died in 1945, she left her artist's and writer's materials to George Clutesi. He was born at Port Alberni in 1905, into a family of Nootka chiefs. He worked as a pile-driver, and broke his back in an accident. But he knew a lot of stories, and he decided that a Nootka man could interpret them as well as any anthropologist. He began to record his people's songs and stories, and to write his own versions in a plain solid English. His books, including Son of Raven, Son of Deer and Potlatch, both published in the late sixties, became famous and presented an authentic narrative of coastal Indian subjects that would provide an example for later Indian writers, and teach white readers that Native stories are not just "folklore" or anthropological "information."

White politicians

Jn the years right after the 1967 Centennial orgy, Prime Minister Trudeau had to take on the sovereigntists in Quebec, and elsewhere. He talked about a "just society" that equated equality with homogeneity. Expansion of French-language services would be one of his tools in discouraging separatism in French-Canada. And in 1969 his government introduced a white paper that outlined the national scheme for assimilating Native communities into the mainstream. The federal government would get out of their relationship with the First Nations, and let the provinces handle the matter of integrating their Native populations. There would be no federal treaties or special considerations based on history. It was a new world, and Canada was a "mosaic," in which none of the tesserae would be of a distinctive shape. The Indians would have to give up their special privileges along with their disadvantages. They would have to settle for what the business community would come to call a "level playing field." One is reminded of the days when Indian reserves were created, on the hillsides well above the valley floors.

George Manuel and the National Indian Brotherhood had a message for Trudeau. All the Indian groups across the country denounced the white paper as a betrayal of their historical rights and the particular legal relationship they had with the Crown. Assimilation, they said, was the response of the European newcomers who had been disappointed in their notion that the Indians were a doomed race. In much of Canada the Indians saw the white paper as a threat to their old treaties. In B.C., where there had been almost no treaties, it was seen as a threat to future land claims. The National Indian Brotherhood suggested an alternative to the white paper—preservation of historical rights along with autonomous Indian government. And they were not talking about a big Indian nation somewhere in Canada. They were talking about a lot of nations and a lot of land in every part of Canada.

Trudeau was, unlike some politicians, educable. He withdrew the white paper, and went about some first steps in Native self-rule. He did not expunge the Department of Indian Affairs, but he removed its Indian agents from Canada's reserves, and allowed them to be replaced by Native band councils. In the seventies the Indians would run their own schools on their reserves, and, if they wanted to, they could teach their children what was left of the languages that had preceded English or French in Canada. Those small victories won, the Native peoples could organize better than they had for almost two centuries. More than two-thirds of the Indian reserves in Canada were in B.C. While consulting with one another, they would each find their own ways to improvement. Many of them elected women as chiefs. Some of them outlawed alcohol. In Kamloops the band took over the big residential school and created the marvellous Secwepemc (Shuswap) Cultural Education Society, forming an alliance with Simon Fraser

University and rebuilding a nation that would serve as a resource for Indians and whites looking for civilization.

For the rest of the twentieth century the Native peoples of British Columbia would have to struggle for their ancient lands, roadblock by roadblock, court paper by court paper. They would take decades to inform "one country, one law" whites about their ancient spiritual valuation of certain and many sites on the surface of the earth.

Coyotes

In 1954 the province removed the bounty on coyotes. In 1980 the Fish and Wildlife Branch of the Ministry of the Environment would publish a "Preliminary Coyote management Plan for British Columbia." It acknowledged that in Indian culture "...much mythology and superstition was based around the coyote." Here is the summary of its policies:

> The coyote will be managed as an integral part of wild ecosystems, as a furbearer and as a game species, generally being allowed to fluctuate naturally. Problem coyotes will be removed locally where they cause losses or harass livestock in established agricultural areas. Wide-scale coyote control will not be practiced unless essential for the survival of another species or to protect public health (i.e. rabies). Control through the use of poison baits will be restricted to trained certified government personnel in a manner and with methods which minimize stress and which are the least harmful to non-target species.

Socialist Hordes

"Pry open that first painful door, move into the political
system at every level, so we can alter the futures for our
daughters."
—Iona Campagnola, MP for Skeena, 1974

Once more into the screech

For ban-the-bombers and rock-and-rollers and smash-the-staters, the sixties did not end with 1970. For their antithesis, the Social Credit movement, things looked pretty good, too. They had won their biggest
election in 1969. W.A.C. Bennett turned seventy in 1970, and was as blustery as ever, fighting Ottawa for off-shore mineral rights, and proposing a
radical new "negative income tax," whereby low income earners would get a
cheque from the government. 1971 was yet another centennial year, and
Bennett thought it would be a good run-up to another election in 1972. By
now the three-year government had become a B.C. tradition, and Bennett
loved the campaign trail with all its photographers and microphones. There
could be no question of retirement; friends and enemies looked in vain for a
plausible successor, especially with Robert Bonner gone into the forest-flat-
tening business. Bennett was a little worried about Phil Gaglardi, who was
the figurehead for the redneck core of the party. The thought of a Premier
Gaglardi horrified the old hardware man who had been for the last few years
tailoring himself as an elder statesman of the centre-right. He found what
seemed to him to be a solution, making Gaglardi the minister in charge of
social assistance, and sure enough, the minister started making wild statements about kicking deadbeats out of the welfare lines and the virtues of the
hard-working self-made man, such as, well, Phil Gaglardi.

For Bennett the campaign trail was really a good old-fashioned salesman's route, and in 1971 he was almost always on the road, glad-handing, asking the photographers for more light on the teeth, please, and selling British Columbia. He did not think of Ottawa as part of his route, and conferences of first ministers were not his priority. He preferred the circus. Thus, on the first day of 1971 he did not celebrate the province's birthday in Victoria, where only the local television cameras might be expected to show up. He was in sunny southern California, riding on top of a grandiloquent B.C. Centennial float in the Tournament of Roses Parade, beaming for the big US networks and their hundred million viewers. After the parade he was at the Rose Bowl game, where he and Gordon Shrum had predicted the Simon Fraser Clansmen football team would soon be playing (small-town hucksters do not let the reality of NCAA conference rules stand in their way). He fidgeted until half-time, and then grabbed his chance. Knowing that the cameras would find California governor Ronald Reagan at that moment, he slipped between the startled bodyguards and shoved a gaudy B.C. flag into the governor's hand. Reagan recoiled, looking around for help, but when he was informed about what was happening, he recovered and said that California welcomed anyone who came there to celebrate something. Television viewers in Kentucky were making their half-time visit to the bathroom and fridge.

Bennett had been premier for nearly twenty years. He was the longest-sitting first minister on the continent. He travelled like a potentate, from continent to continent. He sat in the Folies-Bergère and drank apple juice. Back home he jumped onto his centennial train and visited all his little towns, telling people how good they had it.

Bennett said that his big projects of the fifties and sixties had just been the foundation of the big happy house he was building. Now he was ready to make it more comfortable to live in. In 1970 and 1971 the government brought down bills to increase old-age pensions and welfare checks a little. Civil servants, who were beginning to sound a little like the NDP too often, got a nice little raise. Meanwhile the age of majority was lowered from twenty-one years to nineteen years. Younger people might now go legally into the beer parlour, but they were going to see less beer advertising. In 1971 Bennett brought down a bill banning all advertising for liquor and tobacco. The advertisers and the tobacco companies said that Bennett was an old fuddy-duddy and a tyrant. Bennett said that the advertisers and tobacco companies were a bunch of "pushers." But once again the old-fashioned gent from the sticks was ahead of his time. Besides, was the NDP about to go to bat for the booze merchants and cigarette salesmen?

But perhaps the NDP was not the only threat. In 1971 the unthinkable had happened in Alberta, when Social Credit, which used to control 90 per cent of the seats, and which had been in power almost twice as long as Bennett had, was ousted by Peter Lougheed and the Conservatives. Now a man named

Derril Warren, who had helped elect Lougheed, was in British Columbia, heading the B.C. Conservatives and looking for MLAs. He started with Scott Wallace, a Victoria doctor who, like Bennett two decades earlier, quit the government benches and walked across the House to sit as an independent. Soon Warren talked Wallace into joining the Tories and thus becoming their House leader. Later in 1971 a northern Socred MLA joined him. Bennett remembered 1952. He knew that he had a new kind of fight to handle in 1972—he would have to make sure that the anti-socialist vote was not split so badly that the NDP might squeak in. He also had to condescend to talking with his own MLAs, all those young nonentities that might drift rightward to the Tories.

West coast ice

Jn 1915 the team name "Vancouver Millionaires" was etched into the side of the Stanley Cup, emblem of the Canadian professional ice-hockey championship. Frank and Lester Patrick had raided eastern teams, built ice arenas in Victoria and on Denman Street in Vancouver, and started a whole new league to challenge the easterners for the Cup. In 1915 the Millionaires had shocked the eastern press by easily disposing of the Ottawa Senators. The nicknames should have alerted careful bettors.

But a decade later big-time hockey was gone from the coast. In 1948 a minor professional league was formed in the west, and one of its premier teams would be the Vancouver Canucks. Loyal fans, many of them immigrants from the prairies and Ontario, supported the team at the PNE Forum, but hockey always seemed an out-of-place game in a region that did not know deep snow and frozen ponds.

In 1967 the old six-team National Hockey League, wherein a "western trip" meant a train to Chicago, saw that baseball had proven that you could go west now, and decided to go for the fan dollar in the US, and doubling its size, formed teams in places such as St. Louis and San Francisco. Hockey fans in Vancouver were browned off, and found themselves in the unusual position of playing the nationalist card in that Canadian centennial year. The NHL, which still had its office in Montreal in those days, felt the wind of patriotic emotional blackmail, and promised that Vancouver would be allowed a franchise in any further expansion.

So the people at Pacific National Exhibition built a brand new hockey arena, and called it the Pacific Coliseum, which, if you thought about it, almost seemed to be an oxymoron. In 1968 when it opened, it was, like the Denman Arena half a century earlier, and Empire Stadium a quarter-century earlier, a state-of-the-sport building. Fancy sports palaces would always find a place to sit in Vancouver. It would always be harder to find local owners for its sports teams. In the late sixties a lot of rich people from other cities vied for sponsorship of an expansion NHL team on the Canadian west coast.

While waiting for the next expansion, the owners of the Canucks copied Frank Patrick's technique and raided the east for players, this time buying a whole team from Rochester. They won the Western League championship the next two years.

Then in 1969 the NHL said yes to Vancouver; there was a spot available for six million dollars. Now no one in the city, not even among the usual carpetbaggers, was willing to spend that much to finish in last place. So the league looked around and found a Minnesota businessman named Tom Scallen to pick up the tab. A few years later Scallen was in court, and there were revelations about irregularities in the deal, but hockey fans were not worried about business. The new NHL franchise had become what passes for a reality in hockey in October of 1970, and Vancouver had become a hockey town.

From then on the Vancouver newspapers would run hockey stories on the front page of their sports sections during baseball season. In the early seventies Jimmy Pattison, a local businessman who got along swimmingly with the Socreds, brought the upstart World Hockey League to the Pacific Coliseum, and the Vancouver Blazers thrashed around in a half-filled rink for a couple of years before hightailing it to Calgary. The Canucks' attendees were people from the east or people who had followed hockey on television. When the Montreal Canadiens made one of their rare visits to the Pacific Coliseum, their success was cheered mightily by the crowd. All over the city and especially in the suburbs, boys started to play ice hockey indoors and ball hockey in the streets. Immigrants from the snowy parts of the country were bemused by a curious local phenomenon. Most right-handed hockey players shoot left-handed, and vice versa. But in lower mainland rinks and streets most of the kids were shooting right-handed. Could it be that people in British Columbia were largely left-handed? That would certainly match other statistics in the anomalous province. An interview with a sporting-goods salesman shed some light on the situation. It turned out that most of the tyro hockey players' outfits were bought by their mothers, who had never had hockey-playing brothers or sons. When asked whether their children shot right or left, almost all of them said right.

As the years went by Vancouver hockey fans paid higher and higher prices for their tickets, to see games against teams from even less likely hockey centres such as Anaheim and Miami. They were encouraged, despite a lengthening history, by the fact that the National Hockey League is an outfit that ensures that almost all its teams make the playoffs.

Fat little Dave

The New Democrats made two big mistakes in the run-up to the 1969 election. In the first place the party had been split into two factions—those who supported leader Bob Strachan, and those who supported his more "modern" rival Tom Berger. To observers the leftists seemed to be doing what the fractious branches of socialism were always doing elsewhere in the world—squabbling publicly among themselves. There were disputes inside Socred ranks, too, but the nabob W.A.C. Bennett contrived to keep the arguments inside caucus while maintaining total control of policy in his own hands. Bob Strachan got tired of the fight and resigned as leader, and immediately Tom Berger was challenged by a number of NDPers with various bodies of support ranging from teachers to longshoremen. Prominent among them was a social worker named Dave Barrett, but his challenge was diluted when one of his own friends, Bob Williams, with Strachan's support, joined the lists. Berger became the NDP leader in 1969.

In addition to the heat of its leadership race, the NDP was feeling a lot of warmth from its own expectations. Paid-up party membership was growing fast, and NDPers from across the country were in the province, organizing with fervour not seen since the days before the Coalition. Confidence turned into a sure thing. The NDP made its second mistake. They adopted the campaign slogan: "Ready to Govern." W.A.C. Bennett loved it. He had the handle his tired old organization had been looking for. He went on the warpath against the threat of the "Marxists," and Tom Berger did not even get into the legislature. The Socreds baffled the pollsters and got their highest seat count ever.

In 1970 the NDP let Berger go, and elected Dave Barrett their leader.

Dave Barrett watched Bennett every step of the way, and took notes.

Dave Barrett was a short stocky man with not much of a neck. He called himself "fat little Dave," and he knew what he was doing with such self-directed humour. He was interested in playing the outsider role the way that Bennett had twenty years earlier. His father, he often said, had pushed a vegetable cart around the east end of Vancouver. He never made anything of his Jewish heritage, preferring the image of a generalized immigrant working-class background. Rather than play up the socialist milieu in which he grew up, he stressed his father's hard work and self-reliance. He went to Britannia High School in Little Italy, and then headed south for his university degrees in social work, first at Catholic Seattle University and then at Catholic St. Louis University. In St. Louis he also worked for the Family and Children's Service, and later as a probation officer for juveniles. He would turn his Jesuitical learning and public-aid experiences to a career that would be more humanitarian than Marxist.

Back in British Columbia he got a job as training officer for personnel and staff at the Haney Correctional Institution, a provincially run jail. There he tried to organize a union of jail-workers, and was promptly fired by Attorney General Bonner. So he ran for the CCF in 1960, and easily secured the Dewdney seat, then the new Coquitlam seat, to spend the next ten years as an opposition member, all the time becoming a highly popular representative of his constituents. He spent those ten years studying Bennett, learning what it was about the high-school dropout with no apparent ideology that made the voters go for him.

End of an error

In May of 1972 W.A.C. Bennett eased into his chauffeured black Cadillac, and with his cabinet ministers in tow, set out on a tour of fifty towns in British Columbia, handing out trinkets and promises. Everyone knew that he was planning an election that year because his term was nearly three years old. But this was not an election campaign. That would have been unfair politics. This was just the premier and his ministers showing that they wanted to be in touch with the citizenry. Naturally, the tour wound up in the premier's bailiwick, where Bennett announced his big "Kelowna Charter," which consisted of little raises to the minimum wage and the old-age pension. Folks on Pandosy Street said whoopee, but no one else seemed to be cheering.

In fact the premier and his uncomfortable ministers were met by quite a few mayors, and a lot more hostile demonstrators, who jeered the Cadillac and waved placards announcing their dissent. Civil servants, for instance, shouted their disapproval of the premier's refusal to allow them collective bargaining. The climax came when the entourage returned to the Vancouver area. In front of the Royal Towers Hotel in New Westminster five hundred unhappy electricians and carpenters shouted "*Sieg heil!*" as the premier and his ministers got out of their cars. They raised their arms and offered salutes that had never been seen by the pre-war German dignitaries. Then they turned their placards into cudgels and started administering a thumping to the provincial cabinet. Someone stuck a piece of lumber into the soft part of the retreating Phil Gaglardi. Other ministers were bopped on the head or poked in the stomach. That evening the tour wound up in a victory meeting in Delta, where the wounded cabinet members gingerly held their seats while W.A.C. Bennett proclaimed that the three-thousand-mile tour had received a friendly reception everywhere.

Bennett must have known that his party was in trouble. But he tried his old Red-baiting tactic again. He called a press conference, where he waved his arms and shouted about the Red menace. He said that Dave Barrett had engineered the New Westminster riot, calling the leader of the opposition an extremist, a radical, an anarchist and a leader of violent brigands. Bennett was probably expecting Barrett to shout back, heating up the coming election and rousing the good Socred voters who feared the rowdy commies. Dave Barrett, though he liked to clown around and utter provocative one-liners, was a wily strategist. He promptly sued the premier for slander. Bennett called him a crybaby and an academic who did not have the stomach for real politics. But Barrett was playing inventive politics. During the election campaign the premier was not allowed to talk about the New Westminster episode in public because the matter was before the court. After the election Barrett said oh what the heck, and dropped the suit.

Bennett kept trying to provoke fat little Dave all summer. Noting that Barrett had signed the Waffle Manifesto of a caucus within the NDP, which called for an independent socialist Canada, Bennett started slinging the word "waffle" at the opposition leader. Barrett just laughed and said that if he was a waffle, Bennett was a big pancake. When Bennett claimed that Barrett was a Marxist, Barrett said that his favourite Marx was Groucho, but that he liked Harpo too. His tactic was to suggest that the Socreds could not mount an argument worth confuting. Bennett was not used to this kind of foe. Every time he fired a shot, Barrett moved his head to the side and laughed.

Meanwhile the NDP campaign was kept efficient and quiet. Instructions went out that no one in the constituency offices was to make any suggestions that they expected to win. Barrett went on the stump, even in solid Socred ridings, and tossed off a few jokes. He looked comfortable and sounded friendly. He was a great contrast to Bennett, whose platform demeanour consisted of a stiff body in a dark suit, and who shouted homilies and threats. Barrett stayed away from anything that would frighten an anti-socialist, discussing his plans for day cares and public automobile insurance and rapid transit. He was a social worker who cared about the little person, taking on the guy in the Cadillac.

The last harrumph

The election was called for September, when the socialist teachers would presumably be too busy to cause trouble. In late August, the unpredictable welfare minister Phil Gaglardi gave an amazing interview to *The Toronto Star*. He was quoted as denigrating several of his colleagues, and saying that Bennett was remaining as leader only to block Flyin' Phil's ascension to the premier's chair. The premier persuaded Gaglardi to deny everything and sue the newspaper for libel, saying that his future as a cabinet minister would depend on the success of the suit. Barrett could not believe his luck, but he was not slow to move. He began to suggest this scenario to the voters: Bennett wins the election and then retires, the Socreds staging a leadership race for a new premier. Little Dave tried this phrase out on the populace: "Premier Gaglardi." British Columbia had had some pretty strange men in the premier's chair, but the image provoked laughter and terror across the province.

Now the Socreds tried some damage control. Forests minister Ray Williston announced that he too would be a leadership candidate. The idea was that the voters should be calmed. But now it looked as if Bennett was indeed thinking of stepping aside. Voters would not be voting for him but rather for a successor. During the election campaign it looked as if Bennett were gliding. He campaigned three days a week, and only three hours a day. He showed a Social Credit film called *Twenty Great Years*. He told people to vote for the government so that they might expect improvements in their ridings. He warned again that "the socialist hordes are at the gates." In the cities people began to apply Barrett's technique: they wore lapel buttons proclaiming "I'm part of the socialist hordes."

At ten o'clock on the night of August 30, 1972, W.A.C. Bennett conceded defeat. He blamed the newspapers and the high-school teachers for the end of free enterprise and morality. Eleven of his cabinet ministers had been chucked out of the house. The NDP had won thirty-eight of the fifty-five seats, and the Socreds had won ten. That night, at the NDP constituency headquarters in each riding, old CCFers kept their mouths shut as early returns were tabulated on the television news. While the long-haired young campaign workers cheered each number on the screen, the old CCFers kept their counsel. They had been through this before. When Bennett conceded, they thought about their old union brothers and sisters who had died without ever seeing the promised land. When NDP campaign workers all over the lower mainland converged on Dave Barrett's Coquitlam headquarters, they did not come to drink champagne. The beverage of choice was beer, and lots of it, and straight from the bottle.

Two weeks later W.A.C. Bennett was driven away from the premier's office in a well-waxed black Cadillac. Dave Barrett showed up driving his own Volvo that looked as if it had not been washed lately.

Change in the weather

The history of party politics in British Columbia has been shaped by the ever-growing disparity between feds and provincials. In Ottawa the Liberals and Tories have taken turns running things while appearing not that much apart in nature. If Quebec sends a lot of Liberals to Ottawa, the Liberals run Ottawa. If Ontario sends a lot of Conservatives, the Conservatives run things. Sometimes Quebeckers take a fling on Créditistes or separatists, or there is a surge of rawbone populists from the prairies to scramble the numbers. But usually the prime minister is from Quebec, and the farther west one goes, the less one feels connected with party politics on the Rideau.

In British Columbia, the provincial Liberals and Conservatives grew less and less connected with their federal organizations, and the voters of the province were more and more unlikely to belong to families that identified with the old parties. In the Maritimes you grow up in a Liberal family or a Tory family. In British Columbia you vote for a party that is likely to represent the interests of your class or occupation. In the postwar period that meant that the CCF/NDP would get the working-man's vote and the vote of middle-class people with a socially developed conscience. The Socreds would get the vote of people who believed in individual initiative and the right to property and profits.

In September of 1972 things looked scary to the property and profits people. It was not just that the socialist hordes were inside the gates. There was a feeling of change in the air. The youth movement seemed to be getting more political, and people in their thirties and forties were still in the youth movement. The USAmerican forces were carpet-bombing North Vietnam and spreading the war into Cambodia, as if they were getting desperate about winning. High-school teachers were wearing blue jeans in the classroom. Ottawa was handing out things called OFY grants and LIP grants to local organizers to promote group activities the chamber of commerce would never approve of. In Vancouver, for instance, an LIP grant supplied the equipment for a zany softball revolution called the Kozmik League, which featured rules and costumes never envisioned by the traditional Little Leagues and bank teams.

Vancouver mayor Tom Campbell, a right-winger whose antics seemed bizarre to newspaper readers in the east, was met by unconventional politics he could not understand. When the federal troops went into Montreal to quell the "apprehended insurrection" in late 1970, Campbell tried to invoke the War Measures Act to round up "hippies" in Gastown. In 1971 he had to face the settlers of "All Seasons Park." The Four Seasons Hotel had won easy approval to build a huge development on the waterfront at the entrance to Stanley Park. Young folks went to the cleared area and put up tents and huts, planted trees, and declared a new alternative community. When Campbell visited the site, he was rebuffed. But early in 1972 the bulldozers tore down the last of the trees and huts. Later in the year, though, a plebiscite forced city council to purchase the western half of the site for park use. A similar victory was won by the squatters at the old military barracks at Jericho Beach. When the United States prepared a huge hydrogen bomb blast at Amchitka in the North Pacific, Greenpeacers sailed for ground zero, while thousands of high-school students marched on the USAmerican consulate on Alberni Street.

Like numerous Vancouver mayors, Tom Campbell was a real-estate promoter. He could not understand people who did not equate freeways and concrete towers with progress, and saw them only as some sort of conspiracy. In 1972, just after the NDP had attained provincial power, he was defeated at city hall by a new group called TEAM, more respectable conservatives who were able to appeal to the voters who wanted Campbell out but did not want the left to take over the city.

Inside the gates

For some reason, commentators of various political stripes like to call the Dave Barrett government a failure. On the right there were cries that he was spending money the province did not have, although he did not build any giant dams. On the left there were complaints that he was not all that different from his predecessors, retaining the system of leaving power to the most prominent of his cabinet ministers rather than delivering it openly to the people. In the end, he was brought down by a combination of two main factors: a recession that hit just when he was spending money on invisible planning mechanisms and a coordinated business community that swallowed its pride and created the son of W.A.C.

But in less than three years the first NDP government did take several measures built on principle, and changed the nature of daily life as much as the nationalizing of electric power had done during the first Socred years. The most often mentioned innovation was the creation of the promised Insurance Company of British Columbia, whereby automobile insurance was taken out of the hands of the private insurance companies, most of them branches of huge US companies, and operated by the province. The other newsworthy legislation was the Agricultural Land Use Act, by which the land commission hoped to prevent the converting of agricultural land to quick-profit commercial real estate. A lot of real-estate promoters were upset about that one. The Barrett administration was ridiculed early for buying some sawmills and pulpmills, accused of throwing away the public's hard-earned dough on mills that were going to go under in an orderly proceeding of free-enterprise competition. However, as time went by, most of those mills did well, even during the fluctuations in world markets, as they say.

There were some other changes that did not get the jeering headlines from the Vancouver newspapers, or the mutterings of aging farmers. Barrett's government created the B.C. Petroleum Corporation, which gave the province control of the natural gas business. Civil servants were finally given the right to collective bargaining. A new labour code was set up, and its provisions were related to a new human-rights code (which was called unnecessary by the new opposition, who claimed that citizens were adequately covered by Diefenbaker's Bill of Rights). In the new human-rights code it became illegal to discriminate against minorities in employment, service and accommodation. It was strengthened by a Landlord and Tenant Act, some rent controls and a new Department of Consumer Services. A system of local community resource boards was set up to monitor and administer social services in communities. These things were not as visible as roads and dams, so to keep track of them, Barrett introduced a question period and a daily Hansard into the legislature.

In other words, the Barrett social democrats did not go in for wholesale nationalization, but concentrated on those matters one might expect a sympathetic social worker to consider.

The business community did not like the drift toward social legislation and protection of the consumer. With the Old Man gone and so many cabinet ministers ejected, they had to find a new figure to run for premier. Grace McCarthy, a Vancouver merchant, was their *de facto* leader and party president. She was the best political animal left in the herd, and she had never mentioned Major Douglas in any speech or back room. She was always going on about what a great man W.A.C. had been. Why not ask her to—to—organize a search for a new candidate for the top job?

It's snowing bills!

Wacky Bennett used to introduce about forty bills a year into the house. In his first year Barrett brought down nearly four hundred. The left had been waiting forty years, after all. Barrett and his team were interested in planning and a well-mixed economy; they wanted to create something like Sweden. Cece Bennett had run something like a one-man show; he did not need a big bureaucracy because he made most decisions himself, and dealt with a relatively small number of businessmen. Barrett pretty well ran a one-man show, but he was interested in social programs and community planning, which need lots of people to run them. His cabinet ministers had to compete for funds, so they had to hire a lot of researchers and field people. During Barrett's time in office the provincial budget soared. Unfortunately the world economy was slipping into a recession, even while the USAmerican adventure in Southeast Asia was coming to an end. Barrett was not losing any friends across the province, but he was making enemies among citizens who had got used to expecting more and more good times.

There were farmers who wanted to sell a few acres to the new golf entrepreneurs. There were café owners who did not like the minimum wage. There were people on the religious right who thought that Jesus was in favour of private enterprise. There were people such as an Okanagan housewife I have known all my life, whose husband assured her that the NDP were communists taking directives from overseas. There were folks in small towns and suburbs who had never seen so many dark-skinned people before. The sheer numbers of acts that the NDP sped through the legislative session frightened folks who had been used to size rather than breadth. Besides, the opposition parties and their newspapers were always warning that a huge budget in worsening times spelled disaster for the future of the province. W.A.C. Bennett had done a lot better job of hiding the public debt.

One of Bennett's favourite ploys had been to underestimate resource income, and then pretend surprise when totals "outdid expectations." Barrett proved to be less wily in office than he had been as a campaigner. He tended to underestimate expenditures. The electorate was not as likely to be pleased with his surprises. Acting as his own finance minister, the new premier was not getting very good advice. The legislative bills he brought down had more substance than most of the ones his predecessor had enacted, but the populace, especially in the hinterland, were really interested in the bills their newspapers and commercial radio talkers warned them about. Once again the people in the countryside were lined up against the big city, but this time their animosity was directed toward the imagined hordes of single mothers and jobless youths who were picking up welfare cheques at the Coast.

"I told you, Fuzzy," said a Sunshine Coast bed-and-breakfast operator to her odd-job husband, "those hippies were singing 'We shall overspend, some day!'"

Oh my God, it's alive!

There were analysts, perhaps encouraged by the dissolving of Social Credit in Alberta and Quebec, who said that the Socred government that had replaced the Social Credit movement would not survive an election loss, that its adherents would return to the traditional free-enterprise parties. Perhaps these analysts did not take into account that for middle-aged and younger voters Bennett had been the only premier they could remember until 1972. To these people Social Credit was not some wacky foreign idea with a silly name, but the capitalist party of record. These analysts were perhaps going to be puzzled by the fact that British Columbians would give 1.2 per cent of their vote to Social Credit in the federal election of 1974, and then turn around and give Social Credit 49.2 per cent of their votes in the provincial election of 1975. Social Credit was always just a name. Twenty years later it would re-emerge in the lower Fraser Valley with the name Reform.

In British Columbia the committed left might have differences among their factions, but their votes always would go to the CCF/NDP. The rest of the province's votes would go to whatever group seemed to have the best chance of forestalling or ousting the CCF/NDP. After the beginning of the Great Depression the vote became more and more polarized. In 1983, for instance, the NDP would raise its total to 45 per cent of the popular vote, but the Socreds would get almost 50 per cent. In the years immediately following the 1972 election, the anti-NDP factions were faced with the problem of getting the socialist hordes back outside the gates.

Their greatest fear was that the private-enterprise vote would be split among three parties. Some businessmen bruited a reborn coalition, but the official opposition insisted that it should be called Social Credit. Some anti-NDP organizers suggested that the three parties hold joint nominating meetings and pick the strongest candidate, regardless of party. That manoeuvre might work something like the preferential ballot of the fifties.

But the private enterprise people's instinct for competition overruled all suggestions of unity. The Liberals and Tories subscribed to the notion that the time of Social Credit was over, and the Socreds were remembering very recent victories. They understood the polarization that had shaped B.C. politics, and they had no real federal organization to align themselves with. They knew that they could gather the votes of individuals who wanted to give the federal Tories or Liberals a slap.

There were old party MLAs who could read the situation, too. In later years there would be right-wingers jumping from party to party to enhance careers as anti-socialists, but in the early seventies the pattern begun by W.A.C. Bennett's gathering of two Tories in 1952 was set when Pat McGeer, Garde Gardom and Alan Williams, three of the five Liberals in the house, swallowed whatever pride they might have had and jumped to Social Credit. They were joined by Hugh Curtis, half of the Conservative caucus. There would also be jumpers from outside the legislature; the mayor of Surrey, a Liberal named Bill Vander Zalm, announced that he was a Socred now.

What these jumpers were joining was not W.A.C. Bennett's organization. After his 1972 defeat the Old Man went on a long overseas vacation, and unlike James Douglas in a similar situation, he took his wife along. He announced that when he came back he was going to vacate his seat in the opposition. Grace McCarthy, often called Wacky's "political daughter," was left with the job of rebuilding the party. She was filled with animus for anyone who was not a Social Crediter. She blamed the old parties for splitting the 1972 vote, which resulted, among other things, in her losing her own Vancouver riding. When Bill Bennett, the seemingly unpolitical son of Wacky, announced that he wanted his father's job, McCarthy showed her family loyalty, deciding that a Bennett was the party's best hope.

Psychologists are probably better able than pols to figure out why Bennett's younger son decided to make a grab for his father's chair. He was not outgoing and grandiose as Wacky had been. He was a shy younger brother with a view of the world that saw it as a big hardware store. His father had overcome the inability to utter complete sentences by grinning and waving his arms and shouting slogans. When Bill Bennett went out on the campaign trail for the 1973 by-election around Kelowna, newspaper reporters peeked at each other's spiral notebooks to see whether there was something there that they could piece together. Once in a while the younger Bennett would delight the reporters with sentences such as this one: "This is the party that speaks its mind straight from the shoulder." During his campaign of 1973 he appeared to be entering the political life with reluctance. Later he would say that he wanted to make up for his family's disappointment in 1972. There were those who thought that he might be trying to pay his father back for heading off to Victoria to play father to a bigger family.

But he won the by-election on his father's turf, and in late 1973 Grace

McCarthy crowned him as the new leader of the Social Credit Party in the house. There Dave Barrett enjoyed out-talking the rookie for a year and a half. But behind the scenes, the young Bennett was changing his father's outfit. He was completely without ideology; his business was winning. He hired strategists from Ontario, and he didn't care what private enterprise party they might represent. He lured those four MLAs with a promise of future cabinet posts. Unlike his father, he did not like cameras, and he did not spout challenges that began with the phrase, "My friend...." He saw his party as a firm, and when he raided the Tories and Liberals for candidates, he explained that that was how you got ahead in business.

In public his father said that Bill's rise was a source of pride. But he was watching the organization change in a radical way. It had been built out of the rural people's mistrust of big anything. Cece Bennett's grudges against the Tories, the easterners and the big-city financiers and their lawyers would never fade completely. Now Bill Bennett was cozying up with Howe Street and his technocrats from Ontario. Unlike his puritanical father he did not mind having a few drinks with them too. From now on the running of the province would be a business rather than a religion.

Night of the living Socreds

If people had trouble figuring out why Bill Bennett went into politics, they had even more trouble figuring out why Dave Barrett called an election for December 1975. He had often ridiculed Wacky Bennett for calling elections every three years. Tommy Douglas, the first CCF premier in any province, had warned that the second election was always the most dangerous. And Douglas had found success in his deal with the Saskatchewan voters to hold an election at regular four-year intervals. But the polls had started to look pretty good for the NDP. Maybe there would be so much snow on December 11 that country Socreds would not bother to drive to the rural booths to cast their votes. Apparently Dave Barrett had not noticed that the Bill Bennett Socreds were sharing cocktails with the suits in lower mainland boardrooms.

Dave Barrett made one big mistake in his campaign. Although he had brought down some important social legislation, and the little people were urged not to let big business take it away, he spent most of his time running on his personality. He was trying to play the Wacky Bennett card, hiding his cabinet ministers and ridiculing the opposition's leader as a feckless son. He thought that his rhetorical besting of Bennett, Jr. in the legislature would play well on the stump. Bill Bennett, meanwhile, hid his father in Kelowna and presented himself as his own man with a new kind of Social Credit party made up of young candidates who would put a stop to the extravagant spending of the government. His slogan was "Get British

Columbia moving again." His advisers told him that the populace was more interested in prosperity than in equality. When the NDP proposed that Barrett and Bennett hold a debate on television, Bennett's handlers wisely suggested that he decline the offer.

On election night it did not take long for television to bring the news. Once again the province would have a premier who was not encumbered by a college education. The NDP held onto their share of the popular vote, but the Socred coalition won thirty-five seats, leaving eighteen for the NDP and one each for the old parties.

When Bill Bennett said "Let's get B.C. moving again!" He was speaking in economic terms. A hardware man does not like to see money going for anything but business and expansion. He is interested in seeing profits exceed expenditures. When asked about his plans regarding Barrett's expanded social programs, Bennett replied "economic development is the only social program." That sent a chill through the ranks of people and organizations that were interested in protecting minorities, the disabled, the poor and the environment. They were reminded of Phil Gaglardi's praise for pollution as a necessary part of progress. Bennett, without irony or apology, openly declared that his administration was an arm of business. He did not seem to have his father's Biblical conscience that would at least give an ear to human needs other than material comfort. In the coming years W.A.C. Bennett would almost come to seem a regretted statesman. Education and welfare, two things that the new premier had never felt a need for, fell to the bottom of the government's priorities.

The few old-time Socreds from the bushes felt like wallflowers at their own party. Bennett made no cabinet appointments from the north, consolidating power among his recruits from the cities. His father had not shared much power with his MLAs or operatives in the field, but he had formed policy in the premier's office. Now the son seemed to be using the name Social Credit as a front for the brokers on Howe Street. It was no secret that Bill did not consult the founder of the party. Policy was being shaped by a mysterious ultra-conservative group of economists that called itself the Fraser Institute, and tried to become known as a "think tank." In fact government became almost invisible after 1975. It began to look like the façade of a new glassy bank building. Bill Bennett dressed in seventies style on the weekend, bell-bottom trousers, sideburns, but he was usually seen in a dark suit. The days of flamboyant characters in the premier's seat seemed to be over. Even W.A.C. Bennett was grumpy about the new regime, which his son's handlers called "modern government." He called them "reactionaries" who had no time for "progressive ideas." There were not going to be any folk heroes in Victoria for a while.

Right turn

Certainly, Bill Bennett never became anyone's hero. It was clear to every-one, including himself, that he would never be an outsized figure. The car-toonists were forced to go after other targets. They wished that they had a Gaglardi or an Amor de Cosmos. Barrett had been a problem, but the invis-ible man was no fun, and it was hard to make caricatures of men who just looked like modern economists and lawyers and were always behind oak doors anyway. They had to make do with the premier's five o'clock shadow and a nose that was getting a little red.

Dave Barrett had created a department of consumer affairs. But Bennett was from the supply side. Prices should go up; costs should go down. The bud-get should be balanced or there should be a surplus. Prices went up on things such as ferry fares, hydro bills and automobile insurance, while tight reins were put on public-service salaries and social spending. During the seventies the population continued to move to the cities, and the "favourable eco-nomic climate" saw real-estate prices quadruple in less than a decade. Bill Vander Zalm, the new human resources minister, out-Gaglardied Flyin' Phil, talking about welfare bums, and saying that his ministry would rather hand out shovels than cheques. The cartoonists had found a new subject. A famous caricature showed Vander Zalm tearing the wings off a fly, and from then on nearly all the cartoonists incorporated houseflies in drawings of the Zam.

Bennett's first four years droned on while labour and management became ever more unhappy with each other. The invisible men made rela-tions between Victoria and the forest giants more efficient. More efficient foreign money entered the province and bought resources while trees and minerals once again were treated as the way toward balancing the budget. Following the advice of the invisible men, Bennett became a "tough" guy, resisting the appeals of those parts of the populace that were not efficient. The sixties were long gone; from now on tough guys were going to be elected all over the world. As a product of the business world rather than New Brunswick Christianity, Bennett did not have his father's impatience with scandals among his cabinet ministers. These scandals were the hum-drum ones that one might expect in the business world, small-time travellers fattening their expense accounts on New York night-life of all scales, for instance. The funniest one livened up the Vancouver and Victoria newspa-pers and television stations for a while. Jack Davis, the transport minister and one of the defectors from the Liberal party, was found to have been trad-ing in his airline tickets for cheaper ones and pocketing the difference. Phil Gaglardi must have thought that Davis was a piker.

Cynicism in management, which was the proper new name for govern-ment, was met by cynicism in the underclass. The only people that still flashed the peace sign were Richard Nixon and certain foreigners fighting factional wars in the Third World. The USAmericans had finally decided to use economics instead of bombs against the peoples of Southeast Asia. Students who espoused oppositional politics were looked on as geeks. There were even Social Credit clubs organizing among the business administration students at the universities. The NDP was in disarray, and the New Left was getting older.

Bill Bennett let four years go by before running again. In 1979 the polarization of British Columbia was complete. A few months after W.A.C. Bennett died, the second session of modern government was ensured. The Socreds hung on to thirty-one seats, and the NDP, getting their highest popular percentage ever, attained twenty-six. No third party need apply.

Son of Megaman

For his second term, Bill Bennett decided to make his memory by putting up some big monuments. He would try to continue "restraint" and "modern government" while borrowing huge amounts to get his megaprojects onsite. But first, how about turning the people into financiers? During the seventies it became more and more common to hear political candidates say that they were the best choice to run the government because they had been successful at running a business. These men (usually) seemed not to have thought of the possibility that there were other paradigms for government, perhaps because their reading experience consisted of business books. In the run-up to the 1979 election, Bennett's government decided to train the citizens of B.C. as investors, and made British Columbia Resources Investment Corporation a major campaign promise.

BCRIC, commonly pronounced "brick," gave a whiff of old-time Social Credit thinking. The idea was to take the Crown corporations created by the NDP government and privatize them. Thus the individual citizens of the province rather than the state would be the shareholders. Each citizen of the province would receive five free shares upon applying for them (some people refused to do so for political reasons); then the rest would be put on the market for any Canadian, who could buy up to five thousand of them for six dollars each. At last Bill had proclaimed the "progressive" idea his father had urged the new regime to find. The Socreds and their advisers thought that a brick was the beginning of a solid edifice. Critics suggested that a brick would not float.

David Helliwell was made president of BCRIC, and the corporation distributed ten million free shares and sold eighty million. A lot of people borrowed money to buy shares, figuring that they were like good safe government bonds with the added possibility of soaring values. They had a lot to learn about the stock market. A lot of low-income people sold their free shares immediately, to buy food or cigarettes. "Take my advice—don't sell," said the hardware man. Sure enough, the price shot up by twelve cents in a month. It would go to nine dollars eventually. David Helliwell announced that BCRIC was buying a controlling interest in the mammoth Kaiser Resources, whose shares had lately risen by 25 per cent. Stories got around that friends of the government had sunk a lot of money into Kaiser Resources lately, and happened to do well by the transaction. There was an inquiry, of course, and no one went to jail, but Helliwell was encouraged to resign. The stock-market investigators would not go after Bill Bennett until a few years later. As BCRIC shares started to slide in value, Bennett opened the market to foreign investors, but the brick sank far below the surface, eventually fetching a few cents as a souvenir. Bill Bennett kept busy distancing himself from the whole affair. Critics began to question his acumen as a businessman, his self-proclaimed qualification for office.

Meanwhile, the megason was dreaming of steel and concrete—and Teflon. In the spring of 1980 Bennett announced a series of big building projects. Interestingly, these were set for the Vancouver area, not Wacky country. (Even when the provincially backed Whistler ski resort village was built, it was made for rich hedonists who would drive there from Vancouver.) First there would be a super modern sports stadium built downtown. It would have an inflatable Teflon roof raised in honour of the city's winter weather pattern. Thus Vancouverites could twit the unfortunate people of Seattle who had a stadium with a dreary concrete dome. (Of course, Seattle's Kingdome was home to teams from three or four major league sports.) Next there would be a big flashy trade centre on the waterfront. And Vancouver had landed an international transportation exposition. Wags pointed out that this was an ironic achievement, given the failure of various governments to build a good alternative to the automobile in and out of the city. Not to worry, said Bennett—there would be a rapid transit system in place to wow the visitors to Expo 86, on the city's hundredth birthday.

In November of 1982 Bill Bennett proudly poked the button that turned on the fans that filled B.C. Place Stadium with forced air and raised the puffy white roof. He even grinned for the cameras the way his father had at damsites. Newspaper columnists made cracks about premiers and forced air. The expansive white roof of the stadium would be a prominent feature of downtown, a relief from the relentless towers. But for the next decade and more there would not be much going on there. The B.C. Lions would play for audiences that filled a fifth of the seats. There would be monster trucks and tractor pulls, and some trade fairs. On one occasion Queen Elizabeth II would hear the singing voices of school children who assembled on the artificial turf.

Expo 86 would happen just in time for Bill Bennett's retirement from office. But for now he had another big business deal to pull off, with the poor unsuspecting Japanese.

Socrend

"Look, if somebody makes us an offer we can't refuse
then yes, we'd sell."
—Bill Vander Zalm, 1987

The kid with the curly hair

The puffy-roofed B.C. Place Stadium has a peculiar little monument now standing a short walk from its main west doors. It is a pastel plastic arch that can be reached on concrete steps, an arch that stands by itself with no roadway to straddle nor any real purpose for walking under it. Some people think that it is silly. Others are glad that its surface is relatively easy to remove graffiti from. It has been called "post-modern" by newspaper columnists in the know. It is one of many Canadian monuments built to commemorate an amazing athletic feat that rose above the smaller world of sport in 1980. The arch was put there, some people say, to make up for the fact that the provincial government did not listen to the public that wanted to name the stadium for the young athlete whose name would become synonymous with courage.

Terry Fox is a wonderful name that would be heard across the country every summer after 1980. That year he was twenty-one years old, a former cancer patient, athlete and Simon Fraser student. A curly-haired boy from Port Coquitlam, one of the suburbs that was pushing greater Vancouver eastward into the last forests of the lower mainland. Three years earlier he had lost one of his legs to cancer, and now he wore a metal prosthesis. He liked to wear a running shoe on the end of it. On April 12, 1980, he dipped his artificial leg into the Atlantic Ocean at St. John's, Newfoundland, and

357

started running, or rather hop-skipping across Canada. His announced purpose was to raise consciousness and financial donations for research and treatment of cancer. He had 8,500 kilometres to go on his winding way before he was to reach the Pacific Ocean in his home province, where funding for education and health were being slowed down in the provincial government's "restraint" program.

His run was billed as the "Marathon of Hope," and Fox demanded a gruelling routine of himself, getting up at four every morning to run the equivalent of a marathon. His peculiar hop-skipping gait, arms lifting at every step, became a familiar feature of the nightly television news across the country. Often he would be seen in the spring rain on the side of a Maritimes highway, his curly hair flattened and his shorts soaked. By the time he reached Toronto, he was an enormous media event. Children ran beside him, wearing Marathon of Hope tee-shirts. People in wheelchairs accompanied him. Mayors and club presidents were photographed presenting him with outsized cheques. His entourage included the mobile home in which he slept, and sometimes police cruisers with flashing lights. Often he was drenched and sometimes nearly sideswiped by big trucks. There was a Terry Fox song that became as familiar as the theme song of the US boxing movies about a fictional fighter called Rocky.

By the time he set out along the northern Ontario highway that discourages even motorists in air-conditioned cars, he was easily the most famous man in Canada. The stump of his sacrificed leg was in pain almost all the time. The summer was hot, and the television pictures now showed a young man with a sunburned face. Newspapers featured columns in which journalists explained the difference between real heroism and the concocted heroics of entertainment, the military and professional sports. People across the country were genuinely moved by this young man as they had never been by any individual, and the television cameras brought the image of his pain and determination into almost every home in the country. Everyone was looking forward to autumn, when that battered shoe would step into the Pacific Ocean.

Fox turned twenty-two while running near Parry Sound, Ontario, in the heart of summer. He had done over four thousand kilometres. He was thinking of the long hot stretch of the prairies and then the many mountain ranges of the last province. Politicians were planning to drive up and meet him at the Alberta-B.C. border. But in the days before he got to Thunder Bay he started coughing. His chest was sore and he was not breathing right. Fox was an athlete; he knew that his instrument was not functioning properly. They checked him into a hospital in Thunder Bay, where doctors found cancer in his lungs. He gave a television interview from his stretcher as he was being moved from a plane on the west coast. He had sunburn and insect bites on his face. He said he had done his best, as if he had somehow failed. He did not know that there would be Terry Fox runs every summer after that, that his round face with the curls on top would become a national emblem.

During the winter of 1980–81 Fox continued to work for the campaign that would bring in twenty million dollars that first year. He appeared at hockey games and civic celebrations and hospitals. He described his treatments for the press and broadcasters. His youth was always facing people, and his youth was the main factor in the story of his courage and the sadness of his fate. Now he was seen in blue jeans rather than running shorts, and his youthful ordinariness tore at people's hearts. On June 28, 1981, he died at four in the morning, the hour at which the daily Marathon of Hope had begun.

Coal

Jn January of 1981 the minister for economic development announced the giant coal deal that would open up the north again. B.C. governments are always talking about opening up the north. In this case the figures were grandiose, and B.C. Coal was going to make British Columbians busy and rich. Meetings with the Japanese steel families had been going on for years, and the federal government was brought onside and even managed to get some of the credit in eastern newspapers. The feds signed up for a hundred million dollars to develop a big coal port at Ridley Island just off Prince Rupert. They also agreed to improve the Canadian National rail line to the site. British Columbia would build any necessary new rail links, good northern highways, some more new towns, and the power stations needed to run all this development. Unfortunately the "restraint" administration would have to borrow the money to do the building; it was certainly not going to be done with BCRIC profits.

Big coal pits were gouged at the Quintette and Bullmoose mines near Dawson Creek. Miners and their families moved into the new town with the beautiful name Tumbler Ridge, and the coal started moving to the coast in 1984. It made someone a fortune. The NDP economists pointed out that the whole shebang was going to cost Canadians more than a billion dollars to get up and running. Newspapers were always pointing out the cost over-runs. Opposition MLAs got up and suggested that the government's accounting had never been so imaginative. As one of them, the NDP's Stu Leggatt, said, "Japan gets the coal and we get the hole." The private companies operating the coal pits found something less than runaway profits, and the free-enterprise government had to learn to wing it while keeping up its image as everyone's leader in "restraint." A coal miner living south of Dawson Creek was making good wages, but there was no work for his wife, and prices were high up there. The Canadian dollar was starting to slip.

A resource-based economy can be a headache. If the USAmericans take a rest from house-building, the jobs disappear in the B.C. bush. What would happen to the coal fields if the Japanese took a rest from automobile-building? One northern mayor said that his region was always living in a toilet-seat economy—it was always going up and down. But Bill Bennett said that he was an optimist. The risks, if there were any, would be incurred by private enterprise. In the early eighties Bennett made numerous goodwill trips to eastern Asia, promoting the emerging image of his province as a Pacific Rim power. On television viewers saw lots of government advertisements that depicted huge gleaming machines developing the north. In the late eighties the world price of coal started its fall. The Japanese wanted a new deal, or they would be a lot less eager to think of B.C. in their future plans, in discussions with their tourists and hotel-builders who liked skiing overseas, for instance. In Australia and the US, the Japanese had financed their own coal operations. Stu Leggatt suggested that B.C. would have been better off to tell the Japanese to build their own mines and ports here, and take all the coal they wanted for free.

If you asked the average Bri'sh Columbian about the coal deal, you would find out that the subject was boring, or confusing, or too far away to get much interested in. Bennett had pictured the massive deal as a dandy campaign asset for the 1983 election. He probably did not need it. The deep recession of the early eighties brought on savage battles between Bennett and organized labour, and free-enterprise voters were animated to come out and slap down the unionists who were making exorbitant demands. "Restraint" was always said by the premier with tough pride. While saying it, he could get away with borrowing and expenditure that spooked conservative economists. For example, early in 1983 the flashy new ski resort of Whistler was going bankrupt. Even while the government was distributing a series of "recession fighter" ads to the media, the government created another new Crown corporation, and picked up a twenty-seven-million-dollar tab at the luxury resort. One of its early backers, Bill Vander Zalm, who had scoffed at ideas of public money for the resort, was nowhere to be seen when the announcement was made by a deputy minister bathed in TV camera lights.

Skiing, of course, was seen to be good for international business, while less glamorous and more egalitarian things such as education and health were not. Through 1982 there had been layoffs in those categories, while junketing cabinet ministers were discovered in New York, catching the broadway production of *The Best Little Whorehouse in Texas*, and quaffing numerous bottles of forty-dollar French wine at the taxpayers' expense. People were getting tired of the recession and tired of seeing prices rise sharply. How could the Socreds win Bill Bennett's third election in May of 1983? And where was Bill Bennett? He was living alone, it was said, in a hotel in Victoria. A popular word in the politics business in those days was "charisma." Bill Bennett didn't have any. How was he going to do it? Really, there was nothing to worry about—he was running against Dave Barrett again.

First, the Socreds said that the budget could not be brought down before the election. Maybe it was too complicated to prepare, because for the first time in history it would be running on a billion-dollar deficit. Then Bennett travelled the province all spring, even into labour-intensive ridings, and claimed to be a world leader in the practice of restraint. All the governments in the First World, he said, were looking to B.C. and following suit. For the first time the Vancouver television cameras were broadcasting live from the Kootenays, and just by chance both Bennett and Barrett were working that southeast corner of the province. A television reporter asked Barrett what his plans were for fighting the recession. Barrett gave his usual answers: he was going to repeal the cutbacks in education and health, he was going to create fifty thousand jobs, and he was going to work with business as well as the unions, so that British Columbians of all stripes would work together to pull their society out of the hole. What are you going to do with the Compensation Stabilization Programme, he was asked. The CSP was the bureaucratic name for restraint. The day after the election it was out of here, said the little chubby guy who liked to fire off the one-liners.

The television people were delighted. A smart politician would have mouthed a lot of long sentences with passive verbs and abstract nouns. They had hoped that they could get Barrett to say something quick and rash. On the news that evening the Barrett interview was seen, and then followed by an interview with Bill Bennett, who used the words that his handlers advised. He managed to look shocked rather than thankful, and spread the alarm. He said that Barrett's remarks were dangerous and thoughtless. He said that the socialists were planning to dig a huge deficit and raise taxes like crazy. He equated an attack on restraint with something like treason. He scared the hell out of the voters. In the election the Socreds beat the NDP by thirteen seats and 5 per cent of the ballots.

Serial killer

Terry Fox was not the only name to take on symbolic meaning in 1981. So did Clifford Olson.

On Christmas Day of 1980 someone found a partly decomposed human body protruding from a shallow grave beside the dike next to River Road in Richmond. It was the body of a teenaged girl who had been strangled with a belt and stabbed, and left in that murky place often used by youngsters for fugitive sexual activity. Police were reminded of another body of a teenaged girl found in a makeshift grave on the Sunshine Coast. She had been strangled with a belt. Just after the new year, a teenaged girl complained of being picked up and raped; she furnished the police with a description that matched a man who had been a suspect in earlier attacks on youths of either sex. In this case the attacker had handed the victim a business card with his name on it, and had used a pistol with a silencer to threaten her and take potshots at some teenaged boys. The man was Clifford Olson, and he lived in Coquitlam, the suburb next to Port Coquitlam, where Terry Fox lived.

Olson's face was to become as familiar as Terry Fox's. He was dark-haired, squat and beefy. He had spent all his adult life as a convict or a police informant. He had escaped from jail seven times and broken parole five times. He was just about always a suspect when he was on the outside. When he was on the inside, he got stabbed for ratting on drug dealers. When his wife, Joan, got a $43,000 divorce settlement from an earlier marriage, Olson blew it all in two months. He was a nasty piece of business. He was what the social scientists call a psychopath.

In 1980 and 1981 the police around the lower mainland were looking for ten missing teenagers and one nine-year-old boy, and eventually came to be persuaded that there might be a serial killer on the loose. The newspapers whipped up fear among parents from New Westminster to Hope. Clifford Olson had been a suspect from the beginning, but the publicity seemed to excite him to worse depredations. He tortured the children and killed them savagely, with a hammer or a belt or his bare hands.

Then he contacted the police. He said that he wanted to do some informing. He would complain about a teenager who was doing burglaries, and there were some other crimes he knew about. In the police station he pointed at a picture of the nine-year-old who had disappeared and suggested that the child had been picked up by a pervert. When he was not meeting the police to offer clues, he was being arrested for picking up teenagers, and then released without charge. Then he went a step further, suggesting to the police that he could tell them where the bodies of the missing children were—for reward money. He joked about his arrests and chattered obscenely to a detective who was wearing a wire. The detective wanted bodies. He told Olson that there might be something in it for him. Right after Olson left that meeting, he picked up a teenaged girl hitchhiker and asked her whether she wanted a job with his company in Whistler. She agreed, and he drove north. At the Squamish police station she waited in the car while he went in to demand a gun that the police had confiscated from him earlier. He came out empty-handed, but he had a hammer in the car. He drove the girl to a gravel pit outside Whistler and smashed her head in.

Eventually a missing girl's name was found in Olson's address book, and he was arrested again. Olson wanted to be famous. He talked about giving press conferences. The police interrogators played on his strange mental processes, talking about everything from Olson's baby to the Bible to the details of Canadian jurisprudence. Olson thought that he could always get the best of psychiatrists and anyone else who was talking with him in a little room. He kept feeding them more and more hints. Then he proposed a deal. He would sell shallow graves for ten thousand dollars a grave. If the authorities would give his wife a hundred thousand dollars he would explain ten killings, and throw in an eleventh as a bonus.

Attorney General Allan Williams had a decision to make, the kind that other people are glad that they do not have to consider. It was illegal for police to pay money for a confession. A judge could throw the case out of court, and Olson knew that. Even if Olson were to lead police to the bodies they might not be able to nab him. But they could employ a second detachment of police to gather hard evidence at the graves and among Olson's effects. Williams did not have only the legal problem. How would the press and the public react to the idea of public money going to the family of the killer? On the other hand, how could he forgo the chance to put an end to the anxiety of parents in the lower mainland?

The deal was worked out. Olson knew that there would be those who argued that it would be all right to renege on a deal made with a psychopathic killer. A careful scheme to channel the money through a third party was worked out. The press, who had a sniff of the deal, were warned about contempt of court. Soon Olson was sitting in an office, wearing handcuffs and smoking a cigar. On the table were ninety-nine thousand-dollar bills and two five hundreds. Olson laughed as he checked to see that they were not counterfeit. Then he showed the police where the bodies were.

Olson did not have a media trial. He pleaded guilty and was convicted quickly. He began a career of complaining about the conditions he had to put up with in prison. When he was asked what he would do if he were ever to be released, he said he would pick up where he left off. He became the most hated man in Canada around the time that Terry Fox became the most adulated.

Meanwhile Allan Williams denied that he had paid money for the bodies. He admitted that someone had made a deal, but that his office was not a part of it. He also said that this case was an exceptional one. He did not really have a hole to hide in. His decision, no matter how it might bring relief to police and parents, would cost him his career. Pierre Trudeau said that police pay for information all the time. They do not like to, but sometimes that is the cost of convictions. Parents of the dead children had horror piled on horror, and their situation was the one that the newspapers concentrated on. It was a lot more emotionally appealing than the philosophical arguments. The parents sued Olson for the money, but Olson did not have the money. He was telling jokes in prison. He was watching his own television that his wife had bought for him. The periodic call for the return of the death penalty went up from right-wing politicians and the television viewers of Surrey and Langley.

There were investigations and suits, of course. In 1986 the parents of the dead teenagers, who had been rebuffed all the way, presented their appeal to the Supreme Court of Canada, and were told that the Supreme Court would not consider their case.

And there were lots of recriminations and hindsight. Why had the police not kept a sharp surveillance on Olson from the beginning, especially given his record, their familiarity with him, the accusation of one raped girl and the tips they were getting from other rats? The answer was that the police departments were operating on stretched budgets. "Restraint" happens everywhere except on high-profile construction sites.

Solidarity

After his third election win, and with vapour where Dave Barrett used to be, Bill Bennett's "new government" decided to make restraint even tougher. When the session began in July 1983, the budget announced only a moderate rein on inflation, deep cuts but no knife marks on the bone. But then various ministers rose and introduced the bills that this government would pass. They would be the products of the Fraser Institute's dream: power would be centralized in Victoria, and social legislation would be thrown away as too expensive or inimical to the profit sector. First the unions had to be dealt with. In the old days it had been a little easier, because the unions had been manual labourers and their fates tied to the resource industry. Now most of them were from the service industries, and unwilling to swallow the supply-and-demand argument. One Socred bill would abrogate the government's agreement with the 40,000-member B.C. Government Employees' Union. Another bill said that any of 200,000 public-sector workers could be fired as soon as their collective agreement expired. The Employment Standards Board would be eliminated. Another bill declared that unions could not argue for wage increases above 5 per cent, and the minimum was to be minus 1 per cent.

That was the anti-union package. Then there was the anti-social package. A bill would abolish the office of the rentalsman, and thus all rent controls. Another would abolish the human rights commission. Tax credits for the poor would be abolished, as would safety inspections for automobiles. School boards lost their power to form budgets, and local groups were stripped of input on area land zoning and community college planning. The committee to scrutinize Crown corporations was deleted, and decisions on health and education, the traditional enemies of the "new government," were to be made high up in Victoria. It looked as if Howe Street's Fraser Institute, and Norman Spector, the premier's dark suit from Ontario, were going to install a regime more repressive than any north of the equator.

Labour union halls were packed with angry workers. B.C. Teachers'

Federation telephones were held in hot hands. The word "Solidarity," until now the name of the amazing and romantic opposition to Communist and Russian hegemony in Poland, began to be applied in British Columbia. There were two main groups using the name—Operation Solidarity and the Solidarity Coalition. The former, kicked off by the tough fishermen's union, was the alliance of labour organizations in the province, intent on repealing the government's repealing of the workers' arduously won advances. The Solidarity Coalition was the name for the popular uprising that would throw in with the unions to fight the draconian excesses in the government's attack on human rights. Its most visible group was made up of the province's teachers, but included religious leaders, women's organizations, street wastrels, artists and writers, old-age pensioners, firemen, Maoists, unemployed intellectuals, college students and weekly opposition newspapers. A new paper called *Solidarity Times* featured stories and opinion pieces from all these sectors.

The union organizers tended to think of the non-union groups as ineffectual, and the non-union groups wished that the unions would say more about social and environmental issues, but in the summer of 1983 the Solidarity Coalition did show the Socreds that their new restraint measures were not universally popular, and that protesting crowds in the street were not just part of B.C.'s colourful past. Solidarity was showing signs of becoming the opposition, and the NDP in the legislature would become its voice. Toward the end of July 25,000 people met under banners outside the new football stadium. Outside the legislature in Victoria 25,000 more demonstrated. In early August 45,000 gathered in Empire Stadium, which had been abandoned by the B.C. Lions. All through the province there were demonstrations and marches.

Inside the legislature Dave Barrett and twenty-one other NDP parliamentarians fought Bennett's (Spector's) bills clause by clause. Barrett had announced that he was going to resign as leader, but the government's extreme measures could not be allowed to pass without a fight. The House sat late into the morning hours. The government had to invoke closure over and over. MLAs screamed insults that had not been heard since the days before party politics. On one occasion Dave Barrett was picked up by the speaker's musclemen and deposited on the floor of the corridor outside. When Bill Bennett went to his hotel in the wee hours, he was escorted by large bodyguards. When Solidarityniks marched down a street, the Southam newspapers aimed their cameras at the Communist contingent.

Then came October 15, and the annual Social Credit convention at the staid Hotel Vancouver. In television pictures many of the Socred delegates could be seen staring out hotel windows at a scene on the street that seemed to puzzle them. They were looking at a parade of 60,000 citizens, led by a marching band, a priest and a female civil-rights champion. It is doubtful whether the delegates knew the names of Father Jim Roberts and Renate Shearer. The crowd had marched along Georgia Street, tubas and banners poking above them, taking an hour to pass any given corner, inviting the motorcycle cops to join in. There was a noise both joyous and angry outside the old hotel. Who are all these people, a Social Credit delegate from Summerland was heard to ask. Communists, said an acquaintance from Abbotsford. They certainly weren't the official opposition.

Even William Bennett knew that he had more to worry about than the thrice-defeated NDP. He announced a recess for the House, to give the enemy time to lose their ardour. But on Hallowe'en night 45,000 public workers walked off the job. There was a general strike coming, said Solidarity. Go ahead and try it, said Bennett. A week later the teachers walked out and the schools shut down. Bennett got an injunction against the "illegal strikers." But the teachers could not go back because now other unions were maintaining pickets. Now the government decided to put out feelers to begin talking negotiation, and tried to figure out which Solidarity leaders were the softest. They settled on Jack Munro, the big plug-ugly trash-talking leader of the International Woodworkers of America. Munro had no time for radical interest groups. He ran a loggers' union.

On November 13, a Sunday, Munro got into a government jet and flew to Kelowna, to meet Bill Bennett and his handler Norm Spector. Reporters and cameramen gathered on Bennett's lawn and tried to see what was happening behind the pulled drapes. As the afternoon waned Munro's loud voice was heard less and less often through the walls. Late that night Bennett in a red sweater and Munro in his suit appeared on the porch and announced that they had shook hands on the "Kelowna Accord." It would make some concessions to the unions on the worst of the anti-labour bills, and make vague promises about consultation in the future. There was nothing on paper, and there was nothing said about the devastation of social services. The Solidarity Coalition was lost. Jack Munro, as far as the non-union segments were concerned, had shown his contempt for all the hard work they had done and the concern they felt for pensioners and educators. The hulking man with the big smile would be a cultural hero no more. In fact in a few years he would be working for management in the logging world.

Last of the Bennetts

The partial deal (or sell-out, as it was called by the teachers and others) made by Munro pretty well finished Solidarity, though the word did not disappear immediately into history. It transformed Munro from an unattractive hero to just another prominent enemy of the dissenters, as when he publicly called for the extermination of the desperately few spotted owls who had the unfortunate habit of nesting in trees that could become lucrative lumber. It also seemed to help in the descent of Bill Bennett. A few weeks after the "Kelowna Accord" there was a poll that showed that 30 per cent of British Columbians approved of his restraint program. For the rest of his last term he would run behind his own party in popularity. Alone in his hotel room, he knew that he was disappearing, just as he and his father had from the family scene. He was deciding to bow out, saying that his father had hung around too long, and like his father, he would appoint no heir apparent. He was known to favour a hotshot lawyer from Kamloops, Bud Smith, whom he had made his principal secretary.

But he wanted to go out with what he thought would be a bang. This would be Expo 86, the inflated name of the transportation fair to be held in Vancouver in 1986, to coincide with the city's hundredth birthday. The fair was supposed to exhibit innovations in transportation, but Bennett's biggest project would be the spectacular Coquihalla Highway, which would knife diagonally from Hope to Kamloops, between the Number One that followed the Fraser River, and the Hope-Princeton, which followed the old Dewdney Trail to the South Okanagan. The mighty new highway would offer a high-speed four and sometimes six-lane artery to the middle of the Interior, and shorten communication to the north and east dramatically. In Kamloops the old highwayman Phil Gaglardi cheered the son of the father. But the son and the father were from Kelowna, and a connector would meet the Coquihalla at Merritt and allow people to get to Kelowna fast. Kelowna was doomed. The pretty little lakeside city would become by the nineties a huge traffic jam and franchise shopping mall surrounded by hillsides covered densely with brutish houses rather than spare ponderosa pines.

The highway soared wildly over budget, and delays were threatening to embarrass the government that wanted the road open by the time of Expo. The official government estimate of the cost was 375 million dollars. The actual bill was a billion dollars. The annual interest payments on the loan would be forty million dollars, two times the amount estimated as income from the toll booths. And in the first year that estimate was proven to be unreachable. This information was not offered to the public by the outgoing premier or by his successor. It was dug up out of computer printouts by a Vancouver *Sun* columnist. Even the citizens who refused to drive the new highway for political reasons would pay for it dearly for a long time to come. But it opened in May of 1986, just in time for Expo.

When Bill Bennett, his winter's California suntan still in place, presided over the opening of the fair, the grounds on the north side of False Creek were filled with exhibitors' temporary buildings, thrilling amusement rides and trees trucked into the forested province from elsewhere. A gaudy barge was moored on the little inlet that had been reclaimed from the dirty old mills and warehouses; it was an enormous McDonald's hamburger joint, one of the most prominent buildings on the site. For years afterwards the area on the edge of downtown would be a fenced wasteland of shoved-around light grey dirt, owned, it was said by a Chinese billionaire who had bought it for a fraction of its value.

Bennett emerged from his shadows and presided over the opening of the circus, perhaps imagining that he was a rather young elder statesman. Three weeks later he instructed one of his lieutenants to inform the cabinet that he was resigning from politics. Members of his cabinet knew that Bennett was not doing well in the polls, but they were caught by surprise, and further surprised that Bennett had not made the announcement himself. Grace McCarthy, the long-time Bennett hand, wept, and then persuaded the cabinet to fly to Vancouver to be with the premier. On the trip those Socreds with names looked speculatively at one another, and at their own visages in the washroom mirror.

Zam

The Socreds had to scramble to get a premier and a candidate for the election in the fall. At the party's leadership convention, held symbolically at Whistler in the summer, there were only four real candidates, two guys named Smith, the holder of a comically gerrymandered riding, Grace McCarthy and the "charismatic" Bill Vander Zalm, who had earlier run against Bill Bennett in a Socred leadership race, and who had been out of provincial office since 1983. He had tried to become mayor of Vancouver, though he was an obvious suburbanite. But now he was the spokesman for those old-guard and bushland Social Crediters who resented Bill Bennett's placing the party in the hands of easterners and big-city businessmen. Vander Zalm had left Sheffield High School in Abbotsford just before graduation in 1952 because his father had had a heart attack and it was time to help the family. He knew how to work and he knew how to play his role. He flashed his teeth in an uncanny imitation of Wacky Bennett, and criticized Bennett *fils* for the creation of the blue-suited "new government." Social Credit's second-only leadership convention was the scene in which the schism in the party was played out. The main figures were to be the brash folksy Vander Zalm and Bennett's man, the cool operator Bud Smith. But it was Attorney General Brian Smith that the Zam had to defeat at last. On August 6, 1986, a new Bill was sitting in the premier's chair.

Now Vander Zalm had to contend with two forces within regular politics—the NDP, who had made colourless Bob Skelly their front man, and the delegates who were really federal Tories who had supported first one Smith and then the other at the convention. Vander Zalm would make people remember the weird old days of Wacky and Flyin' Phil. He was not acute in answering questions from the press or allegations from the opposition, but he was a successful flower-grower, and often told the story of eating tulip bulbs during the war in his childhood home of Holland. He had the common touch, and if he was baffled by complicated arguments, so was his constituency. Fortunately for him, the little people of several political stripes were tired of government by blue-suited functionaries. This was the man who had offered shovels to the unemployed. In the October 1986 election the NDP would keep twenty-two seats, the number they had held before the vote, but the Socreds would get forty-seven in the newly enlarged house. Once again other parties were DOA.

Vander Zalm's caucus was made up of florists and car dealers rather than lawyers. The premier let it be known that he was in favour of privatization, ownership, good old Christianity and resistance to federal notions of bilingualism. He himself had built a theme park in Richmond, managing through puzzling legal means to get his agricultural land converted into a strange neverland called "Fantasy Gardens." Drivers on the main highway to White Rock could see a big replica of an open Bible fashioned from flowers, and a windmill poking up behind the tall fence. There were flowers galore, of course, but also a petting zoo and a miniature railroad, a chapel for prayers and colourful weddings, statues of Biblical figures, and all the plants mentioned in the Bible. There was a gift shop in which one could buy all the usual trinkets, plus Bill's book or a copy of his wife's famous trademark headband. The main attraction was the little Dutch village, with real restaurants and stores, and offering a castle, in which the premier and his family would live. The US south might eventually boast places like Elvis Presley's "Graceland" or Dolly Parton's eponymous theme park, but even they would never see a governor's abode like this.

The land commission people and the municipal government of Richmond said that they had no idea that such a peculiar place would be the result when they agreed to slice a few hectares off Mr. Vander Zalm's agricultural holdings. Eventually the splendid place would run into financial trouble with bankrupt stores and restaurants and disaffected minimum-wage workers, and then greater trouble when the premier decided to unload it.

A richness of embarrassments

Now the new premier began his business of embarrassing educated British Columbians. He began by giving solace to the apartheid government of South Africa. The white government there had recently upped their repression of the black residents, declaring martial law and jailing and executing large numbers of black "communists," etc. A Christian leader named Archbishop Desmond Tutu became a hero to democracies around the world and called for economic and diplomatic sanctions against the government that forebade human rights in his country. The world responded. Even Canadian prime minister Brian Mulroney, no friend to labour and dissent, led the Commonwealth in condemning the violent regime. That regime was looking all over the western world for some government of some sort that would offer hospitality to its representative. Bill Vander Zalm was happy to oblige. The emissary of the outlaw regime had a talk with the premier and was escorted away under a police shield. The premier announced that he had made a big deal to ship prefabricated housing to South Africa, despite the boycott of that kind of trade by Canada and all the other provinces. People inside and outside the province could not decide whether the man was a conscienceless businessman or the only person in the western world who had not heard of events in South Africa. Even Jack Munro, whose loggers stood to profit from such a sale, expressed his shock in public.

A key to the premier's, um, thinking might be the choice of words he used to defend his announcement. He said that he did not believe that British Columbia should "discriminate" against South Africa. People willing to give him the benefit of the doubt suggested that he was not aware that the majority of the people in that country were forbidden to vote, much less grow tulips in certain neighbourhoods.

The tenor was set for the atmosphere of the late eighties in British Columbia. During the five years of scandals and incompetence, pundits and readers could not decide whether the Socred leadership was Macchiavellian or ignorant. A good example of the confusion would be Vander Zalm's pronouncements about AIDS.

Acquired Immune Deficiency Syndrome and its astonishing worldwide spread may go down as the biggest story of the eighties. The most horrible plague since the worldwide influenza of seventy years before had been the subject of a million newspaper and magazine stories. It would become an enormous agony among medical people, politicians and religions around the globe. British Columbia, and especially Vancouver, would be hit hard by the dreadful disease. Cities and provinces across the country and governments of all levels in the United States were working to create public-health policies to fight the virus and treat its victims. Vancouver's chief medical officer, Dr. John Blatherwick, would be seen often on the television news, advocating a major education program. A teenaged girl at Point Grey high school said that she could not get AIDS because she was using birth-control pills. In order to combat that kind of appalling ignorance, Dr. Blatherwick proposed information programs in the schools and advertising for the use of condoms. He said that the way things were going, the numbers of cases would double every year.

But Bill Vander Zalm did not know anyone with AIDS. Furthermore, he was a Catholic, and drew much of his support from the evangelical right. He publicly admonished Dr. Blatherwick, saying that he was not an elected person, and therefore not qualified to make public proposals. The newspapers reminded the premier that he was not running a theocratic state. The

Vancouver School Board commissioned a videotape that featured carefully modulated but frank information about viruses, homosexuality, drug use and death. When the premier was eventually persuaded to view the tape, he called it the world's longest advertisement for condoms. Reporters began to ask him whether he thought that his personal beliefs should be the foundation for public policy. Again and again Vander Zalm said that when the people elected him they were endorsing his take on moral issues. Another shudder went through the press corps. What would happen if the premier saw no distinction between, say, his personal business and the business of government?

Tulip boy

Young Vander Zalm was a boy with a North American dream. The fertile Fraser Valley was destined to provide his riches. He got this idea early. During the Second World War he stayed in Holland with his mother, and according to his story, sometimes subsisted on meals of tulip bulbs. But his father, a sociable and energetic man, by all accounts, spent the war years in the Fraser Valley, building up a business in flower bulbs. By the time his refugee family was able to join him after the war, Vander Zalm, Sr. was thriving. When he died, it was left to his son Wim, now called Bill, to carry on the family tradition of palaver and pounce.

Young Bill may not have known that he was training himself as a young W.A.C. He proved to be a sharp businessman like his predecessor, and he enjoyed the heck out of it as the former premier had done. In hindsight we can see one main difference. Where Cece Bennett had turned a religious puritanism into a search for worldly success, Bill Vander Zalm was totally pragmatic. When he expanded from tulip bulbs into real estate, one of his favourite methods of operation was to push at the margins of municipal zoning codes, sometimes to push beyond those margins, to get the edge to be found there. When small-time politicians remonstrated, Vander Zalm pointed out the investments he had made, and suggested that they might be good for the municipality. He was not wracked by guilt; he saw himself as a creative businessman.

Whereas Cece Bennett sometimes suggested that his Protestant God had a hand in his leadership of the big province, Bill Vander Zalm simply said that whatever happened was meant to be. If he became rich, then became mayor of Surrey and eventually premier of British Columbia, he was a person wrapped in history. Except for his too-short nose and unfortunate voice, he was a handsome man. He arrived on the scene at about the time that the term "charisma" as used about politicians had run its course, but he liked the idea. He dressed in snappy suits and had good haircuts. He liked the word "classy." When the leadership convention was being waged in Whistler, leadership hopeful Kim Campbell spoke a line about him that would be

Premier Bill Vander Zalm, an opponent of the federal bilingualism policy, complained about French on corn flake boxes.

quoted for years: "charisma without substance is a dangerous thing." Now Kim Campbell was never accused of being a clothes horse. Bill Vander Zalm said that politics is marketing, and you got your edge in marketing by paying attention to style.

He thought it was pretty classy to live in a castle on the alluvial soil of the Fraser Delta.

Who are these people?

Bill Vander Zalm's favourite word, spoken in the odd post-Dutch accent he delivered in his high voice, was "fantastic." It has been used for a purpose different from Bill's in nearly every book and article about him and his career. It was during his regime that the official tourism people started using a new slogan to promote the province, referring to "Super Natural British Columbia." To these hucksters in power, the words were probably just words. These people were elected by the kind of people who call a mall store "Hollywood West." It's just a name, man.

Fantasy Garden World was the name of the premier's theme park. A visitor to the province, hearing about fantasy and the supernatural, might be forgiven for thinking of British Columbia as ga-ga land. Was the premier's language a sign of his distance from reality, especially reality as it is visited upon the unemployed and the single mothers? It does not make sense to hand shovels to single mothers.

Bill Vander Zalm's other favourite word was "bureaucracy." He hated bureaucracy, but he loved saying the word. As a businessman he saw bureaucracy as a restraint of trade. When marketing boards got in his way, he sold his bulbs across the border. When he found himself in the premier's chair, he looked upon that fortune as the way things were meant to be, and regarded his cabinet as a nest of bureaucracy. The premier's office could get things done faster than the ministries; Zam increased the staff of the premier's office sevenfold. He saw his main job as selling the province to customers, and the province business, especially in a province living on (super) natural resources, was not all that different from the bulb business.

And business should be run by businessmen. Privatization was big business in Thatcher's Britain and other conservative fiefdoms. Vander Zalm admired businessmen, so he wanted them rather than the Crown corporations to maintain highways and tree farms and provincial publishing, eventually to operate car insurance and the medical business. Privatization would mean efficiency; Bill Bennett's restraint measures got rid of a lot of unnecessary jobs, and privatization would eliminate a lot more.

The unions that had persuaded Bennett to privatize his own life would be a problem again, but Vander Zalm had managed to grow a lot of flowers without asking permission from the unions. During his first year in office he introduced Bill 19, which would form the new Industrial Relations Council, and Bill 20, the Teaching Profession Act. The first would appoint a premier's representative who could put an end to any labour dispute that threatened the "public interest," as well as curtailing cooperation among the unions. The second would dissolve the province-wide B.C. Teachers' Federation, and allow teachers to form local unions in their districts. Both bills were obviously designed to prevent big waves.

The NDP opposition and the unions and the teachers asked the government for consultation, informing the premier that legislation without their input could lead to the second coming of Solidarity. But the Zam liked moving fast. When some businessmen and some Social Crediters were telling him that the bills were badly written, the premier scoffed at what he called "philosophy," and pushed ahead.

Meanwhile, the NDP had a quiet leadership convention, where the word "charisma" was not spoken, and the rookie MLA Mike Harcourt was named their new aspirant for the premier's chair. Harcourt had earlier succeeded in his campaign for the mayor's seat in Vancouver, where Vander Zalm had failed. The acceptance of Harcourt, whose outfit TEAM, made up of reformist liberals, had shoved the developers and businessmen out of power in Vancouver, was a signal that the NDP was going to play the moderate card. They were going to look like sane people who cared about the little man and the environment. They were not going to look like hardhats and godless schoolteachers. They were going to campaign calmly in their ridings while the unions and the Zam grabbed newspaper space. With his bald pate and big eyeglasses and pipe-cleaner moustache, pushing a baby carriage in his city's peace march, Mike Harcourt would never be accused of style and charisma.

The war between Vander Zalm and the revived Solidarity people was on. Teachers announced that they would do instruction only, a kind of work-to-rule scheme. Union people held giant rallies, in which they faced Vander Zalm's inflamatory threats with announcements that they would not go quietly. To long-time citizens, it appeared as if the premier had no inkling of the history of union-government relationships in the province. He seemed to see the issue in simple terms, often equating opposition to his legislation with sedition. The "public interest" was a handy term he expected to use against anything organized labour might do in its own interest. The Zam seemed to love confrontation, and seemed to expect that his "charisma" would ensure that he would be seen as the champion of the people. But the newspapers began to make fun of him, and then earnestly advise him to listen to the lawyers in his own party. Polls showed his support dropping rapidly. People noticed that veterans of the party, such as Grace McCarthy, began to look for a little distance.

The unions pointed out the faults of the draft legislation. Some people inside the government were also restive. The newspapers told Bill to consult and modify. The people of the province told pollsters that they already liked Harcourt better than Vander Zalm. Bill Bennett shrugged his shoulders and tended to his stocks on Howe Street. But the premier denounced the traitors, told the workers that he was trying to protect them from the evil geniuses in the B.C. Federation of Labour, and talked about family values.

On June 1, 1987, the workers and teachers went on a one-day general strike. Vander Zalm thought that they were hurting their own cause because the strike was illegal and the government was legal. The workers and teachers thought that they were helping their cause because they were showing that they had been pushed to the extremity of walking out illegally. The polls showed that the premier had overestimated the influence of headbands and white teeth.

A quarter of the workforce, 300,000 employees, went out that day. There were no buses or trains or ferries operating. There were no schools or government offices open. There were no newspapers, and in the pulp mills there were no workers making newsprint for future newspapers. Fish plants and mines and sawmills were quiet. Here, said the workers, is what we can do for a day. And we can do it again. School students held placards that announced that the next generation was not going to be any easier to handle than were their teachers.

Would the premier get the point? Would he moderate his position or would he up the ante? Would he be troubled by the news of his dropping popularity? He said that Jesus Christ would have been low in the polls. He lined Jesus up on his side of the education fence; just like Bill Vander Zalm, he said, Jesus did not have a UBC degree. Presumably the Saviour would have been a sworn enemy of the B.C. Teachers' Federation.

And like Jesus, Bill would not stop in his crusade until they crucified him. On the day of the general strike, the B.C. Supreme Court was open. That day the premier sent his attorney general, Brian Smith, to the Supreme Court to acquire an injunction against any more job action against Bill 19. The language of Smith's writ made the language of the bill seem temperate in comparison. Smith and Vander Zalm decided to use a portion of the Canadian Criminal Code dealing with sedition. The unions and the teachers would be described as revolutionaries trying to overturn the government by *force*. It would, if the writ were successful, make it a *crime* in British Columbia for any worker or teacher to engage in "resisting legislative change" or even "pointing out errors in the government of the province."

Has there been some mistake? asked reporters from provincial newspapers. The attorney general replied that he was trying to prevent an "illegal conspiracy" and a "breakdown of law and order." Jaws dropped, even in rooms not occupied by conspirators with UBC degrees. Presumably, the government and businessmen in the Republic of South Africa would not feel it necessary to "discriminate" against the government of British Columbia.

The judges at the Supreme Court pushed their jaws back up and spent a few days trying to think of a way to bring relative sanity back to the province. Perhaps they were wondering whether they might be next to be named as conspirators. Luckily, they were able to find some fortuitous technicality, and threw the writ back. The unionists and teachers went back to pointing out errors in the government of the province.

Friends in "high" places

It was not so much Vander Zalm's war against the teachers and workers that hurt him; it was his rashness, his impatience with normal legislative and executive practice. He was a man who wanted to go over the top before his agents had assessed the enemy's troop strength. Like Ronald Reagan, he had been elected not as a politician, but as an antidote to politicians. He thought that good looks and a quick punch would win the day; he always went for an early knockout, even against a good counter-puncher.

He had other problems that would lead to a falling away among his Socred team members and the voters. Newspaper columnists noticed that the premier liked to use the word "Faaaantastic!" more and more often, and hardly ever said "Reeeeality!" The reporters liked him because he provided good copy, but there was always a laugh in the story. Thank goodness he was privately successful in business. If he could make money, he must be a capable entrepreneur. The province was a business, and Bill was its CEO. If only he could act a bit more like those Tories in Ontario.

It was bad enough that the premier of British Columbia lived in a castle that looked like a site in a Walt Disney movie for children. Now he wanted to be the star of his own fairy-tale movie. He already had a weekly television show on cable. He had a radio talk-line program in which people were invited to throw questions at the premier. It seemed fairly apparent that the radio audience was salted with callers who would pose the questions that the premier was most eager to answer. The premier also liked to hit the evangelical Christian circuit, giving speeches that suggested that he was the Bible's representative in the B.C. legislature.

But now the premier of British Columbia had his eyes on the movies. During 1986 and 1987 he found time to lend his talents to a made-for-television confection called *Sinterklaas Fantasy*. Sinterklaas is a Dutch version of Saint Nicholas, and also, significantly, a patron saint of businessmen. Vander Zalm's involvement was obvious in the use of that second word in the title. The plot of the movie was interesting, especially in view of the fact that it seemed to tell a fantastic story about the success and heroism of the man who would call an anti-AIDS film a long advertisement for condoms.

Sinterklaas Fantasy was about a poor little Dutch boy who comes to Canada and grows up to be a handsome man and successful merchant. One day, while strolling through his fantasy garden, he gets a message from Sinterklaas, who has found to his chagrin that he has run out of presents to give to the little Dutch children. The handsome gardener rides to the land of his birth on a frozen rainbow, hops onto a snowy white horse, and with his snowy white teeth gleaming, hands out presents to the unfortunate tykes. The story is narrated in the peculiar voice of Bill Vander Zalm. The movie was intended as Christmas television fare, but it has never knocked over the Grinch as an annual favourite.

So now the premier who invited comparison between himself and the Saviour who never graduated from UBC had a new image to present to his worshippers, a kind of cross between Santa and the white knight. Torontonians, who always like to view British Columbia as the home of wackos, nodded their heads inside their parkas at the end of 1987.

While the hero on the white horse was distributing gifts to little children in Holland, the premier of British Columbia was waging a battle against the children of single mothers in his province. When his attempts to challenge the federal legalization of abortion failed, he turned his attention from his reverence for fetuses toward the children who were going to school without lunch. Saying that their mothers were spending all their welfare money on cigarettes and lottery tickets, the premier nixed the subsidized lunch programs at schools. The mothers, said the champion of family values, should go out and get jobs. Hiyo, Silver!

But British Columbia had seen crackpot premiers before. Vander Zalm may have unsettled voters, cabinet ministers and businessmen with his impatience and loose hold on reality, but it would take money-grubbing scandals to bring the premier—and the Social Credit "Movement"—down.

A lot of people wanted to laugh during the descent of Vander Zalm and the Socreds, but their faces were frozen in disbelief, and their hearts were rattled by the sheer pace of the revelations of dishonesty in government. While the premier billed himself as a martyr, and began to persuade newspeople and readers that he really did not see anything wrong with using his office to help his friends and himself, party luminaries would resign. Brian Smith and Grace McCarthy announced their resignations and left the room with glazed eyes. Kim Campbell called the premier "narrow and bigoted." Old-time Socreds in the hills began to think about saving the party from this man.

The prospect of detailing the scandals that wiped out Social Credit is daunting. If that is what it takes to be a historian, I would rather be a novelist. If you read the books of Vancouver political writer Stan Persky, you will get the sordid quotations and facts. Even the wryly cynical Persky seems to stutter with disbelief as he recounts the story of the Zam's premiership.

British Columbia millionaires are just as wacky as British Columbia politicians. They dress in funny clothes and get their pictures taken doing goofy things. They get arrested for fistfights and sexual molestations. They have public divorces and medical operations you don't want to hear about. Their names make ordinary people chuckle. The quiet anonymous suits in Toronto don't want to have anything to do with the Vancouver Stock Exchange. In 1987, the ranks of the comical and suspect B.C. businessmen were joined by one who had always wanted his dealings to take place away from the cameras. This was a fat man named Peter Toigo.

Though his first sharp deals had been made around Prince Rupert, Toigo really got his empire going when he moved operations to the lower Fraser Valley, where he first made friends with William Vander Zalm, the flower king. It was this early association that was to cause trouble for both men during the 1988 "Toigo Affair."

Premier Bennett's super natural highway into the Interior had left an enormous debt to the taxpayers of British Columbia. The site of Expo 86 left another. After the temporary buildings were brought down and the McDonald's barge towed away, there was a desolate crescent of abandoned grey soil filled with mysterious chemicals at the heart of Vancouver, stretching along the north shore of False Creek, from Chinatown to the West End.

It looked like the no man's land near the Berlin Wall. You can be sure that there were businessmen keeping an eye on the Berlin Wall, because if it were ever to come tumbling down, it would leave the most valuable real estate in Europe. The ground along False Creek was fifty square blocks of developers' paradise.

But during Expo 86 the citizens of the city and the province had been assured in government statements that the area would not be handed over to the sharks. There might have been dead soil on the ground but there were grand visions in the air. The Expo site would be developed as a total community, featuring a mixture of private business and social housing, of parkland and cultural development that would save downtown Vancouver from the fate that had been visited on the cores of so many North American cities.

But the B.C. Place Corporation, the government body that owned the domed stadium and the Expo lands, was borrowing money just to pay the interest on its debts. Grace McCarthy's economic development ministry also had the B.C. Development Corporation on its hands. A scattering of developable land throughout the province, it too owed money to the banks. The government merged the two corporations, creating the B.C. Enterprise Corporation. People who had dreams about a social experiment in the middle of Vancouver began to get edgy. Their fears were made worse when McCarthy announced that the government wanted to get out of the development business. Privatization was on the way, and those who had always been suspicious of Expo 86 were noticing that BCEC looked a little like BCRIC.

In August the corporation decided to streamline matters and offer the whole package, ninety hectares, to a single bidder. To hell with local triflers who would want a hectare here for a hotel or a hectare there for a health clinic. The premier would like to get the matter settled, hating bureaucracy as he did, and the corporation wanted to get the debt off its shoulders as soon as possible. If the north shore of False Creek was going to end up looking like Hong Kong, at least it would be a good tax base.

Along came Hong Kong, in the mysterious person of Li Ka-Shing, a billionaire with lots of computer-generated real-estate art. Oh no, said Canadian nationalists, worried that Asian money would grab their city's heart as it was scooping up valuable assets in New York and elsewhere. Along came a shaky consortium of rich locals calling themselves the "Vancouver Land Corporation." Li Ka-Shing dubbed his outfit "Concord Pacific," and put matters in the hands of his son, who lived part-time in Vancouver. These two aspirants began the orderly process of presenting their plans and prices to BCEC.

Now along came Peter Toigo. But he was looking for a way to make an end-run around the Vancouver people and the Concord people. He went straight to the premier and said that he would plop down a half-billion dollars for everything, the Expo lands and all the BCEC holdings elsewhere. There followed an interesting and sometimes incredible series of events, in which the premier spoke to everyone on his friend's behalf, and the attorney general and the minister of economic development explained that such important deals were supposed to be handled with a confidential and legalistic procedure in order to forestall appearances of inappropriate collusion between a businessman and a friend in high places. The premier either did not understand this principle or pretended that he did not, neither alternative particularly encouraging to his cabinet members or to the voters who bothered to read the newspapers.

What is wrong with trying to keep valuable British Columbia property in the hands of true British Columbia citizens? asked the premier. Now even Socred MLAs who could not avoid the reporters began to make remarks that would put a little distance between them and their leader. Vander Zalm began to make comments about crew members with insufficient "moxie." Privately and publically, important party members tried to instruct the recently converted Social Crediter. But Vander Zalm persisted, pushing again and again for Toigo's chances. It was not that he had anything to gain by his friend's success. That was not the problem, he was told. It was that a premier should be letting the BCEC do its own work in a way that will appear fair to all sides.

Even when rumours got into the newspaper that BCEC had asked the RCMP to investigate Toigo's connections, Vander Zalm did not get the point. When Brian Smith told him that it would be unseemly for the attorney general's office to deny the rumours and whitewash the hamburger mogul, Vander Zalm went ahead and did the job himself. Asked about this embarrassing situation, Smith told the press that the principle of neutrality was really kind of hard for a non-lawyer to grasp. But Grace McCarthy, another florist, had it figured out. Like Smith, she was beginning to plan a safe departure from cabinet.

When it looked as if the foreigner was going to get the ground, Toigo happened to decide that he needed to go to Hong Kong on business matters. BCEC phoned Li and urged him not to talk to Toigo. When Li refused to see him, Toigo phoned his friend Vander Zalm and asked what was going on. When all this stuff was leaked to the public, critics were not so much shocked that businessmen would try such shenanigans; they were more perturbed that amateurs were peeing in the pool.

In the end Concord Pacific won the day with a bid of 320,000 million dollars, which, when the sellers paid for cleaning up the site, might come to a third of that sum. Peter Toigo pointed out that the Li family had got the place for about a quarter to a third of the going rate in the neighbourhood.

Almost a decade later most of the site was a fenced-off wasteland with some hardy volunteer grass growing where the Expo site had not been blacktopped.

Bring out the clowns

The heart quails while considering the deposing of the Zam. Perhaps it is a historian's job to describe and analyze the political and psychological details of his last months in office. Or perhaps it is a comic playwright's job. In British Columbia we have a lot of popular historians and political analysts, but for some reason they have not inundated us with the peculiar details of the Zam's scandalous departure from the premier's chair, and the Social Credit debacle. Maybe the pundits, as they like to call each other, did not bother because the comic opera was performed every day in the province's newspapers and television and radio stations. Or maybe their hearts were not up to it because they like to work as satirists, and satirists are snookered by events and characters that are bizarre from the word "dough."

There were scandals growing like the provincial debt, cabinet ministers and other prominent Socreds holding their noses while tiptoing away from their leader. Now when radio listeners turned on the set, they were not sure whether they were listening to that enduring satiric review "The Royal Canadian Air Farce" or the latest news from Victoria. The ongoing laugho-rama included a mysterious Asian billionaire family that wanted to invest in British Columbia, and purchase the premier's Fantasy Gardens while they were at it—for fourteen and a half million dollars. One could be pretty sure that the family was not made up of agriculturists. Then there was a godsend for the newspapers, a real-estate woman named Faye Leung, who seemed to be rolling in dough, but who wore silly clothes, including preposterous hats festooned with giant flowers and stuff. There was also a mysterious wad of cash—twenty thousand dollars—that all the characters tried to shake off their fingers. Pretty soon the loudspoken hat lady was being investigated by the law, and threatening to blow the whistle on the tulip king. When Faye Leung became a folk hero the premier was done.

Mrs. Leung, involved in a tangle of law suits, seemed to love the television cameras, and there were usually a few of them waiting in her front yard. On March 18, 1991, for example, she asserted that Vander Zalm had received the by-then famous twenty thousand bucks from Mr. Tan Yu in August of 1990. For a while the premier said that he didn't know anything about it because his wife, Lillian, owned the property and did all the property's business. Then, under more pressure, he said that as a gallant husband he took care of his wife and her business.

The conflict-of-interest commission that was given the tiresome job of examining all this mess was headed by The Honourable E.N. Hughes, Q.C. No one ever did figure out what the $20,000 was all about, or which of the stories about where it was hidden was true, but Hughes did say this:

> Irrespective of the purpose for which Tan Yu provided the Premier
> with that money I have no doubt that reasonably well-informed per-
> sons could properly conclude that the Premier's ability to exercise
> his duties and responsibilities objectively in the future might appear
> to be compromised given the bizarre circumstances in which the
> money was given to the Premier and the lack of any reasonable
> explanation. Therefore, reasonably well-informed persons could
> properly conclude that the Premier was thereafter beholden to Mr.
> Tan Yu. Even if this is not in fact true, there is certainly an appear-
> ance that it is.

The Asian family tried to back off, probably on a principle of good taste.
People had the goods on each other, and threats were passed through the
news media in code language.

The premier looked older and balder than he had looked when he prevailed in Whistler four years earlier. When the conflict-of-interest commissioner issued his report on the premier's sale of his theme park home, Social
Credit advisers gave up trying to explain the principle to Vander Zalm, and
just told him to resign, so that the party would have time to get ready for an
election. In July of 1991 the party held a leadership convention, and the
Socreds shot themselves in the other foot. Instead of nominating someone
who would show that Vander Zalm was a temporary mistake, someone such
as Grace McCarthy, who could claim respectability simply because she had
been around so long, they went for Rita Johnston. Rita Johnston was the
other MLA from Surrey, and an old ally of the Zam. She was a stocky,
spunky, old-fashioned pol, and she appeared to stand for all those who perhaps did not know the finer points of philosophy and grammar, but knew
what was right and wrong. Like Jesus Christ and Bill Vander Zalm, she did
not have a degree from UBC.

In a couple of years the outgoing prime minister of Canada, having made
voters angry at his party, would pass his job on to a woman from British
Columbia, who would have to preside over the disappearance of her party
in the next election. In August of 1991 the pattern was set. Mike Harcourt
led the "socialist hordes" back into power in Victoria, and Social Credit held
onto only seven seats. Four of those MLAs would jump to the new right-
wing Reform party, and two others would quit politics, so that just before the
1996 election, Cliff Serwa, the MLA for Okanagan West, was the only
Social Crediter left in the house. In 1991 they would not even get a chance
to form the opposition. Businessmen and developers and other people on
the right had found a leader of sorts in a little guy named Gordon Wilson,
and restarted the Liberal party.

But party politics in British Columbia are volatile. In a short time Gordon Wilson would lose his job because of another funny scandal, this one having to do with love and marriage, and he and his paramour would start a new party whose name no one can remember. Meanwhile Bill Vander Zalm looked around the lower Fraser Valley for a party he could lead, and when that did not work out, a party he could join. There were lots of former Socred MLAs starting new parties, but they were not eager to have the tulip king in their ranks.

The New Potlatch

"More disconcerting, the last vestiges of the local—the
Co-op cafeteria—the oldest old men on canes in the sunlight.
And that reality isn't there either, disappears when you look
back to the Indians, back to the land. You realize you look
back at nothing. Again, there is nothing. It is all made up.
Except the forms."
—George Stanley, "Terrace Landscapes," 1995

The new opposition

Mike Harcourt has usually been pictured as boring, and that may have been his strong suit; voters may have grown tired of weird and wacky politicians, and tired of the monkey house sometimes called the British Columbia legislature. Maybe boring could be equated with dependable, the voters thought in 1991. Yes, Mike Harcourt had the sense to set up his constituency office in the east end of Vancouver, and he knew how to eat ethnic food in front of cameras. But he was not a dangerous radical. The NDP got behind him because he was a good antidote to Vander Zalm, and the voters in the centre accepted him because he somehow gave the impression that his administration would be more liberal than socialist. In public interviews Harcourt gave a good impression of an awkward good guy. His timing was perfect—the public did not want another spieler with "charisma."

But dependable as he was, Harcourt would be sacrificed, too. He would have to quit near the end of his term because of a series of scandals that plagued his tenure. It turned out that left-leaning liberals and centre-leaning social democrats are just as much prone to hanky-panky as anyone else. They might not be as much interested in amassing personal fortunes, but they might commit indiscretions that can be found out by agile news reporters.

But it would not be the other political parties that would test the New Democrats in the nineties. There were no other political parties. The rump

383

Socreds were beginning to devolve into some kind of provincial Reform party, an unwelcomed branch of the national party that spoke for rural gun-owners and capital-punishment advocates. The Liberals were trying to decide which man named Gordon they would hail as their chief.

No, the real critics of the government's performance were not much interested in being Her Majesty's Loyal Opposition. They were usually described as interest groups, or by those who would want to dismiss them as "special interest groups." There had long been such groups—the suffragists before the First World War being the first example that comes to mind. Veteran street demonstrators of the sixties and seventies believed that the US military adventure in Indochina had been stopped by the public protests of the hippies and other anti-war activists. In British Columbia, Jack Munro's deal with Bill Bennett told people who acted on the basis of social conscience that they should perhaps try to act without joining any movement led by the unions.

So in the eighties and nineties there developed a tradition of non-party politics, in which interest groups were prepared to take on any government or big business or union. The NDP learned that protesters were not necessarily going to be *their* people. The protesters found out that union people were no more likely to be altruists than were company directors. The interest groups learned that power is made by cameras in the late twentieth century. They could go directly to the public rather than trying to make deals in constituency offices.

The public would get used to lobbying and protests by interest groups, and begin to see their successes as politics for our time. The Burrard Street bridge in Vancouver was often filled with pedestrians, many of them wearing costumes and carrying signs and balloons and children. People without boardrooms wanted recognition and fair treatment, and they knew that if they wanted any kind of power they would not get it at lunch in expensive restaurants or long tables high up in downtown buildings. If they wanted to acquire and display power it had to be in the street, or on a logging road, or in front of a blackboard in a small city.

Politics in British Columbia was coming to mean women's groups, food banks, Gay Pride marches, Native people's blockades of ski resort roads that went through reserves, courageous individuals who spoke up and demanded that police and politicos treat AIDS patients and prostitutes as human beings who deserved to be protected from violence and despair. The ministers of this and that in Victoria were finding out that they had to be ready to talk to the public all the time rather than only during election campaigns.

Of all the interest groups, the two most successful would be the Native people and the environmentalists. The NDP government listened to the environmentalists, especially those who wanted to preserve forests and waterways, and stonewalled the Native people when they showed no signs of relaxing their claims to land. But an interesting pattern was developed by two new alliances: the environmentalists and Natives would join forces as Indian elders and young white friends of the planet stood together on muddy logging roads and tried to stop big trucks from chugging into the forests slated for clear-cut; and now the unionized loggers joined hands with the forest company multinationals in an effort to save jobs in the wood industry. Threatening times bring novel partnerships. The province's political parties, already jumping into the seats vacated by one another, now had to figure out how to please or avoid the most persuasive of the issue politicians.

Nearing the end

Paying attention to party politics in British Columbia in the last decade of the twentieth century can be amusing or depressing, depending on whether the person paying the attention is a cynic or a residual idealist. If that person is also trying to tell some kind of story about the province, he might like to end on a note or two of hope. If people or their environments cannot live happily ever after, they might at least be cheered a little by the survival of the ancient country and the human beings who were its first occupants.

The Skagit Valley is still there

The city of Seattle is romantic and beautiful. It is, in many people's estimation, the most pleasant city in the United States. It it known for cappuccino drinkers and free downtown buses and outdoor arts festivals. But it is also the home of some giant businesses, including the Boeing airplane business and the Microsoft computer business. It requires a lot of electrical power. Because geography writes history on the northwest coast of America, a lot of that electrical power has to come from the rivers of British Columbia.

Southeast of Hope, B.C., there is a beautiful river valley called the Skagit, which begins its descent in Canada and broadens as it flows toward the Pacific in the United States. The forty-ninth parallel of latitude runs across Ross Lake, a body of water created by Ross Dam. In the mid-sixties the city of Seattle and the W.A.C. Bennett government of B.C. worked out an arrangement whereby Seattle would get more power and Victoria would get more US dollars. The Ross Dam would be raised and the valley floor on the Canadian side would have a great big lake.

The Canadian side of the Skagit Valley is home to plant species that do not show up elsewhere, as well as trout that make it a great pleasure to sit in a boat on the river, and cougars and bears and deer and the famous spotted owl that would become the totem of the environmentalists' movement. With high blue mountains and deep forest and a river made of recently melted snow, the valley would probably even soften the heart of Jack Munro.

It melted the heart of Curley Chittenden. In the second half of the twentieth century, if you were talking in the lower Fraser about logging and lumber you would wind up talking about the Chittendens. In 1965 Curley Chittenden was a logging superintendent with the Seattle Light and Power Company. The company told him what they wanted him to superintend: they were going to raise the height of the Ross Dam and flood ten miles of the Skagit Valley on the Canadian side. Curley was directed to clear-cut the valley floor.

Curley Chittenden was not a starry-eyed tree-hugger from the west side of Vancouver. His clothes smelled of cedar. He was going to have a granddaughter named Cedar. He never drank a cup of cappuccino. He was born in St. Catharines, Ontario, but he grew up near Abbotsford, B.C., where he could see those blue mountains. He had relatives across the line. Near Seattle you can find Chittenden Locks, and on the way to Cultus Lake in the lower Fraser you will pass Chittenden Road. Curley was not a politician, either. There was not a drop of oil in the sentences he was known to utter over the sound of a chain saw.

But one day in 1965 he put down the telephone, rolled up his map, and got into his truck. He was not going to clear-cut the Skagit for Seattle Light and Power. That day he did not hold a press conference or issue a manifesto, but his action was well noticed by the newspapers and TV stations and became just as important to environmental history as the first Greenpeace naval expedition into the North Pacific.

The Socreds and the USAmericans did not give up on the power deal. In 1967 they signed a deal to enlarge the dam and inundate the rare foliage. They were going to make the lake even bigger than what the original plans had called for. But then the late sixties were happening. Prominent USAmerican politicians were being shot to death. Ordinary people were joining longhairs to oppose the US bombing of Asian cities and villages. Dissent was a big topic in the newspapers and on television news. In British Columbia people began to find out about the Skagit deal, and protests took place on mountain roads and legislature lawns. Ross Lake gave its name to the central core of the opposition: Run Out Skagit Spoilers.

In 1972 the NDP won its first election. Tom Perry, a young west-side Vancouver MLA, who had spent a lot of time canoeing the Skagit, did the politicking that Curley Chittenden would not and could not do. The provincial government opposed the bigger Ross Dam, and the federal government agreed. The provincial government designated the valley as a recreation area, and ten years later the USAmericans agreed that that was a good idea. But there were no guarantees that logging and mining would not be allowed to shove the spotted owls aside. In fact there were already mine claims in the area, and stories that some of them would prove it worthwhile for someone to smash roads into hillsides.

The tree-huggers massed in the bush, and the newspaper photographers were there. The World Wildlife Federation knocked on people's wooden doors. Curley Chittenden's family spent summer weekends at Cultus Lake, enjoying quiet in the trees. Years went by, and while the Ross Dam did not rise to block the sun, neither did the Skagit breathe easily.

But by the mid-nineties the second NDP government was trying to find ways to preserve symbolic wilderness while holding onto forest union votes. It managed to create a vast wilderness park along the Tatshenshini River, but that was a long way from the United States. Finally, in 1995, the government worked out a deal: the northeast corner of the Skagit Valley would be marked off for mining claims, where gold, silver and copper could be gouged out of the rock—but there would be no mining roads in the valley. The government could demonstrate that it was willing to listen to those who talked about economic development and jobs, while creating a park for canoers and spotted owls.

Tom Perry reminisced about the two-decade campaign while he made the official announcement. Curley Chittenden was in a palliative care hospital, going through the severe pain and consciousness-robbing chemistry of cancer. His son Harold, a forest products man, was able to tell him about the ceremony a few days before he died. Now in Skagit Valley Park there is a Chittenden Bridge and a beautiful Chittenden Meadow.

Myth, history, facts

When I went to high school in the Okanagan in the fifties, I took literature and history and French. After school and on weekends I went for hikes through Chief Manuel Louie's ranch, or I sat in the pool hall, watching Chief Manuel lean his ample belly up against the rail and snap a nine-ball into the corner pocket. The literature I took in school included plays by Shakespeare and sonnets by Keats. I had no idea that there were Okanagan poems and stories. The only Canadian history I ever took was about New France. I learned very little French, and I did not learn more than three words of Okanagan. It was not until I visited the University of Arizona ten years later that I first heard about taking courses on local Native Indian history or arts or languages.

Some politicians and social workers considered it a great advance to bring Indian children out of the Indian schools, where they learned about Euro-Canadian life, to the regular provincial schools, where they sat among white students and learned about Euro-Canadian life. The Battle of Hastings. "The Rime of the Ancient Mariner." The preterite. At the end of school assembly on Monday mornings we sang "God Save the King/Queen."

Oh, did the Red Indians have languages, asks an English educator late in the twentieth century.

In the middle of the twentieth century it looked as if the Indian people were going to stay around, but they would, with the odd heroic exception, be relegated to the margins, to the unpainted reserves, to the mean streets of Vancouver's east end, and when they were permitted to buy alcohol, to the least desirable bars and sidewalks.

In the late-twentieth century the Native Indian people of British Columbia have not overcome all the mistreatment they received after the white miners and settlers followed the fur traders into the area between the Rockies and the Pacific. But they are to be encountered in the newspapers and on television. When they show up in the courtrooms, they might now be suing for land or spiritual property or redress, not just receiving sentences. Now they not only appear in schools and colleges and universities—they appear as course subjects, and they appear as teachers.

The Native people had learned how to communicate with the news media, and the media had somehow come around to considering them newsworthy. In the eighties, and increasingly through the nineties, one of the principal ongoing stories would be the old Indian residential schools. More and more middle-aged Native men and women came forward to describe their mistreatment in those schools, and their troubled lives afterward. The first of the schools opened in 1861 in Mission, and most of them closed in the 1970s, though three lasted into the eighties. The last closed in 1984, and soon afterward the first accusations of sexual abuse and other cruel treatment were heard. Similar stories were being told in other parts of Canada. Former staff members at former schools in Lytton and Williams Lake were convicted of mistreatment.

There was a royal commission. There was a report from the Assembly of First Nations. Finally in 1994 the RCMP was receiving so many complaints about children being deprived, tortured and raped that they decided to enter all such complaints on their computers and set up a twenty-five-member task force to investigate all thirteen of the province's former residential schools. Almost all the complaints in the following years would be delivered in English, the language the children were forced to speak once they had been separated from their families.

The Native people had a lot of things taken away from them during the "settlement" and "development" of the colony and province. The newcomers took away the children and put them in residential schools. They took away land, language, religion and wildlife. They took away the bones of their dead families. They took away art. The things that Native peoples carved and painted and wove have only recently been called art. Before that the businessmen and churchmen and politicians that took away these things called them folklore or artefacts or pagan deviltry. The people from whom they were taken called some of them necessary and some of them sacred. By the eighties and nineties various Native groups, especially those on the coast, had begun to persuade newspaper readers and even some government folk that it was not a bizarre notion to give some of those objects back to the people who had made them.

When Captain James Cook and his men arrived at Nootka Sound in 1778, there were eight thousand people called the Mowachaht and Muchalaht living there. They were whalers and fishermen, and they had a three-hundred-year-old shrine. It contained carvings of two whales and sixty life-sized human figures. By 1904 there were only about fifty people left, and the shrine was in the American Museum of Natural History. (Somehow the carvings, one supposes, were part of the natural world rather than the art world.)

In the 1960s the people were moved by the Canadian government to a town on land that used to belong to them, where they were promised jobs in a pulp mill. But the mill dumped poison on their houses and children. Now there are more than 350 of the people, and half of them are moving to a new village they are building themselves, on land looked over by an eagle nest rather than a smokestack. They wanted their shrine back. It is locked inside a vault in New York City.

In recent years some groups of Native people along the Coast have had their old property returned to them, and have built their own museums to show Native work. There is a beautiful museum at Cape Mudge village on the south end of Quadra Island. The Anglican church returned five objects to the Nisga'a people in the early nineties, after running into opposition to its plan to sell them to pay for renovations to its cathedral in Victoria. The five objects were appraised at $300,000. That kind of monetary figure illustrates the difficulties that Native peoples face in trying to get their masks and rattles and dance aprons back—there is a lucrative market in aboriginal art.

There are also white people who resist the idea of repatriating the valuable things. Museums anywhere in the world hate the idea of losing things that they have collected, except when they have to raise money to maintain their buildings. Individuals who have fallen heir to chief's blankets and jewellery and so on often scoff at the idea that they are not the proper owners. Such an individual was retired businessman Robert Crosby.

Crosby was the grandson of a highly successful missionary, Thomas Crosby, who worked for the Methodist church all over the northern coast of B.C., and was instrumental in the formation of the United Church of Canada. The Reverend Crosby liked to dress up in chief's regalia, and received a houseful of sacred objects. Some people, such as his grandson, claim that these were gifts. Others suggest that the Reverend Crosby demanded that the Native people hand them over when they converted from their "heathen" ways to civilization. He detested the savagery of the potlatch, but he somehow came into possessions that would have made any visitor to a potlatch feel very lucky and very much obliged.

Now there were some people in the United Church who thought that at least some of these objects should be returned to the Tsimshian and other nations who produced them. But Robert Crosby did not like what had been happening in the United Church lately. He was evasive when asked whether he had profited from his grandfather's collection. He said that he may have given some pieces to his family. He admitted selling one object to a museum, but he said that he did not know about the forty pieces called the "Crosby Collection" in Ottawa's Museum of Civilization. His grandfather made enemies in the B.C. government by fighting for Tsimshian land claims, but the grandson thinks that the idea of giving the Indians anything is insane. In an interview with Vancouver *Sun* religion reporter Douglas Todd, he opined that "the whole world's going crazy." The Tsimshian people would probably get most of their things back from the Museum of Civilization, but they were not going to get anywhere with the missionary's grandson.

Manny Jules figured that one way to get something from the Europeans was to charge them taxes. He thought that his ancestors should have started doing that in 1811. Manny Jules was a short man with very long hair and noble stubbornness. He got himself elected chief of the Kamloops band when he was thirty, and talked his community into growing faster than the booming city of Kamloops across the river. He took hold of the moribund church building and the empty residential school and transformed them. The Kamloops band people could not stand watching him jump up and down, so they got to work. Soon there were new buildings around the old school, including a huge pow-wow circle. There was a demonstration village, with sweat lodges and pit houses and kanickanick berries. The school is back in business, but now the Native people are running it, and Simon Fraser University is offering courses there.

As soon as he became chief in 1984, Manny Jules contacted every Native chief in Canada and many in the US. He tirelessly lobbied federal and provincial government departments. He told his people to learn as much as they could about history, because he was working on making it. In the late eighties he got the feds to pass what is familiarly called the "Kamloops Amendment." That means that if Indian bands want to lease some of their land for commercial use by whites, they will not risk losing the special economic laws that govern reserve land. It also means that organized Native peoples can raise taxes from the white businesses or housing that use their land. It also means that the band that taxes the land has to service it with roads and power and the like.

Manny Jules wanted Native peoples all over the country to learn the tax business. For years the white people had been telling the Natives that they ought to pull themselves up to the national standard. Manny Jules noticed that white people kept up their standards by taxing business and real estate. Ten years after Manny Jules became chief of the Kamloops band, the province saw forty bands raising taxes off such things as airports, roads and factories on reserve land. The province passed an Indian Self-Government Enabling Act, which compels the province to get out of the tax business wherever the Native people decide they want to operate.

Manny Jules travelled a lot across the country, helping Quebec Natives learn how to tax shopping centres, or helping Alberta groups write the bills for the oil companies exploring on Indian range. Certain white people, such as Robert Crosby, were getting a little nervous. What if the claim that Native people still owned all of British Columbia were to be proven true? What if they decided to put a retroactive tax on Indian sacred objects that came to rest on shelves in white people's factories.

In the mid-nineties Manny Jules started working on a giant plan for Native real-estate development....

Land claims

As British Columbia felt the approach of the twenty-first century, it was becoming quite clear that the province would have to negotiate seriously with the First Nations people. They were not going to disappear in some Darwinian apocalypse. They had survived smallpox and come back in numbers. They had survived the residential schools, and though many of them were now Christians, they were relearning their language, their spirituality and their history. Their leaders were now lawyers and negotiators and businessmen. They had learned how to get attention and serious consideration by challenging the assumptions of non-Natives who had blithely driven cars across their reserve lands on the way to ski resorts.

Land claims became the key issue in the complex relations between aboriginal peoples and more recent humans. Often there were two extreme positions heard: some people said that the entire province was still Indian land, with the possible exception of the bits bought by James Douglas on southern Vancouver Island; some other people said that the non-Natives did not have to "give" the Indians anything. These latter people were generally the same people who said that England had won the Plains of Abraham fair and square, and did not owe the French-Canadians a thing. (Well, actually, most of the people with that opinion would probably have trouble identifying the Plains of Abraham.)

One could say that there was a connection between the Plains of Abraham and the legal battles for land west of the Rockies nearly two and a half centuries later. In the middle of what Europeans called the eighteenth century, the many nations west of the Rockies never heard much about the

Seven Years' War. In the ten centuries that they had been there they had had a few battles themselves, and worked out a few treaties among them. But the political fate of their descendants would be affected by the Seven Years' War.

The main story of the Seven Years' War was the survival of Prussia against the wishes of its neighbours, Austria, Sweden and the German states. The French backed Austria and the English backed Prussia. The English kept the French and their Spanish friends so busy in Europe that the French could not properly defend their outnumbered garrisons in North America. General James Wolfe perished on newly British land at the Plains of Abraham in 1759, and in 1763 the French were forced to sign the Peace of Paris. That led to two things: the Austrians then had to quit fighting the Prussians, and the British got to enjoy a decade and a half of supreme power in North America.

In 1763 King George III issued a royal proclamation that still reverberates through the rooms in which Native land claims are being negotiated. Having set up administrations in the newly British colonies, his government wanted to ensure that they did not grow too big too fast and thus create problems for London. The proclamation said that the lands lying westward of the colonies were to be preserved for the "tribes or nations" that were using them. These people were not to be "molested," and they were to be entitled to their land until they were "ceded to or purchased" by the Crown. That means that land could not simply be taken away, that there had to be treaties.

There were a lot of treaties east of the Rockies, and it is common knowledge that for many of those treaties the white people had better lawyers. But west of the Rockies the newcomers did not get around to making treaties, except for those fourteen little ones on Vancouver Island. The Hudson's Bay Company had at first been interested in furs, not land, and by the time that they got interested in land, they were pretty used to acting as a private corporation, not a British government.

Then after James Douglas retired, the colony of British Columbia declared that Indians were not human enough to have any rights to land. That would pretty well sum up B.C.'s governmental policy for decades. In 1927 the federal government declared that there was nothing in law to support the idea of land claims. From that point forward the main right-wing argument would be that George III's proclamation did not apply to British Columbia, because no Englishmen had been west of the Rockies in 1763. How could he have made policy about people he had never imagined? For all anyone knew in London, there might not be any land or Indians west of the Rockies.

But the Indians, led by the peoples of the northern coast, never gave up. They got the potlatch back. They got out of the residential schools. In 1949 they were allowed to vote in British Columbia elections, and in 1960 they won the right to vote in federal elections. In 1973 the Supreme Court of Canada admitted that there was such a concept as Native ownership of land. The Court said that before B.C. was invented, the Nisga'a people owned their land, but could only reach a split vote on whether they own it now. In the 1980s some Native groups started winning court cases, including injunctions against big logging companies. And when the NDP became the government in the 1990s, it recognized the principle of aboriginal title and the inherent right of self-government. In 1993 the B.C. Court of Appeal decided that there is some sort of aboriginal title, and left it to the Natives and the government to work out the details.

By 1994 forty-three Native bands had submitted claims, and begun negotiations. This time they had pretty good lawyers.

En'owkin

Native militancy made daily newspaper items through the 1970s. Hand-painted signs appeared at the gates of reserves, to remind drivers that they were about to drive onto Native land. Sometimes taking their models from the American Indian Movement, young Natives put on feathers and made themselves highly visible at municipal meetings. In 1975 at Penticton, Native people from the Penticton Okanagan reserve and elsewhere occupied the local office of the Department of Indian Affairs. Their message was that they pretty well understood how to address problems of housing and welfare and education. They told reporters and politicians that they wanted to be directors rather than clients.

When the people closed down the Indian Affairs office, they looked around and saw that coming together as a community suggested two things: as Okanagan Natives they could make an impact on the surrounding non-Native world, and they could tap ancient social ways to improve their own sense of power and pride. They could make it manifest that surviving Okanagan traditions did not have to be viewed as something that had to disappear if people wanted to get ahead in the world.

The Okanagan elders from bands all up and down the Canadian side of the valley met with the politicized young, and held conferences about their future. They decided that the highest priority would be given to education, not just for the young but for people of every age, and not just in subjects that would help Natives make way in the non-Native world, but in subjects that would make them aware of both versions of their own history. Thus was born the idea for the En'owkin Centre.

"En'owkin" is a stately word in Okanagan, and is not easily translated into English. But it refers to a process of consultation whereby people come together and figure out how to overcome problems, not by debate but as the Okanagan writer Jeanette Armstrong says, to exchange views, to find out how the community thinks. The En'owkin Centre is in the middle of Penticton. It is a good place, because the name of the city means something like "the place where people can live all the year round."

The En'owkin Centre is a school and a resource centre, a social gathering place and a publishing house. It began as a place to gather Okanagan minds, but is now a campus for students and teachers from aboriginal communities across Canada. Jeanette Armstrong, the great-niece of Mourning Dove, is a director of the school of writing and visual arts, which has an association with the University of Victoria. The writer Beth Cuthand is a Cree from Saskatchewan, and teaches poetry and life-writing. Greg Young-Ing is a Cree from Manitoba, and manages Theytus Books, the En'owkin publishing house. Since 1980 Theytus has published fiction and poetry and history books, and since 1990 the journal *Gatherings*, which is subtitled *The En'owkin Journal of First North American Peoples*, and is an invaluable source for the writings of Native people across the country.

Jeanette Armstrong edited a book called *The Native Creative Process*, which describes the difference between Indian and non-Indian art. The school conducts courses in the Okanagan language. The students and faculty and staff are all Native people. It is different in every way from the residential schools. Students who have had unpleasant experience at other schools are offered a sense of safety in which they can explore their personal, spiritual and political selves and culture. Their parents or grandparents may have been taken to a residential school, where they were punished for speaking their parents' language, or practising their home community's spiritual traditions.

In describing the militancy that would lead to the creation of the centre Jeanette Armstrong said that the founders were saying to the larger society: "We're not going to be you, so get used to it."

Bushy tail

In the middle of the last decade of the twentieth century, people in Vancouver and other municipalities in the densely populated southwest were calling on municipal, regional and provincial governments for advice. The subject of their inquiries was *canis latrans*, sometimes called the prairie wolf, most commonly known as the coyote. In recent years he had moved east of the Appalachians, into New York. Now he was being seen in the bushes around Vancouver, and sometimes in back yards. Well-off folks in new luxury houses where the North Shore forest used to be were alarmed by the presence of coyotes. They wanted to know what could be done to make their back yards free of those sneaky animals. Get used to them, the experts replied.

B.C. in Literature

Some important fiction set in British Columbia

Blondal, Patricia. *From Heaven with a Shout*. Toronto: McClelland & Stewart, 1963.

Romance about an impoverished mother who marries into a rich Vancouver Island logging family.

Bowering, George. *Burning Water*. Toronto: Musson, 1980. Reprint. Toronto: Penguin Books Canada, 1994.

Captains George Vancouver and Juan Francisco de la Bodega y Quadra explore the Pacific coast at the end of the eighteenth century.

Carr, Emily. *Klee Wyck*. Toronto: Irwin, 1941. Reprint. Toronto: Stoddart, 1987.

Stories of the Nootka people of Vancouver Island, gathered by the author and written in English under a title that is her name given by the Indians.

Cohen, Matt. *Wooden Hunters*. Toronto: McClelland & Stewart, 1975. Reprint. Toronto: McClelland & Stewart, New Canadian Library, n.d.

An unconventional young woman experiences elemental living among the Natives and whites on an island off the northern coast of British Columbia.

Evans, Hubert. *Mist on the River*. Toronto: Copp Clark, 1954. Reprint. Toronto: McClelland & Stewart, New Canadian Library, 1973.
    A young Gitskan man represents his people in his being pulled in two directions—to his traditional Native village life, and the white world.

Fawcett, Brian. *The Secret Journal of Alexander Mackenzie*. Vancouver: Talonbooks, 1985.
    Stories filled with anger and humour about the Prince George area, where forests and people are endangered by industrial greed and human stupidity.

Fraser, Keath. *Foreign Affairs*. Toronto: Stoddart, 1985.
    Urbane and meticulous stories and novellas about Vancouver and some Asian places that challenge the moral thinking of both characters and readers.

Grainger, M. Allerdale. *Woodsmen of the West*. London: Edward Arnold, 1908. Reprint. Toronto: McClelland & Stewart, New Canadian Library, 1964.
    A realistic novel of the logging industry along the coast in the early years of the twentieth century, by a man who would become B.C.'s chief forester.

Harlow, Robert. *Scann*. Port Clements: Sono Nis Press, 1972.
    In a northern town a newspaperman writes a historical novel, often confusing times with a mixtures of stark realism and bravura sentence-mongering.

Hindmarch, Gladys. *The Watery Part of the World*. Vancouver: Douglas & McIntyre, 1988.
    Linked stories told in immediate language about a young woman who works on a freighter that travels the west coast of Vancouver Island.

Hodgins, Jack. *The Invention of the World*. Toronto: Macmillan, 1977. Reprint. Toronto: McClelland & Stewart, New Canadian Library, 1994.
    A robust tale, both realistic and hallucinatory, about a mysterious Irishman who founds a suspicious spiritual colony on Vancouver Island.

Kogawa, Joy. *Obasan*. Toronto: Lester & Orpen Dennys, 1981. Reprint. Toronto: Penguin Books Canada, 1991.
    A Japanese-Canadian child sees her family become "enemy aliens" during World War II.

Kroetsch, Robert. *The Puppeteer*. Toronto: Random House, 1992. Reprint. Toronto: Random House, 1993.

The bizarre plot swings from Vancouver to the hot springs in the Kootenays and back to Vancouver via Italy and Greece, turning the story on its head.

Laurence, Margaret. *The Fire-Dwellers*. Toronto: McClelland & Stewart, 1969. Reprint. Toronto: McClelland & Stewart, New Canadian Library, 1988.
Innovative narrative techniques deliver the life of a housewife approaching middle age in a frightening world threatening varieties of fire and death.

Lowry, Malcolm. *October Ferry to Gabriola*. New York: World, 1970. Reprint. Vancouver: Douglas & McIntyre, 1988.
Visionary odyssey of a married couple desperate to find a home away from a collapsing world, who flee from edenic Burrard Inlet toward an island.

Marlatt, Daphne. *Ana Historic*. Toronto: Coach House, 1988.
A lyrical novel in which the lives of two immigrants to Vancouver, a nineteenth-century teacher and a twentieth-century schoolgirl, seem conflated.

Mills, John. *The Land of Is*. Toronto: General, 1972.
Our interesting satirist and parodist refigures the story of Shakespeare's *The Tempest*, and sets it in modern Vancouver.

O'Hagan, Howard. *Tay John*. New York: Laidlaw & Laidlaw, 1939. Reprint. Toronto: McClelland & Stewart, New Canadian Library, 1989.
Blending Native Indian mythology with scientific metaphor and experiments in diverging narratives, this novel is influential among later stylists.

Rule, Jane. *The Young in One Another's Arms*. Garden City: Doubleday, 1977. Reprint. Toronto: Collins Totem, 1978.
The story of experimental group living by a range of disaffected young people, and the harassment they receive from the "straight world."

Thomas, Audrey. *Intertidal Life*. Toronto: Stoddart, 1984. Reprint. Toronto: Stoddart, New Press, 1986.
A divorced woman with a daughter lives on a gulf island, facing the fear of a major operation and trying to sort out the strands of late-century life.

Watson, Sheila. *The Double Hook*. Toronto: McClelland & Stewart, 1959. Reprint. Toronto: McClelland & Stewart, New Canadian Library, 1989.
This most honoured precursor among modern Canadian novels reads like ancient myth while telling about poor rural people in the Cariboo.

Wilson, Ethel. *Swamp Angel*. New York: Harper & Bros., 1954. Reprint. Toronto: McClelland & Stewart, New Canadian Library, 1990.

A courageous and moral woman leaves her abusive Burnaby husband and finds a new life at a fishing lodge south of Kamloops.

Some interesting longer poems about B.C.

Belford, Ken. *Sign Language*. Prince George: Gorse Press, 1979.

Detailed and musical long poem about survival and feeling in the winter logging country of the northern Interior.

Birney, Earle. *Trial of a City*. Toronto: Ryerson Press, 1952. Reprinted as *The Damnation of Vancouver*. Toronto: McClelland & Stewart, New Canadian Library, 1977.

Drama in verse and prose in the form of a "public hearing into the proposed damnation of Vancouver." Deposees include Captain George Vancouver, a 1792 Salish chief and Gassy Jack Deighton.

Davey, Frank. *The Clallam*. Vancouver: Talonbooks, 1973.

A USAmerican passenger ship with a USAmerican captain sinks in the Strait of Juan de Fuca, with a loss of fifty Canadian lives on January 4, 1904.

Kearns, Lionel. *Convergences*. Toronto: Coach House Press, 1984.

Taking an incident that occurred between British ships and the Nootka Indians, Kearns weaves documentary, lyric and literary philosophy into a text that also uses many historical illustrations.

Kiyooka, Roy. *Pear Tree Pomes*. Toronto: Coach House Press, 1987.

A sequence of meditations about age and separation, taking as its main image a pear tree in a back yard on the edge of Chinatown in downtown Vancouver. Illustrated throughout by David Bolduc.

Lillard, Charles. *A Coastal Range*. Victoria: Sono Nis Press, 1984.

Descriptive lyrics about the mountains and forests from the San Juan Islands to Alaska.

Livesay, Dorothy. *Call My People Home*. Canadian Broadcasting Company, 1950. Printed in *The Self-Completing Tree: Selected Poems*. Victoria: Press Porcépic, 1986.

Dorothy Livesay is an exponent of the documentary poem as a way of taking part in political struggle. This one is about the forced relocation of Canadians of Japanese extraction during World War II.

Marlatt, Daphne. *Steveston*. Vancouver: Talonbooks, 1974. Reprint. Edmonton: Longspoon, 1984.

The history and present life in a Japanese-Canadian fishing community south of Vancouver. The book contains a portfolio of photographs by Robert Minden.

McKinnon, Barry. *The Centre*. Prince George: The Caitlin Press, 1995.

An account taken of a life half-over at a dead-end job in the B.C. north, but made with poems that snap the way nature can.

Newlove, John. *The Green Plain*. Lantzville: Oolichan Books, 1981. Reprinted in *Apology for Absence: Selected Poems 1962–1992*. Erin: Porcupine's Quill, 1993.

Concentrating on images of stars, rain and forest, this highly lyric meditation considers the place of humans in the natural universe, and human treatment of an erstwhile paradise.

Nichol, bp. *Continental Trance*. Lantzville: Oolichan Books, 1982. Reprinted in *The Martyrology, Book* 6. Toronto: Coach House Press, 1994.

Verse meditations composed during a family trip on the train from Vancouver to Toronto.

Potrebenko, Helen. *Life, Love and Unions*. Vancouver: Lazara Publications, 1987.

Humorous and tough poems about the unemployed and the working poor in the streets of Vancouver.

Roberts, Kevin. *Cariboo Fishing Notes*. Cullompton, Devon: Beau Geste Press, 1973.

An outdoorsy immigrant from Australia goes after rainbow trout in some lakes north of Kamloops.

Sibum, Norm. *Cafe Poems*. Ottawa: Oberon Press, 1988.

Long thoughtful and argumentative lines written in a café on Commercial Drive, in the multi-ethnic centre of Vancouver's east end.

Stanley, George. *Opening Day*. Lantzville: Oolichan Books, 1983.

A poet who belongs to a union and reads European poetry offers several sequences about living in the northwest corner of the province.

Thesen, Sharon. *Confabulations*. Lantzville: Oolichan Books, 1984. Reprinted in *The Pangs of Sunday*. Toronto: McClelland & Stewart, 1990.

A long poem based on the life and writings of Malcolm Lowry, and the conspiracy of breath provoked by the poet's sympathy.

Trower, Peter. *Unmarked Doorways*. Madeira Park: Harbour Publishing, 1989.
Folk-flavoured poems bringing a heroic and romantic eye to the downside of life in logging camps and Vancouver flophouses.

Wah, Fred. *Pictograms from the Interior of* B.C. Vancouver: Talonbooks, 1975.
Using Coleridge's term "transcreation," the poet makes poetic responses to Indian rock paintings as collected in a book by John Corner, *Pictographs in the Interior of British Columbia*.

Webb, Phyllis. *Wilson's Bowl*. Toronto: Coach House Press, 1980.
A sequence of poems dedicated to Lilo Berliner. "Before she committed suicide she left her letters from the noted anthropologist, Wilson Duff, on my doorstep." Duff was famous for his work with Northwest Coast Indian art forms.

Wong-Chu, Jim. *Chinatown Ghosts*. Vancouver: Pulp Press, 1986.
Plain and simple poems about growing up in the Chinese café culture of the Interior and moving to Vancouver's Chinatown as a young man.

Bibliography

(Note: this contains children's books, camping guides, etc., lots of stuff you don't see in a lot of histories.)

"A Successful Digger," *Guide Book for British Columbia, &c.* [No publishing information. This may be an advertising booklet.]

Akrigg, G.P.V., and Helen B. Akrigg. *1001 British Columbia Place Names.* Vancouver: Discovery Press, third edition, 1973.

Allison, Susan. *A Pioneer Gentlewoman in British Columbia: the Recollections of Susan Allison.* Edited by Margaret A. Ormsby. Vancouver: University of British Columbia, 1976.

Anderson, Charles P., Tirthankar Bose and Joseph I. Richardson, eds. *Circle of Voices: a History of the Religious Communities of British Columbia.* Lantzville: Oolichan Books, 1983.

Anonymous. *British Columbia: information for emigrants.* London, [1873].

Anonymous. *Guide to the Province of British Columbia for 1877-8.* Victoria: T.N. Hibben & Co., 1877.

Anonymous. *Kinbasket Country; the story of Golden and the Columbia Valley.* Golden: The Golden & District Historical Society, 1972.

Apollinaire, Guillaume. *Calligrammes.* Paris: Mercure de France, 1918.

Atkinson, R.N. *Penticton Pioneers.* Penticton: The Okanagan Historical Society, 1967.

Balf, Mary. *Kamloops: a History of the District up to 1914.* Kamloops: Kamloops Museum, second edition, 1981. *The Dispossessed: Interior Indians in the 1880's.* Kamloops: Kamloops Museum, 1978.

Bancroft, Hubert Howe. *History of British Columbia, 1792-1887.* San Francisco: The History Company, 1887.

Barlee, N.L., ed. *The Best of Canada West, volume 2*. Langley: Stagecoach Publishing, 1980.

Barman, Jean. *The West Beyond the West*. Toronto: University of Toronto, 1991.

Barman, Jean, and A.J. McDonald, eds. *Readings in the History of British Columbia*. Richmond: Open Learning, 1989.

Berman, Tzeporah, et al. *Clayoquot & Dissent*. Vancouver: Ronsdale, 1994.

Birney, Earle. *Selected Poems*. Toronto: McClelland & Stewart, 1966.

Boam, Henry J. (compiler) *British Columbia: its history, people, commerce, industries and resources*. Edited by Ashley G. Brown. London: Sells Ltd., 1912.

Bouchard, Randy, and Dorothy Kennedy, eds. *Shuswap Stories*. Vancouver: CommCept, 1979.

Bringhurst, Robert. "A Story as Sharp as a Knife, Part 3: The Polyhistorical Mind." *Journal of Canadian Studies*, Vol. 29, No. 2 (Summer 1994): 165-175.

Burns, John. "En'owkin School: learning to write apart." *Quill & Quire*, Vol. 61, No. 12 (December 1995).

Cendrars, Blaise. *Kodak (Documentaires)*. Paris 1924.

Colombo, John Robert. *Colombo's Canadian References*. Toronto: Oxford University Press, 1976.

Cooper, Carol. "Native Women of the Northern Pacific Coast." *Journal of Canadian Studies*. Vol. 27, No. 4 (Winter 1992–1993).

Dangelmaier, Rudi. *Pioneer Buildings of British Columbia*. Madeira Park: Harbour Publishing, 1989.

Davis, Chuck, ed. *The Vancouver Book*. North Vancouver: J.J. Douglas, 1976.

Davis, Earle. *Vision Fugitive: Ezra Pound and Economics*. Lawrence: University Press of Kansas, 1968.

Dawe, Alan. *Pocket Guide to the Wineries of British Columbia*. Kelowna: Sandhill, 1986.

Diaz, Bernal del Castillo. *The True History of the Conquest of New Spain*. Translated by A.P. Maudslay. London: Hakluyt Society, 1916.

Douglas C.H. *Social Credit*. London: Eyre and Spottiswoode, 1933.

Eastman, Sheila, and Timothy McGee. *Barbara Pentland*. Toronto: University of Toronto, 1983.

Falconer, Dickson M., ed. *British Columbia: Patterns in Economic, Political and Cultural Development*. Victoria: Camosun College, 1982.

Fetherling, Douglas. "Road Allowances." *Books in Canada*, XXIV, 3 (April 1995).

Fish and Wildlife Branch. *Preliminary Coyote Management Plan for British Columbia*, Victoria: Ministry of Environment, 1980.

Fisher, Robin. *Contact and Conflict: Indian-European Relations in British Columbia, 1774-1890*. Vancouver: UBC Press, 1977.

Fladmark, Knut R. *British Columbia Prehistory*. Ottawa: National Museum of Man, 1986.

Fraser, Geo. J. *The Story of Osoyoos: September 1811 to December 1952*. Osoyoos: Fraser, 1953.

Friesen, J. and H.K. Ralston, eds. *Historical Essays on British Columbia*. Toronto: Gage, 1980.

Gawthrop, Daniel. *Affirmation: the Aids Odyssey of Dr. Peter*. Vancouver: New Star Books, 1994.

Geddes, Gary, ed. *Skookum Wawa: Writings of the Canadian Northwest*. Toronto: Oxford, 1975.

Gerson, Carole, ed. *Vancouver Short Stories*. Vancouver: University of British Columbia, 1985.

Glanville, Alice, and Jim Glanville. *Grand Forks; the first 100 years*. Grand Forks: Gazette Printing, 1987.

Gosnell, R.E. *The Year Book of British Columbia: and manual of provincial information* (Coronation edition). Victoria: British Columbia Bureau of Provincial Information, 1911.

Gregoire, David, ed. *Gatherings: the En'owkin Journal of First North American Peoples*. Volume 1: Survival issue. Penticton: Theytus, 1990.

Haig-Brown, Roderick. *Captain of the Discovery*. Toronto: Macmillan, 1974.

Hill-Tout, Charles. *The Salish People*. Vols. I–IV. Edited by Ralph Maud. Vancouver: Talonbooks, 1978.

Howay, F.W., et al. *Cariboo Gold Rush*. Surrey: Heritage House, 1987.

Hubert, Henry A., and W.F. Garrett-Petts, eds. *Textual Studies in Canada*. No. 1. Kamloops: The University College of the Cariboo, 1991.

Humber, William. *Cheering for the Home Team: the story of baseball in Canada*. Erin: The Boston Mills Press, 1983.

Johnson, Patricia M., ed. *Canada's Pacific Province: selected sources from early times*. Toronto: McClelland & Stewart, 1966.

Kavic, Lorne J., and Garry Brian Nixon. *The 1200 Days: Dave Barrett and the NDP in B.C*. Coquitlam: Kaen Publishers, 1978.

Keddell, Georgina. *The Newspapering Murrays*. Toronto: McClelland & Stewart, 1967.

Kelsey, Vera. *British Columbia Rides a Star*. Toronto: J.M. Dent, 1958.

Kitagawa, Muriel. *This is My Own, Letters to Wes & other writings on Japanese Canadians, 1941–1948*. Edited by Roy Miki. Vancouver: Talonbooks, 1985.

Lawrence, D.H. *Lady Chatterley's Lover*. Harmondsworth: Penguin Books, 1960.

Leslie, Graham. *Breach of Promise: Socred Ethics Under Vander Zalm*. Rev. ed. Madeira Park: Harbour Publishing, 1991.

Livesay, Dorothy. *Right Hand Left Hand*. Erin: Press Porcépic, 1977.

Lopez, Barry, ed. *Giving Birth to Thunder, Sleeping with his Daughter: Coyote Builds North America*. New York: Avon Books, 1977.

Lower, J. Arthur. *Canada on the Pacific Rim*. Toronto: McGraw-Hill, 1975.

Lyons, Chess. *Mileposts in Ogopogo Land*. Surrey: Foremost Publishing, 1970.

MacIsaac, Ron, Don Clark and Charles Lillard. *The Devil of DeCourcy Island: The Brother XII*. Victoria: Press Porcépic, 1989.

Marlatt, Daphne. *Vancouver Poems*. Toronto: Coach House, 1972.

Marsh, James H., ed. *The Canadian Encyclopedia*. Edmonton: Hurtig Publishers, 1985.

Mason, Gary and Keith Baldrey. *Fantasyland: Inside the Reign of Bill Vander Zalm*. Toronto: McGraw Hill Ryerson, 1989.

Maud, Ralph. *A Guide to B.C. Indian Myth and Legend*. Vancouver: Talonbooks, 1982.

McGeer, Patrick L. *Politics in Paradise*. Toronto: Peter Martin Associates, 1972.

McInnis, Edgar. *Canada: a Political and Social History*. New York: Rinehart, 1947.

McKelvie, B.A. *Pageant of B.C.* Toronto: Thomas Nelson, 1955.

McLeod, Monica, et al. *Merritt & the Nicola Valley: an Illustrated History*. Merritt: Sonotek, 1989.

Meany, Edmond S. *Vancouver's Discovery of Puget Sound*. Portland: Binfords & Mort, 1957.

Milne, David. *The Canadian Constitution*. Toronto: James Lorimer, 1991.

Mitchell, David J. *W.A.C. Bennett and the Rise of British Columbia*. Vancouver: Douglas & McIntyre, 1983.

Molyneux, Geoffrey. *British Columbia: an Illustrated History*. Vancouver: Polestar, 1992.

Morton James. *In the Sea of Sterile Mountains: the Chinese in British Columbia*. Vancouver: J.J. Douglas, 1974.

Mourning Dove. *Coyote Stories*. Edited by Heister Dean Guie. Lincoln: University of Nebraska, 1990. *A Salishan Autobiography*. Edited by Jay Miller. Lincoln: University of Nebraska Press, 1990.

Muir, E. St. C. *Poems of Protest*. North Vancouver. Privately printed, no date.

Mulgrew, Ian. *Final Payoff: the True Price of Convicting Clifford Olson*. Toronto: Seal Books, 1990.

Munro, Jack, and Jane O'Hara. *Union Jack: Labour Leader Jack Munro*. Vancouver: Douglas & McIntyre, 1988.

Murray, Peter. *From Amor to Zalm*. Victoria: Orca, 1989.

Neering, Rosemary. *A Traveller's Guide to Historic British Columbia*. Vancouver: Whitecap, 1993.

Newlove, John. *Black Night Window*. Toronto: McClelland & Stewart, 1968.

Nichol, Kathleen M. *Wines and Vines of British Columbia*. Vancouver: Bottesini, 1983.

Norris, John. *Old Silverton*. Silverton: Silverton Historical Society, 1985.

Olson, Charles. *Mayan Letters*. Palma de Mallorca: Divers Press, 1953.

Ormsby, Margaret A. *British Columbia: a History*. Toronto: Macmillan, 1958.

Parkin, Tom. *West Coast Words*. Victoria: Orca Books, 1989.

Paterson, T.W. *Encyclopedia of Ghost Towns & Mining Camps of British Columbia*. Langley: Stagecoach, 1979. *Lower Mainland*. British Columbia Ghost Town Series. Langley: Sunfire, 1984. *Okanagan-Similkameen*. British Columbia Ghost Town Series. Langley: Sunfire, 1983. *Outlaws of Western Canada*. Langley: Stagecoach, 1977.

Persky, Stan. *Bennett II: the Decline & Stumbling of Social Credit Government in British Columbia 1979–83*. Vancouver: New Star Books, 1983. *Fantasy Government: Bill Vander Zalm and the Future of Social Credit*. Vancouver: New Star Books, 1989. *Son of Socred: has Bill Bennett's government gotten B.C. moving again?* Vancouver: New Star Books, 1979.

Pethick, Derek. *British Columbia Disasters*. Langley: Stagecoach, 1978.

Pethick, Derek, and Susan Im Baumgarten. *British Columbia Recalled*. Saanichton: Hancock House, 1974.

Porteous, H.A. *Oliver 1921–1971*. Oliver: Oliver & District Centennial '71 Committee, 1971.

Pratt, E..J. *Towards the Last Spike*. Toronto: Macmillan, 1952.

Purdy, Al. *The Collected Poems of Al Purdy*. Toronto: McClelland & Stewart, 1986.

Ramsey, Bruce. *Ghost Towns of British Columbia*. Vancouver: Mitchell Press, 1963.

Ray, Verne F. *Cultural Relations in the Plateau of Northwestern America*. Los Angeles: Southwest Museum, 1939.

Richardson, Boyce. *People of Terra Nullius: Betrayal and Rebirth in Aboriginal Canada*. Vancouver: Douglas & McIntyre, 1993.

Robin, Martin. *Pillars of Profit: The Company Province 1934–1972*. Toronto: McClelland & Stewart, 1973. *The Bad and the Lonely*. Toronto: James Lorimer, 1976. *The Rush For Spoils: The Company Province 1871–1933*. Toronto: McClelland & Stewart, 1972.

Robinson, Harry. *Write It on Your Heart: the Epic World of an Okanagan Storyteller*. Edited by Wendy Wickwire. Vancouver and Penticton: Talonbooks and Theytus, 1989.

Rothenburger, Mel. *The Chilcotin War*. Langley: Stagecoach, 1978. *The Wild McLeans*. Victoria: Orca, 1993. *We've Killed Johnny Ussher!* Vancouver: Mitchell Press, 1973.

Safarik, Allan, ed. *Vancouver Poetry*. Winlaw: Polestar Press, 1986.

Sauer, Carl. *Land and Life*. Berkeley: University of California, 1965. *Man in Nature: America Before the Days of the White Man*. Berkeley: Turtle Island, 1975.

Schmidt, Jeremy. "Mongolia's Mysterious Reindeer People." *Equinox* 74, March–April 1994: 38–49.

Schroeder, Andreas. *Carved From Wood: Mission, B.C., 1862–1992*. Mission: The Mission Foundation, 1991.

Schroeder, Andreas, and Rudy Wiebe, eds. *Stories From Pacific & Arctic Canada*. Toronto: Macmillan, 1974.

Sharma, Hari, et al., eds. *Fifth Report: a Great Leap Forward*. Kamloops: Secwepemc Cultural Education Society and Simon Fraser University, 1994.

Shewchuk, Murphy. *Fur, Gold and Opals: a Guide to the Thompson River Valley*. Saanichton: Hancock House, 1975.

Smith, R.D. Hilton. *Northwestern Approaches: the first century of books*. Victoria: The Adelphi Book Shop, 1969.

Smyth, Fred J. *Tales of the Kootenays*. Vancouver: J. J. Douglas, 1977.

Spalding, A.G. *America's National Game*. New York: American Sports Publishing Company, 1911.

Spicer, Jack. *The Collected Lectures of Jack Spicer*. Edited by Peter Gizzi. Typescript.

Stanley, George. *Gentle Northern Summer*. Vancouver: New Star Books, 1995.

Sweet, Arthur Fielding, ed. *Islands in Trust*. Lantzville: Oolichan Books, 1988.

Toye, William, ed. *The Oxford Companion to Canadian Literature*. Toronto: Oxford University Press, 1983.

Trevelyan, George Macaulay. *Clio, a Muse, and Other Essays*. London: Longmans, 1949.

Turnbull, Elsie G. *Ghost Towns and Drowned Towns of West Kootenay*. Surrey: Heritage House, 1988.

Vancouver, George. *A Voyage of Discovery to the North Pacific Ocean and Round the World, 1791–1795*. Edited by W. Kaye Lamb. London: Hakluyt Society, 1984.

Ward, W. Peter. *White Canada Forever*. Montreal: McGill-Queen's University Press, 1978.

Watmough, David, ed. *Vancouver Fiction*. Winlaw: Polestar Press, 1985.

Webber, Jean, and the En'owkin Centre. *Okanagan Sources*. Penticton: Theytus, 1990.

White, Brenda Lea, ed. *British Columbia: Visions of the Promised Land*. Vancouver: Flight Press, 1986.

White, Howard, ed. *Raincoast Chronicles First Five*. Madeira Park: Harbour Publishing, 1976.

Wild, Roland. *Amor de Cosmos*. Toronto: The Ryerson Press, 1958.

Wilson, Ethel. *Hetty Dorval*. Toronto: Macmillan, 1947. *The Innocent Traveller*. London: Macmillan, 1949.

Wilson, Sandy, ed. *Western Windows: a Comparative Anthology of Poetry in British Columbia*. Vancouver: CommCept, 1977.

Woodcock, George. *British Columbia: a History of the Province*. Vancouver: Douglas & McIntyre, 1990. *100 Great Canadians*. Edmonton: Hurtig Publishers, 1980. *Ravens and Prophets*. Victoria: Sono Nis Press, 1993.

Woodward, Meredith Bain. *Land of Dreams: A History in Photographs of the British Columbia Interior*. Banff: Altitude Publishing, 1993.

Wright, Esmond, ed. *History of the World: the Last Five Hundred Years*. London: Bonanza, 1984.

Young-Ing, Greg, ed. *Gatherings: the En'owkin Journal of First North American Peoples*. Volume II: Two Faces. Penticton: Theytus, 1991. Volume III: Mother Earth. Penticton: Theytus, 1992.

W. Kaye Lamb, librarian, historian, Dominion archivist from 1948 until retirement in 1969, holder of 10 honorary degrees, past president of a number of learned societies including the Royal Society of Canada and the Society of Archivists (Great Britain), Officer of the Order of Canada, and editor of a number of journals and collections of letters, on George Bowering's novel about George Vancouver:

"...taking only scant account of historical facts and good taste...he has bespattered his pages with numerous errors of fact that are both pointless and needless...without a shred of supporting evidence...the facts speak for themselves...."

Index